# THE SOCIAL ORGANIZATION

# OF LAW 2<sup>ND</sup> EDITION

# THE SOCIAL ORGANIZATION OF LAW

## 2ND EDITION

EDITED BY

## M. P. BAUMGARTNER

*Department of Sociology*
*William Paterson University*
*Wayne, New Jersey*

ACADEMIC PRESS

San Diego   London   Boston   New York   Sydney   Tokyo   Toronto

*Front cover photograph:* © PhotoDisc.

This book is printed on acid-free paper. ∞

Academic Press
*a division of Harcourt Brace & Company*
525 B Street, Suite 1900, San Diego, California 92101-4495, USA
http://www.apnet.com

Academic Press
24-28 Oval Road, London NW1 7DX, UK
http://www.hbuk.co.uk/ap/

Library of Congress Catalog Card Number: 98-86588

International Standard Book Number: 0-12-083170-8

PRINTED IN THE UNITED STATES OF AMERICA
98  99  00  01  02  03  EB  9  8  7  6  5  4  3  2  1

# CONTENTS

## 1

### INTRODUCTION   1

#### M. P. BAUMGARTNER

# PART I

## LAW AND SOCIAL STRATIFICATION

# 2

## ARBITRARINESS AND DISCRIMINATION UNDER POST-FURMAN CAPITAL STATUTES    35

### WILLIAM J. BOWERS AND GLENN L. PIERCE

# 3

## DISPUTE SETTLEMENT BY THE POLICE    61

### DONALD BLACK

# 4

## SPEECH STYLES IN THE COURTROOM: POWERFUL VERSUS POWERLESS SPEECH   97

### WILLIAM M. O'BARR

# 5

## LAW AND SOCIAL STATUS IN COLONIAL NEW HAVEN, 1639—1665   111

### M. P. BAUMGARTNER

# PART II

## LAW AND SOCIAL MORPHOLOGY

# 6

## MURDER IN SPACE CITY   133

### HENRY P. LUNDSGAARDE

# 7

## THE OVEN BIRD'S SONG: INSIDERS, OUTSIDERS, AND PERSONAL INJURIES IN AN AMERICAN COMMUNITY    157

### DAVID M. ENGEL

# 8

## EVIDENCE AS PARTISANSHIP    183

### MARK COONEY

# 9

## STRUCTURE AND PRACTICE
## OF FAMILIAL-BASED JUSTICE
## IN A CRIMINAL COURT    207

### KATHLEEN DALY

# PART III

## LAW AND CULTURE

# 10

## DEVIANCE AND RESPECTABILITY: AN OBSERVATIONAL STUDY OF REACTIONS TO SHOPLIFTING   229

### DARRELL J. STEFFENSMEIER AND ROBERT M. TERRY

# 11

## LEGAL CONTROL OF MUSIC: THE CASE OF ROCK AND RAP   245

### NANCY A. HEITZEG

# 12

## JUSTICE, CHINESE STYLE   267

### ROGER GRACE

# Contributors

*Numbers in parentheses indicate the pages on which the authors' contributions begin.*

**M. P. Baumgartner** (1, 111) Department of Sociology, William Paterson University, Wayne, New Jersey 07470

**Donald Black** (63) Department of Sociology, University of Virginia, Charlottesville, Virginia 22903

**William J. Bowers** (35) College of Criminal Justice, Northeastern University, Boston, Massachusetts 02115

**Donald A. Clelland** (371) Fort Collins, Colorado 80525

**Mark Cooney** (183) Department of Sociology, University of Georgia, Athens, Georgia 30602

**Kathleen Daly** (207) School of Justice Administration, Griffith University, Mt. Gravatt Campus, Brisbane, Queensland 4111, Australia

**G. E. M. de Ste. Croix** (285) Oxford OX7 3ER, United Kingdom

**David M. Engel** (157) School of Law, State University of New York, Buffalo, New York 14260

**Ronald A. Farrell** (389) Division of Social Science, City College of the City University of New York, New York, New York 10031

**Roger Grace** (267) Rochester, New York 14694

**John Hagan** (343) Faculty of Law, University of Toronto, Toronto, Ontario M5S 1A1, Canada

**John O. Haley** (417) University of Washington School of Law, Seattle, Washington 98195

**Nancy A. Heitzeg** (245) Department of Sociology and Anthropology, College of St. Catherine, St. Paul, Minnesota 55105

**Henry P. Lundsgaarde** (133) Department of Anthropology, University of Kansas, Lawrence, Kansas 66047

**John Lynxwiler** (371) Department of Sociology, University of Tennessee, Knoxville, Tennessee 37996

**William M. O'Barr** (97) Department of Anthropology, Duke University, Durham, North Carolina

**Glenn L. Pierce** (35) Academic Computing, Northeastern University, Boston, Massachusetts 02115

**Reginald S. Sheehan** (323) Department of Political Science, University of South Carolina, Columbia, South Carolina 29208

**Neal Shover** (371) Knoxville, Tennessee 37932

**Donald R. Songer** (323) Department of Political Science, University of North Texas, Denton, Texas 76203

**Elizabeth Anne Stanko** (405) Law Department, Brunel University, Uxbridge, Middlesex UB8 3PH, United Kingdom

**Darrell J. Steffensmeier** (229) Sociology and Crime, Law, and Justice, Pennsylvania State University, University Park, Pennsylvania 16802

**Victoria Lynn Swigert** (389) College of the Holy Cross, Worcester, Massachusetts 01610

**Robert M. Terry** (229) Robert Terry Law Firm, Akron, Ohio 44303

**Denis Chimaeze E. Ugwuegbu** (271) Department of Psychology, University of Ibidan, Ibidan, Nigeria

**Craig Wanner** (309) Deceased.

# PREFACE

It has been 25 years since the first edition of *The Social Organization of Law* appeared in print. Edited by Donald Black and his student Maureen Mileski, it proposed a scientific agenda for legal sociology, one committed to the discovery of facts about law and the development of general and testable theory to explain them. It brought together 20 selections, drawn from the best of the sociological literature about law then available, that illustrated how a number of social factors were intertwined with legal behavior. The accompanying introduction summarized the state of empirical knowledge about law at the time and laid out a blueprint for the kind of discourse about law that sociologists should pursue in the future. In their preface, Black and Mileski claimed that the book contained "nothing more than beginnings," but these beginnings turned out to be extraordinarily fruitful.

In the years since the first edition was published, nothing short of a revolution has taken place in the sociology of law. Extending and developing theoretical ideas presented in rudimentary form in that 1973 work, Donald Black went on in 1976 to publish *The Behavior of Law*, a *tour de force* that offered both a sophisticated paradigm for the sociological study of law and an immense body of predictive and explanatory theory. Subsequent efforts in the field have elaborated, refined, and applied this theory to a variety of subjects, increasing the power of Blackian legal sociology ever more. At the same time, a remarkable explosion in the number and quality of empirical studies about law has occurred, so that today much more is known about legal reality than was the case just a short time ago.

In light of these developments, it is time for a new collection of readings in the sociology of law, one reflecting the field's many recent achievements and introducing them to a new generation of students. It is time for this second edition of *The Social Organization of Law*. Like its predecessor, the present volume arises from a commitment to scientific sociology and includes works that illustrate and advance such an enterprise. It also retains most of the first book's organizational structure. In other ways, however, it is very different. Most noticeable is the fact that its selections are entirely new; only two of the readings in this book had even appeared when the first edition was assembled, and neither was included in it. The theoretical formulations that the readings illustrate are also different in the present edition, because most were only proposed after 1973, primarily in *The Behavior of Law*. The introduction to this edition is able to survey a wealth of ideas about law that did not exist when the first edition came out and to discuss jurisprudential, moral, and practical applications of legal sociology that were barely imaginable then, back in the infancy of the field. Any reader who compares this book with the first edition must surely be amazed at how far and how fast legal sociology has progressed.

The preparation of this second edition of *The Social Organization of Law* has been assisted by a number of parties who deserve acknowledgment and thanks. Donald Black not only developed the paradigm and theory from which the volume arises, but also made valuable contributions at every stage of the project. Mark Cooney, Allan Horwitz, and an anonymous reviewer offered many suggestions that greatly improved the book. J. Scott Bentley of Academic Press encouraged the project and, along with his assistants Beth Bloom and Karen Frost, facilitated it in many ways. Joan Fitzgerald provided outstanding secretarial assistance, and Michele LaMotta helped organize the manuscript's computer files. Finally, financial support for the project was made available through a Faculty Development Grant from William Paterson University.

# 1

# INTRODUCTION

## M. P. BAUMGARTNER

In the United States and elsewhere, thousands of legal events occur everyday. People call the police or attract their suspicion, consult attorneys and file lawsuits, testify in court and complain to administrative agencies. Legal officials pass laws, file reports, make arrests, bring charges, gather and present evidence, issue rulings, pronounce judgments, and impose sentences. Fines are paid, prison terms served, executions carried out. Actions and events like these affect the lives of numerous individuals, sometimes profoundly, and also shape the social climate of entire communities and societies.

Whether and how law becomes involved in people's affairs, and what the outcome of that involvement is, varies considerably across time, space, and incident. Of all the things that law might in theory forbid, for example, only some are actually proscribed, and these are not the same ones everywhere. At the level of individual cases, similar behavior can elicit dramatically different legal responses, ranging from complete inaction to aggressive and punitive intervention. Given the same provocation, only some of the people who could call the police or lodge a complaint proceed to do so. The police arrest only some of the many individuals who come to their attention. Prosecutors bring numerous and serious charges against some persons while deciding not to proceed at all against others. Some criminal defendants are convicted while others go free. In civil matters, some people are ordered to pay huge sums in damages while others are found to owe little or nothing. Further examples of such differential treatment could be multiplied, for the phenomenon is pervasive—indeed, universal. It is observable throughout all stages of the legal process in all legal systems.

This variation cannot be explained simply with the formal laws applicable to the handling of cases. Even when all technical issues are taken into account and all relevant formal rules are applied, much variation in law remains. In the past, this has most commonly been attributed to a kind of sheer arbitrariness or unpredictability arising from the exercise of discretion by legal officials and citizens who bring their own personalities, values, and idiosyncracies to the processing of the cases in which they become involved. From this perspective, many of the differences in case outcomes have extremely complicated origins and are ultimately inexplicable.

There is another way of understanding what happens in legal matters, however, and why their outcomes so often differ. This alternative makes it possible to predict and explain legal variation, which no longer appears mysterious or arbitrary but rather consistent with a set of specifiable laws or principles. This is the sociology of law, which locates the source of legal variation in the social environment within which legal events occur. Applying a scientific method that seeks to establish facts and to develop testable theories about them, it shifts the focus from doctrinal and technical elements of cases to social ones.

This book brings together a number of readings in the sociology of law, each showing how one or more social factors affect the processing of legal cases. The book arises from a theoretical paradigm developed by Donald Black (see especially Black, 1976) and applied to the study of diverse aspects of law by a growing number of legal sociologists. This ambitious and systematic approach lays out exactly what variation the sociology of law needs to explain (i.e., the field's dependent variables), identifies the major social factors that account for this variation (i.e., its independent variables), and offers a number of theoretical formulations about the relationship between the two. Work in the Blackian tradition strives to incorporate a great array of findings about law into a single framework, and to order them all.

This introduction briefly surveys the major features of Black's approach to law, providing a context for the readings that follow. It begins with an overview of the field's history, then turns to the core issues of how law varies and how this variation can be explained. It next considers the jurisprudential, moral, and practical impact of the sociology of law. Finally, it concludes by describing the papers collected in the present volume, highlighting their most significant contributions. Taken individually and as a group, these papers present compelling evidence that the operation of legal systems cannot be understood without reference to the social characteristics of the individuals and settings that become implicated in legal affairs.

## THE HISTORY OF LEGAL SOCIOLOGY

Although legal sociology's greatest advances have come in recent years, its roots reach back for centuries. In 1748, for example, the Baron de Montesquieu was already arguing that the origins of laws must be sought in the customs, experiences, and environments of particular societies (Montesquieu, 1748). In 1762, the French political philosopher Jean-Jacques Rousseau observed that differentials of wealth and power have a great impact on legal systems: "The universal spirit of Laws, in all countries, is to favor the strong in opposition to the weak, and to assist those who have possessions against those who have none" (Rousseau, 1762: 200).

Later and more systematic commentators on the relationship between law and its social environment included such classical sociological theorists as Karl Marx, Emile Durkheim, and Max Weber, all recognized as "founding fathers" of modern sociology. The contributions of these individuals were primarily conceptual and theoretical in nature, since sociological research as we now know it was very rudimentary in their time (that is, in the 19th and early 20th centuries). Each called attention to the importance of one or more social variables for law. Karl Marx and his collaborator Friedrich Engels, for instance, emphasized the significance of social inequality, arguing that law emerged historically with the appearance of social classes, it operates in stratified settings as a tool of domination used by ruling classes over others, and it will ultimately "wither away" when equality is restored to human society (see, e.g., the work of Marx and Engels assembled in Cain and Hunt, 1979).

Emile Durkheim, by contrast, focused on patterns of connectedness and interpersonal association in explaining legal variation. In his most famous work on law, *The Division of Labor in Society* (Durkheim, 1893), he distinguished between two kinds of social solidarity: mechanical solidarity, which is based on the mutual attraction of similar individuals and is found in face-to-face societies, and organic solidarity, which is based on the interdependence of people with specialized skills and is found in more complex societies. Durkheim claimed that each kind of solidarity is linked to a distinctive kind of law, mechanical solidarity to repressive law, which is harsh and inclined to punishment, and organic solidarity to restitutive law, which is tempered and inclined to compensation. While subsequent research has failed to support Durkheim's thesis (see, e.g., Spitzer, 1975), it remains significant for the variables it featured and the kind of theory to which it aspired.

Yet other aspects of social life were singled out as important by the third great classical theorist, Max Weber. Weber called attention to the role of bureaucracy and formal organization in the transformation of modern society and its law (Weber, 1922). For Weber, increased bureaucratization has been a far-reaching trend evident in virtually every aspect of social life. In the legal arena, it has expressed itself in the emergence of rational justice, in which specialized state officials process cases in standardized ways, applying formal rules in a routinized manner. This contrasts with the more personal and informal justice found in earlier societies.

The legacy of the classical theorists to the sociological study of law goes beyond the specifics of these arguments. Collectively, the early theorists helped to establish a larger agenda for the field. All were committed to a study of law that is *empirical,* or concerned with objective facts, and all sought to develop theory that is *general,* that is, that would apply across societies, historical periods, and stages of a legal system. Taken together, they also helped to identify a number of the most important social factors that influence law—social stratification, interpersonal connection, and formal organization. These independent variables are still recognized as critical to the understanding of legal variation.

Other early contributions to the sociology of law emerged from the world of legal scholarship, especially in a movement known as legal realism. During the first decades of the 20th century, legal realists such as Karl Llewellyn and Jerome Frank called attention to the wide gap that exists between how law is supposed to operate in theory and how it actually operates in practice. In doing so, they focused on the differential handling of individual cases, a phenomenon with which the contemporary sociology of law remains centrally preoccupied. The legal realists argued that the source of such variation lies in the fact that law is ultimately a human enterprise, in which decisions are made by people who differ from one another in their social backgrounds, life experiences, and personalities, and whose own behavior can itself vary day by day depending on their personal circumstances at the time (for an overview of legal realism, see Leiter, 1996).

While the classical sociological theorists and the legal realists helped to develop an agenda and a blueprint for the sociology of law, most of the field's accomplishments have been achieved in more recent years. During the last few decades, a substantial research literature has accumulated that reports findings from systematic empirical investigations into the operation of legal agencies in a wide variety of settings and contexts. Scholars from a number of disciplines have helped to build this literature, including not only sociologists but also anthropologists, historians, legal scholars, political scientists, and psychologists. The facts they have uncovered have described legal systems around the world and at various historical moments, and have shed light on the practices of legislatures, police officers, prosecutors, private attorneys, judges, juries, and ordinary citizens embroiled in legal affairs. This wealth of information has made possible an increasingly accurate depiction of legal reality and has provided the necessary foundation for the development of a truly explanatory theory.

As scholars from many backgrounds have worked to build this research literature, many have also sought to explain the patterns uncovered. New theoretical insights have thus accompanied the growth of empirical knowledge. In one famous instance, the anthropologist Max Gluckman generated an important formulation about law on the basis of his research into the courts of the Barotse people in what is now Zambia (Gluckman, 1967). Gluckman observed that among the Barotse, where people were traditionally bound to one another by a multitude of ties and interests—where their relationships were "multiplex"—the courts acted to promote reconciliation and to restore harmony between the parties to legal disputes. The typical legal outcome was a compromise. This contrasts with the way in which courts in the contemporary West tend to dispose of their cases, which commonly involve people who have no prior relationship with one another or who are linked by only a single interest: in this context, authoritative, punitive, and one-sided outcomes abound. Gluckman's work thus showed that multiplex relationships be-

viduals occupy social positions based on the relative amount of wealth and other resources they control. In the contemporary United States, for example, a person's social status is measured by such things as income, wealth, and occupation. Given large average differences in these assets between groups—between men and women, adults and children, or whites and blacks, for instance—certain kinds of group affiliations can also serve as crude indicators of status. Thus, in the United States, men, adults, and whites generally have a status advantage over women, children, and blacks.

When people have legal conflicts, where they stand in a status hierarchy relative to everyone else involved is an important predictor of what is likely to happen. When the status of the offender is the same, for example, offenses against high-status victims are defined and treated as more serious matters than identical offenses against low-status people; when the status of the victim is the same, low-status offenders are treated more harshly. *The most law and the most penal law occur when low-status people offend their status superiors, followed in descending order by cases in which both parties are of high status, then cases in which both parties are of low status, and lastly by cases in which the offenders are of higher status than their victims* (Black, 1976: Chapter 2). The greater the status disparity in cases involving unequal parties, the more extreme the effects of social stratification will be.

Given the importance of the status of *both* parties to a legal matter (see also below, pages 13–14), and in light of how status affects law, it becomes clear that the widespread belief that elite criminal defendants fare better than impoverished ones is simplistic and largely inaccurate. Status matters, but it does not always give the advantage to high-status offenders over low-status ones. It depends on whether there are victims in a case, and, if so, who those victims are: High-status offenders of high-status victims are worse off than low-status people who have offended others equally low. The status of the victim is thus more determinative of legal outcomes than that of the offender, although it is the social standing of both parties in relation to each other that is ultimately most predictive.

### Social Morphology

Social morphology refers to patterns of interpersonal association and connection. Two aspects of social morphology known to be predictive of legal behavior are the degree to which people are integrated into the life of their communities through active social participation, and the kind of prior relationship that existed between them before a case began.

Social participation, or radial status (Black, 1976: 48), is determined by how much an individual adds to the life of the group of which he or she is a part. Some people are good citizens and active participants; others fail to contribute much of anything and may even be a drain on those who do. Thus, some people may be energetic members of the work force, helping to produce the goods and services on which the health of a community depends, while others may not make an economic contribution of any kind. Some may invest in marriage and the rearing and support of children, thereby contributing to the continuity of a society over time, while others remain single. Some may join clubs and associations or otherwise volunteer their time and energy to what are seen as worthy causes—fund raising for charity, supporting political parties, or coaching youthful athletic teams, for instance—while others just stay home. And some people may be friendly, outgoing, and gregarious, forging ties to many individuals and acting to promote the social solidarity of their groups, while others are glum, unfriendly, or withdrawn.

When people become involved in legal matters, their radial status has an effect similar to that of their socioeconomic status. Offenses against active and well-integrated persons are treated as more serious than those against social isolates. *The offenses taken most seriously of all—producing the most law and the most penal law—are the ones committed by marginal people against integrated people, followed by those involving two integrated people, then two isolated people, and lastly those in which an integrated person offends someone who is marginal* (Black, 1976: 48–54).

Prior relationship is also an important predictor of legal outcomes. Before becoming involved in a case, the parties may have been total strangers, brought together only by the offense that one committed against the other. They might have been casual acquaintances or associates, known to each other but not very close. Or some more intimate and enduring tie might have bound them, such as that between friends or family members. The degree of "relational distance"—or intimacy—between the parties is systematically linked to legal variation: *Law is most likely to become involved, to proceed aggressively, and to be penal in style when the parties are strangers; it is least likely to become involved and most likely to be lenient and conciliatory when they are intimates* (Black, 1976: 40–48). Thus, one and the same offense is likely to be seen as a dispute when it occurs between family members but a crime when it occurs between strangers.

## Culture

In all groups, people devote a considerable amount of time and energy to expressive activities—to things that are not a matter of immediate practical importance but that are defined as valuable for their own sake. This is the realm of culture. Among these activities are ones devoted to the creation and appreciation of beauty—aesthetic life—and to the articulation of belief systems and the practices associated with them—notably including religion. Culture also includes the language people speak and the philosophies they articulate. Some degree of involvement in activities of these kinds is virtually a defining characteristic of human beings (see, e.g., Pfeiffer, 1982). At the same time, there is variation in aspects of cultural life within and across groups.

People differ in what they define and appreciate as beautiful, true, or otherwise desirable. One person or group may enjoy a type of music that another person or group finds unappealing. One may prefer a clothing style defined as ugly or outlandish by another. What kind of art people like, what kind of literature they read, what kind of food they relish, what style of home furnishings they select, and similar choices all vary. So, too, does religious conviction and practice. What some people recognize as true and sacred others may reject as untrue, unimportant, or possibly even as heretical. What some see as profound ritual others may reject as silly or sacrilegious. People may be separated from each other, then, by "cultural distance," defined by differences in cultural behavior. Some of these differences may be linked to ethnic identity, since ethnicity represents a distinctive cluster of cultural practices passed down over generations, or they may be linked to membership in different religions, subcultures, or taste systems. Within social settings, the extent of cultural distance is itself variable: Some societies or groups are very homogeneous, consisting of culturally similar people, while others are very diverse or heterogeneous, including culturally dissimilar people.

In diverse settings, a further kind of cultural variation is relevant. This is the degree to which some cultural practices predominate over others. Groups may, for example, consist of a number of different cultures, all of which are equally well-represented, or they may contain a dominant cultural group and one or more cultural minorities.

The outcomes of legal cases depend on the cultural characteristics of the parties involved, relative to those of the other participants. *Law is more likely to become involved in the affairs of culturally dissimilar people than in those of people who are culturally alike.* What happens when law is invoked depends on the cultural affiliations of all concerned. *Law is likely to be most severe and most penal when a member of a cultural minority group offends a member of a more conventional culture, followed by offenses between two members of a conventional group, then offenses between two members of a minority group, and lastly offenses committed by members of a conventional culture against someone from a minority background* (Black, 1976: Chapter 4).

## Organization

Organization is defined by the degree to which people work cooperatively in support of common goals. In modern societies, this aspect of social life is embodied most dramatically in the many formally structured groups, such as business corporations, that pursue a common agenda over long periods of time. These groups are generally characterized by extensive bureaucracy.

In contemporary American law, organizations are defined as "legal persons" just as individuals are. In reality, however, there are important social differences between organizations and individuals. Organizations generally command more wealth, expertise, and other resources than individuals, and their relations with outsiders are likely to be more impersonal and more narrowly focused. In dealings between organizations and individuals, the former generally enjoy an advantage over the latter; a recent book argues, in fact, that American society has become an "asymmetric society" because of the degree to which organizations are able to pursue their interests at the expense of everybody else (Coleman, 1982). Even among organizations, there are disparities, with the largest and most bureaucratized groups dominating over the smaller and the more informally structured.

The benefit of organization can be seen in the legal arena, where case outcomes vary systematically with the degree of organization of the parties. *The cases most likely to enter the legal arena, and to be defined and treated as serious matters, are the ones in which organizations complain against individuals. Next most serious are ones involving two organizations, then ones between two individuals, and lastly, ones in which individuals complain of offenses by organizations* (Black, 1976: Chapter 5). In this last category falls much of what is known as white-collar or corporate crime, behavior long recognized for its ability to escape aggressive prosecution and punishment (see, e.g., Sutherland, 1945; Clinard and Yeager, 1980: Chapters 12 and 13).

## Other Social Control

Law is not the only method people use to deal with behavior of which they disapprove. It is, in fact, only one of a number of techniques of social control that can be employed. Others include such diverse tactics as inflicting violence against an offender through a strategy of self-help, working out a solution with an offender through negotiation or mediation, cutting off interaction with an offender through avoidance, or trying to get help for an offender through therapy. Some combination of these methods, with or without the occasional use of law, appears in families, friendship networks, workplaces, schools, churches, and all other social settings (see Black, 1976: Chapter 6; 1984; 1990; Horwitz, 1990).

When a problem arises that might be handled by legal officials, one factor that predicts what happens is the availability of other forms of social control. *When alternatives to law are abundant and accessible, people are less likely to invoke law in the first place, and, should they do so, officials are less severe* (Black, 1976: 107–111). They are more likely to refer a case to these alternative forums or simply to refuse to do much about it themselves.

All forms of social control entail a condemnation of someone's behavior. The degree to which a person has been subject to social control in the past—including law—defines that person's moral reputation, or "normative status" (Black, 1976: 111). Someone whose behavior has often aroused negative response has a poor reputation, or low normative status; a morally upstanding person whose conduct has been beyond reproach has a good reputation, or high normative status. Like the other kinds of status already discussed, normative status predicts and explains what happens in legal cases. *The most law and the most penal law are found when persons of poor reputation offend those of unblemished character, followed in order by offenses between two morally upstanding people, two disreputable people, and those committed by a person with a high normative status against someone whose reputation is compromised* (Black, 1976: 111–117).

This overview of how social factors shape legal outcomes is necessarily brief and general. A more detailed discussion of the Blackian theory of law can be found in a number of places (e.g., Black, 1976; 1989; Horwitz, 1990: Chapters 8 and 9; Baumgartner, 1992). One issue that remains to be considered here, however, is the question of exactly how these social factors intrude themselves into the legal

tice should be defined (see Black, 1972). At the same time, however, much of its theory is of great relevance to participants in the legal system and to concerned citizens more generally. Many of its claims challenge longstanding conceptions about law, while many of the facts it features raise difficult questions for those concerned with issues of justice and fairness. Work in this tradition even suggests new possibilities for the deliberate manipulation of legal systems in order to bring about intended results, techniques of social engineering likely to become highly controversial as well as highly effective. The impact of the Blackian approach is thus far reaching.

## JURISPRUDENTIAL IMPACT

As legal sociology has evolved, it has put into new perspective many of the most time-honored notions found in the philosophy of law, or jurisprudence. Consider, for example, the concept of discretion, used to refer to the latitude of legal officials when they decide how to handle cases. The traditional understanding of discretion is that it allows officials to decide cases "according to the dictates of their own judgment and conscience, uncontrolled by the judgment and conscience of others" (Black, in *Black's Law Dictionary,* 1968: 553). Discretion is said to introduce a significant measure of unpredictability into legal systems, and much variation in legal processing is attributed to it. In this view, discretion is associated with idiosyncrasy and caprice—products of a human element in legal functioning that is ultimately beyond comprehension or control.

The sociology of law suggests that discretion is really something quite different, and that the traditional understanding is inaccurate and constitutes a myth about how legal systems actually operate (Baumgartner, 1992). As we have seen, legal sociology indicates that the discretionary decisions of officials are not random and capricious, but rather highly regular and patterned. While they may be largely unpredictable in terms of statutes, case law, evidentiary guidelines, and the like, they are quite predictable when analyzed sociologically using Blackian theory. Factors such as the ones discussed above—the social status of everyone involved in a case, the nature of their personal relationships with one another, and so forth—determine how discretion is exercised. Seen in this way, discretion turns out to be something far different from the uncontrolled use of personal judgment, appearing instead as conduct constrained by the dictates of sociological laws.

Another traditional understanding called into question by the sociology of law is that of discrimination. From a jurisprudential perspective, discrimination is regarded as a deviation from the rule of law, something that happens when social factors like wealth or race are allowed to contaminate the legal process. Discrimination is contrasted with what should occur under more normal circumstances—the rigid application of relevant rules in light of the known facts of a case. Blackian sociology of law, however, suggests a different understanding of discrimination (see generally Black, 1989). The weight of the evidence reveals that social influences on legal outcomes are not exceptional, but rather ubiquitous, and that the handling of cases solely in terms of technically relevant criteria is something that essentially never happens. What is more, discrimination is not limited to the effects of social class or race. Legal systems everywhere process cases on the basis of a host of other social characteristics, as described above. Discrimination thus turns out to be vastly more extensive and routine than has commonly been recognized, "an aspect of the natural behavior of law, as natural as the flying of birds or the swimming of fish" (Black, 1989: 21–22).

The sociology of law also has implications for some more limited and technical concepts in jurisprudence. One such concept, for example, is that of the "reasonable person." This hypothetical individual represents the responsible citizen, whose degree of understanding, knowledge, caution, and moral sensitivity serves as a yardstick against which that of other individuals can be measured. The construct of the reasonable person plays a role in the framing and resolution of a variety of legal matters, such as those dealing with allegations of recklessness and negligence. The reasonable person takes on a very different appearance from the traditional one, however, in light of research indicating that what people say and do varies considerably across social groups. Depending on the specifics of a case, men may uphold different standards of what is reasonable than women do, highly educated persons may uphold different standards than less educated people do, blacks may uphold different standards than whites do, and so on (see Kornstein, 1993). The reasonable person thus turns out to be different in different social locations, so that in diverse societies like the contemporary United States there may be no single reasonable person at all. Accordingly, any legal provision that assumes the existence of a common standard of reasonableness is likely to require rethinking.

As significant as the scientific sociology of law is for the understanding of any number of legal concepts like discretion, discrimination, and the reasonable person, it has a still broader jurisprudential relevance as well. This lies in the alternative perspective it provides on the fundamental nature of law itself (see Black, 1989: 19–22). While law is traditionally understood as an affair of rules, the sociology of law sees it as an affair of human beings responding in predictable ways to their social environment. Instead of seeing the rigorous and detached application of formal standards as the heart of legal behavior, it sees instead moral confrontation and moral struggle between adversaries whose chances of success are shaped by their social identities. Rather than formality, logic, and consistency, it sees in law a variability fine-tuned to respond to every social feature of every case. Approached sociologically, then, law itself looks very different from the way in which it has so commonly been portrayed in the past.

## MORAL IMPACT

As a scientific enterprise, legal sociology is not in a position to pass judgment on the facts and patterns it uncovers. Those facts and patterns, however, can possess great moral relevance for participants and critics of a legal system. This is particularly true in societies like the contemporary United States, where it is widely accepted that justice requires similar legal treatment of socially dissimilar individuals, or where, to put it another way, it is largely taken for granted that legal discrimination is always wrong. Where such values prevail, the findings of legal sociology can be very disturbing indeed.

Of course, evidence that legal systems treat people differently on the basis of their social characteristics would not present a challenge to those who find such discrimination morally acceptable. There have, in fact, been many societies in which at least some forms of legal discrimination have been seen as perfectly appropriate by significant numbers of people. One student of law in the Roman Empire has concluded, for example, that "the Romans rejected juridical equality, the equality of all citizens before the law, as easily as they rejected political equality. Cicero viewed as unequal that kind of equality which 'does not recognize grades of dignity'" (Garnsey, 1968: 165). Romans expected their legal system to favor the wealthy and privileged, as indeed it did. In Rome and in many other places, the written law itself explicitly called for the differential treatment of different kinds of people. The earliest known legal code, that of Hammurabi from the ancient Middle East, stipulated penalties of varying severity for an assortment of offenses based on the social standing of both wrongdoer and victim (Harper, 1904). In many societies, then, legal discrimination has been practiced overtly and without apparent guilt of any kind. In these places, the sociology of law would have only limited ability to scandalize.

In most contemporary democratic societies, by contrast, the realities of discrimination revealed by legal sociology and described above are in stark contradiction to the widespread ideological commitment to legal equality. What the sociology of law documents is that the social factors openly acknowledged to dictate legal outcomes in some societies continue to exert a profound effect even when they are officially repudiated or denied. As Donald Black has put it: "Legal sociology therefore invites modern jurisprudence to face reality: Cases are not decided by rules alone" (Black, 1989: 100). A powerful though unwritten and possibly unconscious moral sense guides legal decision making in modern societies, one in which different outcomes are considered appropriate for different kinds of people and different social circumstances. This folk morality not only conflicts with the official one, but appears the stronger of the two, for it is the one that prevails in practice.

Faced with evidence of systematic social variability in modern legal behavior, one possibility is to maintain that all of it is morally wrong and must somehow be eliminated. Another possibility is to survey the range of variability that has been uncovered and to make distinctions between forms of social discrimination considered least acceptable and others considered justifiable after all (see Black, 1989: 100–101). Giving preferential treatment to wealthier people who have legal conflicts with poorer people might be rejected as indefensible, for example, while a moral debate on the effects of factors such as intimacy or reputation might reach a different conclusion. It might be felt that those who offend intimates ought to be treated differently from those who offend strangers, or that special consideration should properly be given to victims who have always lived a blameless life over those who have frequently violated social conventions.

Whatever the outcome of these moral debates might be, it seems likely that the debates will indeed occur as the theories and findings of legal sociology become more widely known. Disagreements may well arise as different people come to different conclusions about the moral relevance of the field. The existence of pervasive social discrimination in the legal system, however, is more and more obvious with every advance in the sociology of law, and coming to terms with this fact is something increasingly difficult to avoid.

## PRACTICAL IMPACT

Legal sociology is a potentially powerful tool available to those who would like to change or control the legal system. In the past, most legal engineering has proceeded on an ad hoc basis, guided only by intuition and conviction, and not surprisingly, much of it has failed to achieve its ends. With legal sociology, however, comes a better understanding of the principles underlying legal behavior and thus new possibilities for effective manipulation. Whether the application of sociological knowledge will be seen as a good thing in any particular instance will depend largely on whether people approve of the goals being sought, but, like it or not, there is no turning back from the new power over law that sociology makes available.

One possible application of legal sociology is "sociological litigation," or the systematic use of sociological knowledge in the day-to-day practice of law (Black, 1989: Chapter 2). Many decisions that lawyers have to make in handling cases could be affected by sociology, including "screening cases for professional attention; scheduling fees; choosing case participants; deciding whether to seek out-of-court settlements; preparing cases for trial; selecting judges, jurors, and venues; devising tactics during trial; and, when losses occur, deciding whether to appeal to a higher court" (Black, 1989: 25). The Blackian sociology of law indicates which people are most likely to win legal cases—high-status people confronting those of low status, respectable people confronting known deviants, formal organizations confronting individuals, and so forth. It points out the social characteristics that make for effective and thus desirable witnesses, as well as ones that make for sympathetic and thus preferable third parties such as judges and jurors. A careful analysis of the social identities of all those involved in a legal matter reveals the sociological strengths and weaknesses of a case, allowing attorneys to determine how good a risk a client is and how best to manage and present a case to maximize the likelihood of success. Lawyers may advise people with sociologically weak cases not to bother pursuing them, may request payment on an hourly rather than a contingency basis should they go ahead in such matters, or may aggressively try to negotiate outcomes in these cases rather than run the risk of a trial. In court, an attorney engaged in sociological litigation can be certain to draw attention to every advantageous fact about the client and disadvantageous one about the op-

William M. O'Barr, provides insight into one of the more subtle ways in which social status becomes a factor in legal cases: how people talk. Using observational and experimental techniques, O'Barr demonstrates that people from different status levels tend to speak differently, and that these differences in turn determine their credibility when they testify in court. Women more than men, and lower-status people more than those of higher status, are likely to use a "powerless" style of speech marked by various hesitations, qualifications, and expressions of deference. When asked to assess the credibility of witnesses in a courtroom setting, research subjects consistently rate powerless speakers as significantly less convincing and trustworthy than those who use a more confident and aggressive "powerful" style. Since both how people speak and how others respond to their speech styles are generally not conscious matters, O'Barr's findings suggest that status enters the legal process through means that are all but undetectable to the parties concerned.

The last reading in this section is "Law and Social Status in Colonial New Haven, 1639–1665" by M. P. Baumgartner. This paper draws on court records from a Puritan colony in 17th-century New England to explore the effects of social stratification on law in a very different setting from that of the contemporary United States. It reports patterns that are essentially the same as those found today: In the New Haven Colony, higher-status persons used law more often, especially against those of lower status, and used it more successfully than less privileged citizens did. The complaints most likely to succeed were those brought by high-status persons against their status inferiors, followed by those brought by high-status people against other high-status people, then by low-status people against other low-status people, and lastly by low-status people against those of higher rank. These patterns appeared in both the criminal and civil matters handled by the court. The article's findings illustrate how Black's theory of law and social stratification transcends the boundaries of particular societies and applies in places widely separated by social and historical distance.

## SOCIAL MORPHOLOGY

The four readings in this section consider the relationship between law and aspects of social morphology addressed in Black's theory, including the degree of intimacy between people involved in a case and the degree of their participation in the life of their communities. "Murder in Space City," by Henry P. Lundsgaarde, focuses on the first of these issues. Lundsgaarde reports findings from a study of homicide in Houston, Texas. Drawing on official case files, he documents that the severity of the legal treatment accorded killers varies with the nature of their ties to their victims. Throughout the stages of the criminal justice process—in the actions of detectives, prosecutors, grand juries, judges, and trial juries, among others—those who kill intimates such as family members are treated more leniently than those who kill friends or casual acquaintances, and those who kill friends or casual acquaintances are treated more leniently than those who kill strangers. The killers of strangers are more likely to be charged with serious crimes such as first or second degree murder, and are more likely to be indicted, convicted, and sentenced to the harshest punishments, such as long prison terms or execution. These findings are consistent with Black's claims about the effects of relational distance on law.

Intimacy is also the major explanatory variable illustrated in the "The Oven-Bird's Song: Insiders, Outsiders, and Personal Injuries in an American Community" by David M. Engel. Engel reports findings from an ethnographic study of personal injury litigation in a small American town. In the community studied, long-time residents are extremely reluctant to sue one another, even when they have sustained injuries that are serious and result in permanent disabilities. In the relatively few cases in which injuries do lead to lawsuits, the parties are almost always separated from each other by some significant measure of relational distance. A resident might sue or be sued by an outsider from another county or state, for example, or one of the parties might be a relative newcomer who is neither personally nor socially close to the other. The behavior of third parties in the town also conforms to Black's theories. Local attorneys, for example, who are closely linked to most prospective defendants, are very reluctant to participate in legal action against them. As a result, plaintiffs' attorneys almost always come from outside the county. And juries composed of local residents are extremely unlikely to find liability in such cases and award substantial judgments to plaintiffs, especially when this would entail a victory for an outsider over a fellow resident. This is consistent with Black's claim that legal agents who are closer to one side than the other will tend to favor that side in their decisions.

"Evidence as Partisanship," by Mark Cooney, explores the social roots of evidence, arguing that what at first appears to be a purely technical matter—the amount of evidence available in a case—is actually the result of the social circumstances under which the case arises. Applying Black's theory of partisanship, which claims that people are most likely to give support in conflicts to individuals of high social status and those to whom they are personally close (Black, 1993), Cooney seeks to explain the amount of evidence that parties to a legal action are able to assemble. He finds that high-status individuals and those who have close ties to many people enjoy special advantages in the production of evidence. They are, for example, better able to recruit witnesses who will provide leads or testify on their behalf during trials, which in turn can only increase their chances of winning their cases. Because the social origins of evidence are often obscured as a case wends its way through the legal process, it may often seem that a matter has been handled on the basis of evidence alone, when in fact social factors have been critical in determining what that evidence is in the first place. Cooney's work highlights more generally the important role played by third parties—people other than the principals themselves—in predicting what happens to a case.

"Structure and Practice of Familial-Based Justice in a Criminal Court," by Kathleen Daly, documents the effect on law of another aspect of social morphology—the degree to which individuals involved in legal matters are active con-the moral status of the victims. Prosecutors claim that respectable citizens are better able to persuade judges and jurors to convict those accused of offending them, while people with bad reputations lack credibility and become a liability to the prosecution. Drawing on ethnographic field work in the office of the Manhattan district attorney, Stanko describes the kinds of victims who have trouble convincing prosecutors to take aggressive measures on their behalf. These include people victimized while buying illegal drugs, members of youth gangs, those with prior convictions of their own, and those who appear to be homosexuals, prostitutes, or alcoholics. People with a higher normative status have a considerably easier time securing the prosecution of those who offend them.

The last selection in the book looks at a different aspect of the relationship between law and other social control. In "Sheathing the Sword of Justice: An Essay on Law without Sanctions," John O. Haley considers how the total amount of law in one society—Japan—is associated with the variety and strength of its nonlegal means of social control. Haley's analysis seems to be a response to an earlier influential work by a Japanese scholar, Takeyoshi Kawashima, who argued that Japan has very little law because it is a society in which nonlegal alternatives like mediation are traditionally available. Haley agrees that Japan has little law, as evidenced by its small number of lawyers, prosecutors, and judges as well as by the extremely weak character of its legal sanctions. But he questions whether this comparative lack of law results from the availability of informal alternatives and suggests instead that the nonlegal alternatives result from the lack of law. Since the Japanese cannot rely on the courts to preserve social order and redress injustice, he argues, they have been forced to find other ways of achieving these ends. Regardless of issues of cause and effect, the Japanese case illustrates Black's claim of an inverse relationship between law and other social control: Where a great deal of one of these is found, there is not likely to be much of the other.

In their various ways, all of the readings in this book support and illustrate one central argument. Law is a social phenomenon. It arises from human activity and can be understood, predicted, and explained with its social environment. It is not immune to science. The Blackian paradigm, and the body of theory that employs it, provide powerful tools for making sense of legal behavior of all kinds, in all societies, at all historical moments. More than the content of the specific readings, it is this underlying message, conveyed by the cumulative weight of all the selections, that the present volume is designed to introduce.

## REFERENCES

Baumgartner, M. P. 1992. "The myth of discretion." Pages 129–162 in *The Uses of Discretion,* edited by Keith Hawkins. Oxford: Clarendon Press.
Bernard, J. L. 1979. "Interaction between the race of the defendant and that of jurors in determining verdicts." *Law and Psychology Review* 5: 103–111.

Black, Donald. 1972. "The boundaries of legal sociology." *Yale Law Journal* 81: 1086–1100.

———. 1976. *The Behavior of Law*. New York: Academic Press.

———. 1979. "A strategy of pure sociology." Pages 149–168 in *Theoretical Perspectives in Sociology*, edited by Scott G. McNall. New York: St. Martin's Press.

———. 1984. "Social control as a dependent variable." Pages 1–36 in *Toward a General Theory of Social Control*, Volume 1: *Fundamentals*, edited by Donald Black. Orlando: Academic Press.

———. 1989. *Sociological Justice*. New York: Oxford University Press.

———. 1990. "The elementary forms of conflict management." Pages 43–69 in *New Directions in the Study of Justice, Law, and Social Control*, edited by the School of Justice Studies, Arizona State University. New York: Plenum Press.

———. 1992. "The social control of the self." *Virginia Review of Sociology* 1: 39–49.

———. 1993. "Taking sides." Pages 125–143 in *The Social Structure of Right and Wrong*. San Diego: Academic Press.

———. 1995. "The epistemology of pure sociology." *Law and Social Inquiry* 20: 829–870.

———, and M. P. Baumgartner. 1983. "Toward a theory of the third party." Pages 84–114 in *Empirical Theories about Courts*, edited by Keith O. Boyum and Lynn Mather. New York: Longman Press.

Black, H. C. 1968. *Black's Law Dictionary*. St. Paul: West Publishing Company.

Bowers, William J., and Glenn L. Pierce. 1980. "Arbitrariness and discrimination under post-*Furman* capital statutes." *Crime and Delinquency* 26: 563–635.

Cain, Maureen, and Alan Hunt. 1979. *Marx and Engels on Law*. London: Academic Press.

Clinard, Marshall B., and Peter C. Yeager (with the collaboration of Ruth Blackburn Clinard). 1980. *Corporate Crime*. New York: Free Press.

Coleman, James S. 1982. *The Asymmetric Society*. Syracuse: Syracuse University Press.

Cooney, Mark. 1994. "Evidence as partisanship." *Law and Society Review* 28: 833–858.

Durkheim, Emile. 1893. *The Division of Labor in Society*. New York: Free Press, 1964.

Garnsey, Peter. 1968. "Legal privilege in the Roman Empire." *Past and Present* 41: 3–24.

Gluckman, Max. 1967. *The Judicial Process among the Barotse of Northern Rhodesia*. Manchester: Manchester University Press (second edition; first edition, 1955).

Harper, Robert Francis (translator). 1904. *The Code of Hammurabi, King of Babylon: About 2250 B.C.* Chicago: University of Chicago Press.

Horwitz, Allan V. 1990. *The Logic of Social Control*. New York: Plenum Press.

Kornstein, Sandy. 1993. The "Reasonable Person": The Link between Cultural Diversity, Law, and Social Science. Unpublished Master's Paper, Department of Sociology, Rutgers University.

LaFree, Gary. 1980. "The effect of social stratification by race on official reactions to rape." *American Sociological Review* 45: 842–854.

Leiter, Brian. 1996. "Legal realism." Pages 261–279 in *A Companion to the Philosophy of Law and Legal Theory*, edited by Dennis Patterson. Oxford: Blackwell.

Levin, Martin A. 1974. "Urban politics and judicial behavior." *Journal of Legal Studies* 3: 339–375.

Montesquieu, Baron de. 1748. *The Spirit of the Laws*. New York: Hafner, 1949.

Nagel, Stuart S. 1962. "Judicial backgrounds and criminal cases." *Journal of Criminal Law, Criminology and Police Science* 53: 333–339.

Pfeiffer, John E. 1982. *The Creative Explosion: An Inquiry into the Origins of Art and Religion*. Ithaca: Cornell University Press.

Rousseau, Jean-Jacques. 1762. *The Social Contract: Or, Principles of Political Right*. Middlesex: Penguin Books, 1968.

Spitzer, Steven. 1975. "Punishment and social organization: a study of Durkheim's theory of penal evolution." *Law and Society Review* 9: 613–635.

Strodtbeck, Fred L., Rita M. James, and Charles Hawkins. 1957. "Social status in jury deliberations." *American Sociological Review* 22: 713–719.

Sutherland, Edwin H. 1945. "Is 'white collar crime' crime?" *American Sociological Review* 10: 132–139.

Uhlman, Thomas M. 1979. *Racial Justice: Black Judges and Defendants in an Urban Trial Court*. Lexington: Lexington Books.

Weber, Max. 1922. *The Theory of Social and Economic Organization,* edited by Talcott Parsons. New York: Free Press, 1964.

# LAW AND SOCIAL STRATIFICATION

# 2

# ARBITRARINESS AND DISCRIMINATION UNDER POST-FURMAN CAPITAL STATUTES*

## WILLIAM J. BOWERS
## GLENN L. PIERCE

In the *Furman v. Georgia* decision on June 29, 1972,[1] the United States Supreme Court held by a five to four margin that capital punishment, as administered under then-existing statutes, was unconstitutional. In separate opinions, the concurring majority variously characterized the imposition of the death penalty as "freakishly rare," "irregular," "random," "capricious," "uneven," "wanton," "excessive," "disproportionate," and "discriminatory." The majority were united in the finding that the death penalty was being used in an "arbitrary" manner. The Court ruled that because death is a supremely harsh and an irrevocable form of punishment, "different in kind from lesser criminal sanctions," such arbitrariness in capital punishment was a violation of Eighth Amendment prohibitions against "cruel and unusual" punishment.[2]

The *Furman* decision did not, however, put an end to capital punishment in the United States. To be sure, two of the concurring majority—Justices Brennan and Marshall—found death as a form of punishment constitutionally unacceptable, but the other three —Justices Douglas, Stewart, and White—limited their objections to existing statutes "as applied." Justice Douglas contended that the Court's intervention was warranted because the existing statutes gave "uncontrolled discretion" to sentencers and provided "no standards [to] govern the selection of the penalty."

---

*See p. 55

[1]*Furman v. Georgia,* 408 U.S. 238 (1972).

[2]The Court had previously held in *McGautha v. California,* 402 U.S. 183 (1971) that discretion in capital sentencing that might result in arbitrary or discriminatory imposition of the death penalty was not a violation of the Fourteenth Amendment "due process" clause. The finding of arbitrariness in *Furman v. Georgia* served, however, to sustain an Eighth Amendment challenge which explicitly incorporated the unique severity and finality of capital punishment.

---

Justice Stewart's opinion also reflected concern with discretion in the sentencing process. In his dissenting opinion, Chief Justice Burger suggested that states could restore capital punishment by drafting new statutes that would narrow and restrict the exercise of discretion in sentencing.

Reacting to the *Furman* decision, state legislatures adopted remedies varying in the restrictions they placed on sentencing discretion. These post-*Furman* capital statutes took two basic approaches: the "mandatory" death sentence, designed to eliminate sentencing discretion altogether, and "guided discretion" statutes, designed to limit or control the exercise of discretion by means of explicit standards to be followed in the sentencing process. Mandatory statutes were narrowly drawn to avoid ambiguity in classifying crimes as capital offenses, and the death sentence was made mandatory upon conviction for such offenses. Guided discretion statutes provide standards, typically in the form of specific aggravating and mitigating circumstances, that must be taken into account before the death sentence can be handed down. These new guided discretion statutes also provide for separate phases of the trial to determine guilt and punishment, and for automatic appellate review of all death sentences.

In *Gregg v. Georgia* and companion cases, decided on July 2, 1976,[3] the United States Supreme Court rejected the mandatory death penalty as provided for by the legislatures of Louisiana and North Carolina, but upheld guided discretion as formulated in the statutes of Florida, Georgia, and Texas. The Court reasoned that making the death penalty mandatory upon conviction removes sentencing discretion that should be exercised in the interest of "individualized" justice and that the total absence of discretion in sentencing may cause the trial of guilt to be colored by considerations of punishment (i.e., jury nullification). By contrast, it reasoned that providing specific sentencing guidelines to be followed in a separate postconviction phase of the trial would free the sentencing decision of arbitrariness and discrimination and, for that matter, free the guilt decision of sentencing considerations. . . .

The present study examines whether the new post-*Furman* capital statutes affirmed by the Supreme Court in the *Gregg* decision have, in fact, eliminated the arbitrariness and discrimination which rendered pre-*Furman* capital statutes unconstitutional. We consider the nature of arbitrariness, the forms it takes, and its sources in the extralegal functions of capital punishment. We then turn to the existing evidence of arbitrariness and discrimination under pre-*Furman* statutes that can serve as a baseline against which the operation of the post-*Furman* statutes may be judged. These steps will set the stage for our report of findings to date from an on-going research project designed to evaluate the application of post-*Furman* capital statutes in terms of arbitrariness and discrimination.

---

[3]*Gregg v. Georgia,* 96 S. Ct. 2909 (1976); *Roberts v. Louisiana,* 96 S. Ct. 3001 (1976); *Woodson v. North Carolina,* 95 S. Ct. 2978 (1976); *Profitt v. Florida,* 96 S. Ct. 2960 (1976); *Jurek v. Texas,* 96 S. Ct. 2950 (1976).

1940, Charles Mangum reported that execution clemency disproportionately favored white as opposed to black offenders condemned to death. With data (supplied to him by Johnson) on commutations of death sentences in the 1920s and 1930s for nine southern and border states—Florida, Kentucky, Missouri, North Carolina, Oklahoma, South Carolina, Tennessee, Texas, and Virginia—Mangum showed that in every state commutations were more likely for whites than for blacks on death row. Thus, in contrast with Garfinkel's study showing differential treatment by race across stages of the criminal justice process in a single state, Mangum showed differential treatment by race across states at a single stage of the process.

Notably, the suppressor effect of victim's race revealed in Johnson's and Garfinkel's studies suggests that Mangum's data may actually have underestimated differences in the use of executive clemency by race of offender. Indeed, a year after the publication of Mangum's work, Johnson actually demonstrated a suppressor effect of victim's race at the postsentencing stage of the process as well. Working with a restricted sample of cases from the period from 1933 through 1939 in North Carolina for which race of victim could be obtained, he tabulated the data for offenders only and for offender/victim combinations (Johnson, 1941: Table 2). "When the data are tabulated merely by race of offender," in Johnson's words, "they show that 71.6 percent of the Negroes and 69.0 percent of the whites get executed. When they are tabulated by offender-victim groupings the picture is different" (ibid: 100). Johnson reported that 80.5% of the blacks who killed whites were executed, compared with only 68.3% of the whites who killed whites. And the difference attributable to race of victim among black offenders was even greater.

These early studies established several things: (1) that there were very substantial differences by race of both offender and victim in the administration of capital punishment in selected southern and border states; (2) that the pattern was repeated with minor variations at successive stages of the criminal justice process; and (3) that the magnitude of racial differences was obscured by the lack of information on race of both offender and victim in the analysis. These studies do not directly control for the possibility that the crimes of blacks and crimes against whites were more serious or aggravated in nature and thus more likely to qualify for the death penalty. The magnitude of racial differences especially at later stages of the process does, however, cast doubt on the possibility that legally relevant factors are responsible for these differences. After all, the defendants who reach each successive stage of the process are, presumably, more nearly alike in personal culpability and the character of their crimes.

## FURTHER EVIDENCE OF SYSTEMATIC ARBITRARINESS

In the years that followed, research on the criminal justice processing of potentially capital cases spread to states in other regions of the country, and investigators focused in more detail on discrete stages of the criminal justice process, explicitly introducing interpretive variables into their analyses in an effort to account for observed racial differences in terms of legally relevant factors. The earliest and most numerous of the studies dealt with the postsentencing stage of the process; the most extensive and detailed dealt with the sentencing stage; the fewest and most recent have examined the presentencing stage of the process. We review them in this order.

The greatest number of these studies have focused on the postsentencing stage of the process, perhaps because data on death row inmates, commutations, and executions are relatively complete and accessible from prison records. Following Mangum's lead, investigators have documented racial differences in the likelihood of execution among death row inmates in Maryland (Maryland Legislative Council, 1962), New Jersey (Bedau, 1964), Ohio (Ohio Legislative Service Commission, 1961), Pennsylvania (Wolfgang, Kelly, and Nolde, 1962), and, for longer periods than Mangum examined, in Texas (Koeninger, 1969) and North Carolina (Johnson, 1957). These studies extend the coverage of Mangum's research to non-southern states with sufficient numbers of blacks sentenced to death for reliable comparisons. Two of these studies are notable for their extensions beyond Mangum's research and refinements of the work he initiated.

The first to appear was carried out by Elmer H. Johnson in 1957 with data on commutations and executions in North Carolina for the period from 1909 through 1956 (Johnson, 1957). He showed substantial differences in execution rates for specific types of offenses, by race of offender within broad offense categories such as murder, rape, and burglary, and by race of victim for the crime of rape. His analysis also traced changes over time in execution rates by race of offender and by reasons for commutation as given in official commutation statements. His analysis did not, however, attempt to account for racial differences in execution rates in terms of interpretive variables nor did it attempt to evaluate the independent effects of offender's and victim's race.

The first study that attempted to interpret racial differences in execution rates among condemned murderers in terms of legally relevant variables was conducted with data on death row inmates in Pennsylvania for the period from 1914 through 1958. In 1962, Marvin Wolfgang, Arlene Kelly, and Hans Nolde examined the possibility that higher execution rates for blacks occurred because black condemned murderers were more likely than their white counterparts to have committed felony-type murders, for which commutations were less apt to be granted (Wolfgang, Kelly, and Nolde, 1962). They found that blacks were, indeed, more likely to have committed felony-type murders, *but* that they were less likely to receive commutations than whites for both felony and nonfelony murders. The investigators also found that the greater incidence of court-appointed as opposed to private defense attorneys among condemned blacks did not account for their higher execution rates. This research carried the analysis of racial differences farther than other studies of the postsentencing disposition of condemned offenders. But it too failed to take the race of victim into account, as Johnson had done (Johnson,

1941), and may therefore have underestimated the extent of execution rate differences by race of offender.

The sentencing phase of the process in capital cases has received the most detailed attention. In 1964, Edwin Wolf examined the sentencing of 159 convicted capital offenders in New Jersey over the period from 1937 through 1961 (Wolf, 1964). He found that blacks convicted of a capital crime were more likely than whites to be sentenced to death—47.5% of the blacks compared with 30.4% of the whites received death sentences. He then introduced type of murder (felony versus nonfelony), murder weapon (gun versus other), and offender's age as possible interpreting variables. The difference in treatment by race of offender remained evident under each of these controls.

In a concluding footnote citing Johnson's work, Wolf indicated that race of victim was available for about half the cases, and presented a tabulation of these data showing that 72% of the blacks who killed whites were sentenced to death as compared with 31.6% of the whites who killed whites. Although he made no effort to examine the effect of interpretive factors on offender/victim differences in the likelihood of a death sentence, it is clear from the magnitude of the disparity that none of the control variables available to him could account for it.

The most extensive and ambitious effort to examine the racial factor in capital sentencing was undertaken in the summer of 1965 by Wolfgang and his associates. They gathered extensive data on some 3000 convicted rapists in selected counties of eleven southern and border states for the period from 1945 through 1965. In various reports of their findings, these investigators have shown that the death sentence was more likely for blacks than for whites, and especially so for blacks whose victims were white (Wolfgang, 1974; Wolfgang and Riedel, 1973; 1975). Furthermore, they have shown that the legally relevant aggravating circumstance of an accompanying felony plays no part in the interpretation of the stark racial differences. For both felony and nonfelony rapes, 39% of blacks with white victims were sentenced to death; for the other three offender/victim racial categories combined, 3% were sentenced to death for felony rape and 2% for nonfelony rape.

The first reports of findings from this study presented felony circumstance as the only interpretive variable, although the investigators have indicated that more thorough analyses confirming marked racial differences were carried out separately for Alabama, Arkansas, Florida, Georgia, Louisiana, South Carolina, and Tennessee. In the latest report of their work, however, Marvin Wolfgang and Marc Riedel included an analysis of the Georgia data with a number of control variables introduced not one at a time but simultaneously (Wolfgang and Riedel, 1975). Using discriminant function analysis, the investigators estimated the independent effects of fourteen variables. Only two—black offender/white victim and felony circumstance—had independent effects that were statistically beyond the .01 probability level.

In 1969, a study of the sentencing of 238 persons convicted in California of first degree murder between 1958 and 1966 shifted the focus from race to social class as a basis for differential treatment (Judson *et al.,* 1969). This study used extensive information on the offender, victim, crime, and trial, coded from court and prison records. Controlling for some 18 other variables by means of partial correlation analyses, the investigators found that by occupation, blue-collar defendants were more likely and white-collar defendants were less likely to be sentenced to death. A broader measure of social class incorporating unemployment, job instability, and education (available in the data set) as well as occupation might show an even stronger sentencing difference. Notably, race of offender and victim was not significantly related to the likelihood of a death sentence in this western state after other correlated variables were partialed out. Could it be that where race is not so prominent a basis of stratification in society, other more prominent bases will be substituted for it?

And, finally, what do studies of the presentencing stages in the handling of potentially capital cases show? The tendency for social class to be a basis for differential treatment before sentencing is reflected in research on convictions in murder cases by Victoria Swigert and Ronald Farrell (Swigert and Farrell, 1976; 1977). With data on 444 persons arrested for criminal homicide in an urban jurisdiction in an unnamed northeastern state for the period from 1955 through 1973, these investigators studied factors affecting severity of conviction (as a five-point ordinal scale from first degree murder conviction and eligibility for capital punishment to acquittal).

They first reported that lower-status occupation of the defendant was a significant determinant of conviction severity, independent of other legally relevant factors controlled by multiple regression techniques (Swigert and Farrell, 1977). They later showed that killings that crossed class lines, particularly those with offenders from lower and victims from upper occupational categories, were more likely to result in conviction on murder charges subject to more severe punishment (Farrell and Swigert, 1978). In effect, they demonstrated that social class of both offender and victim was a significant determinant of conviction level—just as previous studies of the racial factor had indicated that both offender's and victim's race figured in the handling of cases across stages of the process. Again, in this study of a nonsouthern jurisdiction, race of offender and victim was not found to be significantly associated with conviction outcome.

Concerning prosecutorial discretion, in 1979 Steven Boris examined the decision to prosecute or dismiss charges against 383 arrested murder suspects in an unnamed large northern industrial city for the year 1972 (Boris, 1979). The study incorporated data on race and occupation of both offender and victim, as well as other legally relevant control variables. Using multiple regression techniques, Boris found that the decision to prosecute was associated with the status of the offender (disadvantaged) and the status of the victim (advantaged) in terms of both race and occupation, with occupation a stronger determinant than race. By focusing on occupation as an indicator of social class of offender and victim, this research and the work of Swigert and Farrell have suggested a more general tendency for the crossing of social boundaries in murder to be singled out as a reason for especially severe treatment of offenders.

## DATA FOR THE ANALYSIS

In the fall of 1977, the Center for Applied Social Research at Northeastern University began collecting data on capital punishment under post-*Furman* statutes, following a national conference on capital punishment attended by lawyers and social scientists.[7] This meeting underscored the need for a centralized effort (1) to gather the kinds of systematic information that might yield *prima facie* evidence of arbitrariness and discrimination under post-*Furman* statutes, and (2) to build a data archive that would contain the refined and detailed kinds of information needed to develop an integrated and exacting picture of the administration of capital punishment following the *Furman* decision.

In gathering data, we have relied on the cooperation of federal, state, and local agencies of government, the help of trial attorneys, and the paid and volunteered assistance of a number of other individuals. We have obtained systematic data on (1) criminal homicides in all states since the 1972 *Furman* decision; (2) death sentences handed down and appellate review in selected states since *Furman;* and (3) the criminal justice processing of potentially capital cases from charge through sentencing in one state under the post-*Furman* capital statute.

## CRIMINAL HOMICIDE DATA

In 1976 the FBI began to include in the Supplementary Homicide Reports information on arrested and/or suspected offenders. Before 1976, these reports contained information on the offense (e.g., felony circumstances, murder weapon, offender/victim relationship, time and location of the crime, number of offenders and victims) and on the victim (e.g., age, sex, race). In 1976, the reports were modified to include such information on the arrested or suspected offender as age, sex, race, and alcohol involvement, and motive for or purpose of the crime (United States Federal Bureau of Investigation, 1976). Thus, since 1976 both offender and victim characteristics have been available for most killings that could be prosecuted as capital offenses.

The Supplementary Homicide Reports are filled out voluntarily by local police departments and are transmitted to a state crime-reporting agency, which compiles state-level crime statistics and forwards the data to the Uniform Crime Reporting section of the FBI. We have obtained from the FBI the data on all states for the pe-

[7]1977 Death Penalty Conference, Howard University, Washington, D.C. The meeting was jointly sponsored by the NAACP Legal Defense Fund and the Center for Studies in Criminology and Criminal Justice, University of Pennsylvania.

riod from 1973 through 1976, and, from the state-level crime-reporting agencies of Florida, Georgia, Texas, and Ohio, the data for the year 1977.[8]

In Florida, the Supplementary Homicide Reports are filed by all local jurisdictions for full statewide coverage; in Georgia, Texas, and Ohio, they are reported by most but not all local agencies. To correct for the incomplete geographic coverage in the latter states, and to estimate offender characteristics for the pre-1976 period in all four states, we have also obtained the complete willful homicide data from the Vital Statistics programs of these states for the period from 1973 through 1977.[9] With these data, we have developed victim-based adjustments for undercoverage of Supplementary Homicide Reports offender data (see Appendix A).

## DEATH SENTENCE AND APPELLATE REVIEW DATA

In the fall of 1977, we began to compile detailed information on all persons sentenced to death in the states whose capital statutes were specifically upheld in the *Gregg* and companion decisions—Florida, Georgia, and Texas. These three states were responsible for approximately half of all death sentences handed down under post-*Furman* capital statutes in effect at that time. In the spring of 1978, we also began to compile such data for Ohio, which brought the representation of post-*Furman* death sentences to approximately 70%. (These estimates are based on a state by state count of death sentences compiled by the United States National Criminal Justice Information and Statistics Service, 1978.) We have periodically updated our data files and now have death sentence information through August 1980 for Florida and Georgia and through May 1978 for Texas. For Ohio, we were able to obtain information on persons under the sentence of death as of the *Lockett* decision of the United States Supreme Court, which overturned Ohio's capital statute on July 3, 1978 (*Lockett v. Ohio*).[10] With respect to appellate review status, we now have complete information for Florida and Georgia through August 1980.

The data collection effort has involved trial attorneys and others, who have helped in compiling and validating the information in the respective states; with their assistance, we have acquired extensive information on offense, defendant, victim, and processing of the case from indictment through appellate review. In particular, the instruments used to compile these data have provided comparable information on felony circumstances of the crime; race of offender and victim; the statutory, aggravating, and mitigating circumstances found by sentencing authorities; and the current status of the case in the appellate review process.

[8]We subsequently obtained the Supplementary Homicide Reports data on all states for 1977 and 1978 from the FBI, but not in time for the information to be incorporated into this report of findings.

[9]These data are published by the Public Health Service, Department of Health and Human Services.

[10]*Lockett v. Ohio.* Unlike that on Florida, Georgia, and Texas, our information on Ohio does not include data on persons sentenced to death; it is restricted to those persons who were under sentence of death at the time of the *Lockett* decision.

## JUDICIAL-PROCESSING DATA

In the fall of 1977, Professor Hans Zeisel of the University of Chicago Law School, Dr. Linda Foley of North Florida University, and the present authors began collaborating to collect data designed to follow the criminal justice processing of potentially capital cases in Florida from charge through sentencing. In the first stage of this project, information was gathered on all first-degree murder indictments from 1973 through 1976 in 21 Florida counties, accounting for approxinately 75% of Florida's death sentences over that period. Six months later, a second stage of data collection was undertaken to obtain a broader initial sampling of homicide cases, including all homicide charges at arraignment. These data were gathered for the period from 1976 through 1977 in a sample of 20 Florida counties, including some but not all of the counties sampled in the first phase of the data collection.

In both phases, data were collected by law students instructed in the use of a standard form designed to gather information on the disposition of the case at successive stages and to obtain characteristics of the crime, the victim, and the accused defendant. All decisions concerning the coding of verbatim material were reviewed by a consulting attorney.

## SCOPE OF THE ANALYSIS

The upcoming analysis deals with the first 5 years following the *Furman* decision. For Florida, Georgia, Texas, and Ohio, we examine criminal homicides committed between the effective dates (if occurring on the first of the month; if not, tabulations begin with the first of the following month) of their respective statutes (i.e., Florida: December 8, 1972; Georgia: March 28, 1973; Texas: January 1, 1974; Ohio: November 1, 1974) and the end of 1977, and the death sentences imposed under the post-*Furman* statutes for homicides occurring before 1978. The analysis of judicial processing in Florida is restricted to offenses that occurred before 1978 and reached the trial court dockets before the collection of data. Thus, December 31, 1977 is our cutoff date in the sense that offenses occurring after 1977, regardless of sentencing date, are excluded from this analysis.

## ANALYSIS

The stage is now set for the analysis. The questions are clear. Have the new post-*Furman* capital statutes removed the substantial risk of arbitrariness and discrimination present under pre-*Furman* statutes? Have they eliminated differential treatment by race of offender and victim by time and place within a jurisdiction, at presentencing and sentencing stages of the process? Has appellate review corrected differential treatment that might have entered earlier in the process? And, are the different forms that post-*Furman* capital statutes take equally effective in purging the process of differential treatment?

## ARBITRARINESS BY RACE

By far the most substantial and consistent extralegal basis of differential treatment under pre-*Furman* statutes was race. All but a few studies found gross racial differences in the likelihood of a death sentence; race of both offender and victim was associated with differential treatment, and race of victim was a more prominent basis of differential treatment than race of offender. If the post-*Furman* statutes have remedied the previous ills, we should find no substantial or consistent differences by race in the likelihood of a death sentence for criminal homicide under the new statutes.

The likelihood of a death sentence by offender/victim racial categories in Florida, Georgia, Texas, and Ohio is shown in Table 2. It presents the estimated num-

TABLE 2    Probability of Receiving the Death Sentence in Florida, Georgia, Texas, and Ohio for Criminal Homicide, by Race of Offender and Victim (from effective dates of respective post-*Furman* capital statutes through 1977)

| Offender/victim racial combinations | (1) Estimated number of offenders[a] | (2) Persons sentenced to death | (3) Overall probability of death sentence |
|---|---|---|---|
| Florida | | | |
| Black kills white | 240 | 53 | .221 |
| White kills white | 1768 | 82 | .046 |
| Black kills black | 1922 | 12 | .006 |
| White kills black | 80 | 0 | .000 |
| Georgia | | | |
| Black kills white | 258 | 43 | .167 |
| White kills white | 1006 | 42 | .042 |
| Black kills black | 2458 | 12 | .005 |
| White kills black | 71 | 2 | .028 |
| Texas | | | |
| Black kills white | 344 | 30 | .087 |
| White kills white | 3616 | 56 | .015 |
| Black kills black | 2597 | 2 | .001 |
| White kills black | 143 | 1 | .007 |
| Ohio | | | |
| Black kills white | 173 | 44 | .254 |
| White kills white | 803 | 37 | .046 |
| Black kills black | 1170 | 20 | .017 |
| White kills black | 47 | 0 | .000 |

Data sources (keyed to Appendix B): Florida—A1, A2, B1, B2, C1; Georgia—A1, A3, A6, C2; Texas—A1, A5, A8, C4; Ohio—A1, A4, A7, C3.

[a]Based on information submitted by the police in the Supplementary Homicide Reports. The number of offenders is estimated as described in Appendix A, with the following adjustment factors: Florida, 2.861; Georgia, 4.453; Texas, 2.473; Ohio, 1.871.

**TABLE 3**  Probability of Receiving the Death Sentence in Florida, Georgia, and Texas for Felony and Nonfelony Murder, by Race of Offender and Victim (from effective dates of respective post-*Furman* capital statutes through 1977)

| Offender/victim racial combinations | Felony-Type Murder | | | Nonfelony-Type Murder | | |
|---|---|---|---|---|---|---|
| | (1) Estimated number of offenders[a] | (2) Persons sentenced to death | (3) Probability of death sentence | (4) Estimated number of offenders[a] | (5) Persons sentenced to death | (6) Overall probability of death sentence |
| **Florida** | | | | | | |
| Black kills white | 143 | 46 | .323 | 97 | 7 | .072 |
| White kills white | 303 | 65 | .215 | 1465 | 17 | .012 |
| Black kills black | 160 | 7 | .044 | 1762 | 5 | .003 |
| White kills black | 11 | 0 | .000 | 69 | 0 | .000 |
| **Georgia** | | | | | | |
| Black kills white | 134 | 39 | .291 | 124 | 3 | .024 |
| White kills white | 183 | 37 | .202 | 823 | 6 | .007 |
| Black kills black | 205 | 8 | .039 | 2253 | 4 | .002 |
| White kills black | 13 | 2 | .154 | 58 | 0 | .000 |
| **Texas** | | | | | | |
| Black kills white | 173 | 28 | .162 | 171 | 2 | .012 |
| White kills white | 378 | 48 | .127 | 3238 | 8 | .002 |
| Black kills black | 121 | 2 | .017 | 2476 | 0 | .000 |
| White kills black | 30 | 1 | .033 | 113 | 0 | .000 |

Data sources (keyed to Appendix B): See Table 2.
[a] See Table 2.

It appears, then, that among the kinds of killings least likely to be punished by death (i.e., nonfelony killings), the death sentence is used primarily in response to the most socially condemned form of boundary crossing—a crime against a majority group member by a minority group member. Among those offenders more commonly (but not usually or typically) punished by death (i.e., those committing a felony homicide), there is some suggestion that cases of boundary crossing in the opposite direction—with majority group offenders and minority group victims— are selected occasionally against the prevailing race of offender and victim influences for more severe treatment.[19] But this latter pattern is a minor variation on a major theme. The primary point is this: Among felony killings, for which the death penalty is more apt to be used, race of victim is the chief basis of differential treatment.

Table 3 also helps to clarify the effects of differences among the capital statutes of Florida, Georgia, and Texas. We noted in connection with Table 2 that the overall likelihood of a death sentence was somewhat greater in Florida than in Georgia, but that the differences were less for specific offender/victim racial categories. With the control for felony circumstances in Table 3, the differences between corresponding categories are still further reduced for killings under felony circumstances. Thus, compared with Florida, the likelihood of a death sentence in Georgia is 10% lower for black offender/white victim felony killings, 6% lower for white/white felony killings, and 11% lower for black/black felony killings. (The corresponding figures for all homicides in Table 2 are 24, 9, and 17%, respectively.) Among nonfelony killings, for which the death sentence is relatively unlikely, there are greater differences in some of the categories between the two states in relative terms. But by and large, the statutes of these two states yield similar levels and patterns in the use of the death penalty.

Moreover, Table 3 addresses a question raised earlier, about the manner in which the Texas "structured discretion" statute affects the likelihood of a death sentence. It is clear from Table 3 that the death sentence is less likely in Texas than in Florida or Georgia for felony as well as nonfelony killings. Obviously, the low likelihood of a death sentence in Texas is not simply the result of the statutory restrictions on the kinds of killings that qualify for the death penalty. It is evident that, for the kinds that qualify in all three states—namely, felony murders—Texas has relatively fewer death sentences. Apparently, the procedural questions of aggravation the Texas jury must answer have the effect of limiting the imposition of the death sentence in that state. These inferences are, of course, only as strong as the assumption that the killers are no more culpable and their crimes no more heinous in one state than another, or that the prosecutors, judges, and juries in the three states do not differ in their predilection for capital punishment.

The data in this section point to more than arbitrariness and discrimination in

---

[19]In each state the fewest homicides are reported for the white offender/black victim category. Hence, the likelihood estimates for this category are least stable, and comparisons between this category and the others are least reliable.

isolation. They reflect a twofold departure from even-handed justice which is consistent with a single underlying racist tenet: that white lives are worth more than black lives. From this tenet it follows that death as punishment is more appropriate for the killers of whites than for the killers of blacks and more appropriate for black than for white killers. Either discrimination by race of offender or disparities of treatment by race of victim of the magnitudes we have seen here are a direct challenge to the constitutionality of the post-*Furman* capital statutes. Together, these elements of arbitrariness and discrimination may represent a two-edged sword of racism in capital punishment which is beyond statutory control.

## CHAPTER TITLE NOTE

*This study was made possible by the cooperation and assistance of a great many people and organizations, to whom we are deeply grateful. In developing the present analysis, we have consulted with many people. For their assistance and insights, we wish to thank Millard Farmer and Courtney Mullins, of Team Defense; Morris Dees, John Carroll, and Dennis Balske, of the Southern Poverty Law Center; John Boger and Joel Berger, of the Legal Defense Fund; and trial attorneys Bud Siemon and Craig Barnard. We also thank Gwen Spivey, for her work on findings of aggravation in the Florida sentencing process, and we owe special thanks to Carol Palmer, of the Legal Defense Fund, for her constant responsiveness to our numerous and detailed questions. The costs of acquiring and processing the data used in our analysis were covered, in part, by funds from the Southern Poverty Law Center and the Legal Defense Fund.

We gratefully acknowledge the contribution of all the persons listed in Appendix B for providing us with these data. Two individuals do deserve special mention because of their extraordinary effort in this regard. Kay Isaly, of Florida Citizens against the Death Penalty, and Patsy Morris, of the American Civil Liberties Union in Atlanta, who provided information on persons sentenced to death and on the appellate review status of persons who received the death penalty, spent countless hours collecting data used in this analysis. Kay Isaly also obtained the judicial-processing data from selected counties in Florida, aided by William Sheppard and a group of law students who consulted court records. Ms. Isaly supervised this collection of data and checked the accuracy of the information.

We were also helped by people who supplied data not yet directly employed in our analysis. They include Tim Carr, Director of Statistics, Georgia Department of Offender Rehabilitation; Jerry Smith, Chief of Research, Florida Department of Offender Rehabilitation; Cecilia Whitmore and Laura Dixon, of Team Defense, who collected Georgia parole and probation information; and Susan Carey, who collected pre-*Furman* death sentence data in Florida.

The task of preparing the data for analysis has required considerable effort on the part of a number of persons we were fortunate to have working with us. Over the past 3 years, Deborah Good, Elaine Lang, and Keith Dubanevich in turn took primary responsibility for managing, updating, and preparing the various data sets for analysis, and assisted in processing various parts of these data for court testimony. Jacques Parenteau, Elise Bender, and Leslie Moffet supervised and carried out major efforts in data coding and preparation. Barbara Kane provided valuable computer-programming assistance, and Donna-Lee Anderson assisted in preparation of data for this project.

Finally, we wish to thank a number of people for their help in preparing the current study. Carol Cain contributed many hours of invaluable research and editorial assistance. Susan Spaar did much of the computer processing for this paper. Robert Kazarian and Charles Kazarian gave technical and legal advice. Jean Stethem ably typed and retyped countless tables and drafts of the manuscript. Lastly, we wish to thank Sarah Dike, editor of *Crime and Delinquency,* for her painstaking attention to our manuscript.

## APPENDIX A
## ADJUSTMENT PROCEDURES FOR TEMPORAL
## AND CROSS-SECTIONAL UNDERCOVERAGE
## OF HOMICIDE OFFENDER DATA

In 1976 the Supplementary Homicide Reports compiled by local police agencies and filed with the Uniform Crime Reporting Section of the FBI were revised to include information on offenders as well as victims of criminal homicide in those cases where offenders or suspected offenders were arrested or known to the police. Since 1976, offender characteristics have been reported for roughly 85% of all homicide incidents or victims. These Supplementary Homicide Reports are filed on a voluntary basis and not all agencies comply, thus producing cross-sectional undercoverage of homicides.

Since reports may not be filed by all local jurisdictions within a given state (cross-sectional undercoverage) and since the information on offenders was not reported before 1976 in any state (temporal undercoverage), this data source will undercount the number of homicide offenders since the effective date of post-*Furman* capital statutes. To obtain adequate estimates of the numbers of homicide offenders arrested by or known to the police during the effective period of post-*Furman* capital statutes in the states under analysis, we must adjust for temporal and cross-sectional undercoverage.

Our adjustment for undercoverage of homicide offenders is based on full coverage homicide victim statistics. The Vital Statistics Program of the National Center for Health Statistics provides a virtually complete accounting of the victims of willful homicide in all states. Willful homicides as classified or defined by the Vital Statistics Program correspond quite closely to the *Uniform Crime Reports* definition or classification of criminal homicides. (Where coverage is complete for both data sources, the reported number of homicide victims is very nearly the same, 95%, on the average.)

Our victim-based adjustment factor is the number of homicide victims in a state for the period to be studied divided by the number of homicide victims in that state for the period over which offender characteristics are available, where the number of victims for the period of analysis is drawn from the Vital Statistics records or reports and the number of victims during the period for which offender data are available comes from the Supplementary Homicide Reports. The adjustment employed corrects for both temporal and cross-sectional undercoverage when the effective date of the post-*Furman* statute was earlier than 1976 and not all police agencies in the state consistently filed Supplementary Homicide Reports. Where a state has a post-1976 capital statute (as in Alabama), the adjustment is strictly for cross-sectional undercoverage; and where all police agencies in a state file Supplementary Homicide Reports (as in Florida), the adjustment is strictly for temporal undercoverage. In the latter case, homicide victim figures from the Supplementary Homicide Reports provide full coverage of homicide victims and are used in place of Vital Statistics figures to correct for temporal undercoverage.

# 3

# DISPUTE SETTLEMENT BY THE POLICE*

## DONALD BLACK

The police in modern society perform many functions beyond the detection of crime and the apprehension of criminals (see, e.g., Cumming, Cumming, and Edell, 1965; Bittner, 1967a; 1967b; Black, 1968: Chapter 3; Wilson, 1968: Chapter 2). Some of these functions have little or no relevance to deviant behavior and social control—such as the transportation of sick and injured people to the hospital or the removal of dead dogs and abandoned automobiles from the street—but even where an exercise of authority is involved, the role of the police may depart considerably from law enforcement in a narrow sense. This might be seen in the handling of an intoxicated or homeless person sleeping in a public place, a game of dice or cards in an alley, a noisy party, a gang of teenagers loitering where they are not wanted, or any of a variety of interpersonal conflicts, whether between a husband and wife, landlord and tenant, or businessman and customer. Although the police might make an arrest in any of these situations, more often they dispose of the matter entirely in the setting where it occurs. They might simply tell someone to "get moving" or to "keep it down," for example, or they might use force or the threat of it, or admonish, mediate, or arbitrate, or they might do nothing at all.

Police work of this kind—where arrest is typically used as only one among a

*Computer time was provided by the Department of Sociology, Yale University, and other support was provided by the Department's Program in Deviant Behavior, Social Control, and Law, under a grant from the National Institute of Mental Health.

I thank M. P. Baumgartner for assistance in the preparation and processing of the data, and also for commenting on an earlier draft. In February 1980, a synopsis of the report was presented at the Center for Criminal Justice, Harvard Law School, and I thank those who attended for their reactions. In addition, the following people made suggestions for improving the chapter: John Griffiths, Candace Kruttschnitt, Peter K. Manning, Sally Engle Merry, Harold E. Pepinsky, Lawrence W. Sherman, and W. Clinton Terry.

number of possible actions—has been called "peacemaking" or "order maintenance" to distinguish it from "law enforcement" (Banton, 1964: 6–7; Bittner,
1967b: 700, 714; Wilson, 1968: 16–17). It is a major part of the police role in contemporary America and, for that matter, a major part of the legal life of any modern society. Nevertheless, little is known about who calls the police in these situations and why, and who is handled in what way under what conditions (but see,
e.g., Banton, 1964: Chapter 3; Cumming *et al.,* 1965; Parnas, 1967; Wilson, 1968:
Chapter 2). Addressing these questions and others, the following report examines
one variety of peacekeeping by the police: the handling of conflicts between people in ongoing relationships. A study of this kind contributes to knowledge about
police work as such, and also to an understanding of law and dispute settlement in
general.

It is a curious fact that, apart from what happens in courtrooms, we know substantially more about how people settle disputes in tribal and other simple societies than in modern societies such as the United States (see, e.g., Barton, 1919;
Llewellyn and Hoebel, 1941; Gibbs, 1963; Nader and Metzger, 1963; Gluckman,
1967). The concept of "dispute settlement" is rarely even seen in the works of sociologists, but appears primarily in the literature of anthropology. Perhaps this is
because the concept is most appropriate where social control is conciliatory in
style, concerned more with compromise and the reestablishment of social harmony than with who is right or wrong, who wins or loses, or—in the penal style—
who is guilty and deserving of punishment. (For an overview of styles of social
control see Black, 1976: 4–6.) The conciliatory style is especially common where
people are relatively homogeneous, intimate, and equal—conditions often found
in tribal societies but quite unlike many of the situations confronted by the police
in a modern society (see Gibbs, 1963; Gluckman, 1967: 20–21; Black, 1976:
47–48). Accordingly, what is handled by legal agents (and defined by social scientists) as a "dispute" rather than a "crime" may be more a question of who is involved than of the conduct that occurs. Where the police are called upon to handle a conflict between people in an ongoing relationship, then, such as between
members of the same family living in the same residence, it may be expected that
the process and outcome will to some degree resemble patterns of dispute settlement in the simpler societies described by anthropologists. But there is also an important difference between any matter involving the police—at least in a large
city—and a conflict between people in a simple society: the police themselves.
Although the parties in a modern setting may be as intimate as fellow tribesmen
living in the same village, the police are likely to be complete strangers, and socially distant from the parties in other ways as well, such as culturally and economically. In a tribal village, however, every agent of social control—whether a
chief, family head, elder, or whatever—is acquainted with all of the parties involved, and socially similar to them in nearly every respect. For this reason alone,
it should not be surprising that dispute settlement by the police—as described in
this chapter—differs considerably from the patterns found by anthropologists in
tribal and other simple societies.

## THE CASES

This report is based upon a sample of 550 cases recorded by observers who accompanied uniformed police officers on their daily rounds in four American cities. Most of the cases—527—were gathered in Boston, Chicago, and Washington, DC, during the summer of 1966. The remaining 23 cases derive from the author's own observations of the Detroit police during the years 1964 and 1965. Whereas the three-city study was carried out in police precincts inhabited predominantly by lower- and working-class people, the Detroit observations were made in a variety of settings, including middle-class neighborhoods on the periphery of the city. Information for the present analysis was obtained from the observation forms used during the three-city study, specifically from the part of the form (called the "capsule description") in which the observer was asked to provide a detailed report of the incident that occurred in his presence, and from the author's discursive field notes prepared after each of 19 rides with Detroit patrol officers.[1]

All of the 550 cases in the sample involved a conflict between two or more people who were related in some way prior to the matter that resulted in a call to the police.[2] However, not all of these conflicts were in progress when the police ar-

[1]In neither study were the police aware of the purpose of the research, or even that the incidents would be recorded at the end of each day of observation. Rather, they were given to believe that the research was not concerned with the behavior of the police at all, but only with the behavior of citizens—including their requests for service—and with the problems for the police created by citizens. This element of deception was introduced in order to assure that the police would conduct themselves in a natural fashion despite the presence of observers.

Although such deception may be subject to criticism on ethical grounds, it is also possible that it contributed to the quality of the information obtained. This is indicated by the degree to which the officers casually engaged in conduct ordinarily considered improper despite the presence of observers. During the hours after midnight, for example, the officers routinely spent some of their time sleeping in their patrol cars —occasionally missing radio calls—and a number of them drank alcoholic beverages while on night duty, confiscated property for their own enrichment (such as money from dice games or beer from underage drinkers), accepted money, free meals, and other favors from citizens, and carried in their patrol cars weapons that they admitted to observers would be used as false evidence should the need arise. On one occasion, an officer beat himself on the forehead with his nightstick following a minor traffic accident in order to be able to file a claim for an injury sustained in the line of duty. He then offered the nightstick to the observer, explaining that it was "a chance to make some money." It seems unlikely that the police would have so incriminated themselves had they been told that their conduct would be recorded and published. On the other hand, it should be recognized that the mere presence of the observers surely inhibited the officers to some degree.

For additional remarks concerning the methods used in the three-city study, see Reiss (1968; 1971). See also Van Maanen (1978) for a general discussion of problems involved in field research on the police.

[2]Like most incidents, conflicts of this kind typically come to the attention of the police by means of a citizen's telephone call. During the three-city study, they comprised 12% of the cases that the police handled in response to such calls ($N = 4371$). They comprised 17% of the cases originating by telephone in which the police had a face-to-face encounter with one or more citizens ($N = 3055$). These figures should not be taken as precise indicators of the amount of all police work that pertains to interpersonal conflict, however, since the sample was drawn from a limited number of precincts in the cities studied, and, as noted above, these were areas populated mostly by lower- and working-class peo-

rived, and even when they were, not all involved a request for the police to exercise their authority. These features are found together in only a little over one-half
of the cases (58%). From the standpoint of the present study, only these are true
disputes (a total of 317 cases), since they alone explicitly demand a settlement of
some kind by the police who handle them.

## A NOTE ON WHO CALLS THE POLICE

In this study, the typical dispute handled by the police involves a lower-class
black woman complaining against a lower-class black man. Even though the
present sample derives from urban areas heavily populated by low-income people,
the fact remains that middle-class people are underrepresented in the cases, and
the same pattern has been found by other investigators as well (e.g., Cumming *et
al.*, 1965: 280; Parnas, 1967: 915; Westley, 1970: 60; Hutchison, 1975: 10–11).
To understand why this is so, it is necessary to compare the households of middle-
and lower-class people. Consider, in particular, middle-class whites in comparison
to lower-class blacks.

A middle-class white woman is more likely than a lower-class black woman to
live in a condition of dependency in relation to a man. She is more likely to live
on the earnings of her husband, in a dwelling financed by him, and to be, in short,
a "housewife." Such a woman is not readily able to leave her situation one day and
replace it with an equivalent the next. This also applies to a lesser extent among
the many middle-class women who are employed outside the home, since their
earnings are often not adequate to support a household at the level to which they

---

ple. As a consequence, the sampling procedure probably overestimates the number of disputes the police handle. It should also be noted that while observations were made at all hours of the day, on all
days of the week, evenings and weekends were intentionally oversampled. These are times when people tend to be at home, often drinking, and so police work on a Friday or Saturday night in the areas
studied entails the handling of a much larger than average number of disputes. A rough estimate might
be that one-fourth to one-half of all the cases dealt with by the police at such times involve conflicts
between people who know each other. Even this estimate might be conservative: It has been reported
that in Atlanta 60% of the calls during the "morning watch" (midnight-to-8 a.m. shift) pertain to family conflict (Anonymous, 1974). The oversampling of evenings and weekends in the present study is
thus another reason why the number of disputes handled by the police is probably overestimated here.
Nonetheless, another investigator estimates that the frequency with which the police handle family disputes alone "probably exceeds the total number of murders, aggravated batteries, and all other serious
crimes" (Parnas, 1967: 914, note 2).

It might be added that a large proportion of the calls about interpersonal conflict appear to be made
by a limited segment of the population, known to the police as "regulars." For example, the Kansas
City police found in their own survey that one-half of their calls about family matters occurred in households that they had visited at least five times during the previous two years (Anonymous, 1974). Some
of these "regulars" call as often as once a week (see Schulz, 1969: 67), and the police often mention
people who call about once a month. It also has been estimated that as many as one-half of all lower-
class urban black families call the police at least once about their domestic problems (Schulz, 1969:
72, note 16).

TABLE 1    Nature of Dispute according to Race of Parties[a]

| Nature of dispute (in order of frequency) | Race of parties | | Total |
|---|---|---|---|
| | Black | White | |
| Noise or other disturbance | 23 | 41 | 29 |
| Physical injury of woman by man (or threat) | 24 | 12 | 20 |
| Dispute about property (including money) | 9 | 23 | 14 |
| Physical fight or injury (or threat)—other | 13 | 8 | 11 |
| Resident wants nonresident to leave | 8 | 5 | 7 |
| Resident wants fellow resident to leave | 8 | 2 | 5 |
| Dispute about child | 5 | 3 | 4 |
| Request for escort | 3 | 2 | 3 |
| Resident locked out by another resident | 2 | 1 | 2 |
| Other | 5 | 3 | 5 |
| Total percent | 100 | 100 | 100 |
| Total cases | (195) | (113) | (308) |

[a]By percent.

upon the police to settle their disputes—they do so proportionately more than whites—but they are less likely to get what they request, and the police expend less time and energy on their problems. At the same time, they are as likely as whites to be punished.

Blacks and whites call upon the police to handle a comparable array of problems. This can be see in Table 1. Twice as many of the calls from blacks involve women complaining about the violence of men, however, while only half as many pertain to property disputes or noise and other miscellaneous disturbances. These differences by themselves do not demonstrate that black women are beaten or threatened by men more often than are white women, that blacks have fewer disputes about property, or that blacks have quieter neighborhoods, since the propensity of each race to report such matters to the police may differ substantially. The actual patterns of conduct could even be the opposite of what the calls might at first suggest. In any event, the larger similarity in calls from blacks and whites makes it possible to compare how the police respond to people of each race.

Table 2 shows that the major styles in which the police respond to the calls of blacks and whites is quite similar, with about half being handled in a conciliatory style and most of the remainder in a penal style. The behavior of black and white complainants is quite similar as well, with 72% of the blacks and 69% of the whites making a specific request of the police. Even the requests themselves are similar, with, for example, 29% of the blacks and 20% of the whites asking the police to order an alleged offender to leave the setting (usually a dwelling), and 19% of the blacks and 17% of the whites asking them to make an arrest. How the police respond to complainants of each race, however, is not so similar: White complainants are more successful with their requests. Thus, the police comply entirely with the

TABLE 2   Major Style of Social Control Exercised by Police according to Race of Parties[a]

| Style of social control | Race of parties | | Total |
|---|---|---|---|
| | Black | White | |
| Conciliatory | 54 | 51 | 53 |
| Penal | 39 | 45 | 41 |
| Therapeutic | 3 | 2 | 2 |
| Compensatory | 1 | 1 | 1 |
| Preventive action only | 3 | 2 | 3 |
| Other | 1 | — | * |
| Total percent | 101 | 101 | 100 |
| Total cases | (188) | (107) | (295) |

[a] By percent.
*Less than .5%.

complainant's request in 61% of the disputes involving whites, but in only 47% of those involving blacks. They also take a greater interest in the nature of disputes involving whites, investing more time and energy in their settlement.

When the police are conciliatory in style, they are actively so in almost nine-tenths of the disputes involving whites, but this proportion falls to about two-thirds for blacks (see Table 3). In particular, when dealing with whites the police are more likely to act as mediators or arbitrators, striving to resolve the conflict, whereas in the black cases they are more inclined to stand by passively, doing little or nothing of a positive nature. In one case involving whites, for example, a woman explained that a man she "dated" 7 years before had contacted her at the beginning of the year to renew their relationship. At that time he gave her a check for $600, but now that they had broken up again the man wanted his money back. He said it was always meant to be a loan, whereas she claimed that it was a gift that she did not want to accept in the first place. In any event, the man had been making threatening phone calls, demanding an immediate return of the money. The woman told him that she would not be able to get the money until next week, but he was not satisfied. After hearing the entire story—this is only an outline—one of the officers called the man and told him that he should stop making threats, that the woman said she would return the money, and that if she did not do so he should take her to court. Apparently he accepted this resolution, and the complainant also seemed satisfied that the police had settled the matter as well as they could. In another case involving whites, the police arrived to find a couple arguing on the sidewalk. They had been living together until 3 weeks earlier when they fought and the man left. Now he had returned and had "stolen" money from her, kicking in a glass door and cutting his foot in the process. The observer noted that the police "entered the debate." One stated that "it was obvious that they could not get along," and suggested that one of them leave. The woman agreed to do so, without getting her mon-

TABLE 3   Mode of Conciliation by Police according to Race of Parties[a]

| Mode of conciliation | Race of parties | | |
|---|---|---|---|
| | Black | White | Total |
| Passive: little or no positive action | 29 | 11 | 23 |
| Mediation | 37 | 59 | 45 |
| Arbitration | 31 | 29 | 30 |
| Emotional support | 1 | 1 | 1 |
| Refer to nonpolice agency | 2 | — | 1 |
| Total percent | 100 | 100 | 100 |
| Total cases | (139) | (74) | (213) |

[a] By percent.

ey back. (After the incident one of the officers remarked to the observer that 3 weeks before "the situation was reversed," with the woman "stealing" the man's money and he being the one to leave.)

Later it will be seen that under the right conditions the police will engage in even more conciliation than is shown in these examples. In cases involving blacks, however, they are less likely to intervene in this way. On a number of occasions the police frankly expressed their lack of concern for the problems of blacks, including incidents in which someone's physical well-being was apparently in danger. In one case, for instance, a black woman complained that her husband had struck her, and he in turn complained that she had threatened him with a knife. The police told the couple to settle their problem in court, and promptly left, abandoning them to their own devices. One officer then commented to the observer, "If we stayed around them a little longer I think we would have been in the fight." The other added, "Maybe them two big niggers will kill themselves before they get to court and save time for everyone." Another case involved a black man whom the police had taken to the hospital earlier that evening after his wife cut him severely with a pair of scissors. It is unclear in the observer's report what was requested of the police at that time, but the case had been handled entirely as a medical problem, without an arrest or crime report. Later, after getting "stitched up," the man returned to the apartment, and his wife, fearing revenge, called the police. According to the observer, the officers "found the whole matter routine." They suggested that the woman wait and see what her husband would do, and told her that she should take the matter to a civil court. As they were leaving, one of the officers nonchalantly remarked, "We'll be back. She'll kill him." In still another case, a black woman said that her common-law husband had assaulted her, and she wanted him arrested. The police said they could not make an arrest since it was a misdemeanor that did not occur in their presence. They advised the woman to get a warrant, and left her with the alleged offender. Back in the patrol car, one of the officers dismissed the complaint as follows: "She's probably on him because he's been playing around with other women. I doubt if he actually assaulted her." In this report, the observer generalized that in matters involving common-laws, "even serious assaults," the police "like to avoid getting involved in mediating," and that they "usually advise warrants and leave as soon as possible." As one officer said, "I don't fuss with these domestics [family disputes] any more than necessary, especially these common-law setups." This might be taken to apply to disputes involving lower-class blacks in particular, since in modern America the concept of "common-law marriage" is most associated with that group, and many blacks themselves speak of their relationships in the same way. In short, then, although the police are basically conciliatory in style in as many disputes involving blacks as whites, blacks receive, case by case, less active help of this kind.

In regard to the penal style, the conduct of the police toward blacks is not entirely identical to that toward whites, but it is similar. Thus, as Table 4 shows, blacks are slightly more likely to be arrested, while whites are a bit more likely to be scolded or admonished. The police make an arrest or threaten to do so in almost one-half of the cases in which they are penal toward blacks, but in only one-third of the cases involving whites. It might therefore be inferred that the police are more legalistic and coercive toward blacks, even though an order to leave a setting—more frequent for whites—has legalistic and coercive overtones as well. Moreover, this interpretation is consistent with other features of police conduct toward the two races. In particular, the police seem to vacillate between indifference and hostility toward blacks, reluctant to become involved in their affairs but heavy-handed when they do so. Typically they are aloof if not openly contemptuous, and during the observation period most of the officers expressed much dislike of blacks and their way of life (see Black and Reiss, 1967: 132–137). For example, one officer said of a black woman who had asked for help in retrieving her clothes from her former lover's apartment, "She'll be living with another bum tomorrow and call us to bail her out." In another case, the officer spoke of the complainant who called as a "nigger bitch." And an officer remarked after still another encounter, "See how these shines [blacks] live? Like pigs. They're a bunch of drunks. See her friend? Just a boy for tonight."

By contrast, the police seem more likely to identify with the white people they meet. In one instance, the observer noted that the officer "obviously sympathized" with a white woman who bemoaned the fact that she was "trapped in a Negro neighborhood" and "could not afford to move." They also relate to whites in a more personal style, with more camaraderie, whereas blacks are more likely to be treated distantly, as objects rather than people (see Black and Reiss, 1967: 56–60). An observer noted how uncomfortable and embarrassed he himself felt merely to be present during one encounter in which the police "did not so much as acknowledge [the] presence" of several black children who stood watching them.

Although in many cases involving blacks the police do little beyond knocking at the door, when they choose to exercise authority it appears that it is more likely to be coercive in character than in comparable cases involving whites. In one

TABLE 4    Penal Action by Police according to Race of Parties[a]

| Penal action (in order of severity) | Race of parties | | Total |
| --- | --- | --- | --- |
| | Black | White | |
| Arrest | 25 | 21 | 23 |
| Order or remove from setting | 21 | 29 | 24 |
| Threaten arrest | 24 | 12 | 19 |
| Scold or admonish | 18 | 26 | 22 |
| Ask or advise to leave setting | 8 | 2 | 6 |
| Other | 4 | 9 | 6 |
| Total percent | 100 | 99 | 100 |
| Total cases | (125) | (82) | (207) |

[a] By percent.

case, for instance, the police were called by a black woman whose estranged common-law husband had broken into her apartment in order to repossess furniture that he claimed was his. The woman insisted that the property was jointly owned, not his alone. The officers advised the man to bring a lawsuit against the woman, but he did not seem to take the suggestion seriously, and proceeded to carry a television set toward the door. The woman shoved him, and he fell to the floor, at which time the police intervened and placed him under arrest for being "drunk and disorderly." The observer reported that the officers used "quite a bit of force" to handcuff him and move him to the patrol car, and that he struggled against them, striking his head on the cement landing of the stairs in the process. In the car, the officers called the man "nigger," and one added, "worse than that, you're just a common alley nigger." In another case, a black woman wanted a man "thrown out" of her apartment, but he insisted that he lived there and would not leave. One of the officers "had already drawn his blackjack in anticipation of a struggle," and when the man still refused to leave they took hold of him and told him he was under arrest. The observer described in detail the manner in which the man was taken into custody: "They pinned him down and grabbed the back of his belt and started to manhandle him out the door. Somehow the man ended up on the floor, and so he was thereupon dragged down two flights of stairs. A commotion started at the foot of the stairway, and one of the officers hit the man with the blackjack."

In each of these examples the arrest and injury of a person might have been avoided if the police had made a greater effort to work out a solution with the people involved. Moreover, black policemen might have handled these cases in a different manner. Thus, in another case (not included in the sample of disputes), two black officers were dispatched to pick up a black man who had been arrested by a white officer on foot patrol, and they were openly unhappy with how the man had been handled. After they heard the details of what had happened—largely a display of disrespect by the black man—they remarked to the observer that if they

teenagers described the woman as "crazy," and it would appear that the police were in complete agreement. Nevertheless, the observer reported that the officer who talked with her was "understanding" and "patient," and, at her request, left his name and phone number for her to call if the "problem" recurred. He promised to keep her yard under surveillance, consoled her, and was generally reassuring and supportive. He also acted as a go-between to the teenagers, and warned them— apparently "for show"—not to bother the woman in the future. Afterward, the officers commented that the supposed offenders were actually "good kids." It is clear that this woman received considerably more attention than the typical complainant of lower social standing, perhaps more than any lower- or working-class complainant in the entire sample, including some who had been physically injured and others who complained that their lives were in danger. Had she been poor and black, the woman might very well have been reprimanded for bothering the police and also, perhaps, for her conduct in general. But the police excused everything she did as an expression of her "craziness."

The attribution of "mental illness" seems to be a common response of the police to people who, if lower in status, might be subject to punishments, threats, or admonishments. They also seem more willing to accept claims of "mental illness" made by citizens of higher status. Thus, in one case a black minister called the police because his son had been drinking and wanted to take the family car (though he had no driver's license), had been fighting with the minister's son-in-law, and had run out into the street in front of traffic. It was unclear what he wanted the police to do, but he told them that his "boy" had just served two years in the penitentiary, and that this was "too long" and had made him "mentally sick." The police advised the man—whom they always addressed as "Reverend So-and-so"— to take his son to a psychiatrist, and one of the officers suggested to the young man that he go for a walk around the park in order to relax. At no time did the police use coercive tactics of any kind. In another case, a black woman complained that her husband, a preacher, had "gone crazy," threatening her and destroying some of their household belongings. The preacher, locked in an adjoining room, shouted at his wife to get the police out of his home, and they left shortly afterward without saying anything at all to the preacher himself. The police may also use a therapeutic style without specifically employing the concept of "mental illness." In one such case, for example, a white landlord called the police, very upset because his wife had been "taking" money and jewelry from the bedroom of one of their tenants. In relating the details to the police, he alternated between crying and raging about his wife's behavior. What might have been treated as a "theft" under other conditions was in this case treated as a tragedy or burden for the alleged offender's husband. The observer mentioned that the police stayed with the man "longer than was officially necessary" and that "during this time [one of the officers] was exceedingly friendly and provided a great deal of emotional support." The officer handling the incident "went out of his way to avoid any official action in this situation in an attempt to help the citizens solve their problems." The possibility of an arrest was never mentioned, and the woman was not treated as an offender or criticized in any way. She was simply a "problem," and her husband deserved sympathy.

If the police so much as suggest that a middle-class person has behaved illegally and is subject to their coercive authority, they may encounter indignation and possibly even a threat of a lawsuit. Thus, in one case in which a young white woman complained that her father was violating a court order to stay away from her house, an officer rhetorically asked the man what he was doing in her kitchen. The man replied, "What does it look like I'm doing here? I'm sitting here drinking a cup of tea. I don't know anything about a court order. If there is one, then let's see it. If you want to take me in, then you go right ahead, and I'll sue you for false arrest." The observer noted that the officer's "voice weakened," and he assured the man that arrest was not being contemplated: "We're not here to make any arrests, sir. We were called because your daughter said she was afraid because you're here." The officers then went upstairs and talked with the daughter about the situation, but nothing more was said to the man, and he was still glowering in the kitchen when they left. Now compare the response of the police to a lower-class black man's assertion of his rights (after he had allegedly tried to throw his wife out of the house and she called them for help). The man did not want the police to enter, and told them, "This is my house—you can't come in." One of the officers replied, "The hell we can't," and pushed into the house. The man was told to "shut his goddamn mouth," at which time he became more cooperative and made no further complaints.

It appears that people of white-collar status view themselves as different from what were once called the "criminal classes," and so do the police, whereas both take for granted the appropriateness of the penal style for lower- and working-class people. At the same time, the police seem less willing to define lower-status people as "mentally ill," or in any other way to apply the therapeutic style to their problems. For example, in one case a lower-class black woman called the police (from an unspecified public place) to complain that her husband was "insane" and had threatened to kill her. To this the police officer replied that her husband actually was "only drunk," and that if they did not go home immediately both of them would be arrested for "drunkenness." Afterward, the observer recorded that, in his opinion, the man probably was "insane or at least dangerous." But then lower-status people themselves are surely less likely than middle-class people to define one another as "mentally ill" in the first place (see Black, 1976: 29).

Although in many cases involving poor blacks the police simply stood by passively, taking little or no action at all, this did not occur in a single case involving people of middle-class status. These cases also illustrate the range and diversity of responses of which the police are capable. A case involving a middle-class Jewish family shows the extremes to which the police will go under the right conditions: The call over the radio directed the officers to "meet the sergeant," and one of them immediately said, "This is it again." He then explained that this call apparently was another stage in a dispute they had handled earlier in the evening, at which time a young woman (18 years old) had called the police because her parents were keeping her baby at their house and would not give it back. This was the most recent episode in a series of often conflictful events going back to the hospitalization of the daughter as "mentally ill" several years before, her relationship with a fellow whom her father described as "just a no-good bum," her pregnancy and subsequent marriage to the young man (also Jewish and from what an officer called a "real good" and a "real wealthy" family), the breakup of the marriage, and the girl's ultimate return with the baby to her parents' large house in a prosperous neighborhood. Now the parents had "kicked her out" of their house and she was planning to move in with a friend, but they refused to let her take the baby, arguing that she would not give it proper care. On their first visit to the home this evening, the officers had told the daughter that her parents would have to keep the baby until she was "settled" and had enough money to pay for its food. She thereupon went to the police station and complained, saying that she had a right to her own baby. The sergeant was then dispatched to meet with the whole group.

Upon the sergeant's arrival, the father made an apologetic plea for help of a sort rarely seen among people of lower status: "First I want to tell you how sorry we are that you had to come out here, but, honestly, we are in a mess—I never thought it could happen in our family—but God knows we are in a mess, and we just don't know where to turn." The sergeant explained that the police technically had no authority to handle the matter: "I want you to realize that this is not really police business. I can't make any final decisions on this, and when I say something it is strictly off the record. The law says this is not a matter for the police, but I understand the situation you are in, and we'll do what we can." The father seemed to understand the legal character of the dispute: "Oh sure, we're fully aware that this is a civil-law case, but something has got to be done tonight." And the sergeant assured him: "I realize that. We'll see what we can do."

The father continued: "The girl just doesn't know what she is doing. We don't know what's come over her. If she took that baby out of here tonight, God forbid, it could die—the condition she is in. And her husband's not going to care. To give you some idea of what kind of boy he is, he didn't even go to his own son's circumcision [a Jewish ritual]. I don't know if you realize what that means." The mother added, "And our daughter, she doesn't seem to care about her own child either. When she was here with the baby, who had to change the diapers, and who had to feed the poor little thing? I did. My daughter doesn't lift a finger for her own baby." The daughter also presented a case to the sergeant: "My parents hit me with a telephone and threw me out. I'll show you the bump on my head where the phone hit me. I'll go, fine, I'll go, but I know I have a right to my own baby." The sergeant replied, "You have a right to your baby, yes, but only if you can take care of the baby." And she in turn said, "I can take care of it, and I've got a place to live, and money. Now I want my baby." And so it went, on and on. The sergeant seemed to be reluctant to take a firm stand: "Now like I said before, the police can't make decisions in a situation like this. It is something for the courts to decide. We can't do anything unless a law has been broken. So far, there haven't been any crimes committed here that I can see." At this point, the father became more aggressive: "We realize that, sergeant, believe me. But if that girl takes the baby out of here, then there *will* be trouble. If that bum husband of hers comes around here, I swear to God I'll kill him." And the sergeant repeated, "Well, anything I tell you isn't because it's what the law says." He then called the Women's Division for an opinion on the matter (the parents had also called there earlier in the evening). Each party in turn took the telephone and explained the entire affair to a woman officer at headquarters, and the sergeant talked to her when everyone was finished. Finally, he hung up and announced to the father, "You will keep the baby until your daughter gets a court order for you to give it back to her. So, for tonight anyway, you keep it, but if she gets that court order you have to give the baby to her." The daughter said that she was contacting her lawyer and would soon be back for the baby, and she left. The police assured the parents that they would keep their house under surveillance for the rest of the night, made some small talk, accepted the parents' thanks, and left. Back in the patrol car, one of the officers commented that the young woman was "kookie." The entire incident had consumed a good part of the evening, about 2 hours of police time from beginning to end. If the case had involved lower-class blacks, it is doubtful that the police would have spent as much as 10 minutes on it, and much less would they have dispatched a sergeant or other ranking officer to a dispute of this kind.

It might be noted that the police intentionally drive slowly en route to many domestic disputes, hoping the matter will be resolved by the time they arrive. But this practice occurs primarily when the call comes from a lower- or working-class neighborhood. And many police are eager to find excuses to leave the scene of such disputes as soon as possible. They may leave if no one answers the first knock at the door, for example, or if the first person to answer denies that the police were called. In response to a reported dispute in a middle-class neighborhood, by contrast, it is not unusual for more than a single patrol car to be dispatched (as in the case of the Jewish family described above), and in other ways the police may treat the case as a matter of considerable importance. For example, in one case two patrol cars responded to a call indicating a domestic dispute in a middle-class neighborhood. Although no one seemed to be home (or willing to answer the door), the observer commented that the officer "must have knocked for close to five minutes—longer than I've ever seen officers wait before." He also generalized that "a bigger production was made of the family trouble run [dispatch] than I've seen in lower socioeconomic areas."

One of the officers who handled the Jewish family mentioned that in one respect the case was typical: "Most of the time we don't have any trouble with the Jews at all, but when they have trouble, brother, they really go all out." Since it seems unlikely that Jewish disputes are significantly different from those of other people, it may be more accurate to say that the police "go all out," not the Jews. But this would be true only in cases involving wealthier Jews such as those in the incident described above, not poor Jews. Whether Jewish or gentile, black or white, people of the middle or upper class receive more help from the police when they ask for it. The police go to great lengths to satisfy these people, particularly if they can do so in a therapeutic or conciliatory style, without coercion. For reasons suggested earlier, however, generally such people do not call upon the police to settle their disputes. They call the police readily enough about those of lower status, but not about each other.

## HOUSEHOLD STATUS

The vast majority of the disputes in this study occur within single households, and among these the vast majority involve complaints brought to the police by household heads (defined here as those who pay the mortgage or rent for a dwelling). Although many involve a complainant and an alleged offender who are presumed to be joint heads of a household, a considerable number pertain to a complaint by a head of a household against someone else, such as a dependent spouse, child, other relative, or a former spouse or lover. In no case could it be determined that a dependent spouse had complained against the head of the household. Because spouses were considered to be joint heads of households in the absence of information to the contrary, however, some incidents of this kind may have been misclassified (as occurring between joint heads). In any event, it is possible to compare how the police handle complaints between people who appear to be equals in the household with complaints in a downward direction—those in which a superior complains against an inferior.

It can be seen in Table 5 that the style of the police is far more conciliatory in cases between equals than in those involving a downward complaint: Whereas nearly three-fourths of the disputes between equals are handled primarily in the conciliatory style, this is true of fewer than half of the complaints brought by a head of a household against someone else. Instead, inferiors in the household are more likely to be handled in a penal style, whether by arrest or threat of arrest, removal from the dwelling, or a scolding. This pattern prevails despite the fact that disputes between equals are more likely to involve violence: While 60% of them entail some degree of violence, this applies to somewhat fewer than half of the downward complaints. There is violence in only 22% of the complaints by the head of a household against a dependent other than a spouse, for example, in 25% of those against a nonresident, in 32% of those against a former spouse or lover, and in 42% of those against a dependent spouse—and yet these downward complaints are the ones in which the police are especially likely to be penal in their social control (see Table 5). It would seem, then, that it is not the greater violence of household inferiors that increases their vulnerability to punishment. Nor is a difference in intimacy an adequate explanation: Holding constant the intimacy of marriage, it can be observed that spouses who are equals are handled in the penal style in only about one-fourth of the cases, but one-half of the dependent spouses are handled in this way (Table 5). It therefore seems that household status itself predicts and explains how the police respond to disputes. A household is a microcosm of society, where those at the bottom of the social-class system are more likely to be punished.

TABLE 5  Major Style of Social Control Exercised by Police according to Household Status of Parties[a]

| | Household status of parties | | | | | | | |
| | Head of household against: | | | | | Former spouse or lover against head of household | Other | Total |
| Style of social control | Another head | Dependent spouse or lover | Other dependent | Former spouse or lover | Other nonresident | | | |
|---|---|---|---|---|---|---|---|---|
| Conciliatory | 71 | 44 | 32 | 33 | 29 | (4) | 50 | 53 |
| Penal | 23 | 50 | 56 | 67 | 68 | (1) | 44 | 40 |
| Therapeutic | 2 | — | 12 | — | 4 | — | 3 | 3 |
| Compensatory | — | — | — | — | — | — | — | — |
| Preventive action only | 4 | 6 | — | — | — | (3) | — | 3 |
| Other | — | — | — | — | — | — | 3 | * |
| Total percent | 100 | 100 | 100 | 100 | 101 | — | 100 | 99 |
| Total cases | (97) | (18) | (25) | (18) | (28) | (8) | (32) | (226) |

[a]By percent. Figures in parentheses are used whenever the total number of incidents is statistically too small to justify a generalized assertion of rate and for total number of cases.

*Less than .5%.

and walked away in disgust." In another case, a black man went to his former wife's house to remove a table that she claimed was a gift, and hers to keep. The police sided with the woman, saying that the man would have to prove his ownership in court and, meanwhile, "as a stranger with no right to presence in her house," would have to leave.

Several other cases show how a person's status in the household can make the difference between arrest and freedom. In one, a young black man complained that his father and a friend of his father's were "drunk" and had abused and threatened him even though he did "all of the work around the house." The police "talked the father into going to bed," but they arrested his friend for "vagrancy." In a somewhat unusual case, the police arrested a white man for "drunkenness" because a woman, described as "almost hysterical," said that he had broken into her apartment and tried to rape her. The alleged offender said that she was lying and that "she's always invited the boys in so's she could get screwed, but when she's had enough she'd holler for the police." According to the observer, "The police didn't believe her story, but took him in to calm her down." Afterward, the police explained that she was a "regular" who routinely made such complaints, often against the man they handled on this visit, and that they "take it as a joke" and "go over there just to have a little fun." Nevertheless, in her apartment they did what she wanted them to do. Another case also dramatizes how far the police will go to comply with the head of the household: A black woman had locked her son out of her apartment because her "lover" did not want the young man to be present while he was visiting overnight. The police arrived to find the woman berating her son as he sat quietly on the stairs outside her door. (It is not clear who had called the police.) One of the officers suggested that the son "spend the night in the park," but he replied that he was "afraid" to stay in the park, had nowhere else to go, and would prefer to go to jail for the night. To accommodate him (and his mother), the police arrested him for "disorderly conduct." In still another incident, a black woman complained that her common-law husband had locked her out of "her" apartment, but he said that it was "his" apartment. The man was able to convince the police that it was his alone, and they arrested the complainant for "drunkenness" when she refused to leave the setting. The observer added in his report that there was no evidence that the woman had been drinking.

The police behave according to the same principle—supporting the head of the household—in other contexts as well. Thus, in dealing with homosexuals, the police generally side with the partner who is the head of the household. In one case, for instance, a white complainant told the police that she wanted them to remove a drunken woman from her apartment. The officers found the woman in a semiconscious condition in the kitchen, threw water on her, took her to the patrol car, and then drove her to the edge of the precinct where they dropped her off on the street. She was dressed in a masculine fashion, had short-cropped hair, and explained to the police that she was "off men." One of the officers remarked afterward that the women were "lesbians," and that the complainant had probably gotten "ticked off" after having sexual relations. In another incident, a white woman complained that a "lesbian" was in her apartment and had asked her to be "her girl." She said that she wanted nothing to do with this, and requested that the police remove the "lesbian." They agreed to do so, and convinced the second woman to leave by threatening her with arrest for "disorderly conduct."

In general, then, the direction of a complaint in the social structure of a household predicts and explains how the police will respond. Whether male or female, the person who owns the house or pays the rent will usually prevail, and the penal style of social control is likely to be applied to his or her opponent. But if the parties share the economic burden of the household, and so appear to be equals, the police are likely to be conciliatory and to refuse to take sides in the dispute. Dispute settlement by the police serves the interests of the household elite.

## AGE

The great majority of disputes that the police are called upon to handle involve conflicts between adults. Occasionally a complaint will be made by an adult against a juvenile, but hardly ever do the police encounter a complaint by one juvenile against another or by a juvenile against an adult. Since nearly all juveniles are economically dependent upon adults, these patterns again portray the role of the police under conditions of inequality. The following discussion partially overlaps with that of the last section (on household status), since adult–juvenile conflicts often occur in a domestic setting, but the social inferiority of juveniles is so extreme in modern society that their experiences with the police deserve special comment.

The great majority of police encounters with juveniles occur in public places and are in other ways quite unlike the cases in the present analysis (see, e.g., Piliavin and Briar, 1964; Werthman and Piliavin, 1967; Black and Reiss, 1970). Nonetheless, the fate of juveniles involved in disputes is much the same as in the more routine encounters: Juveniles lose nearly all of their conflicts with adults, and in most cases are treated in a penal and moralistic fashion. Moreover, on those rare occasions when a juvenile complains about an adult, he or she is likely to be chastised for even attempting to bring law to bear against an older person.

When an adult complains against another adult, the style of the police is primarily conciliatory in over one-half of the cases, whereas less than one-third of the complaints by an adult against a juvenile are handled in this way. Instead, as Table 7 shows, a juvenile is most likely to be handled in the penal style. Beyond this, the penal actions taken by the police are somewhat different in cases involving a juvenile as the alleged offender (see Table 8). While a bit less likely than an adult to be arrested and considerably less likely to be threatened with arrest, he or she is correspondingly more likely to be scolded or admonished. It is in this sense that the police are comparatively moralistic toward juveniles, while treating adults— if they handle them in the penal style at all—in a more legalistic fashion. The police give very few lectures to adults about how they should behave. They are unlikely to invoke standards of right and wrong at all, even when making an arrest

TABLE 7   Major Style of Social Control Exercised by Police according to Age of Parties[a]

| Style of social control | Age of parties | | Total |
| | Adult against juvenile[b] | Adult against adult | |
| --- | --- | --- | --- |
| Conciliatory | 31 | 54 | 52 |
| Penal | 62 | 39 | 41 |
| Therapeutic | 7 | 2 | 3 |
| Compensatory | — | 1 | 1 |
| Preventive action only | — | 3 | 3 |
| Other | — | * | * |
| Total percent | 100 | 99 | 100 |
| Total cases | (29) | (253) | (282) |

[a]By percent.
[b]Under 18 years old.
*Less than .5 percent.

or threatening to do so. If they exercise their authority, then, they usually do so in an impersonal and bureaucratic manner, without explicit reference to their own values. This does not apply to juveniles, however. In these cases the police readily give lectures and exhortations about the proper way for a young person to behave, particularly toward his or her elders. Typically the elders in question are parents.

In one case, for example, a worried white woman called the police because her 15-year-old son had left the house in the afternoon, saying that he would be back in "a little while," and hours later he had yet to return. While the police were in the house, the boy arrived and explained that he had been on a bicycle trip with a friend. His mother raised her voice and said, "Do you know how much worry you put us to? How could you do a thing like this?" The boy "snarled" at her in a loud voice, "Oh, get off my back. Why do you have to make such a big thing out of it?" At this, one of the officers got up from his chair and said, "Just a minute, buddy. You tell me where you learned to act like that to your mother. Don't you know how to behave when your mother talks to you?" The boy replied, "Well, she doesn't have to get so excited about nothin', does she?" This prompted the officer to continue: "Listen here, your mother can say what she pleases, how she wants to, to her son. You know that? My mother never would have allowed me to act the way you do. She would've smacked me in the face. One thing you better get straight— you only have one mother in your life, and you better remember that. You better start respecting her right now. At least you're going to show respect when *I'm* here. You got that?" The boy said, "Yes, sir," and immediately everything quieted down. The woman thanked the police warmly. Afterward, one of the officers remarked that "the trouble" was that "there's no man in the house."

TABLE 8 Penal Action by Police according to Age of Parties[a]

| | Age of parties | | |
|---|---|---|---|
| Penal action (in order of severity) | Adult against juvenile[b] | Adult against adult | Total |
| Arrest | 17 | 24 | 23 |
| Order or remove from setting: citizen complies | 29 | 25 | 25 |
| Threaten arrest | 4 | 22 | 20 |
| Scold or admonish | 46 | 18 | 22 |
| Ask or advise to leave setting | — | 7 | 7 |
| Other | 4 | 4 | 4 |
| Total percent | 100 | 100 | 101 |
| Total cases | (24) | (174) | (198) |

[a]By percent.
[b]Under 18 years old.

In another case involving a white family, a woman called to complain that her teenaged daughter was staying out too late—violating the city's curfew law—and creating other unspecified "problems" as well. The daughter was sitting outside in a car with her boyfriend when the police arrived, and both were asked to come into the mother's apartment. According to the observer, the officers "tried very hard to convince the girl that she was hurting herself and her poor working mother's well-being by such recurring trouble." The girl was "openly nasty" to the police and told them, "Too bad. I don't like curfews." Before leaving, the police gave her a ticket for curfew violation and warned her that future violations could mean that she would be sent away to an institution.

Another case illustrates what seems to be the typical response of the police to a juvenile who complains about the conduct of a parent: A 16-year-old black girl called the police to complain that she had been struck by her father. The observer inferred that she had "talked back" to her father, he had "hit" her, and now "her pride was hurt." The police "found the girl in the wrong," and proceeded to "belittle" her and to try to "shame" her, admonishing her to "grow up" and to "get rid of her smart attitude." They also "made her apologize" to her father. The observer added that, in the end, the girl's "pride was further hurt" because the police had "degraded" her. In a similar case, a black girl tearfully complained that her mother had "whipped" her, and the officer—with a show of disgust—grumbled, "Whip her again," and walked out the door.

In sum, the police readily use their authority against a juvenile who is criticized by a parent, but when the situation is reversed—with a juvenile complaining against an adult—they show no sympathy at all, and usually treat the complaint itself as an offense. Patterns of this kind should be expected wherever one person or group is far below another in social status, as is true of slaves and women in many societies (see Black, 1976: 18–19, 28). In modern America, however, hardly anyone is lower than juveniles.

## THE RELEVANCE OF THE WRITTEN LAW

Thus far, the disputes the police handle have been presented and analyzed almost entirely without regard to the written law. It was noted earlier that close to one-half of the cases involve violence, and that almost one-fifth involve the use of a weapon, but little effort has been made to classify them according to the categories that might be used by a lawyer or a judge. Moreover, the actions taken by the police have not been viewed from the standpoint of the rules of legal procedure or formal obligations of any other kind (compare, e.g., Goldstein, 1960; La Fave, 1965). The purpose of this study has been to understand dispute settlement by the police from the perspective of social science rather than law. Nevertheless, how these materials appear in the light of the written law of modern America might be of interest to the reader, if only to provide a legal perspective for its own sake. Since police officers commonly refer to the written law to explain their actions, it is also possible to assess the factual value of their version of how they make decisions. It will be seen that however much the written law is used to justify what the police do in handling disputes, it does not seem to correspond closely to how they actually behave.

All of the 317 cases in the sample were classified by whether or not they presented grounds for legal action of any kind and, if so, whether these grounds were civil or criminal. If criminal, a case was further classified as a "felony" or a "misdemeanor" (the former to designate a crime punishable by more than one year in prison). It is important to emphasize, however, that the proper application of these categories is a matter of opinion, not fact. In addition, it should be noted that unless the factual details of an incident were evident to the observer, the classification is based upon the complainant's version of what happened. With these qualifications, then, it may be generalized that in about one-fourth of the disputes there are no grounds for legal action of any kind, criminal or civil (26%). Another 9% of the cases have no apparent criminal elements but may be viewed as falling within the province of civil law, such as disputes pertaining to the custody of a child or the division of property after a marital separation. Thus, over one-third of the cases have nothing to do with the criminal law. At the other extreme, almost one-fifth involve felonies (18%), nearly all of which are violent in nature, such as an assault involving a weapon or a threat to kill. Over one-third of the cases may be classified as misdemeanors, divided about evenly between violent and nonviolent offenses (respectively 17% and 20%). Finally, the remaining cases could not be assigned to any of these major categories, either because the observers' reports did not include enough details about incidents of criminal violence (6%), or because the disputes did not fit adequately under any of the headings (5%). Of the latter sort, for instance, was the case involving a middle-aged couple who had possession of their daughter's baby and would not give it back. Another such case involved an elderly black man who wanted a young man and his girlfriend to move out of his apartment. The two were not related to him by either blood or marriage, nor were they paying rent, but they claimed that they had been "taking care" of the man for 6 months, that he was "old and blind" and had "no one to look after him," and therefore they refused to leave. (On learning that they were not related, the police said that they did not "legally live" in the apartment and would have to move out, and stayed until they packed and left with their belongings in a cab.) Such cases are subject to so many interpretations that they are better left unclassified in the present analysis.

The written law of arrest in American jurisdictions authorizes the police to make an arrest without a formal warrant when they have "reasonable grounds" to believe that someone has committed a felony. In the case of a misdemeanor, they must witness the offense or have a sworn complaint from a citizen before they can make a legal arrest. Since the conditions for a felony arrest are less restrictive, and since a felony is more "serious" in the sense that it is subject to a more severe penalty, it might be expected that the police would normally make an arrest when a felony appears to have occurred and the alleged offender is available to them (as was true of the cases analyzed here). Nevertheless, as Table 9 shows, more often than not apparent felons are allowed to remain free, and they are only slightly more vulnerable to arrest than those who have seemingly committed misdemeanors. An arrest is made in a little over one-fourth of the cases involving a violent felony and in nearly one-fifth of those involving a violent misdemeanor. The highest rate of arrest (over 40%) occurs in the cases involving an unspecified degree of violence. Civil matters and nonviolent misdemeanors have the lowest rates (each about 1 in 20). Finally, it is noteworthy that an arrest occurs in 17% of the cases that appear to have no grounds for legal action of any kind, criminal or civil. The vast majority of people formally susceptible to arrest are allowed to keep their freedom, then, but a substantial minority of those who do not seem to have commited any illegality at all, criminal or civil, are taken to jail.

The written law also poorly predicts the style in which the police handle disputes. Their style is primarily conciliatory in a little over one-half of the cases involving a violent felony, a proportion nearly the same as that for cases that have no apparent grounds for legal action of any kind, and only slightly lower than in civil matters (see Table 10). Conciliation is less likely in crimes with an unspecified degree of violence, and least likely of all in cases of a nonviolent misdemeanor. It is most likely in violent misdemeanors. Hence, the written law has limited relevance to whether a case is handled as an offense or merely as an interpersonal conflict.

In addition, the behavior of the police generally does not conform closely to the written law in cases where the alleged offender is not immediately available for arrest. When a woman complains that she has been beaten or otherwise injured by a man who is not present, for example, the police almost never define the incident as a crime by writing an official report about it. The same applies when the alleged offender is known to be available at a nearby tavern or behind a locked door. When no such action is taken, a follow-up investigation, arrest, and prosecution cannot occur. Such cases are not even entered into the crime rate published by each city.

Still more evidence bearing upon the relevance of the written law is provided by cases involving weapons. Although disputes involving a gun result in an arrest more than those involving no weapon at all (36% versus 13%), and although the same is true for makeshift weapons (35%), cases involving a knife or similar weapon are not significantly more likely to result in arrest (17%). What is more, although cases involving makeshift weapons are somewhat less likely to be handled in the conciliatory style than those involving no weapon at all (41% versus 52%), those involving a gun or a knife are actually more likely to be handled in this way (64% and 61%, respectively). In other words, in most cases involving a gun or a knife—even with the party wielding the weapon present in the encounter—the police do not invoke the criminal law. Typically in such cases they do not define anyone as an offender of any kind. Examples include cases in which the police preferred not to invoke the law against a colleague who had chased his wife down the street with a drawn service revolver, and one in which they retreated from a man who pointed a gun at them and refused to let them in his house. Similarly, the police labeled one of the cases involving a knife threat as a "civil matter," and explained that for this reason it was "not for them to settle."

Perhaps a few more cases should be mentioned as well. In one of these, a black woman complained that her husband had menaced her with a drawn gun, then left when she threatened to call the police. Just as the officer was leaving the building after talking with the woman, the man returned and proceeded to deny his wife's allegation. The observer noted that he had an "obvious bulge on his hip (possibly a gun), and when he withdrew his hands from his pockets a bullet fell out." Nonetheless, the officer did not search the man, and refused to arrest him on the ground that he "had no gun when encountered." The officer also decided not to search the man's car on the ground that such a search would be "illegal."

In another instance, a black woman complained that "her husband had held a gun to her face." The gun was not immediately visible to the police, however, and the officers said that "as this was a misdemeanor, no search could be made." (Surely they knew the reported offense was actually a felony.) The police thereupon left the woman with her husband, telling her to go downtown and swear out a warrant if she wanted him arrested. They reported the case as a "domestic disturbance." In a third case, the police were dispatched to a "man with a gun" and found two black men—father and son-in-law—fighting and swearing to kill each other. The observer described the conflict as follows: "The father had a sexual affair with his daughter before her marriage to her husband. Since the marriage, the father has continued to bother his daughter, mostly by phone calls. Such a phone call triggered the fight between them." When the police arrived, the younger man had a knife, but there was no outward evidence of the gun that one of the disputants reportedly had been wielding. The officers disarmed the son-in-law (remarking that the older man was "not worth it"), told him to see a detective about his father-in-law, and ordered the latter to stay away from his daughter's house. They did not inquire about a gun, however, nor did they explicitly recognize the sexual behavior of the father and daughter as incest. No crime report was filed.

In another case, in which a woman had "come after" her neighbor with an ice pick, the officers told the parties that "they should not expect the police to solve their personal problems." One of the stabbings serves as yet another example: A black man was standing on his front porch "hustling" a woman when his wife came downstairs in a jealous rage and stabbed him in the chest with a butcher knife. The man responded by knocking her to the floor, kicking her, and seizing the knife. The wife then called the police and wanted her husband "thrown out" for treating her that way "in public." Although the police ignored the woman's request and asked the man if he wanted to press charges, one of them commented, "Look, if we step in you'll be sorry tomorrow. Now you don't want that." He also said, "You were fooling around, weren't you? You probably deserved it." In the end, the police suggested that the man "take a long walk" until his wife "sobered up and cooled off," and he agreed. The case was reported as a "family fight."

Apart from numerous assaults, the police ignored cases of burglary, malicious destruction of property, larceny, and other matters of a technically criminal nature. In one case of "threatening phone calls," for instance, the complainant (a black woman) gave the police the name and address of the alleged offender, but they reported the incident as "threatening phone calls—caller unknown," thereby assuring that no further action would be taken. Many more examples could be mentioned. It is apparent, however, that the cases in the sample provide abundant evidence that the police routinely ignore violations of the written law. Moreover, in some cases they lie in order to make this seem reasonable to the people concerned. And when they do invoke the law by making an arrest, they often lie about what happened (see Manning, 1974). Thus, a number of people were arrested for "drunkenness" in private settings, though in each of the cities studied drunkenness is prohibited by the written law only when it occurs in a public place. Some arrested for this crime did not even show any signs of drinking. Still others were arrested for "disorderly conduct" when they were entirely peaceful by normal standards.

In sum, the written law has limited value as a predictor of what the police will do from one case to the next. They nevertheless often make reference to the law, and use it to justify much of their behavior. This is illustrated especially well by a case not included in the sample of disputes. The police stopped to investigate three white teenagers in a parked car. Afterward, the observer asked the officer who handled it whether he had given the driver a ticket. The officer replied, "No, I didn't find anything wrong. Well, I mean, if it would've been somebody else I could've found plenty wrong, but that guy was a pretty good Joe." So it is in dispute settlement and, for that matter, in all police work. Whether the police find that the written law has been violated often depends on how they choose to exercise their authority, rather than the other way around.[9] And this choice in turn depends on their location in social space.

[9]It might be argued that the interpretation of the written law by the police functions in much the same way as the invocation of myth: "Myth . . . can attach itself not only to magic but to any form of social claim. It is used always to account for extraordinary privileges or duties, or great social inequalities, for severe burdens of rank. . . .The function of myth is not to explain but to vouch for, not to satisfy curiosity but to give confidence in power" (Malinowski, 1925:84).

# REFERENCES

Anonymous. 1974. "Cops and couples." *Newsweek* 84 (July 8): 79.

Banton, Michael. 1964. *The Policeman in the Community*. London: Tavistock.

Barton, Roy Franklin. 1919. *Ifugao Law*. Berkeley: University of California Press.

Baumgartner, M.P. 1985. "Law and the middle class: evidence from a suburban town." *Law and Human Behavior* 9: 3–24.

———. 1988. *The Moral Order of a Suburb*. New York: Oxford University Press.

Bittner, Egon. 1967a. "Police discretion in emergency apprehension of mentally ill persons." *Social Problems* 14: 278–292.

———. 1967b. "The police on skid-row: a study of peace keeping." *American Sociological Review* 32: 699–715.

Black, Donald. 1968. Police Encounters and Social Organization: An Observation Study. Unpublished doctoral dissertation, Department of Sociology, University of Michigan.

———. 1976. *The Behavior of Law*. New York: Academic Press.

———. 1979. "A strategy of pure sociology." In *Theoretical Perspectives in Sociology,* edited by Scott G. McNall. New York: St. Martin's Press. Reprinted in *The Social Structure of Right and Wrong.* San Diego: Academic Press, 1993.

Black, Donald, and Albert J. Reiss, Jr. 1967. "Patterns of behavior in police and citizen transactions." In U. S. President's Commission on Law Enforcement and Administration of Justice, *Studies in Crime and Law Enforcement in Major Metropolitan Areas,* Field Surveys III, Volume 2. Washington: U. S. Government Printing Office.

———. 1970. "Police control of juveniles." *American Sociological Review* 35: 63–77.

Cumming, Elaine, Ian Cumming, and Laura Edell. 1965. "Policeman as philosopher, guide and friend." *Social Problems* 12: 276–286.

Doo, Leigh-Wai. 1973. "Dispute settlement in Chinese-American communities." *American Journal of Comparative Law* 21: 627–663.

Engels, Friedrich. 1884. *The Origin of the Family, Private Property and the State: In the Light of the Researches of Lewis H. Morgan.* New York: International Publishers, 1942.

Farley, Reynolds, and Albert I. Hermalin. 1971. "Family stability: a comparison of trends between blacks and whites." *American Sociological Review* 36: 1–17.

Frazier, E. Franklin. 1948. *The Negro Family in the United States.* New York: Citadel Press (revised and abridged edition; first edition, 1939).

Friedrich, Robert James. 1977. The Impact of Organizational, Individual, and Situational Factors on Police Behavior. Unpublished doctoral dissertation, Department of Political Science, University of Michigan.

Gelles, Richard J. 1972. *The Violent Home: A Study of Physical Aggression between Husbands and Wives.* Beverly Hills: Sage.

Gibbs, James L., Jr. 1963. "The Kpelle moot: a therapeutic model for the informal settlement of disputes." *Africa* 33: 1–10.

Gluckman, Max. 1967. *The Judicial Process among the Barotse of Northern Rhodesia.* Manchester: Manchester University Press (second edition; first edition, 1955).

Goldstein, Joseph. 1960. "Police discretion not to invoke the criminal process: low-visibility decisions in the administration of justice." *Yale Law Journal* 69: 543–594.

Gulliver, P. H. 1963. *Social Control in an African Society: A Study of the Arusha, Agricultural Masai of Northern Tanganyika.* Boston: Boston University Press.

Hannerz, Ulf. 1970. "What ghetto males are like: another look." In *Afro-American Anthropology: Contemporary Perspectives,* edited by Norman E. Whitten, Jr. and John F. Szwed. New York: Free Press.

Hutchison, Ira W. 1975. "Police intervention in family conflict." Paper presented at the annual meeting of the American Sociological Association, San Francisco.

Komarovsky, Mirra. 1940. *The Unemployed Man and His Family—The Effect of Unemployment upon the Status of the Man in Fifty-Nine Families.* New York: Dryden Press.

La Fave, Wayne R. 1965. *Arrest: The Decision to Take a Suspect into Custody.* Boston: Little, Brown.

Liebow, Elliot. 1967. *Tally's Corner: A Study of Negro Streetcorner Men.* Boston: Little, Brown.

Llewellyn, Karl N., and E. Adamson Hoebel. 1941. *The Cheyenne Way: Conflict and Case Law in Primitive Jurisprudence.* Norman: University of Oklahoma Press.

MacDonald, John Stuart, and Leatrice MacDonald. 1978. "The black family in the Americas: a review of the literature." *Sage Race Relations Abstracts* 3: 1–42.

Malinowski, Bronislaw. 1925. "Magic, science and religion." In *Magic, Science and Religion and Other Essays.* Garden City: Doubleday, 1954.

Manning, Peter K. 1974. "Police lying." *Urban Life and Culture* 3: 283–306.

Merry, Sally Engle. 1979. "Going to court: strategies of dispute management in an American urban neighborhood." *Law and Society Review* 13: 891–925.

Nader, Laura, and Duane Metzger. 1963. "Conflict resolution in two Mexican communities." *American Anthropologist* 65: 584–592.

Parnas, Raymond I. 1967. "The police response to the domestic disturbance." *Wisconsin Law Review* 1967: 914–960.

Piliavin, Irving M., and Scott Briar. 1964. "Police encounters with juveniles." *American Journal of Sociology* 70: 206–214.

Rainwater, Lee. 1966. "Work and identity in the lower class." In *Planning for a Nation of Cities,* edited by Sam Bass Warner, Jr. Cambridge: MIT Press.

———. 1970. *Behind Ghetto Walls: Black Families in a Federal Slum.* Chicago: Aldine Press.

Reiss, Albert J., Jr. 1968. "Stuff and nonsense about social surveys and observation." In *Institutions and the Person: Papers Presented to Everett C. Hughes,* edited by Howard S. Becker, Blanche Geer, David Riesman, and Robert S. Weiss. Chicago: Aldine Press.

———. 1971. "Systematic observation of natural social phenomena." In *Sociological Methodology, 1971,* edited by Herbert L. Costner. San Francisco: Jossey-Bass.

Schulz, David A. 1969. "Some aspects of the policeman's role as it impinges upon family life in a Negro ghetto." *Sociological Focus* 2: 63–72.

Simmel, Georg. 1908. *The Sociology of Georg Simmel,* edited by Kurt H. Wolff. New York: Free Press, 1960.

Skolnick, Jerome K. 1966. *Justice without Trial: Law Enforcement in Democratic Society.* New York: John Wiley.

Stack, Carol B. 1974. *All Our Kin: Strategies for Survival in a Black Community.* New York: Harper and Row.

Suttles, Gerald D. 1968. *The Social Order of the Slum: Ethnicity and Territory in the Inner City.* Chicago: University of Chicago Press.

United States Department of Labor, Office of Policy Planning and Research. 1965. *The Negro Family: The Case for National Action.* Washington: U. S. Government Printing Office. ("The Moynihan Report.")

Van Maanen, John. 1978. "On watching the watchers." In *Policing: A View from the Street,* edited by Peter K. Manning and John Van Maanen. Santa Monica: Goodyear.

Weber, Max. 1922. *The Theory of Social and Economic Organization,* edited by Talcott Parsons. New York: Free Press, 1964.

Werthman, Carl, and Irving Piliavin. 1967. "Gang members and the police." In *The Police: Six Sociological Essays,* edited by David J. Bordua. New York: John Wiley.

Westley, William A. 1970. *Violence and the Police: A Study of Law, Custom, and Morality.* Cambridge: MIT Press.

Wilson, James Q. 1968. *Varieties of Police Behavior: The Management of Law and Order in Eight Communities.* Cambridge: Harvard University Press.

# 4

# SPEECH STYLES IN THE COURTROOM: POWERFUL VERSUS POWERLESS SPEECH

## WILLIAM M. O'BARR

The phenomenon termed here *powerless speech* was derived from an initial investigation of differences between male and female witnesses. The term *powerless speech* is gaining currency among other researchers, suggesting both the appropriateness of this concept for discussions of courtroom speech styles and the saliency of the style across a wide variety of contexts.[1]

### BACKGROUND

Differences in the speech characteristics of men and women have been reported by anthropologists and linguists in the United States (Fischer, 1958) and in other cultures (Haas, 1944). The proliferation of studies of language and gender during the 1970s was due both to the general development of sociolinguistic interest in patterns of language variation and to the women's movement (Philips, 1980). Robin Lakoff's book, *Language and Woman's Place* (1975), provided a catalyst and encouragement for many other researchers with rudimentary interests in the way women and men speak differently. By the mid-1970s, the fact that there are gender-based differences in speech was beginning to be recognized by people who had previously given little or no thought to it.[2]

---

[1]For example, see Philips (1980: 535) and McConnell-Ginet (1980: 18, 25, footnote 35) for more general discussions of the power associated with speech styles and Newcombe and Arnkoff (1979) and Poythress (1979) for more specific applications of the concept of *powerless speech* styles in social psychological and legal contexts.

[2]Philips (1980) and McConnell-Ginet *et al.* (1980) contain useful reviews of the development of

For the study of language in the courtroom, Lakoff's work heightened awareness of possible differences in the speech of men and women and provided a beginning point for investigation of empirical differences in court. Unlike many other studies, this effort was not primarily an attempt to understand language and
gender differences. Rather, gender-related differences were one of the kinds of
variation that current sociolinguistic issues led us to focus on and to consider. In
addition, interest in the way women in particular speak in court was further kin-
dled by the discovery that many trial practice manuals often contain special sections on how female witnesses behave differently from males and what special
kinds of treatment they require as a consequence. This advice includes the following:

1. BE ESPECIALLY COURTEOUS TO WOMEN. "Even when jurors share the cross-
examiner's reaction that the female witness on the stand is dishonest or otherwise
undeserving individually, at least some of the jurors are likely to think it improper for the attorney to decline to extend the courtesies customarily extended to
women" (Keeton, 1973: 149).

2. AVOID MAKING WOMEN CRY. "Jurors, along with others, may be inclined to
forgive and forget transgressions under the influence of sympathy provoked by the
genuine tears of a female witness" (Keeton, 1973: 149). "A crying woman does
your case no good" (Bailey and Rothblatt, 1971: 190).

3. WOMEN BEHAVE DIFFERENTLY FROM MEN AND THIS CAN SOMETIMES BE
USED TO ADVANTAGE. "Women are contrary witnesses. They hate to say yes. . . .
A woman's desire to avoid the obvious answer will lead her right into your
real objective—contradicting the testimony of previous prosecution witnesses.
Women, like children, are prone to exaggeration; they generally have poor memories as to previous fabrications and exaggerations. They are also stubborn. You
will have difficulty trying to induce them to qualify their testimony. Rather, it
might be easier to induce them to exaggerate and cause their testimony to appear
incredible. An intelligent woman will very often be evasive. She will avoid making a direct answer to a damaging question. Keep after her until you get a direct
answer—but always be the gentleman" (Bailey and Rothblatt, 1971: 190–191).

These comments about women's behavior in court and their likely consequences in the trial process further raised our interest in studying the speech behavior of women in court. Having been told by Lakoff that women do speak differently from men, we interpreted these trial practice authors as saying that at least
some of these differences can be consequential in the trial process. Thus, one of
the kinds of variation we sought to examine when we began to observe and tape
record courtroom speech was patterns unique to either women or men. We did not
know what we would find, so we started out by using Lakoff's discussion of
women's language as a guide. First, it would be necessary to determine ethno-

these interests. A bibliography of major writings on gender-based differences in language can be found
in McConnell-Ginet (1980: 20–21, footnote 2).

graphically how women's speech in court is different from men's—if indeed it is. Second, one or more experiments would need to be designed and conducted to determine what, if any, consequences women's language has on the reception of testimony. The stage was thus set for the examination of the . . . pattern of language use and its role in the legal process.

## LAKOFF'S MODEL OF WOMEN'S LANGUAGE

What Lakoff proposed was that women's speech varies from men's in several significant ways. Although she provided no firm listing of the major features of what she terms *women's language* (hereafter referred to as WL), the following features were said to occur in high frequency among women. This set of characteristics provided a baseline for investigating gender-related speech patterns in court.

1. HEDGES: *It's sort of hot in here; I'd kind of like to go; I guess. . . .; It seems like. . . .;*and so on.
2. (SUPER)POLITE FORMS: *I'd really appreciate it if. . . .; Would you please open the door, if you don't mind?*; and so on.
3. TAG QUESTIONS: *John is here, isn't he?* instead of *Is John here?*; and so on.
4. SPEAKING IN ITALICS: Intonational emphasis equivalent to underlining words in written language; emphatic *so* or *very*; and the like.
5. EMPTY ADJECTIVES: *Divine, charming, cute, sweet, adorable, lovely* and others like them.
6. HYPERCORRECT GRAMMAR AND PRONUNCIATION: Bookish grammar and more formal enunciation.
7. LACK OF A SENSE OF HUMOR: Women said to be poor joke tellers and frequently to "miss the point" in jokes told by men.
8. DIRECT QUOTATIONS: Use of direct quotes rather than paraphrases.
9. SPECIAL LEXICON: In domains like colors where words like *magenta, chartreuse,* and so on are typically used only by women.
10. QUESTION INTONATION IN DECLARATIVE CONTEXTS: For example, in response to the question, *When will dinner be ready?,* an answer like *Around 6 o'clock?,* as though seeking approval and asking whether that time will be okay.

## "WOMEN'S LANGUAGE" OR "POWERLESS LANGUAGE"?

Although most lawyers observed in the North Carolina courts were men, the sex distribution of witnesses was more nearly equal. On looking for the speech patterns described by Lakoff, it was readily apparent that some women spoke in the court in the manner described, but it was also apparent that the degree to which women actually exhibited these characteristics varied considerably. Cases observed during the 10 weeks [of courtroom observation conducted during the study] included a variety of misdemeanors and felonies—traffic ordinance violations, drug possession, robbery, manslaughter, and rape—and varied in length from a few hours to a week or more. The cases covered a good cross section of the kinds of trials, and hence witnesses, who regularly appear in a superior criminal court. Despite the number of hours of testimony included, 10 weeks is not enough to produce a large number of witnesses. It is not unusual for a single witness to testify in direct and cross-examinations for several hours. Add to this the fact that the court spends much time selecting jurors, hearing summation remarks, giving jury instructions, and handling administrative matters. Thus, the 150 hours of tapes collected provide a better basis for understanding the range of speech typical in the court than a means for making a precise frequency count of persons falling into various stylistic categories. The discussion in this section thus concentrates on a description of the range of variation and complements it with some nonstatistical impressions regarding frequency.

Observation of courtroom speakers shows a continuum[3] of use of the features described by Lakoff. Initially, it was not clear why some speakers should conform rather closely to Lakoff's proposed model of speech characteristic of American women while others depart in critical ways from it. Before suggesting an interpretation of this finding, let us examine some points along the continuum from high to low incidence of *women's language* features.

## A

Mrs. A,[4] a witness in a case involving the death of her neighbor in an automobile accident, is an extreme example of a person using WL in testifying. She displays nearly every feature described by Lakoff and certainly all those appropriate for the courtroom. Her speech contains a high frequency of INTENSIFIERS (*very* close friends, *quite* ill, etc., often with intonation emphasis); HEDGES (frequent use of *you know, sort of like, maybe just a little bit, let's see,* etc); EMPTY ADJECTIVES (this *very* kind policeman); and other similar features. This typical example[5] of her speech shows the types of intensifiers and hedges she commonly uses:

---

[3]Each feature should actually be treated as a separate continuum since there is not perfect covariation. For convenience, we discuss the variation as a single continuum of possibilities. However, it should be kept in mind that a high frequency of occurrence of one particular feature may not necessarily be associated with a high frequency of another.

[4]Names have been deleted and are indicated by a letter only in order to preserve the anonymity of witnesses. However, the forms of address used in court are retained.

[5]These examples are taken from both direct examinations and cross-examinations of the witnesses, although Table 1 uses data from only direct examinations. Examples are selected to point out clearly the differences in style. However, it should be remembered that the cross-examination of a witness is potentially a more powerless situation than a direct examination.

Q. *State whether or not, Mrs. A, you were acquainted with or knew the late Mrs. X.*
A. *Quite well.*
Q. *What was the nature of your acquaintance with her?*
A. *Well, we were, uh, very close friends. Uh, she was even sort of like a mother to me.*

By contrast, this rewritten version of the same testimony illustrates what her speech might be like without these features.

Q. *State, whether or not, Mrs. A, you were acquainted with the late Mrs. X.*
A. *Yes, I was.*
Q. *What was the nature of your acquaintance with her?*
A. *We were close friends. She was like a mother to me.*

Table 1 summarizes the frequency of several features attributed to WL by Lakoff. Calculated as a ratio of WL forms per answer, this witness's speech contains 1.14—among the highest incidences we observed.

## B

The speech of Mrs. B, a witness in a case involving her father's arrest, shows fewer WL features. Her ratio of features per answer drops to .84. Her testimony contains instances of both WL and a more assertive speech style. Frequently, her speech is punctuated with responses such as: *He, see, he thought it was more-or-less me rather than the police officer.* Yet it also contains many more straightforward and assertive passages than are found in A's speech.

## C

The speech of Dr. C, a pathologist who testifies as an expert witness, exhibits fewer features of WL than either of the other two women. Her speech contains the lowest incidence of WL features among the female witnesses whose speech was analyzed. Dr. C's ratio of WL features is .18 per answer. Her responses tend to be straightforward, with little hesitancy, few hedges, a noticeable lack of intensifiers, etc. (see Table 1). Typical of her speech is this response in which she explains some of her findings in a pathological examination:

Q. *And had the heart not been functioning, in other words, had the heart been stopped, there would have been no blood to have come from that region?*
A. *It may leak down, depending on the position of the body after death. But the presence of blood in the alveoli indicates that some active respiratory action had to take place.*

What all this shows is that some women speak in the way Lakoff described, employing many features of WL, whereas others are far away on a continuum of pos-

per answer is .46. His no-nonsense, straightforward manner is illustrated in the following excerpt, in which a technical answer is given in a style comparable to that of Dr. C.

Q. *You say that you found blood of group O?*
A. *The blood in the vial, in the layman's term, is positive, Rh positive. Technically referred to as a capital r, sub o, little r.*

Taken together these findings suggest that the so-called women's language is neither characteristic of all women nor limited only to women. A similar continuum of WL features (high to low) is found among speakers of both sexes. These findings suggest that the sex of a speaker is insufficient to explain the incidence of WL features.

Once it had been noted that WL features were distributed in such a manner for witnesses of both sexes, the data were examined for other factors that might be associated with a high or low incidence of the features in question. First, it was noted that *more* women fall toward the high end of the continuum. Next, it was discovered that all the women who were aberrant (that is, who used relatively few WL features) had something in common—an unusually high social status. Like Dr. C, they were typically well-educated, professional women of middle-class background. A corresponding pattern was noted among aberrant men (i.e., those high in WL features). Like Mr. D, they tended to be men who held either subordinate, lower status jobs or were unemployed. Housewives were high in WL features whereas middle-class males were low in these features. In addition to social status in the society at large, another factor associated with low incidence of WL is previous courtroom experience. Individuals C and F testify frequently in court as expert witnesses, that is, as witnesses who testify on the basis of their professional expertise. However, it should be noted that not all persons who speak with few WL features have had extensive courtroom experience. Thus, a powerful position may derive from either social standing in the larger society and/or status accorded by the court. Careful ethnographic observation revealed these patterns to hold generally.[7] A little more about the background of the persons described confirms the observed pattern.

**A** is a married woman, about 55 years old, who is a housewife.

**B** is married, but younger, about 35 years old. From her testimony, there is no information that she works outside her home.

**C** is a pathologist in a local hospital. She is 35–40 years old. There is no indication from the content of her responses or from the way she was addressed (always *Dr.*) of her marital status. She has testified in court as a pathologist on many occasions.

---

[7]We do not wish to make more of this pattern than our data are able to support, but we suggest that our grounds for these claims are at least as good as Lakoff's. Lakoff's basis for her description of features constituting WL are her own speech, speech of her friends and acquaintances, and patterns used in the mass media (1975: 4).

**D** is an ambulance attendant, rather inexperienced in his job, which he has held for less than 6 months. Around 30 years old, his marital status is unknown.

**E** is D's supervisor. He drives the ambulance, supervises emergency treatment, and gives instructions to D. He has held his job longer than D and has had more experience. About 30–35 years old, his marital status is unknown.

**F** is an experienced member of the local police force. He has testified in court frequently. He is 35–40 years old and his marital status is unknown.

These data indicate that the variation in WL features may be related more to social powerlessness than to gender. Both observational data and some statistics show that this style is not simply or even primarily a gender-related pattern. Based on this evidence, it appears that the phenomenon described by Lakoff is more appropriately termed *powerless language,* a term that is more descriptive of the particular features involved and of the social status of those who speak in this manner, and one that does not link it unnecessarily to the sex of a speaker.

Further, the tendency for more women to speak "powerless" language and for men to speak it less is due, at least in part, to the greater tendency of women to occupy relatively powerless social positions.[8] Social status is reflected in speech behavior. Similarly, for men, the greater tendency to use the more powerful variant (which we will term *powerful language*) is probably linked, at least in part, to the fact that men much more often tend to occupy more powerful positions in society than women.

## SOME CONSEQUENCES OF USING POWERLESS LANGUAGE

Part of our study of courtroom language entailed experimental verification of hypotheses about the significance of particular forms of language used in court.[9] We conducted this part of our research by designing social psychological experiments based on what we had actually observed in court. First, we located on the original tapes recorded in the courtroom a segment of testimony delivered by a witness in the powerless style. For this study, we chose the testimony given under direct examination by witness A described earlier. Her original testimony was used to generate the test materials needed for the experiment.

The original, powerless-style testimony was edited slightly to make it more

---

[8]That a complex of such features should have been called *women's language* in the first place reflects the generally powerless position of many women in American society, a point recognized but not developed extensively by Robin Lakoff (1975: 7–8).

[9]This research on powerful versus powerless speech as well as experimental studies of other speech variables reported in this chapter have been discussed in previously published journal articles (Conley *et al.,* 1978; Erickson *et al.,* 1978; Lind *et al.,* 1978; O'Barr and Conley, 1976), conference proceedings (O'Barr *et al.,* 1976), and book chapters (Lind and O'Barr, 1979; O'Barr and Atkins, 1980; O'Barr and Lind, 1981).

suitable for use in the experiment.[10] The testimony was then recorded on audio tape with actors playing the parts of the lawyer and the witness. In this recreation of the testimony the actors strove to replicate as closely as possible the speech characteristics found in the original testimony. Another recording was then made using the same actors; however, most of the features that characterize the powerless style—the hedges, hesitation forms, intensifiers, and so on—were omitted from the witness's speech, producing an example of testimony given in the powerful style. It is important to note that the powerful and powerless experimental style differed only in characteristics related to the speech style used by the witness. In both samples of testimony exactly the same factual information was presented.

The first two columns of Table 2 present the results of linguistic analyses of the two experimental testimony tapes described earlier. As may be seen, they differed markedly on each of the features that distinguish the two styles. Differences between powerful and powerless modes are illustrated by the original (powerless) and the rewritten (powerful) excerpts on page 101.

The original testimony on which the experimental tapes were based was delivered by a female witness. To have conducted the experiment only with a female witness would have limited the conclusions to be drawn from the results. To determine whether any particular effects of the speech style factor were restricted to only one sex, the process described above was followed using a female and male acting as the witness. The four tapes thus produced presented the same information from the point of view of content. The differences consisted of a female and a male witness speaking in either the powerful or the powerless style.

As may be seen from Table 2, for both witnesses the intended differences between powerful and powerless styles are present in the tapes used in the experiments. The characteristics summarized in Table 2 show that powerful versions of the testimony taped by the male and female actors are quite similar. The male and female versions of the powerless tapes, however, contain some important differences. The male version has relatively fewer powerless characteristics than the female. It contains, for example, fewer hesitations and intensifiers. In general, the male powerless tape contains many elements of powerless language, but it is a less extreme variant of the style than that used by the original witness and replicated in the female experimental version. These differences between male and female powerless versions were built into the experimental tapes because members of the research team were in agreement that a faithful replication of the original female witness's speech style and powerless mannerisms—although suitable for a female witness—were not within the normal range of acceptable male usage.

[10]This editing involved only minor changes in the testimony. Specifically, we changed the names, dates, and locations mentioned in the original testimony to fulfill our promise to the court that we would protect the privacy of those involved in the actual taped trials. In addition, we removed attorney objections and the testimony to which the objections were addressed. The removal of this material was prompted by our observation in an early stage of the study that objections tended to divert attention from the relatively brief segment of testimony used in the experiment. We are currently investigating the effects of objections as a style topic in its own right.

TABLE 2   Comparison of Linguistic Characteristics of the Four Experimental Tapes
(Powerful versus Powerless Language)

| | Female witness | | Male witness | |
|---|---|---|---|---|
| | Powerful | Powerless | Powerful | Powerless |
| Hedges[a] | 2 | 22 | 2 | 21 |
| Hesitation forms | 13 | 73 | 18 | 51 |
| Witness asks lawyer questions | 2 | 5 | 2 | 6 |
| Use of *sir* by witness | 0 | 3 | 0 | 4 |
| Intensifiers | 0 | 35 | 0 | 31 |
| Running time of tape[b] | 9:12 | 11:45 | 9:35 | 12:10 |

[a]For definitions, see Table 1.

[b]Time given in minutes and seconds.

Once the four experimental tapes had been produced, it was possible to proceed with the experimental test of the results of the two styles. Ninety-six undergraduate students at the University of North Carolina at Chapel Hill served as mock jurors in the experiment.[11] The participants reported to the experimental laboratory in groups of five to seven at a time. Upon arriving, they were given written instructions describing the experiment. Read aloud by the experimenter, these instructions explained to the participants that they would hear a segment of testimony from an actual trial. The instructions then briefly outlined the details of the case and the major issues to be decided.

The case involved a collision between an automobile and an ambulance. The patient in the ambulance, already critically ill and en route to the hospital, died shortly after the collision. The experimental participants were told that the patient's family was suing the defendants (both the ambulance company and the driver of the automobile) to recover damages for the patient's death. The participants were also told that the witness they would hear was a neighbor and friend who had accompanied the now-deceased patient in the ambulance and was therefore present during the collision. The participants were informed that they would be asked questions about their reactions to the testimony after listening to the trial segment. Note taking was not allowed.

The participant-jurors then listened to only one of the four experimental tapes described above. After the participants had heard the testimony, the experimenter distributed a questionnaire asking about the participants' reactions to the case and to the individuals involved. The responses to these questions formed the basis for several conclusions concerning the effects of the style in which testimony is delivered.

The average-rating-scale responses to each of five questions about the witness

[11]Of the 96 participants, 46 were males and 50 were females. The experiment was later repeated at the University of New Hampshire with essentially similar findings.

TABLE 3    Average Rating of Witness Using Powerful
and Powerless Language

|  | Female witness | | Male witness | |
| --- | --- | --- | --- | --- |
|  | Powerful | Powerless | Powerful | Powerless |
| Convincingness | 3.00[a] | 1.65 | 3.52 | 2.09 |
| Truthfulness | 3.70 | 1.88 | 4.24 | 2.86 |
| Competence | 2.61 | 0.85 | 2.44 | 0.18 |
| Intelligence | 2.57 | 0.23 | 1.80 | 0.18 |
| Trustworthiness | 3.04 | 1.65 | 3.48 | 2.00 |

[a]All differences are significant at $p \leq .05$.

are shown in Table 3. For each of these questions, a rating of $+5$ indicates a very strong positive response to the question, whereas a rating of $-5$ indicates a strong negative response. The effects of the testimony style on impressions of the female witness may be seen by contrasting the first and second columns of the table. The results for the male witness are presented in the third and fourth columns of the table.

Statistical analyses[12] confirm the patterns of testimony style influences seen in the table. These analyses permit us to state with a generally high degree of certainty that "jurors" who heard the female use the powerful style indicated that they believed the witness more ($p < .01$), found her more convincing ($p < .001$), and more trustworthy ($p < .02$) than did those who heard her give her testimony in the powerless style. Obviously, the female witness made a much better impression when she used the powerful than when she used the powerless style.

The same pattern of results was found in the comparison of the male's use of powerful versus powerless testimony styles. Again the statistical analyses indicate with high certainty that participants who heard the powerful style responded more favorably than those hearing the powerless style to questions asking how much they believed the witness ($p < .05$) and how convincing they thought the witness was ($p < .05$). As was the case with the female witness, participants thought the male witness testifying in the powerful style was more competent ($p < .001$), more intelligent ($p < .005$), and more trustworthy ($p < .02$). It is therefore apparent from the results of the experiment that, for both male and female witnesses, the use of the powerless style produced consistently less favorable reactions to the witness than did the use of the powerful testimony style. Thus, this experiment demonstrates that the style in which testimony is delivered strongly affects how

[12]The significance of the results reported in this section was assessed by the appropriate multivariate or univariate analysis of variance technique. Only differences reported to be significant should be regarded as "true" or real differences. Social scientists interested in more details of the analyses should consult the other published reports of this research; see footnote 9.

favorably the witness is perceived, and by implication suggests that these sorts of differences may play a consequential role in the legal process itself.

## REFERENCES

Bailey, F. Lee, and Henry B. Rothblatt. 1971. *Successful Techniques for Criminal Trials.* Rochester: The Lawyers Co-operative Publishing Company.

Conley, J. M., W. M. O'Barr, and E. A. Lind. 1978. "The power of language: presentational style in the courtroom." *Duke Law Journal* 78: 1375–1399.

Erickson, Bonnie, E. Allan Lind, Bruce C. Johnson, and William M. O'Barr. 1978. "Speech style and impression formation in a court setting: the effects of 'powerful' and 'powerless' speech." *Journal of Experimental Social Psychology* 14: 266–279.

Fischer, J. L. 1958. "Social influence in the choice of a linguistic variant." *Word* 14: 47–56.

Haas, M. R. 1944. "Men's and women's speech in Koasati." *Language* 20: 142–149.

Keeton, Robert. 1973. *Trial Tactics and Methods* (2nd edition). Boston: Little, Brown.

Lakoff, Robin. 1975. *Language and Woman's Place.* New York: Harper and Row.

Lind, E. A., J. Thibaut, and L. Walker. 1978. "Social attributions and conversational style in trial testimony." *Journal of Personality and Social Psychology* 36: 1558–1567.

Lind, E. A., and W. M. O'Barr. 1979. "The social significance of speech in the courtroom." In *Language and Social Psychology,* edited by Howard Giles and Robert St. Clair. College Park: University Press.

McConnell-Ginet, Sally. 1980. "Linguistics and the feminist challenge." In *Women and Language in Literature and Society,* edited by Sally McConnell-Ginet, Ruth Borker, and Nelly Furman. New York: Praeger.

———, Ruth Borker, and Nelly Furman. 1980. *Women and Language in Literature and Society.* New York: Praeger.

Newcombe, Nora, and Diane B. Arnkoff. 1979. "The effects of speech style and sex of speaker on person perception." *Journal of Personality and Social Psychology* 37: 1293–1303.

O'Barr, William M., and Bowman K. Atkins. 1980. "'Women's language' or 'powerless language'?" In *Women and Language in Literature and Society,* edited by Sally McConnell-Ginet, Ruth Borker, and Nelly Furman. New York: Praeger.

O'Barr, William M., and John M. Conley. 1976. "When a juror watches a lawyer." *Barrister* 3: 8–11, 33.

O'Barr, William M., and E. A. Lind. 1981. "Ethnography and experimentation—partners in legal research." In *The Trial Process,* edited by B. D. Sales. New York: Plenum.

O'Barr, William M., Laurens Walker, John M. Conley, Bonnie Erickson, and Bruce R. Johnson. 1976. "Political aspects of speech styles in American trial courtrooms." In *Working Papers in Culture and Communication* (Philadelphia: Temple University Department of Anthropology) 1: 27–40.

Philips, Susan U. 1980. "Sex differences and language." *Annual Review of Anthropology* 9: 523–544.

Poythress, Norman G. 1979. "A proposal for training in forensic psychology." *American Psychologist* 34: 612–621.

# 5

# LAW AND SOCIAL STATUS
# IN COLONIAL NEW HAVEN,
# 1639–1665*

## M. P. BAUMGARTNER

Law is unevenly distributed in social life. There is, for example, variation in the degree to which individuals invoke the law or are summoned to appear before it, the risks of conviction and of punishment that they run, and the nature of penalties to which they are subject. It has often been suggested that social status is a major predictor of variation of this kind (see, e.g., Carlin, Howard, and Messinger, 1966; Chambliss and Seidman, 1971; Quinney, 1974; Black, 1976: Chapter 2). Most relevant evidence for this claim, however, derives from a limited number of modern societies, and there is a need to evaluate its broader applicability (but see Rusche and Kirchheimer, 1968; Garnsey, 1968; Samaha, 1974). With this end in view, the following is an historical study: It begins with a brief description of 17th-century New Haven and its legal system, and then examines the relationship between aspects of law and social status in a colonial court.

## THE NEW HAVEN COMMUNITY AND ITS LAW

New Haven was settled in 1638 by a group of English Puritans. A year later, a civil government was established and, in 1643, the town was joined by several others to form the short-lived Colony of New Haven. In 1665, only a little more than two decades after its formation, the Colony was absorbed into neighboring Connecticut and the town of New Haven entered the jurisdiction of that government. The population of the town ranged from about 800 persons at the time of settle-

*I thank Donald Black for advice at each stage of the research reported here, Rita J. Simon for comments on an earlier draft of the paper, and the New Haven Colony Historical Society for assistance in the location of the data upon which the study is based.

ment to a few thousand by 1665 (Atwater, 1881: 154, 75). Within this population, there was considerable diversity. Some individuals were much wealthier than others: The richest 25% of the town in the early 1640s controlled 70% of the wealth, while the poorest quarter owned but 1% (Shumway, 1968: 31). Some held title to land and had access to property and services communally owned, while others did not. Some were engaged in more prestigious occupations than others, being professionals or merchants rather than farmers, craftsmen, or, lowest of all, common laborers or servants (see Calder, 1934: Chapter 8; Shumway, 1968: 26). In addition, some citizens were distinguished by membership in New Haven's Congregational Church and some by political enfranchisement, or freemanship. Finally, some were married and had families while others were single or childless, an important distinction in a community which held marriage and parenthood in high esteem.

New Haven had a reputation for moral stringency, even among other Puritan communities. Social control was exercised by several agents, only one of which was the town court whose records are analyzed below. Family control by the male heads of households, for instance, was strong (see Morgan, 1966). In matters between families, informal sanctions such as gossip, reprimands, and ostracism were routine. Finally, for church members, there was the additional social control of the church itself, including formal sanctions of censure and excommunication (see generally Oberholzer, 1956). Each of these types of social control drained potential cases from the court, though little can be known about how many this involved.

The laws of New Haven, like those of other New England colonies, were "a syncretization of biblical precedent and a complex English heritage" (Haskins, 1968: xi). Although not codified until 1656, in substance they proscribed violent crimes and crimes against property as well as a large array of morals offenses. In civil matters, damages were required for such wrongs as defamation, neglect, endangerment, and failure to repay debt, among others. In addition, there was a large body of ordinances. Generally, then, the scope of law in New Haven was broad.

The present study is based upon the records of the New Haven Particular Court, or Town Court, a court of first instance. Before 1643, when the town consolidated with several others to form the New Haven Colony, this court heard all cases, whether serious or trivial. Thereafter, capital cases and civil cases involving extremely large sums of money were removed from its jurisdiction and channeled to superior courts. The court consisted of a preeminent magistrate and four deputies, all equally responsible for the settlement of cases. Their decisions were subject to appeal only in civil affairs. (For an overview of the court system, see generally Levermore, 1886.) In matters of procedure, the court was very informal. Trial by jury was unavailable, as were attorneys in the modern sense of paid, professional advocates. Magistrates assumed a prosecutorial stance, questioning witnesses, and, frequently, expressing moral judgments at any stage of the hearing. Standards of relevancy in testimony were broad (see Townshend, 1950: 221), and accused persons might even be convicted and sentenced on the spot for long-past offenses incidentally revealed during their trials for other misdeeds. In all of these regards, the New Haven court exhibited patterns common to the courts of many tribal and other intimate communities (see, e.g., Cohn, 1959; Gluckman, 1967; Fallers, 1969; Nader, 1969).

## THE COURT RECORDS

The present study analyzes the social characteristics, the issues, and the outcomes in the cases heard before the New Haven Town Court between the years 1639 and 1665. It excludes from consideration routine ordinance violations and estate cases, cases involving juveniles, and the few capital cases heard before 1643, prior to their becoming the concern of higher courts. Since cases involving strangers are subject to separate analysis at the end of this chapter, all major generalizations apply to court actions in relation to town citizens. Beginning with the first records of the court, this study concludes with the 1665 absorption of the Colony of New Haven into Connecticut. It is important to end the study with that event, since the merger involved the adoption of Connecticut law, which differed substantively and procedurally from that of New Haven.

Most previous work on early New England law has centered on statute and procedure, especially as these compared to English law of the same period (see, e.g., Goebel, 1931; Haskins, 1942; 1968). By contrast, this study deals with the New Haven court as an agency of social control in the ongoing life of the town, addressing itself specifically to variation in complaints, outcomes in civil and criminal matters, and the nature and severity of sanctions administered. It explains this variation with the social status of the participants, as measured by various features of their location in the social life of the community. An index of social status is used that includes information on two broad aspects of status—vertical location and radial location. Vertical location refers to rank or position in a system of inequality, and radial location to integration into group life (see Black, 1976: 16–21, 48–49). For this study, rank is measured by land ownership, sex, and the mode of address accorded an individual, which was determined by wealth and occupation ("mister" being the highest term of respect, "goodman" an intermediate one, and no honorific title at all an indication of lowest status). Integration is measured by whether or not a person was a church member, a freeman, a spouse, or a parent, and by the number of his or her children. Since women were rarely landed proprietors and never freemen, their status is measured by that of their family head on these two attributes, whereas, for all other matters, they are treated independently. Citizens who were of high status on more than half of these dimensions are considered of composite, or overall, high status. Those remaining are of composite low status. For instance, to take extremes, a landowning man referred to as "mister" who belonged to the church, had taken the freeman's oath, and was the head of a large family would be of composite high status, while an unmarried female servant accorded no title of respect and without church membership would be of low status. In addition, citizens who were of high status on any of these dimen-

cluding disturbance of the peace, violation of public duty, and other like delicts. Lastly, there were crimes of general misconduct. Rather than being on trial for the commission of one or two easily described misdeeds, persons accused in this category were found innocent or guilty of a series of annoying acts that together constituted their misbehavior. These were the persons "not fitt to live in the Plantation," since they did not "behave themselves well and righteously amonge their neighbours" (Town of New Haven, 1917: 285). They were brought into court, for instance, because their children were improperly reared, or because they entertained servants too often, or for "endeavoring to make discord among neighbors," one of the offenses for which Goodwife Bailey was held accountable:

> For her makeing differenc amonge neighbours, she one time came to Goodwife Merrimans, and said Thomas Barnes hath killed many duckes, and intimated that it was not kindely done that he gave her none: Goodwife Merriman said, she looked for none; then she went to Goodwife Barnes, and intimated to her that Goodwife Merriman was troubled that her husband killed so many ducks and gave her none, and the like carriage she used betwixt Goodman Barnes and some other of his neighbours about some porke wch Thom Barnes had killed (Town of New Haven, 1917: 245).

Offenses of this sort are most likely to be prosecuted in intimate communities. Moreover, it has been observed that people in some societies who commit such offenses and gain reputations as undesirables run high risks of being accused of witchcraft. This applies, for example, to patterns of witchcraft accusation among various tribal people (see, e.g., Wilson, 1963: 104) as well as in 17th-century England (Thomas, 1971: 526–534) and parts of Puritan New England (Demos, 1970). Goodwife Bailey herself, accused of causing dissension among neighbors, was told that she was "very suspitious in poynt of witchcraft. . . ." (Town of New Haven, 1917: 245). By no means was witchcraft the only possible charge against offenders of this type, however; many were processed as public nuisances of a more conventional type. In Puritan New Haven, good citizenship was an ideal tended by the court as worthy of enforcement in its own right.

## THE PARTIES

It is often difficult to tell from the court records which private citizen, if any, complained about a defendant on trial. In a community as small as New Haven, news of misbehavior diffused quickly throughout the town, making a particular complainant superfluous in many instances. This applied, however, only to crimes, since the magistrates took no initiative in civil cases and did not act unless the wronged party demanded redress. In addition, some complaints, both civil and criminal, are lost to history through omissions in the records.

A striking pattern in the cases is the extent to which the court served New Haven's elite. Thus, most identifiable criminal complainants—over three-fourths—were of high status. Although the full significance of this finding cannot be known without information on who was most likely to be victimized, it should be noted that persons of high status comprised only a minority of the total population. On the other hand, the overwhelming majority of criminal defendants were of low status. Similarly, the majority of civil cases for which the complainant is known were initiated by plaintiffs of high status, whereas less than half the civil defendants were high in standing. Comparable differentials in modern society are often partly explained by varying access to and attitudes toward quality lawyers across the classes (see, e.g., Smith, 1919; Carlin and Howard, 1965), but this pattern prevailed in colonial New Haven despite a complete absence of lawyers.

It is also possible to describe the direction of complaints in social space, that is, to describe them as passing from one social location, such as a status, to another (Black, 1976: 21–24, 49–54). In the present context there are four possible categories of direction: a high-status citizen against a low-status citizen, a high-status citizen against another high-status citizen, a low-status citizen against another low-status citizen, and a low-status citizen against a high-status citizen. It has been proposed that downward complaints (from a high social position against a person lower in social standing) are more likely than upward complaints in all legal systems (ibid), and this was true in colonial New Haven (see Table 2).

By far the most common criminal complaint in the New Haven court, representing almost three-fourths of the cases, was that in which a person of high status brought a person of law status to court. Next most frequent were complaints made by low-status citizens against other low-status persons. Equally unlikely were criminal complaints made by either high- or low-status persons against high-status people. In civil matters, most complaints were downward. Slightly fewer in number were complaints passing between two high-status citizens, followed closely by those between two persons of low status. Least frequent were those made by low-status citizens against those of higher social standing than themselves.

Since many differences of law are differences of style rather than quantity (see generally Black, 1976: 4–6), other features of the New Haven cases might be noted as well. For instance, most high-status citizens brought to court were ac-

TABLE 2   Percentage of Cases According to Type of Complaint, by Status of Complainant and Defendant, in the New Haven Town Court, 1639–1665

| Direction of complaint by status | Type of complaint | | |
|---|---|---|---|
| | Criminal | Civil | Total |
| Low against low | 18 | 25 | 22 |
| Low against high | 5 | 14 | 10 |
| High against low | 71 | 33 | 51 |
| High against high | 6 | 28 | 17 |
| Total percent | 100 | 100 | 100 |
| Total cases | (103) | (112) | (215) |

cused of civil wrongs, while most low-status defendants were on trial for crimes (again, see Table 2). At the same time, complainants of high standing usually complained about crimes, but low-status persons, when they complained at all, were more likely to be plaintiffs in civil suits. In terms of direction, the vast majority of complaints made by high-status citizens against others of high status were for civil wrongs, as were those made by low-status individuals against those above them. By contrast, complaints by low-status people against others of their standing were about equally civil and criminal, and most of those brought by high-status citizens against those below them were for crimes. In modern society, high-status persons are more subject to civil law and low-status persons to criminal law (Sutherland, 1940: 35), and the patterns of complaint in the colonial New Haven court reveal a similar correlation.

The greater willingness of both high- and low-status persons to complain against high-status defendants in civil cases may reflect differentials in the commission of offense in the community, or it may reflect differentials in the likelihood of a complaint of one type or the other given a similar rate of offense. Which of these explanations is the better, or whether the patterns result from a combination of both factors, could be revealed only by knowledge of the type and amount of victimization in New Haven, irrespective of the court statistics. In any event, however, this does not affect the fundamental social reality revealed by these findings: The civil type of law, compensatory in its style, was more likely to be brought to bear against persons of high status in New Haven than was criminal law, which was disproportionately applied to persons of low social standing. This affinity between the penal style of law and persons of low status, on the one hand, and other less punitive styles and those of high status, on the other, will be seen to have been of great importance in other workings of the New Haven court as well.

## LITIGIOUSNESS

The significance of the likelihood that a plaintiff or complainant would be of high status becomes more vivid when an examination of repeat complainants is made. Although some persons have concluded that the early New Englander was a litigious person (e.g., Powers, 1966: 43), it is not clear what the empirical grounding for this assertion is. Nevertheless, it is possible to describe degrees of litigiousness within the New Haven population itself. Of those who used the court at all during the years from 1639 through 1665, most used it only once. A fourth of the total number of complainants brought two complaints, while about a fifth were responsible for the initiation of three or more cases. The latter group accounted for nearly half of all the complaints received by the court. In addition, a fourth of this group, comprising only 5% of all complainants, brought five or more complaints each. They were thus responsible for a fifth of all instances of accusation.

It is clear that the repeat accuser made a large part of the business that the court was called upon to handle. For purposes of the following analysis, all persons who brought three or more cases are considered litigious. In addition, all citizens who brought the same ratio of complaints in relation to their residence in New Haven as did a person who lived there for the entire period from 1639 through 1665 and made three accusations is also considered such in this analysis. That is, if a person averaged one or more complaints every nine years, he or she was, for these purposes, litigious. This insures that the category of litigiousness is more than an artifact of length of residence.

By this definition, there were 41 litigious people who used the court during the period in question. Since the likelihood of a complaint increased with social status (see above), it is not surprising that a disproportionate number of litigious people were of higher status (compare, more generally, Galanter, 1974). Over three-fourths of the litigious people in New Haven were of composite high status; all were of at least partially high status. In other words, no one without some characteristics of the upper strata was a frequent user of the court.

It might be noted that, in particular, litigiousness in New Haven varied with occupation. Among those litigious people whose work can be determined, the least numerous were ministers and farmers at 7 and 10% of the total. This constitutes overrepresentation for ministers and decided underrepresentation for farmers. Next were craftsmen, comprising slightly less than a third of all litigious people. By far the most prominent users of the court were the merchants, greatly overrepresented at half the total. Beyond this, some of the litigious nonmerchants were involved in trade to a degree; some dabbled in it while retaining primary commitment to a craft, while at least one of the litigious farmers had been a London merchant before coming to New Haven. It should be observed that wealth differences alone cannot account for this pattern, since farmers in New Haven were wealthier than the more litigious craftsmen (Shumway, 1968: 30). Moreover, farmers and craftsmen were not so low in social standing that status could be a sufficient explanation. A person's occupation was independently associated with the use of law in colonial New Haven.

## THE COURT'S WILLINGNESS TO SETTLE DISPUTES

It should never be assumed that law is available to all who call upon it for help. Thus, although the New Haven Town Court always honored criminal complaints, many civil complaints were turned away: " . . . the Court itself seemed anxious that disputes should be settled, if possible, out of court" (Levermore, 1886: 143). "Every possible attempt was made to have parties settle out of Court. They were frequently enjoined by the Court to do so. . . ." (Townshend, 1950: 222). For example,

> An action was entered by Allen Ball against Jeremiah Whitnell and Jeremiah Johnson for the loss of a cow of his the last Spring, as he conceives by their neglect who kept the heard that day and the Court heard sundrie debates on both sides, and understanding that they had

before bine upon some treaty to put it to arbytration, advised them thereunto, to wch they
all agreed. . . .(Town of New Haven, 1917: 327).

Or, more succinctly, "A difference betwixt Mr. Craine and Captain Turner refered
to bro: Gilbert and bro: Newman to arbitrate" (Town of New Haven, 1857: 41).
Sometimes, the court merely "advised them to agree it themselves" (ibid: 403).
The major difficulty in this course of action was delay; one plaintiff appeared before the court and explained that in 2 years the arbitrators had not been able to settle his claim. The court asked him to give arbitration another chance (Town of New
Haven, 1917: 230).

Differences in the court's willingness to handle civil suits may be understood
as a differential in the amount of law involved across the cases. What predicts lawsuits should therefore predict the court's willingness to hear cases. Thus, it might
be expected that the third of all civil cases submitted to outside arbitration would
contain a disproportionate number of disputes between low-status parties. But this
was not the case: Although high-status persons were more likely to invoke the law,
the court was more likely actually to settle the disputes of low-status citizens. In
other words, the pattern of referral to outside arbitration was not the same as the
pattern of complaint (see Table 3).

Specifically, the court refused to settle over a third of the cases involving two
parties of high status. The proportion of disputes between people of unequal status, one high and one low, referred to extralegal arbitration was similar, but the situation for cases brought by two disputants of low social status was different. The
court was significantly more willing to hear the arguments and settle the quarrels
of two persons of low standing, with only 16% of such cases turned away by the
court. To summarize this differently, the court made judgment on the issues presented to it in 64% of the civil cases involving two high-status persons, 62% of
those involving two persons of mixed rank, and 84% of the cases involving parties of low social standing. There are several possible explanations of this pattern.

It appears, for one thing, that law increases as other social control decreases
(Black, 1971: 1108). This means, for instance, that law is more active in the lives of
persons subject to comparatively few alternative means of social control. Since high
status in New Haven is itself partly defined by church membership and participa-

TABLE 3    Percentage of Civil Cases According to Status of Parties,
by Response of Court, in the New Haven Town Court, 1639–1665

| Response of court | Status of parties | | | Total |
|---|---|---|---|---|
| | Low | Mixed | High | |
| Referral | 16 | 38 | 36 | 32 |
| Court settlement | 84 | 62 | 64 | 68 |
| Total percent | 100 | 100 | 100 | 100 |
| Total cases | (32) | (58) | (39) | (129) |

tion in family life, the quantity of other social control available in these contexts was necessarily greater for higher-status people. Hence, the hesitancy of the court to involve itself in the affairs of persons of high social standing may have been a response to the greater access to other means of dispute settlement which they had.

Another possible explanation may lie in the social relationship between citizens and legal officials in New Haven, since this varied with the status of the citizens. Magistrates in colonial New Haven were always of high status, and so were socially closer to the disputants of high position who appeared before them than to those of low status. Judge and high-status litigant were more likely to be intermarried, to share an occupation, to sit near each other at church services, and to socialize. Together they might steer the course of municipal affairs at town meetings and vote on candidates for admission to the church. In sum, there was little social distance between them. Since law is less likely among intimates than among persons more distant from each other (Black, 1970: 740), the magistrates may have drawn back from cases involving their high-status associates. If this explanation has merit, high-status people in contemporary societies should not be as likely to have their cases turned away by legal agencies, since they no longer have such rich relational ties to most legal agents.

## DECISIONS IN CIVIL CASES

The status of participants in civil suits predicts other features of their handling in the New Haven court as well. In their decisions, magistrates had two broad options open to them. They could decide against one or the other of the litigants in the suit, declaring that person the loser and supporting his or her opponent, or they could hand down a compromise decision, finding both parties partially right and granting neither of them full victory. An instance of such compromise occurred when Thomas Powell accused John Punderson of causing the death of one of his cows:

> Thomas Powell declared that John Ponderson (sic) was warned to keepe cows wth the keeper one day, and he attended it so farr as to goe forth wth them in ye morning, but it rained and he returned home and fell to his occasions, and though aboute one a clock it left raining, yet he went not againe to attend his worke in preserving the cattell, so as the heard came home he had a cow swamped, wch was the occasion of her death (Town of New Haven, 1917: 314).

John Punderson countered that the cow was weak and that this was really to blame for her fate. The court decided that plaintiff and defendant were "to beare the loss betwixt them,"

> . . .and so the cow was to be prised by indifferent men chosen betwixt them, who knew the cow the morning she went out, and what was made of her by hide, tallo, or otherwise, being deduckted, the pure neat loss is to be equally divided (ibid).

Of the cases settled by the court, about three-fourths ended with winners declared and the rest with a compromise decision. Considering all civil cases, however, in-

TABLE 4    Percentage of Civil Cases According to Status of Parties, by Outcome, in the New Haven Town Court, 1639–1665

| Outcome | Status of Parties | | | Total |
|---|---|---|---|---|
| | Low | Mixed | High | |
| Compromise | 30 | 8 | 36 | 23 |
| Winner/loser | 70 | 92 | 64 | 77 |
| Total percent | 100 | 100 | 100 | 100 |
| Total cases | (27) | (36) | (25) | (88) |

cluding those sent to outside arbitrators, about half involved the selection of a winner and 15% a compromise. As with the court's refusal to handle certain cases, so its willingness to define a winner varied with the social status of the parties (see Table 4).

It was much more likely to seek a compromise if both disputants were of the same status than if they were of mixed status. Thus, of the cases that it settled between two high-status litigants, over a third involved compromise and the rest the selection of a winner. The likelihood of compromise was about the same when the parties were both of low social standing. Between people of different status, however, compromise was far less likely, with only 8% of the cases ending in this way. Moreover, the court's greater reluctance to compromise mixed-status cases applied whether the complaint was upward or downward. This is consistent with the suggestion that conciliation is more likely among equals than among people of different rank (Black, 1976: 30).

Social variables predict not only whether and how a case is handled but also who wins. For instance, it has been proposed that downward complainants are more likely to win than are upward complainants (ibid: 22–23). Thus, in colonial New Haven, over four-fifths of the winners in all mixed cases were of high status. Downward complaints ended with decisions in favor of the plaintiff 91% of the time, whereas the plaintiff won only half of the 8 cases in which a lower-ranking citizen complained about a superior.

In sum, the status of participants in civil suits affected the judicial process in several ways. Persons of high status were more likely than those of low status to be referred to outside arbitration, whatever the status of their adversaries. Disputes between persons of different status more often ended with the declaration of a winner and a loser than did disputes between equals, which were more likely to end with a compromise. Finally, when winners were selected in mixed status cases, they were more likely to be of high status than of low status. Overall, these patterns reveal that high-status persons were more immune to law than were those of lower social position.

## DECISIONS IN CRIMINAL CASES

The New Haven court was a difficult one in which to win an acquittal of criminal charges: 90% of all criminal cases resulted in guilty verdicts, with another 5% referred to a higher court. Only 5% ended with a verdict of not guilty, and, furthermore, this was often reluctantly given. It should be noted that in modern America most defendants are convicted as well, with about 90% bargaining a plea of guilty in return for a lowered charge or penalty (Newman, 1956). In colonial New Haven, however, there were no bargains of this kind, and every criminal complaint was given a full hearing.

As in civil cases, differences in the status of the parties predict outcomes in the criminal cases. Acquittal is a type of victory for the defendant, and high-status people were more often acquitted than were those lower in standing. In fact, the chance of acquittal was some five times as great for a defendant of high social position as for a low-status person (see Table 5). It is also possible to provide another kind of comparison by social status through dividing the criminal defendants into persons of partially high status and those without any characteristics of the elite. This results in a similar, though less extreme, finding (again, see Table 5).

Although the defendant's status by itself predicts his or her fate in criminal

TABLE 5   Percentage of Criminal Cases According to Status of Defendant, by Outcome, in the New Haven Town Court, 1639–1665

| | Status of defendant | | |
|---|---|---|---|
| Outcome | Composite low | Composite high | Total |
| Acquittal | 3 | 15 | 4 |
| Referral to higher court | 5 | 5 | 5 |
| Conviction | 92 | 80 | 90 |
| Total percent | 100 | 100 | 99 |
| Total cases | (208) | (20) | (228) |

| | Status of defendant | | |
|---|---|---|---|
| Outcome | Completely low | Partially high | Total |
| Acquittal | 3 | 8 | 4 |
| Referral to higher court | 3 | 12 | 5 |
| Conviction | 95 | 80 | 91 |
| Total percent | 101 | 100 | 100 |
| Total cases | (153) | (65) | (218) |

cases, the direction of the criminal complaint, when it can be ascertained, predicts this all the more strikingly. Of those cases in which the complaint issued from a high-status person against a low-status defendant, only 1%—a single case—ended in acquittal, with 7% referred to a higher court and the rest resulting in conviction. This contrasts with the outcomes of cases in which both complainant and accused were of low standing, where 11% of the defendants were acquitted, 5% referred to a higher court, and 84% convicted. As noted earlier, few low-status people complained about those above them. High-status people were accused by those of lower status in only five instances; in addition, they were complained of by other high-staus people only six times. Of the high-status defendants accused by others equal in standing, all were found guilty. Of those complained against by low-status people, however, three were acquitted, one was sent to a higher court, and only one was convicted. Hence, there were three times as many acquittals in five complaints made by low-status people against those of high status as there were in 73 complaints in the opposite direction.

High-status people were thus very successful in their complaints, whatever the status of their opponents, and, overall, they were more likely to be acquitted than were those beneath them in the status hierarchy. As in the civil cases, then, here too high status conferred an advantage in court.

## CRIMINAL SANCTIONS

Sanctions meted out to the guilty also vary with social status (see Rusche and Kirchheimer, 1968). Since there were only a few defendants of composite high status tried for crimes in the New Haven court, variations are examined in the sentences of those of completely low and partially high status. These comparisons are made on the basis of a proportionately matched sample of crimes committed by the two ranks. A sample of this kind, containing equal percentages of a variety of crimes for both statuses, serves to hold offense constant in the absence of a sufficient number of cases of any one crime to permit separate analysis.

In New Haven, both the nature of the sanction and its severity differed with the social standing of the convicted. Every type of sanction was different across the strata (see Table 6).

Thus, although punishments of humiliation were not very common in the sample (or, for that matter, in the court at all), when they appeared they were applied to persons of low social standing. No one of partially high status was sentenced to the stocks or to wear locks or halters, for instance, but this happened to about a tenth of the completely low-status defendants. In addition, miscellaneous penalties, such as temporary imprisonment, the posting of peace bonds, and simple multiple restitution for cases of theft, came to a fifth of the sanctions of the higher-status defendants in the sample but did not appear in the punishments of the completely low in status. Admonition alone was given to lower-status persons upon a few occasions, but never to the higher-status people.

TABLE 6  Percentage of Matched Sample of Crimes
Resulting in Sanction According to Status of Offender, by
Type of Sanction, New Haven Town Court, 1639–1665

|  | Status of offender | |
| --- | --- | --- |
| Type of sanction | Completely low | Partially high |
| Admonition | 6 | 0 |
| Humiliation | 8 | 0 |
| Corporal punishment | 49 | 20 |
| Fine | 37 | 60 |
| Miscellaneous | 0 | 20 |
| Total percent | 100 | 100 |
| Total cases | (63) | (30) |

As in Massachusetts courts of the time (Powers, 1966: 415), however, the two major sanctions in the New Haven court were fine and corporal punishment: 35% of the sanctions administered to all defendants for all crimes were fines and 41% were corporal punishments, sometimes combined with fines as well. These varied with status, too, so that whippings were disproportionately inflicted upon those of completely low status and fines more often exacted of the partially high-status people. Magistrates used their considerable discretion in such a way that the likelihood of whipping decreased as rank increased. Specifically, in the matched sample analyzed here, fines accounted for 60% of the sanctions given the partially high-status defendants, but only about a third of those given to people of completely low standing. Correspondingly, exactly a fifth of the higher-status citizens received corporal punishment, compared to half of the lower-status ones. Since higher-status persons in New Haven were also less likely to be tried in the first place for crimes that usually elicited corporal punishment, such as morals offenses of all kinds, they were extremely unlikely to receive that sanction. For lower-status persons, the situation was reversed, and whipping was especially likely for them.

Although the style of punishment varied with status, so that physical sanctions were favored for the lowly and fines for more substantial citizens, this was not a simple matter of differential severity. Whether punished corporally or fined, higher-status citizens received more severe degrees of their sanctions. For example, the whippings that partially high-status people did receive for the crimes they committed in the sample were more likely to be designated by the magistrates as "severe." Unlike at least some Massachusetts courts (Powers, 1966: 415), the New Haven court did not specify a certain number of lashes when sentencing, though the law decreed that forty was a maximum. The court did, however, distinguish between whipping and severe whipping. For the group of identical crimes, four of the six whippings given partially high-status defendants were designated severe, while only a third of the 31 inflicted upon completely low-status people were so labeled. Fines also became heavier with rank, though the greater ability of high-status people to afford large fines makes difficult any comparison of the actual deprivation inflicted by monetary penalties on the different statuses. Fines of one pound or less constituted 61% of all higher-status persons' penalties, but 83% of those given lower-rank defendants. A tenth of the fines of those of higher social standing were greater than five pounds, while none of the ones demanded of their social inferiors was so high. Finally, and aside from the matched sample under analysis, it should be noted that although no one of composite high status ever received corporal punishment in the New Haven court, the fines which members of this group received were heavier than those demanded of people only partially high in social standing. In sum, the style and severity of sanction fell unevenly across the New Haven citizenry in court.

## STRANGERS

In addition to the cases involving only New Haven residents, 33 involved strangers. For this purpose, a stranger is any individual, whether Dutch, English, French, or Indian, who did not reside in the New Haven Colony. (Cases involving residents of the Colony from towns other than New Haven are not considered here or elsewhere in this study.) In the nature of the case, strangers were persons of extremely low radial status, or integration. However well-integrated they might have been in their own home towns, they were at a great distance from the center of New Haven's social life. Beyond this, certain aspects of their vertical status at home, such as land ownership, were less relevant in New Haven. They occupied a far different social position from that of either high- or low-status persons who lived in the town and participated in its daily activities. In this, they were like strangers in all times and places.

In other respects, however, the condition of strangers varies from one society or community to another. In pre-Norman England and in some African kingdoms, for example, strangers in the realm were under the direct protection of the king or chief (Maitland, 1883: 305ff.; Gluckman, 1965: 216), and thus enjoyed a special status. On the other hand, legal harshness toward strangers has been reported in some rural and primitive social settings (see, e.g., Beidelman, 1967). In New Haven, the court reacted to outsiders in the former fashion, extending certain privileges to them. Despite their low integration, strangers received treatment in the court similar to that received by genuinely high-status natives. They were even, in some regards, treated more like high-status people than were the actual high-status citizens themselves. This was true, however, primarily in their dispositions. When it came to accepting their disputes for settlement, the court related to them in a fashion similar to that used for low-status New Haven residents. It accepted all of these cases, referring none to extralegal modes of social control such as arbitration.

Much like the higher strata of New Haven, strangers won nearly all of the lawsuits in which they were involved—six of the seven that they brought against New Haven citizens and two of the four that residents brought against them. Hence, New Haveners stood in relation to strangers as parties of lower status did to those of higher status in disputes among themselves. Further, like stratified disputes, those between strangers and New Haven residents were more likely to be settled with the declaration of a winner than the issuance of a compromise. In fact, there were no compromises in any of the 11 suits involving townspeople and outsiders.

The acquittal rate for the 20 criminal cases with foreign defendants was higher than that for any group of New Haven residents. As mentioned previously, completely low-status persons were acquitted less than 3% of the time, people of partially high status 8% of the time, and those of composite high standing 15% of the time. Strangers, by contrast, were acquitted in 25% of their trials. Even when convicted and sentenced, they received treatment like that accorded natives of high standing. Thus, over half of the punishments inflicted upon strangers were fines, but less than a third were corporal punishments. These percentages are similar to those for persons of partially high status in New Haven. In addition, such whippings as were received by strangers, like those given higher-status New Haven citizens, were often severe, with two of the four they received so specified by the court. Their fines tended to be large as well.

Finally, there were two instances of criminal complaint brought by strangers against New Haveners, both of which issued from Indians and both of which were successful. The special concern of the court with the treatment of outsiders is shown in the handling of a white settler accused by an Indian of stealing venison he had killed. The magistrates were harsh, explaining their severity with the nature of the victim, in that the settler

> had done it to an indian, & to a poore indian, & when himselfe had noe need of it & soe often denieing it etc. Whereby he makes the English & their Religion odious to the heathen & thereby hardens them (Town of New Haven, 1919: 77).

## SUMMARY

The main findings of this study may be summarized in the following generalizations. First, in colonial New Haven high-status citizens initiated a disproportionate number of legal cases, both civil and criminal, while low-status citizens were more likely than their high-status neighbors to have complaints brought against them. The most frequent complaint involved a high-status complainant and a low-status defendant; the least frequent was the reverse. Beyond this, the most litigious people were of high status, and merchants were most litigious of all.

In civil disputes, cases involving at least one high-status individual were more likely than those involving two low-status parties to be referred to outside arbitration. When the court did decide a civil case, disputes between equals of any status were more likely than disputes between persons of different status to end with compromise, and when it selected a winner in the context of a mixed-status dis-

# LAW AND SOCIAL MORPHOLOGY

# 6

# MURDER IN SPACE CITY

## HENRY P. LUNDSGAARDE

### THE RESEARCH

My curiosity was first aroused in 1970 when I went to live and teach in Houston. As a stranger to the community, I noticed almost constant but exceptionally brief accounts of slayings in and around the city in the news media. These accounts indicated that homicides occurred almost daily somewhere in the city. I was continuously struck by two facts: (1) Except for truly sensational slayings, homicides were not treated as front page news. (2) Despite the cursory nature of most such reports, it could be seen that the killings resulted from seemingly trivial victim provocations. For example, one man killed another because the latter stole the parking space desired by the killer-to-be. Another man shot a bartender after an argument over a five-cent increase in the price of beer during the hours of entertainment. An off-duty police officer working as a security guard was shot when he asked a man to lower the volume of his piano playing after midnight. The officer, in turn, killed the piano player and the incident was classified as a justifiable homicide. The frequency of homicides arising from such slight provocation called my attention to homicide as a subject worthy of anthropological inquiry.

Some of the principal assumptions that have guided the study include: (1) Homicide differs from other forms of violent behavior primarily in the mode of expression and seriousness of outcome; (2) homicide, as exemplified in the 1969 data, requires the broadest possible analytical perspective if explanation is to be attempted; (3) homicide, as a cultural phenomenon, requires a separate analytical treatment because it represents the extreme point on a hypothetical continuum of interpersonal violence. In the City of Houston, the ratio of homicides to other offenses against the person is approximately one to 32. Homicide, therefore, is much like the tip of the proverbial iceberg because it is the most readily evident form of violent human behavior.

During 1972, I received permission from the chief of police to review all 268 official homicide cases on file for the year 1969 in the Homicide Division of the Houston Police Department. This particular year was chosen for several reasons. First, three sociological studies of homicide in Houston, Bullock (1955), Caldwell (1963), and Pokorny (1965), as well as the publication in 1969 of the voluminous study of the National Commission on the Causes and Prevention of Violence, permit comparison of the 1969 Houston data with both a local and a national sample. Second, it was not possible to include cases still under police investigation or cases still in the process of adjudication before the criminal courts. As it turned out, I was able to discover the final outcome for all but 29 cases. Some of these had not yet been solved by the police or prosecuted by the district attorney.

The individual case data, because of their confidential nature, could not be reproduced or removed from the premises of the Homicide Division. I was, however, permitted free access to the 1969 case files provided that I would work on the premises of the Homicide Division, where a small interrogation room was made available to me. This arrangement proved advantageous since it made it possible to seek supplementation and clarification of the file data from homicide detectives. Each case was read in its entirety and the significant facts were directly taped on a tape recorder. To ensure anonymity of all the principals in a case, including the detectives responsible for the case reports, all names have been fictionalized. A case numbering code was adopted to allow any investigator with access to the police files to check or expand on the information summarized in the case descriptions.

The individual case data were also supplemented by interviews with homicide detectives, forensic pathologists, and lawyers familiar with the peculiarities of the Texas system of criminal justice. Official court records were examined to obtain information on sentencing and court disposition. During brief periods in 1972, 1974, and finally after January 1, 1976, I also observed the investigation procedure itself to learn, at firsthand, how different detectives working together on one case collected information and decided what information was to be treated as relevant or irrelevant for their purposes. After I had taped all the known cases for 1969, I accompanied different homicide detectives, working both day and night shifts, on their investigations of current cases. Observation of homicide scenes around the city, and my presence during police interrogation of killers and eyewitnesses to homicide, made me increasingly aware of both the limitations and potentialities of information contained in the previously recorded data. Homicide officers, in addition, significantly enlarged my appreciation of the homicide investigation by accompanying me to such novel but to them familiar scenes as the emergency ward and morgue at the Ben Taub Hospital, the dispatcher's office at police headquarters, and the city jail. Finally, I was given "the guided tour" through high crime localities and neighborhoods.

Police files are not organized for scientific research, but the record of the entire

husband, according to his daughter, had recently been released from a Texas hospital following a lengthy treatment for alcoholism. Both parents were reported to be alcoholics.The police noted a large garbage can filled with empty beer cans in the apartment and the best explanation for the act seems to be that the homicide-suicide was committed in an alcoholic stupor. The autopsy report attached to the case indicated that no alcohol was found in the blood of the wife. No autopsy report on the husband was filed with the police.

The next case, No. 167, bears a striking resemblance to the above. An elderly white couple was found dead by their daughter. The woman's age was given as 69 but the man's age was not given. The wife was dressed in her nightgown and she was shot with a .38 caliber revolver in the back of the head. She was seated before the television set, which was still running when the bodies were found. The daughter told the police that her father had a violent temper and that her deceased mother took special pleasure in needling him. What finally precipitated the man to act and kill his wife is unknown. The fact that the husband killed himself may say something about his way of solving problems. The ready availability of a firearm also must have made his fatal decision somewhat easier to execute. One can only guess that in both cases, which presumably involved persons who had been married for a long time, the homicide-suicide solution seemed easier than separation, divorce, or the continuation of an unsatisfactory and mutually frustrating relationship.

The homicide division telephone answering service is kept continually busy with complaints of marital fighting and brutality. The official response is bureaucratic: The police can only respond to formal complaints or those executed in writing at the police station. There is some indication from the case data and conversations with homicide detectives that many incidents that begin with a complaint to the police eventually terminate in a killing. Spouses who formally "file" against each other have a distinctive advantage, legally, if the relationship sometime in the future results in the killing of an abusive spouse. The record of violence has been established by the recognition of the threat and it can help the assailant in a self-defense plea. In the following case a husband kills his wife with a shotgun. The police in this case found sufficient grounds for bringing the facts of the case before a grand jury. That jury, in turn, issued a no bill (a decision not to indict) for the husband. His killing was well inside the boundaries of a legally excusable act.

A black male, age 70, killed his 55-year-old wife by shooting her in the chest and throat with his 16-gauge shotgun. According to witnesses, neighbors in the apartment complex where the couple resided, the couple had a loud and continuous argument the night before the killing. Their verbal arguments had erupted into a fight during which the woman took a knife and cut her husband's finger. The finger was stitched at the hospital, but later in the day the fight continued and this time the woman shattered a mirror in her husband's face. Witnesses report that the husband was heard yelling at his wife indicating in no uncertain terms that he would kill her. The wife left the house and returned shouting that she was going to kill her husband. The man didn't take any chances. He shot her through the screen door and according to one eyewitness the man came outside to look at her and said, "There she is, I told her I was going to do it." Another neighbor who called an ambulance said that the man came out in the yard and said, to the people in the crowd, "Call somebody to come and get her or I will shoot her again." Other witnesses and neighbors interviewed by the police reported that the elderly couple drank heavily and had quarreled since the day they moved into the apartment complex. This was not the first time that others had heard one of the two threaten the life of the other. After the husband had been cleared by the grand jury he wrote a formal letter to the authorities: "I, _____, hereby give my permission to Arthur Brown to pick up and keep my shotgun out of the property room at the city of Houston, Harris County, Texas, in connection to the charge of murder filed against me." The shotgun was released to the legally exculpated killer.

In Case No. 92 the police made a thorough investigation because there was considerable doubt whether the victim, a 46-year-old black female, was killed with a .32 caliber pistol by her husband or if she committed suicide in her husband's presence. The circumstances of the case were sufficiently complicated by circumstantial evidence and by the fact that the principal witness was the woman's young son by a previous marriage. The assailant, a black male, age 46, was indicted by a grand jury but found "not guilty" after the trial of his case. The 10-year-old boy's verbatim statement encapsulates the sad facts of the marital relationship.

> My name is Daniel Drury. I am 10 years old. I live at . . . with my mother and stepfather. I am in the 5th grade and go to Houston Gardens Elementary School. Yesterday evening, about 6:30 p.m. or 7:00 p.m., my mother wanted to go see my brother who is in Ben Taub Hospital but my stepfather did not [want to go]. My parents left home and dropped my stepfather at Phillip's Place on the way home and stayed for about 30 minutes. I don't think my mother or stepfather had any trouble while at the beer joint (Phillip's). We went on home and I went on to bed which was about 9:00 p.m. She told me to go to sleep and not eat anything. She was going somewhere. I then went to sleep. My daddy came home about 10:00 p.m. and I woke up when he came in the door. He asked me where my mother was. He had been drinking. He told me over and over that I lied. He then went and got the pistol. He said that she could not outsmart me [him] and that he was smarter than she was. They argue a lot about my daddy not working and going out and spending his money getting drunk. He then left. He called back and asked me on the phone where my mother was and I told him that I did not know. I then went back to sleep. I woke up again by my mother and daddy arguing. They were in my room. My daddy slapped my mother in the face and then went out of my room. I heard them argue more and heard mother tell him that she had seen him kiss another lady. The next thing I heard a shot and heard my mother say "Oh, Henry, you shot me." I heard daddy go call an ambulance and say that a lady had been shot while he and her had been wrestling over a gun. He called back again for an ambulance. He went into the bathroom and got a wet towel and went back where mother was and I don't know what he did then. He then went next door and got Mr. G to come over. The ambulance and the police came and I told them what happened. I went and stayed until about 3 a.m. with Mrs. G. My uncle came and got me. Later I was brought to the police station and told Detective A what happened.

The follow-up investigation, among other things, revealed that the victim's husband had been seen by eyewitnesses to physically assault his wife on at least 10 previous occasions and that the husband was a heavy drinker. The autopsy did not reveal any alcohol in the wife's blood or spinal fluid. The husband's police record indicated that he had been arrested for carrying a pistol and that he had been listed as a material witness in a cutting. In 1962, before he was married to his now deceased wife, he was wanted for aggravated assault. The wife's circumstances at the time of her death were not too encouraging. Her other son was hospitalized at the Ben Taub psychiatric ward, she had a daughter who was serving a prison sentence in an Austin city jail, and her stepson—who was married to her daughter imprisoned in Austin—was serving a jail sentence elsewhere. Perhaps the Houston jury found enough loose ends in this case not to render a guilty verdict against the husband or perhaps they were persuaded by defense lawyers that the deceased was crazy enough to have precipitated her own death. One cannot know the details of this and similar cases but we can begin to see the very subtle interplay between the public sanctions that define marriage as an institution and the private sanctions exerted by individuals who, by choice, live within the broad guidelines outlined by their culture.

The victim in Case No. 67, a young married black female, age 21, met her death by strangulation. Her 30-year-old husband was apprehended by the police and remains, at the time of this writing, either a prime suspect or a defendant now represented by an attorney. In many cases, as we shall see, a case is incomplete or disjointed as is this case. Many factors are at work: the police work necessary to uncover legal grounds for an arrest, the time schedules of crowded courts and busy prosecutors and defense attorneys, and last but not least, the medieval recording system that frequently makes it impossible to discover the final outcome of certain cases. The police are not routinely notified of the outcome of a case once it has left the homicide division and is turned over to the district attorney. Obfuscation by a slow-moving bureaucracy is the fate of many police cases once they have been processed by the judicial machinery.

Case No. 168 seems particularly tragic in that it is a homicide that involves two 18-year-old Mexican-Americans, recently married, with a 5-month-old baby. The young wife furthermore was found to be 4 months pregnant with a second child and the shooting was a tragic mistake. The young husband was charged with negligent homicide and sentenced to serve 3 months in jail. What had happened, briefly, was this. He was in the kitchen of the couple's small apartment together with three of his friends. The atmosphere was friendly and the wife was preparing a meal of pancakes. The husband casually took a .22 rifle from behind the refrigerator and began to toy with it. He pointed it around the room and the rifle went off. The bullet entered the right eye of his wife and the young woman died on the kitchen floor. The husband's friends called the police.

The details of Case No. 102 were quickly pieced together at the scene of the killing. A 32-year-old black man shot his wife with a .32 caliber revolver as they were struggling over possession of the "family pistol." The killing was witnessed by the couple's 15-year-old daughter who submitted a written affidavit to the police. According to the young girl, her parents were arguing over the family budget. The girl's statement read as follows:

I live with my mother and stepfather together with my two brothers and two sisters. I attend Baldwin Junior High School where I am in the eighth grade. . . . This morning my mother told my stepfather that she was going to cash a check. He told her that he was going to cash the check to pay the car note. Mother told him that he could not pay the car note this week because he had other bills to pay. Mother was sitting on the footstool in the living room reading the paper. My stepfather was sitting in another chair in the same room. He got up and went into the bedroom and got the gun off the bookcase at the headboard of the bed. He told mother that he was tired of this goddamn shit and he said that when he had the gun in his hand. He put the gun in his pocket. Mother told him, "That is what I wanted you to do. Now that you have got the gun, use it!" She told me to go gather up the clothes for the laundry. I left the room and went to get the clothes. I heard three shots. I ran back into the room to see what had happened. My stepfather told me that he had killed my mother and for me to go and call the police . . . mother was lying on the floor in front of the dresser and her eyes were closed. I called her but she did not answer.

The defendant was tried in the court without a jury, found guilty, and sentenced to serve a 7-year sentence in the Texas Department of Corrections. Can we conclude that the homicide was "victim-precipitated" or perhaps "situation-precipitated"? The technology for an expedient killing was readily available, the argument over money focused other strains and tensions between the couple, and the wife's "I dare you" was more than a kind verbal dig. Why did it happen?

Case No. 191 begins as a domestic quarrel. A 37-year-old white woman and her 42-year-old husband were drinking and quarreling. The woman first ran next door to her sister's apartment but only found her 11-year-old nephew awake. She left her sister's house to seek assistance from a neighbor. Her husband intercepted her as she crossed their driveway, a further argument ensued, and the woman shouted for help as she walked away from her husband. The neighbors found the woman lying bleeding on the sidewalk and called an ambulance. The husband told police that the whole thing had started because his wife didn't love him anymore. The husband's interpretation of their relationship, together with the ensuing quarrel fueled by the mutual consumption of alcohol, finally led him to pull out a pocketknife and stab his wife in the chest. The husband was indicted, tried, found guilty of murder, and sentenced to serve a 10-year term in the Texas Department of Corrections. Expressions like "I don't love you anymore" clearly have the potential for initiating an argument. They challenge the *raison d'etre* of the relationship and must therefore be retrieved, rationalized, or simply erased if the relationship is to continue. It is also possible, as was evident in Case No. 191, that the two principals, rather than negotiating back and forth to achieve a status quo or facilitate a détente, will readily escalate from emotional threat to physical action. In the following case, the husband responded to a similar but more serious emotional injury by killing his wife without further argument or negotiation.

The spouses in Case No. 233, a black male, age 25, and a black female, age 22, were engaged in sexual intercourse when the wife continually called out the name of another man who was known by the husband to be a former boyfriend. The husband, according to his statement to police officers, completed the act then got up and put on his clothes. He took out his .22 automatic pistol and shot his wife in the chest. The couple's two 3-year-old twin daughters were at the scene when the killing took place. The man, at first, told police officers that a neighbor had killed his wife. Sufficient doubt was raised by the husband's conflicting statements, and the absence of an eyewitness or other direct evidence supporting his story, that the first jury trial was declared a mistrial. A second trial was held and the husband was found guilty of murder in the first degree. He was sentenced to serve a life sentence in the Texas Department of Corrections.

We cannot second-guess the two juries or the two judges charged with evaluating the circumstances of the killings in this and the previous case. One element, however, seems bothersome; that is, the different judicial weight assigned to the initial provocation. Does the provocation of words like "I don't love you anymore" and calling somebody else's name during the height of intercourse mean a difference between spending 10 years and a lifetime in jail? But this must raise the question of possible judicial capriciousness and arbitrariness in assessing the degree of victim provocation, assailant response, and final punishment.


## WIFE-HUSBAND KILLINGS

Nearly twice as many wives as husbands killed their spouses in 1969. Since men, as both assailants and homicide victims, outnumber women by a ratio of 4:1, the wife-husband type of killing is the most typical form of homicide involving women as assailants. The most interesting statistic concerns the disposition of homicides in which the wife became the principal assailant. Nine of 15 wives were brought before the Houston Grand Jury and no billed, the police did not file a charge in one case and dismissed another, one case was brought to an inconclusive trial (the outcome, at the time of this writing, is still undetermined), one wife received a 3-year probationary sentence, and the outcome or legal disposition of two other cases remains unknown. Insofar as the available data permit, we shall look at each case and search for any motivational and situational factors that led these wives to terminate the marital relationship by homicide.

Case No. 2 adds a touch of chivalry to the marital tragedy. At 9:15 a.m. on October 17, 1969, a 29-year-old black woman shot her husband in the stomach with a .22 caliber revolver. After the shooting, which evolved in the course of an argument over money, the woman drove her husband to the Veterans' Administration Hospital where he was interviewed by the detectives from the Houston Homicide Division. Prior to his death on January 9, 1970, the husband executed a handwritten affidavit that, in part, reads as follows: "On Friday, October 17, 1969 at 9:30 a.m. my wife and I had an argument over money matters and in this argument we had a gun. In the scuffling over the gun it accidentally was discharged, the bullet striking me in the stomach. Being her husband, I do not want to file any charge against her, and if I do not get well I still do not want the law to file any charge against her." The husband's statement by itself could not exonerate his wife and did not preclude official police action. The police arrested the wife on January 12,

1970, and referred the case to the grand jury. The grand jury in turn issued a no bill and thus closed the case.

Case No. 159 closely approximates Wolfgang's definition of victim-precipitated homicide. The husband was intoxicated (0.27 percent alcohol level in his blood), he verbally provoked his wife by threatening to kill her with a knife, and he physically assaulted her by trying to choke her. It appears that the husband, a 50-year-old black male, had arrived home around 1:30 a.m. His 45-year-old wife offered to prepare some food for him but he began to use abusive language, calling her a "smart bitch" among other things, and he began to beat her. She fled into the bathroom but he followed her and continued to beat her. She escaped once more but her husband ran to the kitchen and picked up a steak knife, which he said he would use to kill her. The woman managed to retrieve their .22 caliber pistol from the closet and she fired six shots at her husband. The bullets hit his chest, back, and left arm. Although it appears that the first bullet stopped her husband's attack it is evident, from the bullet entry in his back, that she continued to fire the pistol after he had turned away. The grand jury did not make an issue of the obvious "overkill" factor and dismissed the case with a no bill.

It is impossible to reconstruct the mutual understandings and misunderstandings about a workable marital relationship from the acts of the principals in Case No. 15. A man is prepared to choke and beat his bride of 6 weeks and yet emotionally unprepared to grant her a divorce. The husband, a 37-year-old black male, was killed with a .22 caliber pistol by his 27-year-old wife at 11:05 a.m. in the family residence. The wife had five young children from a previous marriage. The wife's mother lived in the house next door and it is evident that the victim had failed to get along with either his wife's children or his mother-in-law since the marriage. During the short duration of the marriage the husband had managed to threaten the children, alienate his mother-in-law, and physically maltreat his wife on several occasions. The husband had threatened his wife and added that he would kill her if she ever dared file charges (of assault) against him with the police. One Sunday, after he had once again beaten and choked his wife, the woman moved next door to her mother. The husband unsuccessfully tried to talk his wife into coming back to him, but she resisted and finally went to see an attorney for the purpose of obtaining a divorce. After visiting her attorney she called her husband, who at the time was working as a gas station attendant, to advise him of her actions. His reply was brief: "I will fix you when I get home." In response, the woman and her mother together with the children locked themselves in the house fearing what would happen next. The husband showed up and he asked to be let in. His mother-in-law refused. He got angry and said that he would kill his wife. The mother-in-law went away from the door to call the police. As she left, the man pulled off the screen door and broke down the front door. The wife, in the meantime, had armed herself and she met her husband in the hallway. The man began once again to curse her and he repeated his threat that he would "fix" her. She emptied the magazine of the automatic weapon and her husband fell dead on the floor. It turned out that the pistol was on file with the police department as a stolen weapon. The wife was arrested and booked on suspicion of murder. The grand jury reviewed the facts of the case and issued a no bill on February 19, 1970.

The facts in Case No. 38 were related to the police by the assailant and her 17-year-old daughter who had witnessed the killing in their home. The husband, a 48-year-old black male, was killed by his wife, age 45, at 2:50 a.m. following a fight. The couple had two children. The argument that led to the killing apparently got under way early in the evening. Finally, after the couple had retired together, the husband kicked his wife out of bed and told her to sleep in their daughter's bedroom. On the way to the bedroom the wife secured the family revolver, which, she said, she placed under the mattress of her daughter's bed. Shortly thereafter she went to get a drink of water in the kitchen. She brought the revolver with her—just in case! Her husband left his bed and came after her. The wife fired two shots hitting him once in the head and once in the back. She explained to the police that her husband had come straight at her and that she fired in self-defense. The instant widow first called the deacon of their church and he, in turn, informed the police. The Houston Grand Jury did not find any grounds for indicting the woman so the case was no-billed.

Such familistic killing sometimes occurs outside the home, as in Case No. 49. Here a woman, a 35-year-old black female, had gone to a local cafe to get her husband to come home. Her husband, age 53, left the cafe and was heard arguing with his wife outside the cafe. She apparently yelled that she was tired of seeing her husband fooling with "them whores" in the cafe and he was overheard to shout that she should remove her eyeglasses. They fought on the sidewalk and during the fight the woman took a .22 caliber pistol from her purse and fired. A witness said that the man tried to raise himself after the first shot had been fired and that the woman then shot him once more. The woman threw the weapon into a nearby car and then waited for the ambulance that took them both to Ben Taub Hospital. Homicide detectives were able to interview the husband before he died and he stated that he was willing to prosecute the person who had shot him but that he didn't know who had done it! One of the eyewitnesses swore to the police that he had shouted to the woman not to shoot the man when he saw she had a gun. The grand jury's finding of insufficient cause, a no bill, must have viewed the woman's armed defense as well within the law or, could it possibly be that the jury is responding stereotypically to killings among intimates as an affair between private persons and not within the purview of the public interest?

The principal eyewitness to Case No. 64 was a 12-year-old girl. She had the misfortune to become, on the one hand, a part of the argument that led to the killing and, on the other hand, to witness firsthand the ugly scene of a homicide. The girl's mother, a 28-year-old black female, and her stepfather, age 28, were arguing. The argument escalated and suddenly intensified when the man began to hit his stepdaughter. The woman contested his authority and got a small pocketknife from the kitchen drawer. As the couple argued further, blows were exchanged, and the wife used the small knife to make two penetrating stab wounds. One in the neck and one in the right side killed her husband. The woman was arrested, advised of her legal rights, and put in the city jail. She did not feel that she needed an attorney and she volunteered a written confession, which the police presented to the district attorney, who, in turn, used the confession and the two eyewitness reports to present the case to the grand jury. Both eyewitness reports, one by the defendant's 12-year-old daughter and another by a friend of the couple, were deemed sufficient grounds for issuing a no bill. It is of further interest to note that the second witness's account indirectly tells us something about the neutral or noninterventionist pose frequently adopted by persons who become the perhaps unwilling witnesses to an act of violence. The witness, a male, was visiting this family with his wife and three small children. He and the family stayed long enough to witness the couple's fighting and they saw the victim hit the defendant's little girl. The case report contains no further comment about the role of the outside visitors.

The reader should now recall the warning that it is much too simple to use single variables, such as race or sex, to explain violence and homicide. Case No. 93 exhibits many of the characteristics of the previous cases except that the couple here is a white male, age 45, and his 41-year-old wife. The couple had two teenage daughters who stated to the police that they had become so accustomed to their parents' frequent fights that they had learned to sleep through the noise. On this fatal morning, at 2:15 a.m., the two girls were awakened by a shot. The police were called and they found the girls' father lying, still conscious, on the bedroom floor. As the police officers entered they could not help but notice that the couple was still arguing! The woman told the police that she had shot her husband because he had been abusive and tried to beat her. Her husband told the police that they had been arguing because she had been drinking and had called him a son of a bitch. The man then told the police officers that he felt sure that he was going to die but that he did not want to file charges against his wife. The woman was taken to the homicide division while her husband was rushed to the hospital. When the husband died on the following day the police filed murder charges against the widow who had already secured the services of an attorney and had been released on bond. On December 18th, the grand jury dismissed the case with a no bill *and* the grand jury wrote an official note to the police ordering the release of her .22 caliber pistol.

In reading and studying these homicide cases one gets the feeling that the actors in these strange social scenarios are indistinguishable from ordinary people, yet they seem to walk around as sticks of dynamite that may go off at the slightest disturbance or provocation. In Case No. 140 that triggering device is a $42.00 loan. The actors are husband, a black, age 44, and wife, age 52. It all started quite innocently. The couple, who had their home in Belville outside of Houston, were dining at the home of the defendant's cousin. According to this cousin, who became a principal eyewitness to the killing, the couple arrived on time as expected. The husband bent down for something and a piece of paper fell out of his pocket onto the floor. His wife saw the paper and announced that it was a receipt from a loan company in Houston for the amount of $42.00. The husband and his wife started to argue over the note, she complained that he had been borrowing money without her knowledge, and the husband picked up a knife from the kitchen counter. The wife's cousin took the knife away from him. The man's wife then grabbed her husband by the wrist and held him. The husband started to kick and bite. He bit his wife on the nose, causing a small cut. The wife was frightened, although her husband stopped biting her after she had pleaded with him to let her go. She went into another room where she removed a knife from her purse. She explained to the police that she knew that her husband carried a knife with him and that he, on previous occasions, had pulled his knife on her. The husband approached and he apparently tried to get his own knife out of his pocket. His wife held his wrist and they struggled over control of the wife's knife. In the scuffle the knife lodged in the husband's chest. He exclaimed, "I've been stabbed. I'm feeling weak" as he dropped to the floor. The woman's knife had entered the heart necessitating open-heart surgery at the Ben Taub Hospital. The operation was a success but a member of the medical staff called the homicide division and announced that the man had died in his hospital bed at 3:30 a.m. The subsequent autopsy showed no trace of either alcohol or barbiturates in the husband's body. The wife was no-billed by the grand jury.

Domestic quarrels do not always occur within the privacy of the home. In Case No. 69 a black couple, a woman, age 43, and her husband, also 43, settled their differences in a public bar. The bartender, who nearly got shot himself when the woman began firing a small .22 caliber pistol at her husband, told the police that he was talking to the man when his wife came into the barroom and told him, the bartender, to move over. The loud background music muffled the conversation between the two but it was clear to witnesses that the woman's purpose was to talk her husband into leaving the bar. She left the bar and returned minutes later with a pistol. She walked over to her husband and said something to the effect that he was a S.O.B. and that even if he had come home with her, she would shoot him. After shooting her husband she turned around and took a shot at the bartender, grazing his shoulder with the bullet. She then left the bar. The husband raised himself up from the barstool, walked slowly toward the pool table, and fell dying to the floor as he attempted to hold onto the pool table. The official outcome of the case, I conclude, must reinforce the behavior and form of dispute settlement witnessed in this case. The woman was charged with her husband's murder as well as unlawful possession of a firearm. The bartender apparently did not file a complaint with the police although he was nearly killed himself. The case went to trial, without a jury, and the presiding judge found the defendant not guilty after he heard the testimony. Charges are still pending against the woman for carrying a pistol. The reader may wonder why this woman, unlike all the assailants in the previous cases, was charged for illegally carrying a pistol. Texas law is vague on this point. If you merely possess and use a gun in your own territory it is within the law. In some cases, or if the police want to make an issue out of it, a person will face several different charges relating to the commission of a crime. Unfortunately, this practice opens the way to expedient plea bargaining procedures, which, in the end, speeds official and bureaucratic processing of criminals but, alas, makes mockery of justice.

The principals in Case No. 86, a black male, age 31, and his wife, age 28, were both unemployed and on welfare. They shared a small apartment with their six children. The killing here also evolved as part of an unsatisfactory marital relationship and the victim's body was found in his bed. In this case, the wife stated to the police on their arrival that she had waited until her husband was asleep before she shot him with a shotgun. The events, as related in the wife's affidavit, were roughly that the husband had come home intoxicated around 10:30 the previous evening. He accused his wife of seeing another man during the day and, as a gesture, he picked up his shotgun and held it against his wife's head while he allegedly said, "I ought to shoot you right now." He then put the gun on the bedroom dresser, crawled into bed, and then said that he would get her before the night was over. One of the six children tried to interfere with the parents with the result that the man got out of bed and spanked her using his belt. Sometime later, in yet another scene with the children, the wife's brother came to the house. He left at 11:30 p.m. The husband finally went to sleep. His wife waited about 15 minutes, then she entered the bedroom, removed the shotgun from the dresser, held it about 15 inches away from her husband's chest, and fired one fatal shot. She then left the house but was talked into going back by a neighbor. The neighbor called the police, who arrived at 1:10 a.m. The wife, who explained further to the police that her husband had hit her with a tire iron during their earlier fight, was arrested and booked for murder. The case went to trial and the wife was found guilty. *She received a 3-year probationary sentence.*

The outcome in the two remaining cases within the wife-husband category has not been determined. But each case is quite explicit about the relationships between the principals who, as it may be recalled, are seeking to enforce their conceptions of the relationship upon the situation and the reciprocal person in the status relationship.

Case No. 117 involves a triadic or three-way relationship between a white woman, her divorced daughter, and the woman's present husband (the daughter's stepfather). The divorced daughter, age 21, had recently obtained her divorce and subsequently moved into the apartment occupied by her mother, age 43, and her stepfather, age 48. The threesome began to drink together around four o'clock in the afternoon and eventually left the apartment to continue their drinking at the Stampede Club on Alabama Street. The older woman got quite intoxicated; she began to quarrel with both her daughter and her husband, accusing them among other things of sleeping together, and, in the daughter's own words: "Mother tried to get me to dance with Bob and I finally did dance [with him] one time. After this, Mother got real mad and accused me of trying to make out with Bob. She stayed mad until we left about 11:00 p.m. Just before we got into my car, I grabbed her and shook her and told her that this was the last time she was going to accuse me of trying to fuck any man of hers. . . ." The quarrel continued and the mother threatened to take her own life. She also said that she would blow her husband's brains out. Bob was sitting on a lawn chair when the .22 caliber bullet ended his life. The autopsy revealed a 0.09 percent alcohol content in the victim's blood. The wife was arrested but apparently not searched thoroughly. The next morning she was found comatose in her jail cell. She was rushed to Ben Taub Hospital and treated for a suspected overdose of sleeping pills. She recovered in the emergency ward while her husband's body was being dissected in the morgue one floor below.

The last case of a wife-husband killing involves a black woman, age 21, and her 21-year-old husband. The killing occurred at 10:00 p.m. with one eyewitness. According to the eyewitness, who was the next-door neighbor, the couple did not get along because the husband was very jealous of his wife and they had many fights. On the fatal evening, the wife asked her husband for his permission to attend a "Jewelry Party." At first he gave his permission and the woman took their 9-month-old child next door to the babysitter. While she was there the husband came over and suddenly grabbed her by the throat. They left the apartment physically fighting. The wife had armed herself with a steak knife and while they were fighting outside by the driveway she stabbed her husband in the chest. The wound was fatal. Several bystanders could have stopped the fight but nobody interfered. In fact, in reflecting on all the cases in which third parties have been present, it seems that only young children have tried to physically intervene in a fight.

## THE LEGAL DISPOSITION
## OF DOMESTIC KILLINGS

In most killings within domestic groups it is known precisely who did what to whom and how. Although it cannot be known exactly why one person decides to take the life of another, one must acknowledge, in passing, the importance and recurrence in different cases of such motives as jealousy, anger, frustration, and passion.

To take the life of a close relative ought theoretically to be equivalent to taking the life of a stranger. Yet, as can be seen from the data summarized in Tables 1, 2, and 3 in the Appendix, the final legal disposition of a case, with very few and notable exceptions, varies directly with the killer-victim relationship. The closer, or more intimate, the relationship is between a killer and his victim the less likely it is that the killer will be severely punished for his act. Conversely, the more distant the killer-victim relationship is, as when the killer and victim are strangers, the more likely it is that the killer will be severely punished for his act. Although punishment may vary greatly from one case to another, within any given offender category, there is a certain uniformity to the outcome in similar and analogous cases. If this were not so the system of criminal justice would be wholly arbitrary.

Similar interpersonal relationships, or status equivalence, between killers and victims, and analogous situational contexts in which the final homicide drama is played out, generally evoke similar kinds of official response. An official response refers to the actions of the police in apprehending and processing a suspect together with the subsequent acts of attorneys, grand jury members, jurors, judges, and all other persons called upon to finally dispose of a homicide case. The decision on the part of these officials, individually and collectively, to formally disapprove the actions of a particular killer is governed by very complex cultural rules. It must suffice here to say that given certain kinds of homicidal acts (involving kinspeople, friends or associates, or strangers) and a limited range of judicial alternatives or outcomes (no bill, innocent, or guilty) we can infer how different cultural attitudes and values influence the decision-making choices of both killers and officials.

As a first step, 200 killer–victim relationships from 1969 have been classified into three broad categories that distinguish three principal kinds of killer–victim status relationships. This procedure, which excludes cases for which the final legal outcome remains unknown, yields three broad categories: (1) *Kinspeople or relatives*—those individuals who are related to each other by consanguineal or affinal ties; (2) *Friends or associates*—those individuals who prior to the killing have known each other in some informal or formal capacity (e.g., paramour, neighbor, co-worker, or roommate); and (3) *Strangers*—those individuals who prior to the killing have neither encountered each other or otherwise participated as reciprocals in a social relationship.

Because it proved impossible to categorize the relationships between some of the principals in a number of cases, we are left, for the purposes of statistical analysis, with a distribution of killer-victim relationships within each category as follows: 77 cases involving kinspeople, 68 cases involving friends and associates, and 55 cases involving strangers. The relatively even numerical distribution of cases among the three principal relationship categories provides a fair sample for proving whether the killer–victim relationship delimits the relative severity in the judicial outcome for individual homicide cases.

> Hypothesis I: The killer–victim relationship does not affect the final legal disposition of a homicide case.

This null-hypothesis, which in effect asserts that there is no significant relationship between the two variables, could be accepted as valid if the data displayed no significant differences in outcome for killers in the three offender status categories. The tabulated frequency data in Tables 2 and 3 in the Appendix clearly indicate that there is indeed a significant difference in the final outcome for killers in the three categories. The null-hypothesis therefore is rejected.

> Hypothesis II: The killer–victim relationship significantly affects the final legal disposition of a homicide case.

The tabulated data in Table 2 illustrate the relationships between the three major killer–victim relationship categories and 12 possible case disposition outcomes. The severity of outcome, which might be considered a continuum ranging from "no charge" to death or a literally enforced "life sentence," is unevenly distributed among the three offender categories. It must be noted and emphasized that the severity of the outcome correlates inversely with the degree of intimacy between killer and victim.

In other words, if a person kills a close relative he is more likely to escape punishment than if he kills a complete stranger. The most notable exception to this general rule is to be found in cases in the relative category where the relationship specifically involves two persons who are status reciprocals in a parent–child relationship. In parent–child homicides parents receive a disproportionately lighter sentence for killing their children than do children for killing their parents.

The number of kinspeople, together with persons listed as friends and associates, who escape any form of negative sanctioning is *four* times greater than that of killers in the "stranger" category. To test Hypothesis II, therefore, it is necessary to look closely at those cases in all three categories that resulted in some kind of legal sanction. Yet even here, as summarized in Table 3, the data fail to seriously challenge the explanatory power of the hypothesis.

The 1969 data show that there is a direct causal relationship between a killer's membership in a particular status category, the situational context in which the victim is killed, and the severity of official punishment applied to the killer.

## APPENDIX

TABLE 1    Disposition of Homicide Cases in Terms of the Status Category of Killers

| Killer's status category | Case number | Disposition |
| --- | --- | --- |
| Husband | 125 | suicide |
| | 167 | suicide |
| | 70 | no bill* |
| | 92 | not guilty |
| | 67 | charge pending |
| | 168 | 3-month jail sentence |
| | 102 | 7-year jail sentence |
| | 190 | 10-year jail sentence |
| | 233 | 90-year jail sentence |
| Wife | 2 | no bill |
| | 15 | no bill |
| | 38 | no bill |
| | 49 | no bill |
| | 64 | no bill |
| | 93 | no bill |
| | 140 | no bill |
| | 159 | no bill |
| | 198 | no bill |
| | 82 | no charge filed |
| | 69 | dismissed |
| | 76 | reset for trial |
| | 86 | 3 years' probation |
| | 117 | outcome undetermined |
| | 9 | outcome undetermined |

(*continues*)

TABLE 1   (*Continued*)

| Killer's status category | Case number | Disposition |
|---|---|---|
| Father | 193 | 10-year jail sentence |
| Mother | 164 | 5-year jail sentence |
| Son | 99 | life sentence |
| | 63 | 99-year jail sentence |
| Brother | 206 | no bill |
| | 42 | no charge filed |
| | 170 | nolle prosequi |
| | 225 | 2-year jail sentence |
| | 131 | outcome undetermined |
| Uncle | 129 | no bill |
| | 226 | no bill |
| | 105 | nolle prosequi |
| Tertiary relatives | 17 | 5 years' probation |
| | 35 | 12-year jail sentence |
| Boyfriend | 73 | suicide |
| | 43 | no bill |
| | 50 | 3-month jail sentence |
| | 75 | 20-month jail sentence |
| Girlfriend | 74 | suicide |
| | 179 | no bill |
| | 227 | no bill |
| | 234 | no bill |
| | 11 | probation |
| Cohabitant | 132 | no bill |
| Close friend | 94 | no bill |
| | 145 | no bill |
| | 171 | no bill |
| | 220 | dismissed |
| | 44 | 3-month jail sentence |
| | 77 | 3-year jail sentence |
| | 183 | 5-year jail sentence |
| | 19 | 10-year jail sentence |
| Casual acquaintance | 23 | no bill |
| | 48 | no bill |
| | 65 | no bill |
| | 96 | no bill |
| | 101 | no bill |
| | 114 | no bill |
| | 187 | no bill |
| | 210 | no bill |
| | 57 | nolle prosequi |
| | 20 | 3 years' probation |
| | 148 | 5 years' probation |
| | 97 | 1-year jail sentence |

(*continues*)

TABLE 1    (*Continued*)

| Killer's status category | Case number | Disposition |
|---|---|---|
| | 52 | 2-year jail sentence |
| | 62 | 3-year jail sentence |
| | 209 | 4-year jail sentence |
| | 89 | 5-year jail sentence |
| | 110 | 5-year jail sentence |
| | 36 (2)** | 12-year jail sentence |
| | 36 (2)** | 75-year jail sentence |
| | 32 | outcome undetermined |
| | 37 | outcome undetermined |
| | 68 | outcome undetermined |
| | 211 | outcome undetermined |
| Friend, closeness undetermined | 230 | no bill |
| | 212 | nolle prosequi |
| | 154 | 5 years' probation |
| | 203 | 2-year jail sentence |
| | 84 | 5-year jail sentence |
| | 121 | 5-year jail sentence |
| | 87 | 10-year jail sentence |
| | 144 | 40-year jail sentence |
| Gambling associate | 95 | nolle prosequi |
| | 178 | not guilty |
| | 239 | not guilty |
| | 109 | 5 years' probation |
| | 138 | 2-month jail sentence |
| | 85 | 3-year jail sentence |
| | 91 | life sentence |
| Neighbor | 56 | no bill |
| | 122 | nolle prosequi |
| | 143 | nolle prosequi |
| | 142 | 1-year jail sentence |
| | 47 | 3-year jail sentence |
| Colleague | 13 | suicide |
| | 185 | no bill |
| | 152 | 3 years' probation |
| Roommate | 135 (2)** | 8-year jail sentence |
| | 135 | 10-year jail sentence |
| Employer | 161 | no bill |
| | 83 | life sentence |
| Employee | 195 (2)** | not guilty |
| Customer | 22 | nolle prosequi |
| | 34 | 5-years' probation |
| | 169 | 5-year jail sentence |
| | 238 | 10-year jail sentence |
| | 127 | 25-year jail sentence |
| | 61 | 40-year jail sentence |

(*continues*)

TABLE 1    (*Continued*)

| Killer's status category | Case number | Disposition |
|---|---|---|
| Proprietor | 16 | no bill |
| | 147 | no bill |
| | 165 | no bill |
| | 228 | no bill |
| | 54 | 3 years' probation |
| | 29 | 2-month jail sentence |
| | 60 | 3-year jail sentence |
| | 130 | 5-year jail sentence |
| | 166 | charge pending |
| Husband | | |
|   Separated or divorced | 224 | suicide |
| | 26 | dismissed |
| | 66 | dismissed |
| | 98 | 4-year jail sentence |
| | 180 | 4-year jail sentence |
| | 18 | 5-year jail sentence |
| Wife | | |
|   Separated or divorced | 24 | 3 years' probation |
| Ex-boyfriend | 103 | 10 years' probation |
| | 115 | 10-year jail sentence |
| Ex-girlfriend | 157 | no bill |
| | 217 | 2 years' probation |
| Paramour | 106 | no bill |
| | 40 | nolle prosequi |
| | 123 | nolle prosequi |
| | 176 | nolle prosequi |
| | 137 | 5 years' probation |
| | 194 | 5-year jail sentence |
| | 223 | 5-year jail sentence |
| | 172 | outcome undetermined |
| | 177 | charge pending |
| Common-law husband | 200 | no bill |
| | 71 | reset for trial |
| | 25 | 5-year jail sentence |
| | 182 | 19-year jail sentence |
| Common-law wife | 46 | no bill |
| | 53 | no bill |
| | 55 | no bill |
| | 120 | no bill |
| | 213 | no bill |
| | 134 | not guilty |
| | 195 | not guilty |
| | 33 | 5 years' probation |
| | 186 | outcome undetermined |
| Stepfather, Father-in-law | 139 | not guilty |
| | 205 | outcome undetermined |

(*continues*)

TABLE 1    (*Continued*)

| Killer's status category | Case number | Disposition |
| --- | --- | --- |
| Stepmother, Mother-in-law | 196 | 7 years' probation |
| Stepson, Son-in-law | 181 | no bill |
|  | 146 | not guilty |
|  | 80 | outcome undetermined |
| Stepdaughter, Daughter-in-law | 112 | outcome undetermined |
| Brother-in-law | 126 | no bill |
|  | 215 | no bill |
| Sister-in-law | 1 | referred directly to grand jury |
| Stranger | 222 (2)[†] | 50-year jail sentence |
|  | 27 | no bill |
|  | 51 | no bill |
|  | 128 | no bill |
|  | 175 | no bill |
|  | 192 | no bill |
|  | 207 | no bill |
|  | 235 | no bill |
|  | 3 | nolle prosequi |
|  | 10 | nolle prosequi |
|  | 30 | dismissed |
|  | 118 (2)[†] | dismissed |
|  | 231 | not guilty |
|  | 174 | not gulty |
|  | 14 | 3 years' probation |
|  | 107 | 5 years' probation |
|  | 133 | 7-month jail sentence |
|  | 10 (3)[†] | 3-year jail sentence |
|  | 113 | 4-year jail sentence |
|  | 229 | 5-year jail sentence |
|  | 31 | 7-year jail sentence |
|  | 90 | 10-year jail sentence |
|  | 7 | 15-year jail sentence |
|  | 8 | 15-year jail sentence |
|  | 8 (2)[†] | 15-year jail sentence |
|  | 39 (2)[†] | 30-year jail sentence |
|  | 118 | 30-year jail sentence |
|  | 45 (2)[†] | 40-year jail sentence |
|  | 8 (3)[†] | 50-year jail sentence |
|  | 222 (2)** | 50-year jail sentence |
|  | 10 (2)** | 65-year jail sentence |
|  | 45 | 90-year jail sentence |
|  | 218 | 99-year jail sentence |
|  | 150 | life sentence |
|  | 39 | death penalty |
|  | 59 | death penalty |
|  | 81 | death penalty |
|  | 136 | death penalty |

(*continues*)

TABLE 1   (*Continued*)

| Killer's status category | Case number | Disposition |
|---|---|---|
| | 237 | death penalty |
| | 12 | charge pending |
| | 156 | charge pending |
| | 219 | charge pending |
| | 78 | outcome undetermined |
| | 163 | outcome undetermined |
| Relationship unknown | 111 | suicide |
| | 188 | suicide |
| | 28 | no bill |
| | 41 | no bill |
| | 58 | no bill |
| | 88 | no bill |
| | 116 | no bill |
| | 119 | no bill |
| | 151 | no bill |
| | 153 | no bill |
| | 189 | no bill |
| | 199 | no bill |
| | 204 | no bill |
| | 236 | no bill |
| | 201 | nolle prosequi |
| | 201 (2)** | nolle prosequi |
| | 210 (2)** | nolle prosequi |
| | 210 (2)** | nolle prosequi |
| | 221 | nolle prosequi |
| | 5 | dismissed |
| | 4 | not guilty |
| | 232 | not guilty |
| | 184 | 3 years' probation |
| | 160 | 5 years' probation |
| | 162 | 5 years' probation |
| | 197 | 5 years' probation |
| | 158 | 10 years' probation |
| | 124 | 6-month jail sentence |
| | 79 | 5-year jail sentence |
| | 173 | 5-year jail sentence |
| | 202 | 7-year jail sentence |
| | 149 | 10-year jail sentence |
| | 155 | 15-year jail sentence |
| | 208 | 15-year jail sentence |
| | 237 (2)** | 30-year jail sentence |
| | 214 | charge pending |
| | 141 | outcome undetermined |

*A grand jury issues a "no bill" if it finds the evidence against an accused person insufficient for indictment.

**Two defendants.

†Two or three defendants.

TABLE 2 Three Major Killer and Victim Relationships Expressed in Reference to Final Case Disposition

| Case disposition | Relatives | | Friends/Associates | | Strangers | |
|---|---|---|---|---|---|---|
| | frequency | percent | frequency | percent | frequency | percent |
| Offender deceased | 3 | 3.90 | 3 | 4.41 | | |
| No bill | 24 ⎫ | | 20 ⎫ | | 10 ⎫ | |
| No charge filed | 2 ⎬ 31 | 40.26 | ⎬ 25 | 36.77 | ⎬ 13 | 23.64 |
| Nolle prosequi | 5 ⎭ | | 5 ⎭ | | 3 ⎭ | |
| Dismissed | 3 | 3.90 | 2 | 2.94 | 1 | 1.82 |
| Not guilty | 5 | 6.49 | 3 | 4.41 | 2 | 3.64 |
| Probation | 8 | 10.39 | 6 | 8.82 | 4 | 7.27 |
| Death penalty | | | | | 5 | 9.09 |
| Outcome undetermined | 8 | 10.39 | 2 | 2.94 | 2 | 3.64 |
| Charge pending | 2 | 2.30 | | | 4 | 7.27 |
| Life sentence | 1 | 1.29 | 2 | 2.94 | 1 | 1.82 |
| Sentenced | 16 | 20.78 | 25 | 36.77 | 23 | 41.82 |
| Total | 77 | 100.00 | 68 | 100.00 | 55 | 100.00 |
| Average sentence (years) | 13* | | | | | |
| | 8** | | 10 | | 28 | |
| | 20 | | | | | |

*Case No. 63 excluded.
**Cases Nos. 63 and 233 excluded.

TABLE 3 Statistical Values for Prison Terms in Years among the Three Principal Offender Categories

| | Relatives ($n = 13$) | Friends/ associates ($n = 22$) | Strangers ($n = 21$) |
|---|---|---|---|
| Mean | 7.62 | 10.09 | 27.90 |
| Standard deviation | 4.52 | 16.01 | 28.75 |
| Maximum | 19.00 | 75.00 | 99.00 |
| Minimum | 2.00 | 1.00 | 3.00 |
| Range | 17.00 | 74.00 | 96.00 |

## REFERENCES

Bullock, Henry A. 1955. "Urban homicide in theory and fact." *Journal of Criminal Law, Criminology, and Police Science* 45: 565–575.
Caldwell, Harry. 1963. The Relationship of Houston Homicide to Racial Segregation and Total Crime. Unpublished Master's Thesis, University of Houston.

National Comission on the Causes and Prevention of Violence. 1969. *To Establish Justice, to Insure Domestic Tranquility: Final Report of the National Commission on the Causes and Prevention of Violence.* Washington: U.S. Government Printing Office.

Pokorny, Alex. 1965. "A comparison of homicides in two cities." *Journal of Criminal Law, Criminology, and Police Science* 56: 479–487.

# 7

# THE OVEN BIRD'S SONG:

# INSIDERS, OUTSIDERS,

# AND PERSONAL INJURIES

# IN AN AMERICAN

# COMMUNITY*

DAVID M. ENGEL**

## INTRODUCTION

Although it is generally acknowledged that law is a vital part of culture and of the social order, there are times when the invocation of formal law is viewed as an *anti*social act and as a contravention of established cultural norms. Criticism of what is seen as an overuse of law and legal institutions often reveals less about the quantity of litigation at any given time than about the interests being asserted or protected through litigation and the kinds of individuals or groups involved in

*The title refers to Robert's Frost's poem "The Oven Bird," which describes a response to the perception of disintegration and decay not unlike that described in this article. The poem portrays a woodland scene in midsummer, long after the bright blossoms and early leaves of spring have given way to less attractive vistas and to age, fallen leaves, and "highway dust." With the approach of fall (in both of its senses), the "loud song" of the oven bird echoes through the woods. "The question that he frames in all but words/Is what to make of a diminished thing."

**I am deeply grateful to the residents of "Sander County" for their generous participation in this study. I would also like to thank the following friends and colleagues who read and commented on this article at one stage or another in its development: Richard L. Abel, James B. Atleson, Guyora Binder, Donald Black, Marc Galanter, Fred Konefsky, Virginia Leary, Richard O. Lempert, Felice J. Levine, John Henry Schlegel, Eric H. Steele, Robert J. Steinfeld, and Barbara Yngvesson. I am also grateful to Linda Kosinski for her skill and patience in typing and retyping the manuscript.

The research on which this article is based was supported by the National Science Foundation under Grant No. SOC 77–11654 and by the American Bar Foundation. Opinions, findings, and conclusions are those of the author and not of the supporting organizations.

cases that the courts are asked to resolve. Periodic concerns over litigation as a "problem" in particular societies or historical eras can thus draw our attention to important underlying conflicts in cultural values and changes or tensions in the structure of social relationships.

In our own society at present, perhaps no category of litigation has produced greater public criticism than personal injuries. The popular culture is full of tales of feigned or exaggerated physical harms, of spurious whiplash suits, ambulance-chasing lawyers, and exorbitant claims for compensation. Scholars, journalists, and legal professionals, voicing concern with crowded dockets and rising insurance costs, have often shared the perception that personal injury litigation is a field dominated by overly litigious plaintiffs and by trigger-happy attorneys interested only in their fee (Seymour, 1973: 177; Tondel, 1976: 547; Perham, 1977; Rosenberg, 1977: 154; Taylor, 1981; Gest et al., 1982; Greene, 1983).

To the mind agitated by such concerns, Sander County (a pseudonym) appears to offer a quiet refuge. In this small, predominantly rural county in Illinois, personal injury litigation rates were low in comparison to other major categories of litigation[1] and were apparently somewhat lower than the personal injury rates in other locations as well.[2] Yet Sander County residents displayed a deep concern with and an aversion toward this particular form of "litigious behavior" despite its rarity in their community.[3]

[1] By "litigation" I mean simply the filing of a formal complaint in the civil trial court, even if no further adversarial processes occur. The annual litigation rate for personal injuries was 1.45 cases filed per 1000 population as compared to 13.7 contract cases (mostly collection matters), 3.62 property-related cases (mostly landlord-tenant matters), and 11.74 family-related cases (mostly divorces). All litigation rates are based on the combined civil filings for 1975 and 1976 in the Sander County Court. Population figures are based on the 1970 census and are therefore somewhat understated. That is, the actual litigation rates for 1975 and 1976 are probably lower than those given here.

[2] McIntosh reports a rate of approximately 6 tort actions per 1000 population in the St. Louis Circuit Court in 1970. He does not state what proportion of these involved personal injuries (McIntosh, 1980–81: 832). Friedman and Percival (1976: 281–82) report 2.80 and 1.87 cases filed per 1000 population in the Alameda and San Benito Superior Courts (respectively) in 1970 under the combined categories of "auto accidents" and "other personal injuries." The two California courts had original jurisdiction only for claims of $5000 or more, however, while the Sander County figures include personal injury claims of all amounts. Friedman and Percival do not indicate what proportion of the auto accident cases involved personal injuries as opposed to property damage only. Statewide data for California and New York, compiled by the National Center for State Courts (1979: 49,51) for tort cases filed in 1975, also tend to indicate litigation rates higher than Sander County's. However, these aggregate litigation rates are understated in that they exclude filings from small courts of limited jurisdiction in both states and are overstated in that they fail to separate personal injury cases from other tort actions. Litigation rates for tort cases filed per 1000 population in 1975 are: California, 3.55; and New York, 2.21 (but in 1977, when additional lower court dockets were included in the survey of tort cases filed, the rate reported for New York more than doubled to 4.47; see National Center for State Courts, 1982: 61). In comparing the Sander County litigation rates to those in other cities or states, it should also be remembered that, because Sander County was quite small, the *absolute number* of personal injury actions filed in the county court was also very small compared to more urban areas.

[3] I use the term "community" somewhat loosely in this discussion to mean the county seat of Sander County and the surrounding farmlands. Since Sander County is rather small, this takes in most of the county. There are a handful of very small towns elsewhere in the county. Although they are not far from

Those who sought to enforce personal injury claims in Sander County were characterized by their fellow residents as "very greedy," as "quick to sue," "as people looking for the easy buck," and as those who just "naturally sue and try to get something [for] . . . life's little accidents." One minister describing the local scene told me, "Everybody's going to court. That's the thing to do, because a lot of people see a chance to make money." A social worker, speaking of local perceptions of personal injury litigation, particularly among the older residents of Sander County, observed: "Someone sues every time you turn around. Sue happy, you hear them say. Sue happy." Personal injury plaintiffs were viewed in Sander County as people who made waves and as troublemakers. Even members of the community who occupied positions of prestige or respect could not escape criticism if they brought personal injury cases to court. When a minister filed a personal injury suit in Sander County after having slipped and fallen at a school, there were, in the words of one local observer:

> [A] lot of people who are resentful for it, because . . . he chose to sue. There's been, you know, not hard feelings, just some strange intangible things. . . .

How can one explain these troubled perceptions of personal injury litigation in a community where personal injury actions were in fact so seldom brought? The answer lies partly in culturally conditioned ideas of what constitutes an injury and how conflicts over injuries should be handled. The answer is also found in changes that were occurring in the social structure of Sander County at the time of this study and in challenges to the traditional order that were being raised by newly arrived "outsiders." The local trial court was potentially an important battleground in the clash of cultures, for it could be called on to recognize claims that traditional norms stigmatized in the strongest possible terms.[4]

## SOCIAL CHANGES AND THE SENSE OF COMMUNITY

Sander County in the late 1970s was a society that was strongly rooted in its rural past yet undergoing economic and social changes of major proportions. It was a small county (between 20,000 and 30,000 population in the 1970s), with more than half its population concentrated in its county seat and the rest in several much

---

the county seat and are linked to it in many ways, it is probably stretching things to consider them part of a single "community." I should add that the problem of defining the term "community" as a subject of empirical study has vexed social scientists for many years, and I aspired to no conceptual breakthrough in this regard. My interest was in finding a research site where the jurisdiction of the court was roughly congruent with a social unit comprising a set of meaningful interactions and relationships.

[4]Hostility towards personal injury litigation as a form of "hyperlexis" may also have been influenced in Sander County by mass media treatment of this form of legal claim. Yet the attitudes and antagonisms I describe had deep roots in the culture of Sander County itself as well as in the popular culture of the country as a whole. A critical appraisal of the hyperlexis literature, which parallels this discussion in some respects, is found in Galanter (1983).

smaller towns and rural areas. Agriculture was still central to county life. Sander County had 10% more of its land in farms in the mid-1970s than did the state of Illinois as a whole, but the number of farms in Sander County had decreased by more than one-third over the preceding 20 years while their average size had grown by almost half. Rising costs, land values, and taxes had been accompanied by an increase in the mechanization of agriculture in Sander County, and the older, smaller farming operations were being rapidly transformed. At the same time, a few large manufacturing plants had brought blue collar employees from other areas to work (but not always to live) in Sander County. Also, a local canning plant had for many years employed seasonal migrant workers, many of whom were Latinos. In recent years, however, a variety of "outsiders" had come to stay permanently in Sander County, and the face of the local society was gradually changing.

To some extent these changes had been deliberately planned by local leaders, for it was thought that the large manufacturing plants would revitalize the local economy. Yet from the beginning there had also been a sense of foreboding. In the words of one older farmer:

> A guy that I used to do business with told me when he saw this plant coming in down here that he felt real bad for the community. He said, that's gonna be the end of your community, he said, because you get too many people in that don't have roots in anything. And I didn't think too much about it at the time, but I can understand what he was talking about now. I know that to some extent, at least, this is true. Not that there haven't been some real good people come in, I don't mean that. But I think you get quite a number of a certain element that you've never had before.

Others were more blunt about the "certain element" that had entered Sander County: union members, southerners and southwesterners, blacks, and Latinos. One long-time rural resident told us, "I think there's too many Commies around. I think this country takes too many people in, don't you? . . . . That's why this country's going to the dogs." Many Sander County residents referred nostalgically to the days when they could walk down Main Street and see none but familiar faces. Now there were many strangers. An elderly woman from a farming family, who was struggling to preserve her farm in the face of rising taxes and operating costs, spoke in troubled tones of going into the post office and seeing Spanish-speaking workers mailing locally earned money to families outside the country. "This," she said, "I don't like." Another woman, also a long-time resident, spoke of the changing appearance of the town:

> [It was] lots different than it is right now. For one thing, I think we knew everybody in town. If you walked uptown you could speak to every single person on the street. It just wasn't at all like it is today. Another thing, the stores were different. We have so many places now that are foreign, Mexican, and health spas, which we're not very happy about, most of us. My mother was going uptown here a year ago and didn't feel very well when she got up to State Street. But she just kept going, and I thought it was terrible because the whole north side of town was the kind of place that you wouldn't want to go into for information or for help. Mostly because we've not grown up with an area where there were any foreign people at all.

There was also in the late 1970s a pervasive sense of a breakdown in the traditional relationships and reciprocities that had characterized life in Sander County. As one elderly farmer told me:

> It used to be I could tell you any place in Sander County where it was, but I can't now because I don't know who lives on them. . . . And as I say in the last 20 years people don't change work like they used to—or in the last 30 years. Everybody's got big equipment, they do all their own work so they don't have to change labor. Like years ago . . . why you had about 15 or 20 farmers together doing the exchange and all.

Many Sander County residents with farming backgrounds had warm memories of the harvest season, when groups of neighbors got together to share work and food:

> When we had the threshing run, the dining room table it stretched a full 17 feet of the dining room, and guys would come in like hungry wolves, you know, at dinner time and supper again the same thing. . . . And they'd fire the engine up and have it ready to start running by 7:00. . . . You know, it was quite a sight to see that old steam engine coming down the road. I don't know, while I never want to be doing it again, I still gotta get kind of a kick out of watching a steam engine operate.

And all could remember socializing with other farming families on Saturday evenings during the summertime. In the words of two long-time farmers:

> A: Well, on Saturday night they used to come into town, and the farmers would be lined up along the sidewalk with an ice cream cone or maybe a glass of beer or something. . . .
> B: If you met one to three people, you'd get all the news in the neighborhood. . . .
> A: If you go downtown now, anytime, I doubt if you'll see half a dozen people that you know. I mean to what you say sit down and really, really know them.
> B: You practically knew everybody.
> A: That's right, but you don't now.
> B: No, no, no. If you go down Saturday night. . . .
> A: Everything is dead.

## THE STUDY

I shall argue in this chapter that perceptions of personal injury claims in Sander County were strongly influenced by these social changes as local residents experienced them and by the sense that traditional relations and exchanges in the community were gradually disintegrating.[5] I cannot say that the frequent condemnation of personal injury litigation elsewhere in the United States is linked to a similar set of social processes, but investigation in other settings may disclose some parallels. The sense of community can take many forms in American society, and when members of a community feel threatened by change, their response may be broadly similar to the kind of response I describe here.

[5]The sense of social change and disintegration in Sander County helped crystallize a set of values opposed to personal injury litigation. These values were almost certainly rooted in long established norms, but the targets of their expression and the intensity with which they were asserted may have been new. This article focuses on how and why such values came to be expressed and acutely felt in the late 1970s by many Sander County residents. See note 19 infra.

My discussion is based on fieldwork conducted from 1978 to 1980. Besides doing background research and immersing myself in the community and in the workings of the Sander County Court, I collected data for the study in three ways: (1) A sample of civil case files opened in 1975 and 1976 was drawn and analyzed.[6] (2) Plaintiffs and defendants in a subsample of these civil cases were contacted and interviewed in broad-ranging, semistructured conversations.[7] (3) Strategically placed "community observers" were identified and interviewed at length. These were individuals who had particular insights into different groups, settings, occupations, or activities in the community.[8] Discussions with them touched on various aspects of the community, including the ways in which the relationships, situations, and problems that might give rise to litigated cases were handled when the court was not used. The insights derived from the community observer interviews thus provided a broader social and cultural context for the insights derived from the court-based research.

Personal injuries were one of four major substantive topics selected to receive special attention in this study.[9] It soon became apparent, however, that personal injuries were viewed quite differently from the other topics, and the differences appeared to be related to the fundamental social changes that were taking place in Sander County. Focusing on personal injuries in this chapter makes it possible to examine the role played by formal law in mediating relationships between different groups in a changing society and to consider why the rare use of formal legal institutions for certain purposes can evoke strong concern and reaction in a community. The answer, I shall suggest, lies in the ideological responses of longtime residents of Sander County whose values and assumptions were subjected to profound challenges by what they saw as the intrusion of newcomers into their close-knit society.

## INJURIES AND INDIVIDUALISM

For many of the residents of Sander County, exposure to the risk of physical injury was simply an accepted part of life. In a primarily agricultural community,

[6]A 20% sample was taken for the years 1975 and 1976 within each of the 12 civil categories mandated by the Administrative Office of the Illinois Courts: (1) Law (claim over $15,000); (2) Law (claim $15,000 or less); (3) Chancery; (4) Miscellaneous Remedies; (5) Eminent Domain; (6) Estates; (7) Tax; (8) Municipal Corporations; (9) Mental Health; (10) Divorce; (11) Family; (12) Small Claims. After the sample was drawn, the cases were reclassified into the substantive categories referred to throughout the article.

[7]Parties in 66 cases were interviewed. Wherever possible, all parties to each case were included. Particular attention was given to the individuals themselves, the relationship between them, and to the origin, development, and outcome of each case.

[8]Among the 71 community observers were judges, lawyers, teachers, ministers, farmers, a beautician, a barber, city and county officials, a funeral parlor operator, youth workers, social service workers, various "ordinary citizens" from different segments of the community, a union steward, a management representative, agricultural extension workers, doctors, a newspaper reporter, the members of a rescue squad, and others.

[9]The other three substantive areas were injuries to reputation, contracts, and marital problems.

**163**

which depended on hard physical work and the use of dangerous implements and machinery, such risks were unavoidable. Farmers in Sander County told many stories of terrible injuries caused by hazardous farming equipment, vehicles of different kinds, and other dangers that were associated with their means of obtaining a livelihood. There was a feeling among many in Sander County—particularly among those from a farming background—that injuries were an ever-present possibility, although prudent persons could protect themselves much of the time by taking proper precautions.

It would be accurate to characterize the traditional values associated with personal injuries in Sander County as individualistic, but individualism may be of at least two types. A rights-oriented individualism is consistent with an aggressive demand for compensation (or other remedies) when important interests are perceived to have been violated. By contrast, an individualism emphasizing self-sufficiency and personal responsibility rather than rights is consistent with the expectation that people should ordinarily provide their own protection against injuries and should personally absorb the consequences of harms they fail to ward off.[10]

It is not clear why the brand of individualism that developed over the years in Sander County emphasized self-sufficiency rather than rights and remedies, but with respect to personal injuries at least, there can be no doubt that this had occurred. If the values associated with this form of individualism originated in an earlier face-to-face community dominated by economically self-sufficient farmers and merchants, they remained vitally important to many of the long-time Sander County residents even at the time of this study. For them, injuries were viewed in relation to the victims, their fate, and their ability to protect themselves. Injuries were not viewed in terms of conflict or potential conflict between victims and other persons, nor was there much sympathy for those who sought to characterize the situation in such terms. To the traditional individualists of Sander County, transforming a personal injury into a claim against someone else was an attempt to escape responsibility for one's own actions. The psychology of contributory negligence and assumption of risk had deep roots in the local culture. The critical fact of personal injuries in most cases was that the victims probably could have prevented them if they had been more careful, even if others were to some degree at fault. This fact alone is an important reason why it was considered inappropriate for injured persons to attempt to transform their misfortune into a demand for compensation or to view it as an occasion for interpersonal conflict.

Attitudes toward money also help explain the feelings of long-time residents of Sander County toward personal injury claimants. While there might be sympathy for those who suffered such injuries, it was considered highly improper to try to "cash in" on them through claims for damages. Money was viewed as something one acquired through long hours of hard work, not by exhibiting one's misfortunes to a judge or jury or other third party, even when the injuries were clearly caused by the wrongful behavior of another. Such attitudes were reinforced by the perva-

[10]This distinction between the two types of individualism emerged from an ongoing dialogue with Fred Konefsky, whose contribution to this conceptualization I gratefully acknowledge.

sive sense of living in what had long been a small and close-knit community. In such a community, potential plaintiffs and defendants are likely to know each other, at least by reputation, or to have acquaintances in common. It is probable that they will interact in the future, if not directly then through friends and relatives. In these circumstances it is, at best, awkward to sue or otherwise assert a claim. In addition, in a small community one cannot hide the fact of a suit for damages, and the disapproving attitudes of others are likely to be keenly felt. Thus, I was frequently assured that local residents who were mindful of community pressures generally reacted to cases of personal injury, even those that might give rise to liability in tort, in a "level-headed" and "realistic" way. By this it was meant that they would not sue or even, in most cases, demand compensation extrajudicially from anyone except, perhaps, their own insurance companies.[11]

Given the negative views that local juries adopted toward personal injury cases, terms such as "realistic" for those who avoided litigation were indeed well chosen. Judges, lawyers, and laypersons all told me that civil trial juries in the county reflected—and thus reinforced—the most conservative values and attitudes toward personal injury litigation. Awards were very low and suspicion of personal injury plaintiffs was very high. A local insurance adjuster told me:

> [T]he jury will be people from right around here that are, a good share of them will be farmers, and they've been out there slaving away for every penny they've got and they aren't about to just give it away to make that free gift to anybody.

And one of the leading local trial lawyers observed:

> [T]here's a natural feeling, what's this son of a bitch doing here? Why is he taking our time? Why is he trying to look for something for nothing? . . . . So I've got to overcome that. That's a natural prejudice in a small [community], they don't have that natural prejudice in Cook County. But you do have it out here. So first I've got to sell the jury on the fact that this man's tried every way or this woman's tried every way to get justice and she couldn't. And they now come to you for their big day. . . . And then you try like hell to show that they're one of you, they've lived here and this and that.

The prospects for trying a personal injury case before a local jury, he concluded, were so discouraging that, "If I can figure out a way not to try a case in [this] county for injury, I try to."

[11] I heard of only a few cases where injured persons negotiated compensatory payments from the liability insurance of the party responsible for their harm. In these cases expectations (or demands) appeared to be modest. One involved a woman who lived on a farm. When visiting a neighbor's house, she fell down the basement stairs because of a negligently installed door, fractured her skull, was unconscious for 3 days, and was in intensive care for 5 days. As a result of the accident she suffered a permanent loss of her sense of smell and a substantial (almost total) impairment of her sense of taste. Her husband, a successful young farmer, told me that their own insurance did not cover the injury. Their neighbor had liability insurance, which paid only $1000 (the hospital bills alone were approximately $2500). Nevertheless, they never considered seeking greater compensation from their neighbor or the neighbor's insurance company: "We were thankful that she recovered as well as she did. . . . We never considered a lawsuit there at all. I don't know what other people would have done in the case. Possibly that insurance company would have paid the total medical if we would have just, well, I have a brother who is an attorney, could have just wrote them a letter maybe. But, I don't know, we just didn't do it, that's all." Further discussion of the role of insurance in the handling of personal injuries in Sander County appears in the next section.

Where there was no alternative as to venue, potential plaintiffs typically re-signed themselves to nonjudicial settlements without any thought of litigation. And, as I have already suggested, for many in the community the possibility of lit-igation was not considered in any case. One woman I spoke with had lost her child in an automobile accident. She settled the case for $12,000 without filing a claim, yet she was sure that this amount was much less than she could have obtained through a lawsuit. She told me that since she and her family knew they were go-ing to stay permanently in the community, the pressure of the local value system foreclosed the possibility of taking the matter to court:

> One of the reasons that I was extremely hesitant to sue was because of the community pres-sure. . . . Local people in this community are not impressed when you tell them that you're involved in a lawsuit. . . . That really turns them off. . . . They're not impressed with peo-ple who don't earn their own way. And that's taking money that they're not sure that you deserve.

Others had so internalized this value system that they followed its dictates even when community pressures did not exist. A doctor told me that one of his patients was seriously burned during a trip out of state when an airline stewardess spilled hot coffee on her legs, causing permanent discoloration of her skin. This woman refused to contact a lawyer and instead settled directly with the airline for medical expenses and the cost of the one-week vacation she had missed. Regarding the pos-sibility of taking formal legal action to seek a more substantial award, she said sim-ply, "We don't do that." This same attitude may help to explain the apparent re-luctance of local residents to assert claims against other potential defendants from outside Sander County, such as negligent drivers or businesses or manufacturers.

Thus, if we consider the range of traditional responses to personal injuries in Sander County, we find, first of all, a great deal of self-reliant behavior. Injured persons typically responded to injuries without taking any overt action, either be-cause they did not view the problem in terms of a claim against or conflict with another person or because membership in a small, close-knit community inhibit-ed them from asserting a claim that would be socially disapproved. Some sought compensation through direct discussions with the other party, but such behavior was considered atypical. When sympathy or advice was sought, many turned to friends, neighbors, relatives, and physicians. The County Health Department, the mayor, and city council representatives also reported that injured persons occa-sionally sought them out, particularly when the injuries were caused by hazards that might endanger others. In such cases, the goal was generally to see the haz-ard removed for the benefit of the public rather than to seek compensation or oth-erwise advance personal interests.

## INSURING AGAINST INJURIES

Persons who had been injured often sought compensation from their own health and accident insurance without even considering the possibility of a claim against another party or another insurance company. As a local insurance adjuster told me:

> We have some people that have had their kid injured on our insured's property, and they were not our insured. And we call up and offer to pay their bills, because our insured has called and said my kid Tommy cracked that kid over the head with a shovel and they hauled him off to the hospital. And I called the people and say we have medical coverage and they are absolutely floored, some of them, that it never even crossed their minds. They were just going to turn it in to their own little insurance, their health insurance, and not do anything about it whatsoever, especially if [Tommy's parents] are close friends. . . .

By moving quickly to pay compensation in such cases before claims could arise, this adjuster believed that she prevented disputes and litigation. It helped, too, that the adjuster and the parties to an accident, even an automobile accident, usually knew each other:

> In Chicago, all those people don't know the guy next door to them, much less the guy they had the wreck with. And right here in town, if you don't know the people, you probably know their neighbor or some of their family or you can find out real quick who they are or where they are.

The contrast between injuries in a face-to-face community and in a metropolis like Chicago was drawn in explicit terms:

> I think things are pretty calm and peaceful as, say, compared to Chicago. Now I have talked to some of the adjusters in that area from time to time and I know, well, and we have our own insureds that go in there and get in an accident in Chicago, and we'll have a lawsuit or at least have an attorney . . . on the claim within a day or maybe two days of the accident even happening. Sometimes our insured has not any more than called back and said I've had a wreck but I don't even know who it was with. And before you can do anything, even get a police report or anything, why you'll get a letter from the attorney. And that would never, that rarely ever happens around here.

This adjuster estimated that over the past 15 years, her office had been involved in no more than 10 automobile-related lawsuits, an extraordinarily low number compared to the frequency of such cases in other jurisdictions.[12] Of course, once an insurance company has paid compensation to its insured, it may exercise its right of subrogation against the party that caused the accident, and one might expect insurance companies to be unaffected by local values opposing the assertion or litigation of injury claims. It is not entirely clear why insurance companies, like individuals, seldom brought personal injury actions in Sander County, but there are some clues. This particular adjuster, who had grown up in Sander County, shared the local value system. Although she did not decide whether to bring suit as a subrogee, she may well have affected the decisions of her central office by her own perceptions and by her handling of the people and documents in particular cases. Furthermore, her insurance company was connected to the Farm Bureau, a

---

[12]In Sander County as a whole, the litigation rate for automobile-related personal injury cases in 1975 and 1976 was 0.88 cases each year per 1000 population. For *all* automobile-related tort actions, including those where there was no personal injury claim, the litigation rate was 1.87 cases per 1000 population. In the absence of reliable or meaningful comparative data, it is difficult to say how low or high these countywide rates are; but my hunch is that these are rather low for a jurisdiction in which no-fault approaches were *not* used for motor vehicle cases.

membership organization to which most local farmers belonged. The evident popularity of this insurance carrier in Sander County (over 75% of the eligible farm families were estimated to be members of the Farm Bureau; it is not known how many members carried the insurance, but the percentage was apparently high) meant that injuries in many cases may have involved two parties covered by the same insurance company.

Occasionally, an insurance company did bring suit in the name of its insured, but given the unsympathetic attitudes of local juries, such lawsuits seldom met with success in Sander County. The adjuster mentioned above told me of a farm worker from Oklahoma who was harvesting peas for a local cannery. He stopped to lie down and rest in the high grass near the road and was run over by her insured, who was driving a pick-up truck and had swerved slightly off the road to avoid a large combine. When the fieldworker's insurance carrier sought compensation, the local adjuster refused, claiming that the injured man should not have been lying in the grass near the road and could not have been seen by her insured, who, she insisted, was driving carefully. The case went to trial and a jury composed largely of local farmers was drawn:

> I was not even in there because our lawyers that represent us said, how many of those people do you know out there? And I said, I can give you the first name of everybody on the jury. He said, you stay over there in the library . . . don't let them see you. . . . So I stayed out in my little corner and listened to what went on and we won, we didn't pay 5 cents on it.

Thus, even a lawsuit involving insurance companies on both sides was ultimately resolved in a manner that accorded with traditional values. The insurance companies' knowledge of jury attitudes in Sander County undoubtedly affected their handling of most injury cases.

## LAWYERS AND LOCAL VALUES

Sander County attorneys reported that personal injury cases came to them with some regularity, although they also felt that many injury victims never consulted an attorney but settled directly with insurance companies for less than they should have received. When these attorneys were consulted, it was by people who, in the opinion of the attorneys, had real nonfrivolous grievances, but the result was seldom formal legal action. Most personal injury cases were resolved, as they are elsewhere (Ross, 1970), through informal negotiation. Formal judicial procedures were initiated primarily to prod the other side to negotiate seriously or when it became necessary to preserve a claim before it would be barred by the statute of limitations. The negotiating process was, of course, strongly influenced by the parties' shared knowledge of likely juror reaction if the case actually went to trial. Thus, plaintiffs found negotiated settlements relatively attractive even when the terms were not particularly favorable.

But expectations regarding the outcome of litigation were probably not the only reason that members of the local bar so seldom filed personal injury cases. To some extent Sander County lawyers, many of whom were born and raised in the area, shared the local tendency to censure those who aggressively asserted personal injury claims. One attorney, for example, described client attitudes toward injury claims in the following terms: "A lot of people are more conducive to settlement here just because they're attempting to be fair as opposed to making a fast buck." Yet this same attorney admitted that informal settlements were often for small amounts of money and were usually limited to medical expenses, without any "general" damages whatever.[13] His characterization of such outcomes as "fair" suggests an internalization of local values even on the part of those whose professional role it was to assert claims on behalf of tort plaintiffs.

The local bar was widely perceived as inhospitable to personal injury claimants, not only because there were few tort specialists but because Sander County lawyers were seen as closely linked to the kinds of individuals and businesses against whom tort actions were typically brought. Although plaintiffs hired Sander County attorneys in 72.5% of all nontort actions filed locally in which plaintiffs were represented by counsel, they did so in only 12.5% of the tort cases.[14] One lawyer, who was frequently consulted by potential tort plaintiffs, lived across the county line in a small town outside of Sander County. He told me, "I get a lot of cases where people just don't want to be involved with the, they perceive it to be the hierarchy of Sander County. . . . I'm not part of the establishment."

Thus, even from the perspective of insurance company personnel and attorneys, who were most likely to witness the entry of personal injury cases into the formal legal system in Sander County, it is clear that the local culture tended in many ways to deter litigation. And when personal injury cases were formally filed, it usually was no more than another step in an ongoing negotiation process.

Why was the litigation of personal injury cases in Sander County subjected to disapproval so pervasive that it inhibited the assertion of claims at all stages, from the moment injuries occurred and were perceived to the time parties stood at the very threshold of the formal legal system? The answer, I shall argue, lies partly in the role of the Sander County Court in a changing social system and partly in the nature of the personal injury claim itself.

[13]This is particularly striking since Laurence Ross' observation of insurance company settlement practices in automobile accident cases suggests that general damages are a standard part of the settlement "package" and are rather routinely calculated "for the most part . . . [by] multiplying the medical bills by a tacitly but generally accepted arbitrary constant" (Ross, 1970: 239).

[14]These figures are from a sample of cases for the years 1975 and 1976. See note 6 *supra*. From these data alone one cannot conclude that Sander County attorneys were less often *approached* by potential personal injury plaintiffs, since the data consist only of cases that were filed and tell us nothing about cases brought to an attorney but not filed. We know that Sander County attorneys were sometimes reluctant to bring such actions even when approached by prospective plaintiffs. Attorneys elsewhere, particularly those who were tort specialists, may not have shared this reluctance and may have filed a higher proportion of the Sander County claims that were brought to them.

## THE USE OF THE COURT

In the recent literature on dispute processing and conflict resolution, various typologies of conflict-handling forums and procedures have been proposed. Such typologies usually include courts, arbitrators, mediators, and ombudsmen, as well as two-party and one-party procedures such as negotiation, self-help, avoidance, and "lumping it" (see, e.g., typologies in Abel, 1973; Felstiner, 1974; Steele, 1975; Nader and Todd, 1978; Black and Baumgartner, 1983; Galanter, 1983). Analyses of these alternative approaches incorporate a number of variables that critically affect the ways in which conflict is handled and transformed. Such variables include, among others, procedural formality, the power and authority of the intervenor, the coerciveness of the proceedings, the range and severity of outcomes, role differentiation and specialization of third parties and advocates, cost factors, time required, the scope of the inquiry, language specialization, and the quality of the evidence that will be heard. When variables such as these are used to analyze various approaches to conflict resolution, the result is typically a continuum ranging from the most formal, specialized, functionally differentiated, and costly approaches to the most informal, accessible, undifferentiated, and inexpensive. The court as a forum for dispute processing and conflict resolution is typically placed at the costly, formalistic end of such continua.

Yet common sense and empirical investigations consistently remind us that trial courts rarely employ the adjudicative procedures that make them a symbol of extreme formalism. Very few of the complaints filed in courts are tried and adjudicated. Most are settled through bilateral negotiations of the parties or, occasionally, through the efforts of a judge who encourages the parties to reach an agreement without going to trial. This was true of the Sander County Court, as it is of courts elsewhere, and it applied with particular force to the relatively infrequent personal injury complaints that were filed in Sander County. Adjudication on the merits was extremely rare. In my sample only one of 15 personal injury cases went to trial, and the judges and lawyers to whom I talked confirmed the generality of this pattern. Yet the court did play a crucial role in the handling of personal injury conflicts. It did so by providing what was perhaps the only setting in which meaningful and effective procedures of any kind could be applied. To understand why this was so, we must examine some distinctive characteristics of the relationships between the parties in the personal injury cases that were litigated in Sander County.

Among the relative handful of personal injury cases filed in the Sander County Court, almost all shared a common feature: the parties were separated by either geographic or social "distance" that could not be bridged by any conflict resolution process short of litigation.[15] In at least half of the 15 personal injury cases in

[15]In this discussion of geographic and social distance and their impact on patterns of legal behavior, I draw upon a body of theory that has been developed in several earlier studies. See Black (1976); Perin (1977); Engel (1978); Todd (1978); Greenhouse (1982).

the sample, the plaintiff and the defendant resided in different counties or states. These cases were evenly split between instances in which the plaintiff, on the one hand, and the defendant, on the other hand, was a local resident. In either situation, geographic distance meant that the parties almost certainly belonged to different communities and different social networks. Informal responses by the injured party, whether they involved attempts to negotiate, to mediate, or even to retaliate by gossip, were likely to be frustrated since channels for communication and shared value systems and acquaintance networks were unlikely to exist. This is reflected in the disproportionate presence of parties from outside the county on the personal injury docket.[16]

A more elusive but no less significant form of distance was suggested by interviews with the parties as well as by the court documents in several personal injury cases. In these cases, it became apparent that "social distance," which was less tangible but just as hard to bridge as geographic distance, separated the parties even when they were neighbors.

Social distance could take many forms in Sander County. In one personal injury case, the plaintiff, who lived in one of the outlying towns in Sander County, described himself as an outsider to the community although he had lived there almost all his life. He was a Democrat in a conservative Republican town; he was of German extraction in a community where persons of Norwegian descent were extremely clannish and exclusive; he was a part-time tavernkeeper in a locality where taverns were popular but their owners were not socially esteemed; the opposing party was a "higher up" in the organization for which they both worked, and there was a long history of "bad blood" between them.

In a second personal injury case, a Mexican immigrant and his family sued a tavernkeeper under the Illinois Dram Shop Act for injuries he had suffered as a bystander in a barroom scuffle. Latino immigration into the community had, as we have seen, increased greatly in recent years to the displeasure of many local residents. Cultural misunderstandings and prejudice ran high, and little sympathy could be expected for a Latino who was injured in the course of a barroom fight. Thus, the plaintiff's wife was quite worried about bringing the lawsuit. She feared that they would create more trouble for themselves and told me, "I was afraid that maybe they'd say our kind of people are just trying to get their hands on money any way we could. . . ." The decision to sue was made because they believed that people behind the bar had contributed to the injury by passing a weapon to the man who had struck the plaintiff (although, under the Dram Shop Act, the tavern could have been found liable without fault), and because they saw no other way to recover the income they had lost when the plaintiff's injury had kept him from working.

[16]The disproportionate number of cases involving geographically distant adversaries is especially striking when one considers the relative infrequency of interaction between persons living in separate counties and states as compared to persons living in the same county or town. In absolute terms, injurious interactions must have occurred far more frequently between neighbors than between distant strangers, yet injurious interactions between distant strangers ended up in the Sander County Court about as often as those involving local residents (compare Engel, 1978:142–144).

The tavernkeeper, who considered herself a member of the social underclass (although in a different sense from the Mexican immigrants), was bitter about the case and about the Dram Shop Act. When I asked her how the plaintiffs had known that she was liable under the Act, she answered, "I haven't any idea. How do they know about a lot of things is beyond me. They know how to come here without papers and get a job or go on welfare. They are not too dumb, I guess."

In this case, then, the two parties were separated from each other and from the community by a great chasm of social distance. One person was set apart from the general community by ethnicity and was well aware that his injuries were unlikely to be regarded with sympathy. The other party was also, by self-description, a "second class citizen." As a tavernkeeper, she told me, "you come up against many obstacles, prejudices, and hard times, you wouldn't believe." Both descriptions of social alienation were accurate. Yet the defendant had an established place in the traditional social order. She owned a small business in a town dominated by the ethos of individual enterprise. Her line of work was widely recognized and accepted, although not accorded great prestige, in a community where taverns were among the most important social centers. Her acquisition of Dram Shop insurance made her a "deep pocket" comparable to other local business enterprises that might provide substantial compensation in appropriate cases to injured persons. The plaintiffs in this case, far more than the defendant, were truly social "outsiders" in Sander County. For them, nonjudicial approaches appeared hopeless, and passively absorbing the injury was too costly. Only formal legal action provided a channel for communication between the two parties, and this ultimately led, despite the defendant's reluctance, to settlement.

Social distance also played a part in an action brought by a woman on behalf of her 5-year-old daughter, who had suffered internal injuries when a large trash container fell on her. The little girl had been climbing on the trash container, which was located behind an automobile showroom. The plaintiff and her husband were described by their adversaries as the kind of people who were constantly in financial trouble and always trying to live off somebody else's money. The plaintiff herself stated frankly that they were outsiders in the community, ignored or avoided even by their next-door neighbors. As she put it, "Everybody in this town seems to know everybody else's business . . . but they don't know you."

Her socially marginal status in the community precluded any significant form of nonjudicial conflict resolution with the auto dealer or the disposal company, and the matter went to the Sander County Court, where the $150,000 lawsuit was eventually settled for $3000. Since initiating the lawsuit, the plaintiff had become a born-again Christian and, from her new perspective on life, came to regret her decision to litigate. The little money they had obtained simply caused her to fight with her husband, who sometimes beat her. She came to believe that she should not have sued, although she did feel that her lawsuit had done some good. After it was concluded, she observed, signs were posted near all such trash containers warning that children should not play on them.

In my interviews with local residents, officials, community leaders, and legal

professionals, I presented the fact situation from this last case (in a slightly different form, to protect the privacy and identity of the original participants) and asked
them how similar cases were handled in the segments of the community with
which they were familiar. From our discussion of this matter there emerged two
distinct patterns of behavior which, the interviewees suggested, turned on the extent to which the aggrieved party was integrated into the community. If the parents
of the injured child were long-time residents who were a part of the local society
and shared its prevailing value system, the consensus was that they would typically take little or no action of any sort. Injuries, as we have seen, were common
in a rural community, and the parents would tend to blame themselves for not
watching the child more carefully or, as one interviewee put it, would "figure that
the kid ought to be sharp enough to stay away" from the hazard. On the other hand,
if the parents of the injured child were newcomers to the community, and especially if they were factory workers employed in the area's newly established industrial plants, it was suggested that their behavior would be quite different. One
union steward assured me that the workers he knew typically viewed such situations in terms of a potential lawsuit and, at the least, would aggressively seek to
have the auto dealer and the disposal company assume responsibility for the damages. Others described a kind of "fight-flight" reaction on the part of newcomers
and industrial blue collar workers. One particularly perceptive minister said,
"Those . . . that feel put down perceive everything in the light of another putdown
and I think they would perceive this as a putdown. See, nobody really cares about
us, they're just pushing us around again. And so we'll push back." He also noted,
however, that it was equally likely that aggrieved individuals in this situation
would simply move out of the community—the "flight" response.

There was, then, some agreement that responses involving the aggressive assertion of rights, if they occurred at all, would typically be initiated by newcomers to the community or by people who otherwise lacked a recognized place in the
status hierarchy of Sander County. Such persons, in the words of a local school-
teacher, would regard the use of the court as a "leveler" that could mitigate the effects of social distance between themselves and the other side. Persons who were
better integrated into the community, on the other hand, could rely on their established place in the social order to communicate grievances, stigmatize what they
viewed as deviant behavior, press claims informally, or, because they felt com-
fortable enough psychologically and financially, simply absorb the injury without
any overt response whatever.

Interestingly, this was precisely the picture drawn for me by the evangelical
minister who had converted the mother of the 5-year-old girl to born-again Christianity. Lifelong residents of the community, he told me, reacted to stressful situations with more stability and less emotion than newcomers to the community who
were less rooted and whose lives were filled with pressures and problems and what
he called, "groping, searching, grasping." For this minister, born-again Christianity offered socially marginal people a form of contentment and stability that was
denied them by their lack of a recognized position in the local society. He argued

that external problems such as personal injuries were secondary to primary questions of religious faith. He told me, "[I]f we first of all get first things straightened out and that is our relationship with God and is our help from God, all of these other things will fall into order." This was precisely the message that the plaintiff in this case—and many other socially marginal people in the community like her—had come to accept. On this basis, many social outsiders in Sander County could rationalize passivity in the face of personal injuries, passivity that was at least outwardly similar to the typical responses of Sander County's long-time residents.

The picture of the Sander County Court that emerges from this brief overview of personal injury cases differs substantially from that which might be suggested by conventional typologies of conflict resolution alternatives. In processual terms litigation, although rare, was not strikingly different from its nonjudicial alternatives. It was characterized by informal negotiation, bargaining, and settlement in all but the extremely infrequent cases that actually went to trial. Yet these processes occurred only as a result of the filing of a formal legal action. Because of the distance separating the parties, nonjudicial approaches, even with the participation of lawyers, sometimes failed to resolve the conflict. Resorting to the Sander County Court could vest socially marginal persons with additional weight and stature because it offered them access to the levers of judicial compulsion. The very act of filing a civil complaint, without much more, made them persons whom the other side must recognize, whose words the other side must hear, and whose claims the other side must consider. The civil trial court, by virtue of its legal authority over all persons within its jurisdiction, was able to bridge procedurally the gaps that separated people and social groups. In a pluralistic social setting, the court could provide, in the cases that reached it, a forum where communication between disparate people and groups could take place. In so doing, it substituted for conflict-handling mechanisms which served the well-integrated dominant group but which became ineffective for persons who were beyond the boundaries of the traditional community.

The communication that the court facilitated could, however, give rise to anger and frustration. Plaintiffs often viewed the process negatively, because even when they went to court they could not escape the rigid constraints imposed by a community unsympathetic to claims for damages in personal injury cases. Thus, the plaintiff whom I have described as a Democrat in a Republican town told me that the experience of filing and settling a personal injury claim was "disgusting . . . a lot of wasted time." Low pretrial settlements were, not surprisingly, the rule.

Defendants viewed the process negatively because they were accustomed to a system of conflict resolution that screened out personal injury cases long before they reached the courthouse. Even though settlements might turn out to be low, defendants resented the fact that personal injuries had in the first place been viewed as an occasion to assert a claim against them, much less a formal lawsuit. Being forced to respond in court was particularly galling when the claimant turned out to be a person whom the core members of the community viewed with dislike or disdain.

In short, the Sander County Court was able to bridge gaps between parties to personal injury cases and to promote communication between those separated by social or geographic distance. It did so, however, by coercion, and its outcomes (particularly when both parties resided in the community) tended to exacerbate rather than ameliorate social conflict. In the court's very success as a mechanism for conflict resolution we may, therefore, find a partial explanation for the stigmatization of personal injury litigation in Sander County.

## THE PRESERVATION AND DESTRUCTION
## OF A COMMUNITY

In rural and archaic Japan . . . people used to believe that calamity that attacked the community had its origin in an alien factor inside the community as well as outside it. The malevolent factor accumulated in the community. It was related also to the sins committed wittingly or unwittingly by members of the community. In order to avoid the disastrous influence of the polluted element, it was necessary for the community to give the element form and to send it away beyond the limits of the village. However, the introduction of the alien element, which could turn into calamity at any time, was absolutely necessary for the growth of the crops. Thus the need for the alien factor had two facets which appear contradictory to each other on the surface: that is, the introduction of the negative element of expiation as well as the positive element of crop fertility (Yamaguchi, 1977:154).

The social and economic life of Sander County had undergone major changes in the years preceding this study, and the impact of those changes on the worldview of local residents and on the normative structure of the community as a whole was profound. Small single-family farms were gradually giving way to larger consolidated agricultural operations owned by distant and anonymous persons or corporations. The new and sizeable manufacturing plants, together with some of the older local industries, now figured importantly in the economic life of Sander County and were the primary reasons why the population had become more heterogeneous and mobile.

These changes had important implications for traditional concepts of individualism and for the traditional relationships and reciprocities that had characterized the rural community. Self-sufficiency was less possible than before. Control over local lives was increasingly exercised by organizations based in other cities or states (there were even rumors that local farmlands were being purchased by unnamed foreign interests). Images of individual autonomy and community solidarity were challenged by the realities of externally based economic and political power. Traditional forms of exchange could not be preserved where individuals no longer knew their neighbors' names, much less their backgrounds and their values. Local people tended to resent and perhaps to fear these changes in the local economic structure, but for the most part they believed that they were essential for the survival of the community. Some of the most critical changes had been the product of decisions made only after extensive deliberations by Sander County's elite. The infusion of new blood into the community—persons of diverse racial, ethnic, and cultural backgrounds—was a direct result of these decisions. The new residents were, in the eyes of many old-timers, an "alien element" whose introduction was, as in rural Japan, grudgingly recognized as "absolutely necessary" to preserve the well-being of the community.

The gradual decay of the old social order and the emergence of a plurality of cultures and races in Sander County produced a confusion of norms and of mechanisms for resolving conflict. New churches were established with congregations made up primarily of newcomers. Labor unions appeared on the scene, to the dismay and disgust of many of the old-timers. New taverns and other social centers catered to the newer arrivals. Governmental welfare and job training programs focused heavily (but not exclusively) on the newcomers. Newcomers frequently found themselves grouped in separate neighborhoods or apartment complexes and, in the case of African-Americans, there were reported attempts to exclude them from the community altogether. The newcomers brought to Sander County a social and cultural heterogeneity that it had not known before. Equally important, their very presence constituted a challenge to the older structure of norms and values generated by face-to-face relationships within the community.

## PERCEPTIONS OF CONTRACT AND PERSONAL INJURY CLAIMS

The reaction of the local community to the assertion of different types of legal claims was profoundly affected by this proliferation of social, cultural, and normative systems. The contrast between reactions to claims based on breaches of contract and those based on personal injuries is especially striking. Contract actions in the Sander County Court were nearly 10 times as numerous as personal injury actions.[17] They involved, for the most part, efforts to collect payment for sales, services, and loans. One might expect that concerns about litigiousness in the community would focus upon this category of cases, which was known to be a frequent source of court filings. Yet I heard no complaints about contract plaintiffs being "greedy" or "sue happy" or "looking for the easy buck." Such criticisms were reserved exclusively for injured persons who made the relatively rare decision to press their claims in court.

In both tort and contract actions, claimants assert that a loss has been caused by the conduct of another. In contractual breaches, the defendant's alleged fault is usually a failure to conform to a standard agreed upon by the parties.[18] In personal injury suits, the alleged fault is behavior that falls below a general societal standard applicable even in the absence of any prior agreement. Both are, of course, long-recognized types of actions. Both are "legitimate" in any formal sense of the word. Why is it, then, that actions to recover one type of loss were viewed with approval

[17]Four percent of my case sample were personal injury cases and 37.5% were contract cases.

[18]On many occasions, of course, courts import external standards into contracts and impose them on the parties regardless of their agreement or disagreement with such terms.

in Sander County, while far less frequent actions to recover the other type of loss were seen as symptomatic of a socially destructive trend toward the overuse of courts by greedy individuals and troublemakers? The answer appears to lie in the nature of the parties, in the social meanings of the underlying transactions, and in the symbolism of individuals and injuries in the changing social order.

Most of the contract litigation in Sander County involved debts to businesses for goods and services. Typically, the contracts that underlie such debts are quite different from the classic model of carefully considered offers and acceptances and freely negotiated exchanges. Yet many townspeople and farmers in the community saw such obligations as extremely important (Engel, 1980). They were associated in the popular mind with binding but informal kinds of indebtedness and with the sanctity of the promise. Long-time Sander County residents viewed their society as one that had traditionally been based on interdependencies and reciprocal exchanges among fellow residents. Reliance upon promises, including promises to pay for goods and services, was essential to the maintenance of this kind of social system. One farmer expressed this core value succinctly: "Generally speaking, a farmer's word is good between farmers." Another farmer, who occasionally sold meat to neighbors and friends in his small town, told me:

> We've done this for 20 years, and I have never lost one dime. I have never had one person not pay me, and I've had several of them went bankrupt, and so on and so forth. I really don't pay any attention to bookkeeping or what. I mean, if someone owes me, they owe me. And you know, I've never sent anybody a bill or anything. I mean, sooner or later they all pay.

In these interpersonal exchanges involving people well known to one another there was, it appears, some flexibility and allowance for hard times and other contingencies. On the other hand, there was a mutual recognition that debts must ultimately be paid. When I asked a number of people in the community about a case in which an individual failed to pay in full for construction of a fence, the typical reaction among long-time residents was that such a breach would simply not occur. Of course, breaches or perceptions of breaches did occur in Sander County and the result could be, in the words of one farmer, "fireworks." I was told stories of violent efforts at self-help by some aggrieved creditors, and it was clear that such efforts were not necessarily condemned in the community (Engel, 1980: 439–440). A member of the county sheriff's department observed that small unpaid debts of this kind were often viewed as matters for the police:

> We see that quite a bit. They want us to go out and get the money. He owes it, there's an agreement, he violated the law. . . . You see, they feel that they shouldn't have to hire an attorney for something that's an agreement. It's a law, it should be acted upon. Therefore, we should go out and arrest the man and either have him arrested or by our mere presence, by the sheriff's's department, a uniformed police officer, somebody with authority going out there and say, hey, you know, you should know that automatically these people give the money and that would be it. So therefore they wouldn't have to go to an attorney. Boy, a lot of people feel that.

Other creditors, particularly local merchants, doctors, and the telephone company, brought their claims not to the police but to the Sander County Court. In some cases, contract plaintiffs (many of whom were long-time residents) appeared to litigate specifically to enforce deeply felt values concerning debt and obligation. As one small businessman explained:

> I'm the type of a person that can get personally involved and a little hostile if somebody tries to put the screws to me. . . . I had it happen once for $5 and I had it happen once for $12. . . . I explained to them carefully to please believe me that it wasn't the money, because it would cost me more to collect it than it'd be worth, but because of the principle of it that I would definitely go to whatever means necessary, moneywise or whatever, to get it collected. And which I did.

Even those creditors for whom litigation was commonplace, such as the head of the local collection agency and an official of the telephone company, shared the perception that contract breaches were morally offensive. This view appeared to apply to transactions that were routinized and impersonal as well as to the more traditional exchanges between individuals who knew each other well. As the head of the collection agency said, "When you get to sitting here and you look at the thousands of dollars that you're trying to effect collection on and you know that there's a great percentage of them you'll never get and no one will get, it's gotta bother you. It's gotta bother you." Certainly, business creditors felt none of the hesitancy of potential tort plaintiffs about asserting claims and resorting to litigation if necessary. Equally important, the community approved the enforcement of such obligations as strongly as it condemned efforts to enforce tort claims. Contract litigation, even when it involved "routine" debt collection, differed from tort litigation in that it was seen as enforcing a core value of the traditional culture of Sander County: that promises should be kept and people should be held responsible when they broke their word.

## CONCLUSION

In Sander County, the philosophy of individualism worked itself out quite differently in the areas of tort and contract. If personal injuries evoked values emphasizing self-sufficiency, contractual breaches evoked values emphasizing rights and remedies. Duties generated by contractual agreement were seen as sacrosanct and vital to the maintenance of the social order. Duties generated by socially imposed obligations to guard against injuring other people were seen as intrusions upon existing relationships, as pretexts for forced exchanges, as inappropriate attempts to redistribute wealth, and as limitations upon individual freedom.

These contrasting views of contract and tort-based claims took on special significance as a result of the fundamental social changes that Sander County had experienced. The newcomers brought with them conceptions of injuries, rights, and obligations that were quite different from those that had long prevailed. The traditional norms had no doubt played an important role in maintaining the customary social order by reinforcing longstanding patterns of behavior consistent with a parochial world view dominated by devotion to agriculture and small business. But the newcomers had no reason to share this world view or the normative structure associated with it. Indeed, as we shall see, they had good reason to reject it.[19] Although they arrived on the scene, in a sense, to preserve the community and to save it from economic misfortune, the terms on which they were brought into Sander County—as migrant or industrial workers—had little to do with the customary forms of interaction and reciprocation that had given rise to the traditional normative order. The older norms concerning such matters as individual self-sufficiency, personal injuries, and contractual breaches had no special relevance or meaning given the interests of the newcomers. Although these norms impinged on the consciousness and behavior of the newcomers, they did so through the coercive forces and social sanctions that backed them up and not because the newcomers had accepted and internalized local values and attitudes.

Indeed, it was clear that in the changing society of Sander County, the older norms tended to operate to the distinct disadvantage of social outsiders and for the benefit of the insiders. Contract actions, premised on the traditional value that a person's word should be kept, tended to involve collection efforts by established persons or institutions[20] against newcomers and socially marginal individuals. Such actions, as we have seen, were generally approved by the majority of Sander County residents and occurred with great frequency. Personal injury actions, on the other hand, were rooted in no such traditional value and, although such claims were infrequent, they were usually instituted by plaintiffs who were outsiders to the community against defendants who occupied symbolically important positions in Sander County society. Thus, a typical contract action involved a member of "the establishment" collecting a debt, while the typical personal injury action was an assault by an outsider upon the establishment at a point where a sufficient aggregation of capital existed to pay for an injury. This distinction helps to explain the stigmatization of personal injury litigation in Sander County as well as its infrequency and its ineffectiveness.[21]

[19]Were personal injury lawsuits in the late 1970s, although relatively infrequent, more common than they had been before the recent influx of social "outsiders" in Sander County? Because of the unavailability of reliable historical data, it is impossible to say, nor is the answer central to the analysis presented here. It is true that recent social changes in Sander County had brought striking juxtapositions of insiders and outsiders, and some increase in the frequency of tort claims may have resulted; but in earlier periods there may have been other kinds of outsiders as well, and some of them may have brought personal injury actions. In this article, I am interested in the past primarily as it existed in the minds of Sander County's citizens at the time of my study. It is clear that current perceptions of Sander County's history and traditions, whether accurate or not, played a crucial role in constructing and justifying responses to the problems that now faced the community, and such perceptions were often invoked to support the assertion of "traditional values" in opposition to behavior that provoked long-time residents.

[20]Frequent plaintiffs in collection cases were doctors, hospitals, merchants, collection agencies, and the telephone company. Cases of this type constituted 76.5% of all contract actions. The remaining 23.5% of contract cases involved actions based on construction contracts, promissory notes, wholesale transactions, and other less frequent kinds of contractual transactions.

[21]Sander County tort and contract cases are not unique, of course, in these basic structural differences. In other localities one might also expect to find that the majority of tort plaintiffs are individuals asserting claims against "deep pocket" defendants, while the majority of contract plaintiffs are business organizations attempting to collect debts from individuals. See, for example, Galanter (1974) and

Yet personal injury litigation in Sander County was not entirely dysfunctional for the traditional social order. The intrusion of "the stranger" into an enclosed system of customary law can serve to crystallize the awareness of norms that formerly existed in a preconscious or inarticulate state (see Fuller, 1969: 9–10, and Simmel, 1908). Norms and values that once patterned behavior unthinkingly or intuitively must now be articulated, explained, and defended against the contrary values and expectations of the stranger to the community.

In Sander County, the entry of the stranger produced a new awareness (or perhaps a reconstruction) of the traditional normative order at the very moment when that order was subjected to its strongest and most devastating challenges. This process triggered a complex response by the community—a nostalgic yearning for the older world view now shattered beyond repair, a rearguard attempt to shore up the boundaries of the community against alien persons and ideas (compare Erikson, 1966), and a bitter acceptance of the fact that the "stranger" was in reality no longer outside the community but a necessary element brought in to preserve the community, and therefore a part of it.

Local responses to personal injury claims reflected these complexities. In part, local residents, by stigmatizing such claims, were merely defending the establishment from a relatively rare form of economic attack by social outsiders. In part, stigmatization branded the claimants as deviants from the community norms and therefore helped mark the social boundaries between old-timers and newcomers. Because the maintenance of such boundaries was increasingly difficult, however, and because the "alien element" had been deliberately imported into the community as a societal act of self-preservation, the stigmatization of such claims was also part of a broader and more subtle process of expiation (to borrow Yamaguchi's [1977] term), a process reminiscent of rituals and other procedures used in many societies to deal with problems of pollution associated with socially marginal persons in the community (Douglas, 1966; Turner, 1969; Perin, 1977: 110–115).

Local residents who denounced the assertion of personal injury claims and somewhat irrationally lamented the rise in "litigiousness" of personal injury plaintiffs were, in this sense, participating in a more broadly based ceremony of regret that the realities of contemporary American society could no longer be averted from their community if it were to survive. Their denunciations bore little relationship to the frequency with which personal injury lawsuits were actually filed, for the local ecology of conflict resolution still suppressed most such cases long before they got to court, and personal injury litigation remained rare and aberrational. Rather, the denunciation of personal injury litigation in Sander County was significant mainly as one aspect of a symbolic effort by members of the commu-

---

Yngvesson and Hennessey (1975). It is possible that outside of Sander County perceptions of the legitimacy and illegitimacy of contract and tort actions are also influenced by these basic structural differences. In Sander County, however, this set of distinctions between the parties to tort and contract actions combined with local reactions to recent societal changes to produce a powerful symbolism of insiders and outsiders and of injuries and individualism. The extent to which a similar symbolism may be found in other localities is a subject for further investigation.

nity to preserve a sense of meaning and coherence in the face of social changes that they found threatening and confusing. It was in this sense a solution—albeit a partial and unsatisfying one—to a problem basic to the human condition, the problem of living in a world that has lost the simplicity and innocence it is thought once to have had. The outcry against personal injury litigation was part of a broader effort by some residents of Sander County to exclude from their moral universe what they could not exclude from the physical boundaries of their community and to recall and reaffirm an untainted world that existed nowhere but in their imaginations.

# REFERENCES

Abel, Richard L. 1973. "A comparative theory of dispute institutions in society." *Law and Society Review* 8: 217–347.

Aubert, Vilhelm. 1963. "Competition and dissensus: two types of conflict and of conflict resolution." *Journal of Conflict Resolution* 7: 26–42.

Black, Donald. 1976. *The Behavior of Law*. New York: Academic Press.

Black, Donald, and M. P. Baumgartner. 1983. "Toward a theory of the third party." In *Empirical Theories about Courts*, edited by Keith Boyum and Lynn Mather. New York: Longman.

Douglas, Mary. 1966. *Purity and Danger*. London: Routledge and Kegan Paul.

Engel, David M. 1978. *Code and Custom in a Thai Provincial Court*. Tucson: University of Arizona Press.

———. 1980. "Legal pluralism in an American community: perspectives on a civil trial court." *American Bar Foundation Research Journal* 1980: 425–454.

Erikson, Kai T. 1966. *Wayward Puritans*. New York: John Wiley and Sons.

Felstiner, William L.F. 1974. "Influences of social organization on dispute processing." *Law and Society Review* 9: 63–94.

Friedman, Lawrence M., and Robert V. Percival. 1976. "A tale of two courts: litigation in Alameda and San Benito counties." *Law and Society Review* 10: 267–301.

Fuller, Lon L. 1969. "Human interaction and the law." *American Journal of Jurisprudence* 14: 1–36.

Galanter, Marc. 1974. "Why the 'haves' come out ahead: speculations on the limits of legal change." *Law and Society Review* 9: 95–160.

———. 1983. "Reading the landscape of disputes: what we know and don't know (and think we know) about our allegedly contentious and litigious society." *UCLA Law Review* 31: 4–71.

Gest, Ted, Lucia Solorzano, Joseph P. Shapiro, and Michael Doan. 1982. "See you in court." *U.S. News and World Report* 93 (December 20): 58.

Greene, Richard. 1983. "Caught in the better mousetrap." *Forbes* 132 (October 24): 66.

Greenhouse, Carol J. 1982. "Nature is to culture as praying is to suing: legal pluralism in an American suburb." *Journal of Legal Pluralism* 20: 17–35.

McIntosh, Wayne. 1980–1981. "150 years of litigation and dispute settlement: a court tale." *Law and Society Review* 15: 823–848.

Nader, Laura, and Harry F. Todd, Jr. 1978. "Introduction." In *The Disputing Process—Law in Ten Societies*, edited by Laura Nader and Harry F. Todd, Jr. New York: Columbia University Press.

National Center for State Courts. 1979. *State Court Caseload Statistics: Annual Report, 1975.*

———. 1982. *State Court Caseload Statistics: Annual Report, 1977.*

Perham, John. 1977. "The dilemma in product liability." *Dun's Review* 109 (January): 48.

Perin, Constance. 1977. *Everything in Its Place*. Princeton: Princeton University Press.

Rosenberg, Maurice. 1977. "Contemporary litigation in the United States." In *Legal Institutions Today: English and American Approaches Compared*, edited by H. Jones. Chicago: American Bar Association.

Ross, H. Lawrence. 1970. *Settled Out of Court*. Chicago: Aldine Publishing Co.

Seymour, Whitney North, Jr. 1973. *Why Justice Fails*. New York: William Morrow and Co.

Simmel, Georg. 1908. "The stranger." In *On Individuality and Social Forms: Selected Writings,* edited by David Levine. Chicago: University of Chicago Press, 1971.

Steele, Eric H. 1981. "Fraud, dispute and the consumer: responding to consumer complaints." *University of Pennsylvania Law Review* 123:1107–1186.

Taylor, Stuart, Jr. 1981. "On the evidence, Americans would rather sue than settle." *New York Times* (July 5): Section 4, page 8.

Todd, Harry F. Jr. 1978. "Litigious marginals: character and disputing in a Bavarian village." In *The Disputing Process—Law in Ten Societies,* edited by Laura Nader and Harry F. Todd, Jr. New York: Columbia University Press.

Tondel, Lyman M., Jr. 1976. "The work of the American Bar Association Commission on Medical Professional Liability." *Insurance Counsel Journal* 43: 545–551.

Turner, Victor W. 1969. *The Ritual Process*. Chicago: Aldine.

Yamaguchi, Masao. 1977. "Kingship, theatricality, and marginal reality in Japan." In *Text and Context: The Social Anthropology of Tradition,* edited by R. Jain. Philadelphia: Institute for the Study of Human Issues.

Yngvesson, Barbara, and Patricia Hennessey. 1975. "Small claims, complex disputes: a review of the small claims literature." *Law and Society Review* 9: 219–274.

# 8

# EVIDENCE AS
# PARTISANSHIP*

## MARK COONEY

Demonstrating the importance of the social characteristics of the parties is the central theme—and achievement—of the microsociology of law (see especially Black, 1976; 1989). Work at this level has undermined the traditional idea that law is concerned only with what people do, and not who they are. An imposing body of literature establishes that the way cases are handled varies systematically with, for example, the intimacy (e.g., Lundsgaarde, 1977), social standing (e.g., Farrell and Swigert, 1978), organizational status (e.g., Wanner, 1974; 1975), race (e.g, Baldus, Woodworth, and Pulaski, 1990), gender (e.g., Daly, 1987), integration (e.g., Engel, 1984), and moral reputation (e.g., Holmstrom and Burgess, 1983) of the parties.

Yet there are also limits to what has been accomplished. Sociological factors can explain only so much of the variation in case outcomes. Some portion must be attributed to the components emphasized by traditional legal thought. Evidence, in particular, clearly matters. The party with the most and the most credible evidentiary support generally wins (see, e.g., Myers and Hagan, 1979; Reskin and Visher, 1986). Oddly, though, relatively little of a scientific nature is known about evidence. Legal scholars have argued for some time that fact-finding is an uncertain human process (e.g., Frank, 1949; Posner, 1990: 203–219), but they have not elaborated this insight into a body of data or an explanatory theory. Social scien-

*Earlier versions were presented at the 1991 and 1992 Law and Society Association annual meetings and to the Departments of Sociology of Purdue University and the University of Georgia. My thanks to all who offered comments, and to the following people who read and criticized previous drafts: M. P Baumgartner, Donald Black, Ian Donovan, Paul Gallagher, John Herrmann, Allan Horwitz, Calvin Morrill, Martha Myers, Joachim Savelsberg, Barry Schwartz, Roberta Senechal de la Roche, James Tucker, and several anonymous reviewers.

tists have investigated the important issue of the social biases inherent in the eval-uation of testimony (Stanko, 1981–82; O'Barr, 1982; Wolf and Bugaj, 1990), but neither they nor any other group have looked in depth at where evidence comes from in the first place.

I seek here to advance the microsociological understanding of law by explor-ing the social origins of evidence. The argument presented assumes that the same empirical events can give rise to very different amounts and types of evidence. But the social process by which events are transformed into legally relevant informa-tion is neither random nor inscrutable. Litigants vary systematically in their abil-ity to attract evidence, a pattern that manifests itself at several stages of the legal process: the investigation of the facts by lawyers and police officers, the willing-ness of citizens to involve themselves as witnesses, and the presentation of evi-dence by citizens and legal officials alike. All of this conduct can be considered a form of support or partisan behavior for one party to a dispute. As such, it falls within the jurisdiction of a theory of partisanship recently formulated by Black (1993) to predict and explain the amount of support that people attract from oth-ers in times of conflict. Applying this theory to a diverse set of empirical materi-als yields my central empirical claim: that people with extensive social ties and people with elevated social status have advantages in attracting the evidence nec-essary to sustain their legal cases.

This discussion represents an initial attempt to identify some of the major so-cial patterns in the production of evidence. Its purpose is to open up an area of in-quiry, not to provide a definitive overview of a well-researched subject. It there-fore neither surveys all relevant explanatory variables nor presents quantitative estimates of the effects reviewed. Incomplete though the data presented are, they nonetheless indicate that sociological effects are deeply embedded within the le-gal process. Not only do people's social characteristics and ties affect their chances of winning once their case is presented to legal officials, but they also help to ex-plain the evidentiary strength of the cases themselves. In this way, a kind of dou-ble disadvantage operates against low status and socially isolated litigants.

## THE SOCIOLOGY OF EVIDENCE

### EVIDENCE SCHOLARSHIP

Though often considered a narrow and technical subject, the law of evidence in fact generates a diverse set of scholarly perspectives. Much of the scholarship is doctrinal, focusing on the interpretation of cases and statutes (e.g., Carlson, Imwinkelried, and Kionka, 1991; Kaplan, Waltz, and Park, 1992). But there is also a tradition of philosophical work analyzing the ultimate bases of evidence law: its foundations in logic, its rational justifiability, its social purposes (e.g., Bentham, 1827; Gulson, 1905; Twining, 1983; Twining and Stein, 1992). In recent years, this jurisprudential perspective has generated analyses of the interpretation of legal facts (e.g., Scheppele, 1988: Chapter 5; 1991) and a debate about the nature and role of probability theory and mathematics in establishing legal proof (e.g., Cohen, 1977; Eggleston, 1983; Tillers and Green, 1988).

Evidence scholarship also has a well-developed empirical dimension. Social psychologists work on various aspects of evidence (e.g., Kassin and Wrightsman, 1985) and have devoted particular attention to investigating experimentally the trustworthiness of eyewitness identification (e.g., Loftus, 1979; Wells and Loftus, 1984; for a review of the literature, see Williams, Loftus, and Deffenbacher, 1992). A second issue addressed by social scientists is the related question of witness credibility—how it varies with, for instance, the social characteristics (Stanko, 1981–82; Wolf and Bugaj, 1990) and speech patterns (O'Barr, 1982; Morrill and Facciola, 1992) of those giving testimony. A third is the manner in which legal officials construct legal truth (e.g., Frank, 1949; Cicourel, 1968; McBarnet, 1981; Ericson, 1981; 1982; Rosen, 1980–81: 219–227; 1989: 20–38; Geertz, 1983; A. Sanders, 1987; McConville, Sanders, and Leng, 1991). Finally, scholars from a number of disciplines have analyzed the features of historical and cross-cultural settings responsible for variation in the means of obtaining evidence—ordeals, trial by battle, torture, oaths, witness cross-examination, and so on (e.g., Lea, 1892; Roberts, 1965; Brown, 1975; Langbein, 1977; Bartlett, 1986; Caenegem, 1991).

Broad though it is, all of this work begins from the evidence presented in the case. While scholars have analyzed the second phase of fact-finding—the evaluation of evidence—they have rarely explored the prior stage—the production of evidence—though it is extremely important in the practice of law (e.g. Jeans, 1992: Volume 1, 191–269).

## BLACK'S THEORY OF PARTISANSHIP

Scholars have long been interested in the role third parties play in conflict (e.g., Barton, 1919: 87–88; Evans-Pritchard, 1940: 152–176; Colson, 1953; Eckhoff, 1967; Caplow, 1968; Merry, 1982; Lewicki, Weiss, and Lewin, 1992). There seem to be two major third-party orientations (Black and Baumgartner, 1983; see further Black, 1993: 138–139). First, third parties may seek to settle disputes through mediation, arbitration, adjudication or some other process. Second, third parties may seek to advance the cause of one of the principals in a partisan manner. Although the former have received more scholarly attention, the latter can also profoundly affect the way conflict is handled. For instance, cross-cultural evidence suggests that the structure of partisan support enjoyed by spouses shapes the amount and severity of domestic conflict, including the willingness of men to use violence against their wives (Baumgartner, 1993).

A theory of partisanship would explain variation in the amount of support people generate in times of conflict. To that end, Black (1993) treats partisanship as a form of "social gravitation" by which one social actor is attracted to another. Consistent with his earlier theoretical work on law (1976) and other subjects (1979), Black conceives of social gravitation in general and structural terms. Thus, his theory does not address the subjective dimensions of why disputants attract support in particular situations, but concentrates on the underlying social conditions that explain attraction, regardless of whether it occurs in a remote New Guinea jungle or in a 21st-century urban agglomeration. Just as gravitational attraction in physical space is a function of the mass of objects and the distance between them, so, for Black, gravitation in social space is a function of status and social distance. His theory of partisanship therefore reduces to a single proposition (1993: 127): "Partisanship is a joint function of the social closeness and superiority of one side [of a conflict] and the social remoteness and inferiority of the other" (emphasis omitted).

For present purposes, this proposition encapsulates three main ideas. First, the status and relational characteristics of both parties predict the behavior of partisans. Second, partisans tend to gravitate toward the higher-status party and the party with whom they are more intimate. Third, the degree of support that a partisan provides increases with the status difference between the parties, as well as the closeness of one party minus the distance of the other (e.g., people give more support when they are close to one party and distant from the other than when they are close to or distant from both).[1] In general, then, higher-status parties ought to attract more support than lower-status parties, and parties with extensive ties of intimacy ought to attract more than social isolates.

## THE PRODUCTION OF EVIDENCE

The production of evidence is one type of support behavior (Black and Baumgartner, 1983: 111–112; Moore, 1992: 36–38). In most legal disputes, the testimony of the principal parties appears to be the largest and most partisan source of evidence. This is consistent with the above hypothesis because people are most intimate with themselves (Cooney, 1988: 41–46; compare Black, 1993: 142, note 16). This essay, however, concentrates on the more problematic role played by individuals other than the principals. (Hence, in this article the term "witness" refers to a third party who provides testimony.) Black's theory predicts that the amount of evidentiary support the parties attract from third parties in civil and criminal cases increases with their social status and the number and intimacy of their social ties. "Social status" is defined broadly, referring to matters such as the wealth, organization, and respectability (i.e., lack of a record of deviance) of a social actor. These elements are assumed to have independent and cumulative effects (e.g., a wealthy and respectable individual is more advantaged than one who is wealthy but unrespectable.)[2] "Intimacy" or relational distance refers to the frequency and intensity of contact between people, the degree to which their lives are entangled.

---

[1]"Social remoteness" also includes a variable not discussed here—the cultural distance (as defined in Black, 1976: 65, 70, 74) between party and partisan.

[2]A task for the future is to assess the relative strength of the component dimensions of social status. For further details on both social status and intimacy, see Black (1993: 126–127; 1976: Chapters 2–6).

Evidence varies not just in quantity but also in quality, or credibility. Credibility depends, in part, on the social source of the evidence, on who presents it. The evidence of high-status and relationally distant witnesses tends to carry more weight than that of witnesses with the opposite characteristics (Stanko, 1981–82; O'Barr, 1982; Black, 1983b; Wolf and Bugaj, 1990). Since support is predicted to flow upward rather than downward, high-status litigants ought to be advantaged in attracting high-status witnesses. I also propose that litigants with extensive distant social ties attract more support from relationally distant witnesses.[3]

The following sections illustrate these principles at work in three different areas of the evidentiary process: the factual investigation of cases by legal officials, the provision of evidence by citizens, and the variable content of evidence presented by legal officials and by citizens.[4]

## INVESTIGATION

### TIES TO THE POLICE

The amount of evidence available to legal officials varies greatly. In some cases, there is an enormous volume of information about the parties and the alleged offense; in others, virtually none. The events in dispute do not determine how much evidence there is. One reason for this is that the effort legal officials put into generating evidence through the investigation of facts is not constant across cases (Black, 1980: 14–18; see also W. Sanders, 1977: 95–96). As one legal sociologist has noted:

> Both officials and nonofficials often think of evidence as a fixed commodity attached to the case. Thus, attorneys routinely speak about "how much evidence" there is in a particular case or suggest that "the evidence shows" something. In actual practice, evidence is not a fixed commodity but a purposefully constructed set of documents, testimony, and material objects. In no case is only one set of evidence possible. Moreover, evidence does not cre-

[3]Perhaps a number of clarifications about the ultimate scope of the argument might be useful. First, although the theory applies both to direct support that buttresses a litigant's story and to indirect support that implicates the other litigant in wrongdoing, only the former is addressed here. I do not consider, therefore, how the social characteristics of the parties explain variation in the attraction of hostile evidence. Second, I emphasize oral testimony, often the most common form of evidence (see, e.g., Ericson, 1981: 92; Simon, 1991: 16), but my argument extends to legal evidence in general and thus embraces cases, for instance, in which documentary evidence dominates (e.g., intercorporate litigation). Third, because evidence affects each procedural stage, from the initial statement of a grievance to its final resolution, the analysis is pertinent whenever officials (including jurors) take legal action.

[4]Indeed, although no data are presented on the point, the theory should, in principle, also explain patterns of evidence presentation in nonlegal conflicts, such as disputes among family members, friends, neighbors, and co-workers. Note, however, that the more informal (i.e., the less reliance placed on explicit rules) the setting, the less important evidence appears to be. Nader (1969: 84–88) reports, for example, that courts handling disputes between low-status Mexican Indians are more concerned with reconciling the parties than with establishing clearly what happened in the past. Thus, in some nonlegal conflicts (e.g., formal hearings within an organization) evidence may play a central role, while in others (e.g., peacemaking within families), it may be largely irrelevant.

ate itself. Its generation requires human labor and interpretation and, usually, economic resources. Because evidence must be generated, officials create more or less of it depending
on their conceptions of cases. Cases that they are less interested in winning, for whatever
reasons, generally receive less work and thus generate less evidence. Conversely, more evidence can also be generated (LaFree, 1989: 105–106).

The theory applied here suggests that the generation of evidence increases with
the status of the principal parties and their intimacy with the investigators. The limited amount of available information supports this. Consider, first, police investigation.

Although even small amounts of intimacy appear to increase partisan behavior,
a point elaborated later, close relationships produce the strongest effects. Thus,
when police officers are victims[5] of crimes, their ties to police detectives (whether
based on personal acquaintance or, more indirectly, on common organizational
membership) generally ensure that the case will be vigorously investigated (e.g.,
Simon, 1991: 127–150). The clearest example is the killing of an officer by an unknown assailant (e.g., Matthiessen, 1983: 192–218; McAlary, 1990: 79–164;
Adams, Hoffer and Hoffer, 1991: 12–14). An ethnographer of the police comments:

> Policemen take the death of colleagues seriously. . . . [They] want . . . killers of policemen
> caught, and the department makes extraordinary efforts to achieve their capture. . . . [The]
> captain . . . orders the men to go out and "bring everyone walkin' around with a swinging
> pair" in for investigation. . . . Patrolmen, detectives, special-unit officers, everyone [goes]
> out doing the job, closing up the bars and clubs, hitting the speaks, pinching the junkies, the
> gamblers, the prostitutes, closing down the area, "squeezing them for information" (Ru-
> binstein, 1974: 335–336).

The killing of a police officer may be thought an extreme illustration, but, as
many police researchers have noted, the police take seriously all offenses against
their authority (e.g., Piliavin and Briar, 1964: 210; Chevigny, 1969: Chapter 3;
Black, 1971: 1097–1101, 1102–1104, 1108–1109; 1980: 36–40). In a modern
English case, for example, a defendant let the air out of a police car tire. Observers
note that the police "went to great lengths to secure evidence," including obtaining "a written report from their maintenance department" in order to sustain a
charge of attempted criminal damage (McConville, Sanders, and Leng, 1991:
159).

## BIG CASES

Investigation also varies with the social characteristics of civilian victims (e.g.,
Simon, 1991: 19–20). The police treat some cases as "big" or important and in-

---

[5]This section focuses on victims, but the theory predicts that were information available, the
amount of supporting evidence defendants attract would increase with their status and ties. For instance,
English researchers have found that West Indians (who are disproportionately of low income) are more
likely than whites to be sentenced without a Social Inquiry Report, a document used by defense lawyers
in making pleas of mitigation at sentencing hearings (Hood, 1992: 150–156).

vestigate them in considerable detail. Crimes committed against high-status victims are especially likely to be treated this way (e.g., Skolnick, 1966: 176–177). A clear example is the assassination of a political leader or a media celebrity. Here investigation by police and others may continue for decades or even centuries. But the same principle applies, less dramatically, in crimes against ordinary citizens. When wealthy, respectable people are victimized, police are likely to "seek physical evidence such as fingerprints, tire tracks, and hair samples at the scene of the crime, interview large numbers of potential witnesses and informants, and conduct extensive interrogations, polygraph ("lie detector") tests, and "line ups" (sessions at which suspects are viewed by victims or witnesses through a one-way mirror)" (Black, 1980: 16).

As the victim's social status declines, the probability that these investigatory measures will be undertaken decreases. Thus, in cases where the victims are of decidedly low status, even the most obvious investigative leads may not be pursued, regardless of the legal seriousness of the incident. A study of homicide in a rural Mexican community, where the victims are poor farmers, reports: "There is never any questioning of suspects or attempt to solve the crime by officials" (Nash, 1967: 461). Similarly, minimal investigation also appears to follow homicides committed on American Indian reservations (Matthiessen, 1983: 193) and skid row (Black, 1989: 6–7). In a Georgia case I observed,[6] a young black man, whom the police strongly suspected of being a drug dealer, shot and killed a close friend, another young black male also believed to be in the drug business. The killer turned himself in to the local jail on the day after the shooting, and told the authorities he was prepared to make a statement to the police. Seven months later, when the case came up for trial the prosecuting attorney complained that the investigating officer had still not taken a statement from the defendant. Busy with other cases, the killing of one street-level drug dealer by another was simply not high on the detective's list of priorities.

That evidence is uncovered is no guarantee that it will be useful or important. A considerable amount of legal strategy revolves around excluding or suppressing information that is available to at least one party (see, e.g., Mann, 1985). However, without investigation legal actions are difficult to sustain. In the above case, for instance, the lack of evidence resulted in the assistant district attorney accepting a plea of involuntary manslaughter instead of pursuing the murder conviction he had initially sought.

Another aspect of social status affecting the thoroughness with which cases are investigated is the victim's respectability. One student of police homicide investigators has noted that "nothing deflates a detective more than going back to the office, punching a victim's name into the admin office terminal and pulling out five or six computer pages of misbehavior, a criminal history that reaches from eye lev-

<hr>

[6]This case comes from my observation of a prosecutor's office in a medium-sized Georgia town (population 80,000). I spent some 120 hours observing the seven prosecutors preparing their felony cases and presenting them in court, paying particular attention to evidence collection and the testimonial behavior of witnesses.

el to the floor" (Simon, 1991: 177). But any deviation from conventional standards of behavior can weaken a victim's claim. A study of Canadian detectives cites the following two cases to illustrate this point. In the first, an alleged rape, the detectives "spent five hours trying to talk the victim into following through with her complaint and giving a written statement on it. . . . [They] willingly worked a continuous 16 hour period on this case, on behalf of a victim they characterized as 'naive' and 'respectable' and in need of police assistance to develop and sustain the case" (Ericson, 1981: 106). In the second, an alleged assault, a young man got into a fight while attending a party, receiving injuries which necessitated him spending four days in hospital. The detectives spent a total of 15 minutes on the case. After visiting the victim in his disheveled apartment a detective commented, "Did you see the way he lives? He's probably glad he got hurt so that he had an excuse not to be working." Although the case was one of the most violent encountered during the research, the detectives filed the case without ever contacting the two eyewitnesses or the suspect. The reason they cited: lack of evidence (Ericson, 1981: 106–107).

Legal officials often cite lack of evidence as a reason for the attrition of criminal cases. Examples such as these demonstrate that the designation has an evaluative component linked to the social status of the parties, and that statistical presentations which employ it tend to contain embedded partisan effects (see, e.g., Boland, Mahanna, and Sones, 1992: 35–48).

## DEFENSE ATTORNEYS

Applying Black's theory of partisan behavior to defense attorneys yields the prediction that those who represent family members and friends will, all else the same, investigate in more depth than those who represent strangers. Though plausible, this claim awaits empirical confirmation. Some data exist, however, to support the second hypothesis: that the status of the defendant is correlated with the depth of the attorney's investigation.[7] Thus, a survey of 60 death penalty attorneys (whose clients are virtually all low income) in six states found that 25% reported that they did not have enough time to prepare adequately for the trial, 27% did not call character or expert witnesses at the penalty phase, and 54% felt that the court provided insufficient funds for investigation of the facts and for expert witnesses (Coyle, Strasser, and Lavelle, 1990: 40). This is not confined to death penalty cases. A number of writers have noted that attorneys who usually represent low-income people tend not to engage in extensive searches for evidence favorable to their clients (e.g., Carlin and Howard, 1965: 416). Regardless of whether this is caused by lack of time or lack of interest on the attorney's part, it can result in considerable disadvantages to the client, as illustrated by a case heard by a lower court in Scotland:

---

[7]This observation does not apply to civil law jurisdictions (e.g., the countries of continental Europe)—where state officials, not the party's lawyer, gather defense evidence.

McD. had been so adamant he was innocent that he and his mother had hired a lawyer at their own expense. And in their view, "it was the easiest £30 I ever saw anyone earning." There *was* a witness, a stranger, who, according to the defendant, had in fact been committing the offense, and had been prepared to give evidence that McD. had arrived *after* the event. He had pleaded guilty, but recognized that McD. was not and gave a statement to that effect to the lawyer. Summoning him was left to the defendant's mother. Neither she nor the witness had a phone. She sent her seven-year-old son with a note.

The witness's father took it at the door. She never knew if the witness himself received it. He certainly did not turn up. In court, the defense lawyer merely noted, "I had hoped to have some supporting evidence but unfortunately for one reason or another it is not available." The magistrate, not surprisingly, saw "no reason why I should doubt the evidence given by the policeman." And the family even less surprisingly concluded: "People like us don't have rights" (McBarnet, 1981: 151; emphasis in original).

By contrast, attorneys who represent high-status defendants typically explore the facts in considerable detail, perhaps even employing their own investigators, a point documented by Mann's (1985) ethnographic study of the elite New York white-collar defense bar.[8] In one case Mann discusses, for example, an attorney representing a client suspected of land fraud stated that he undertook the following steps:

First of all, I had to learn the land business from A to Z—selling, buying, and investing. I had to go there and see the land with my own eyes, study what they had been doing, what the geography was like, what representations were being made to people; was there really egregious misrepresentation or really nothing at all? I had to interview salesmen, buyers, talk to state and federal regulators. It was a tremendous operation. . . . I sent my associate to their main office with instructions that he be given access to all records—memoranda, drafts, plans, letters, interim reports . . . whatever. . . . Then I later had him interview salesmen; there were over 50 of them (Mann, 1985: 68).

The depth of this investigation was not exceptional:

Attorneys repeatedly stated that it was very hard to convey the complexity, length, and detailed nature of an examination of records in a case that involved substantial business transactions. Some attorneys described the physical quantity of records delivered to their offices by clients—"They had three large filing cabinets sent here" or "We had one room in the office devoted completely to housing the corporate records, and they were worked on in that room by us." Other attorneys detailed the number of people and hours used for examining the records—"Three associates worked on the accounts for over two months" or "We billed over 150 hours in three months on that case, all in the investigative stage." And still others searched for superlatives to emphasize the obstacles—"It was absolutely impossible to handle all the records in the sixty-day period we had to comply with the subpoena" (ibid: 68–69).

Despite being on opposite sides, then, officials working for the defense and for the state exhibit broadly similar patterns of differential attraction to cases.[9] In this

[8]The higher fees paid by high-status clients appear to explain some, but not all, of the differential investigatory effort of lawyers. To test this, one could compare, for example, the effort exerted on behalf of a sample of wealthy drug dealers with that exerted on behalf of a sample of wealthy conventional businesspeople.

[9]If the theory is correct, lawyers should also put varying degrees of effort into other aspects of the case (e.g., researching the legal doctrine).

they are not alone. As the next section indicates, ordinary citizens also appear to gravitate to some parties more than others, and the principles that underlie their behavior appear to be largely the same as those that govern the partisanship of legal professionals.

## COMING FORWARD

Just because an incident occurs in the presence of onlookers is no guarantee that it will generate witnesses. People are not always willing to come forward and give evidence to legal officials. One study of detectives, for instance, describes a homicide in which a person was shot to death in a crowded bar in the presence of 100 people. Not a single person voluntarily came forward to testify (Waegel, 1981: 269–270). In a study of homicide I conducted in Virginia, the failure of witnesses to appear was a common theme in interviews conducted with defendants, relatives, and law enforcement officials.[10] In one case, for instance, the killing took place in a crowded public park on a Saturday afternoon during a festival. The defendant estimated that about 100 people witnessed the killing. Of these, only one was willing to testify in court.

The willingness of witnesses to come forward appears to increase with the status of the litigant. Thus, people at the top of corporations faced with allegations of white-collar criminal violations can usually rely on receiving evidentiary assistance from their subordinates (Mann, 1985: 67, 73). When Claus von Bulow, a wealthy European well known in East Coast high-society circles, was charged with the attempted murder of his wife, the defense received unsolicited offers from several people who offered to testify about anything that would help the defendant (Dershowitz, 1986: 225). Conversely, those with low social standing, such as the morally unrespectable, find it more difficult to attract witnesses. In a California case, for example, the owner of a restaurant that employed topless female dancers was threatened with closure. Seeking the support of customers and friends, he found that people were unwilling to testify on his behalf, citing the negative impact it would have on their own affairs (Feynman, 1985: 273–274). Likewise, when people are killed in low-income communities, their cases often generate lit-

---

[10]In 1989 and 1990, I conducted lengthy face-to-face interviews with 75 randomly selected people incarcerated for homicide in Virginia in 1988. The interviews focused on the background and context of the killing and the legal and informal social control to which it gave rise. I asked the defendants about their statements to the police, the identity of any eyewitnesses, the people who gave testimony and for which side they gave it, and the substance of the factual arguments on both sides. To supplement the information obtained, I read the available presentence investigation reports ($n = 50$), interviewed 42 members of some of the defendants' families by telephone, and conducted in-depth face-to-face interviews in Richmond with three homicide detectives and one homicide prosecutor. For further details, see Cooney, 1991: 19–27.

tle evidence (see, e.g., Simon, 1991: 147). The same is true when prison inmates are assaulted or killed (see, e.g., Porter, 1982: 16; Shakur, 1993: 309–310).[11]

Witnesses will also come forward to support their intimates. Indeed, intimates usually do not have to be persuaded to testify; they volunteer. In the Virginia case mentioned above, for instance, out of the hundred people who, the defendant estimated, witnessed the killing, the only one prepared to testify in court was the victim's girlfriend. Social isolates will therefore often be at a disadvantage in modern society, as they were in earlier settings in which people ("compurgators") swore oaths to the truth of their kinfolk's legal claims (e.g., Pollock and Maitland, 1898: Volume 2, 600–601; Black, 1993: 143, note 21).

Although intimates will not always provide support, they are typically easier to attract to the case than strangers. A legal anthropologist has noted that among the Tiv of Nigeria, people are slow to intervene in the disputes of unacquainted others, with the result that litigants have "trouble in getting witnesses of this sort, even though the number of people who have seen an act is legion" (Bohannan, 1957: 39). The same is true in America today. Although strangers sometimes volunteer their services, more typically the party or the attorney must first locate and then appeal to the witness's sense of justice or civic duty. If persuasion fails, the witness may have to be coerced. But coercion can harm as much as it helps. Many lawyers operate with the rule of thumb that "reluctant witnesses make bad witnesses" (Vera Institute of Justice, 1977: 69).

When witnesses have ties to both sides, the relative strength of their ties helps to determine whether they are willing to come forward and, if so, on whose behalf. To demonstrate this rigorously requires more detailed information than I can present, but a number of examples from my Virginia study suggest that it is a factor of some importance. Thus, witnesses with ties to both sides that are of unequal strength tend to come forward to support the litigant to whom they are more closely tied. In one case, for instance, a witness who was intimate with the victim and merely acquainted with the defendant provided central evidence for the state. By contrast, witnesses who have ties of approximately equal strength to both sides are more likely to stay back. In two other Virginia cases, witnesses who found themselves in this position refused to get involved: As one defendant said, evoking a pattern of neutrality familiar to students of extra-legal conflict (e.g., Senechal de la Roche, 1990: 146–147), "it wasn't their beef; they didn't want nothing to do with it." Moreover, the willingness of witnesses to come forward may change as their ties to the litigants evolve. In a Virginia child custody case, for instance, a friend agreed to testify to seeing the wife with bruises during the marriage. After the wife moved to another town, the friend and her husband began socializing with the divorcing husband. Caught more squarely in the middle, the friend became reluctant to testify on the wife's behalf.

---

[11]An additional factor that may serve to suppress evidence in prison and in low-income communities is witness intimidation (see, e.g., Graham, 1985: Chapter 1). See further note 14 below.

## THE CONTENT OF EVIDENCE

### THE WEAKNESS OF STRONG TIES

When witnesses do provide evidence, its content will typically vary in its degree of partisanship. Although sensitive measures have yet to be devised, the principal elements of evidentiary partisanship are clear. Some witnesses give evidence that advances neither cause very much; others testify to matters that clearly support one side rather than the other. And some witnesses base their evidence squarely on empirical events, while others fabricate it. The least partisan evidence is truthful and neutral; the most partisan is false and supportive of only one side.

Given the same set of facts, the partisanship of testimony and other evidence ought to increase with the status of the party attracting it. Consistent with this, anthropologist Max Gluckman (1967: 111) notes that among the Lozi, a tribal group resident in present-day Zambia, judges "believe that witnesses are liable to favor the powerful against the weak." Though it has never been investigated, this observation seems to apply to modern societies as well. Recall the "witnesses" who wanted to appear for Claus von Bulow—it is difficult to see what they could have said in support of his defense without telling outright lies. Equally difficult to imagine is a case in which a low-status person—an unemployed drug addict, for instance—accused of attempting to murder his wife would generate similar testimony from total strangers.

The Lozi also "believe that people will distort their evidence, and even commit perjury, to favor their kin, though it is wrong to do so" (Gluckman, 1967: 110; see also Just, 1986: 48). This belief is common today. A number of European countries prohibit close relatives from testifying on each other's behalf because of the likelihood of bias (see Beckstrom, 1989: 23). In the United States, testimony by close relatives is generally allowed, but legal professionals commonly assert that witnesses typically frame their testimony to favor their intimates, consciously or not. The defendant's intimates thus tend to emphasize mitigating circumstances and to deemphasize aggravating circumstances. Appearing for a person accused of murder, for example, they will ensure that the legal officials know that the victim initiated the fight that resulted in his or her death. They will readily agree to appear as character witnesses, drawing attention to commendable features of the defendant's biography. And should the defendant fabricate a defense, they are the most likely people to support it. Only one defendant in my Virginia sample admitted that he lied to the police, prosecutor, and court, but it is noteworthy that the people who were prepared to back up his story were his younger brother and closest friend (see also, e.g., Shakur, 1993: 27).

Conversely, the more intimate a witness is with the victim, the more supportive of the victim's case, and the more damaging to the defendant's case, the testimony tends to be. The victim's intimates typically move aggravating circumstances to center stage and mitigating circumstances to the wings. They will emphasize any predatory elements in the homicide, for instance, and down-play any involvement the victim had in his or her own demise. Note, however, that strongly partisan testimony for one or both principals tends to be found only when the witnesses are close to one side and distant from the other. When the witnesses have strong ties to both sides, the testimony is typically more guarded, less clear-cut.

A Georgia case I observed exemplifies some of these patterns:

> The defendant, Ben, is a young man accused of murdering a friend, Victor. Ben maintains that he killed in self-defense. A number of witnesses are called, each of whom has a different relationship to the parties. The most intimate with the victim is his girlfriend, Joy, who volunteers that the defendant started the fight. The most intimate with the defendant is his brother who, though he did not himself witness the killing, tells the court that Ben came to him after the event and told him that he shot Victor after Victor had choked him and stomped him in the face. Caught in the middle is Ben's ex-girlfriend, Sally, who is a close friend of Joy. Sally appears to be very uncomfortable on the witness stand, turning the chair to the side where she is able to look away from Ben. Her responses are brief and lack detail, but she does say that Victor slammed Ben to the ground in the fight.

To combat the effects of intimacy, lawyers on the other side often point to the relationship between litigant and witness as a reason for disbelieving testimony (see, e.g., Allen, 1977: 121). The following exchange (reconstructed from my written notes) took place after the defendant's brother attempted to repudiate an earlier statement he had made to the police that was more damaging to the defendant's case than his court testimony:

> Prosecutor: "You don't want your brother to go to jail, do you?"
> Witness: "No."
> Prosecutor: "And you certainly don't want him to go on your testimony, do you?"
> Witness: "No."
> Prosecutor: "No further questions."

Thus, while intimates tend to be reliable witnesses, they are not especially effective ones. Although their testimony can be crucial if none other is available, it can be discredited by that of more distant witnesses: strong ties have their weaknesses. Legal success therefore often depends on attracting strangers and other credible witnesses to the case. Litigants differ in their ability to do this. But before I take up this issue, I must briefly address two further points.

## TYPES AND AMOUNTS OF INTIMACY

Testimonial partisanship based on intimacy is not confined to family members and close friends. Police officers, for instance, almost invariably support one another's testimony (e.g., Hunt and Manning, 1991: 61–62). Moreover, they often distrust outsiders because of their uncertainty about how citizens might perceive and report events. In one incident, for example, detectives were unwilling to allow a social scientist to undertake an observation study of them at work because they were concerned, among other things, about any court testimony the researcher might be required to give. A senior detective told a researcher seeking research access that "[the detectives] just don't know who you're going to support in a situation like that. I'm not saying that they lie, but they want someone on their side. You're not a policeman" (Ericson, 1981: 32). A second detective, who was willing to allow the researcher full access to his professional activities on condition that the researcher participate and not just observe, said to him: "Of course, I would expect any good partner to be—you know what I mean—he would have to tell my version of what happened in court" (Ericson, 1981: 33; see also Smith and Gray, 1985: 355).

Whatever its basis, a relatively small amount of intimacy can begin to increase the partisanship of testimony.[12] In common-law countries, such as England and most of its former colonies (including the United States), witnesses are called by the parties rather than by the court. Jerome Frank (1949: 19)—himself a judge—endorsed the observation of a number of legal writers who argued that one of the most pervasive sources of "unconscious partisanship" is the honest witness who repays the confidence placed in him by the person calling him with supporting testimony. Expert witnesses may be subject to the same tendency (e.g., Haward, 1982: 61). Even a small amount of pretrial contact with a lawyer may increase partisanship. Again, in common-law countries the parties or their lawyers must find and interview their own witnesses. Experimental evidence suggests that witnesses with no previous tie to a litigant who are interviewed by a lawyer prior to the trial may, without being aware of it, articulate their evidence in a manner supportive of the lawyer's client (Sheppard and Vidmar, 1980).[13] Thus, although strongly partisan evidence, such as lying, requires a high degree of intimacy, relatively small magnitudes of the variable can serve to increase the supportiveness with which testimony is proffered.

## ATTRACTING CREDIBLE EVIDENCE

Evidence varies in quality as well as quantity. The quality of evidence has a social dimension: all else being the same, the testimony of high-status witnesses is more credible and has a greater impact on the outcome of the case than that of low-status witnesses (Stanko, 1981–82; O'Barr, 1982; Black, 1983b; Wolf and Bugaj, 1990: 8–10). The same appears to be true of relationally distant witnesses (Black, 1983b). The observation that "an unrelated witness is regarded as more valuable and objective than a close relative of either of the litigants" (Pospisil, 1971: 237) is as true of legal actors in modern America as it is of their counterparts among the Kapauku of New Guinea, the people about whom it was made.

---

[12]This appears to be true of helping behavior more generally (see Black, 1993: 142, note 6).

[13]It is thus an advantage for a lawyer to interview a witness before the opposing attorney does: "he who arrives first gets a better interpretation of the facts" (Mann, 1985: 162).

## WITNESSES FOR THE STATE

Litigants differ in their ability to attract the kind of high-quality evidence which helps to make a strong legal case. High-status litigants, individual and organizational, seem to be particularly advantaged in this respect. The state, a party to every criminal action, is an example of a high-status litigant by virtue of its wealth and degree of organization. Researchers have noted that its agents, especially the police, rely heavily on the community for information about crime.[14] They routinely receive intelligence from the owners of businesses, people who manage apartment complexes, school principals, former victims, and the like (Ericson, 1981: 117–127).[15] Typically, these people have no relationship to the victim the state presently represents and have good standing in the community. If called on to testify, they tend to be highly effective witnesses. The state also enjoys ready access to professional evidence. Both police and prosecutors often employ their own investigators, have access to forensic laboratories and large bodies of computer-stored information, and are connected to a network of expert witnesses (e.g., firearms specialists, pathologists).

The net result is that in the typical criminal case the prosecution has five witnesses and the defense two (Kalven and Zeisel, 1966: 136).[16] This makes a difference. Experimental research shows that both sides' chance of success increases with the number of witnesses they call (Calder, Insko, and Yandell, 1974; Wolf and Bugaj, 1990). Moreover, the prosecution has higher quality witnesses: police appear for the state in three out of every four trials and experts in one out of every four. By contrast, the typical defense witnesses are the defendant (82%) and his or her family and friends (47%). Experts appear for the defense in only 6% of cases (Kalven and Zeisel, 1966: 137–140). Thus, by comparison with the defense attorney, the prosecutor generally "does not face a problem of credibility with respect to his evidence since most of his witnesses are agents who are higher in the hierarchy of credibility" (Ericson and Baranek, 1982: 206). Nine out of every ten felony defendants facing a trial therefore plead guilty (Boland, Mahanna, and

[14]The state is sometimes at a disadvantage in recruiting evidence from groups with less influence, such as the young, the poor, minorities, and prisoners. Observers have noted, for example, that members of ethnic and racial minorities in societies as diverse as the United States, Finland, and Israel are reluctant to provide legal officials with accurate information about crimes (see Simon, 1991: 34, 399–400; Gronfors, 1986: 108; Ginat, 1987: 120). Though the authorities often consider this behavior to indicate a lack of civic responsibility, to the people themselves it appears to represent an ongoing attempt to retain control over their own conflicts (see generally Black, 1983a).

[15]Consequently, the backing of state officials can be of help to anybody seeking evidence. An investigator working for a civil rights group, for example, reports that he received significantly more cooperation from legal officials and citizens after he was issued an identification card by his local police department (Stanton, 1992: 152–153).

[16]It might be argued that the reason the state typically has more witnesses than the defense in criminal cases is that the state bears the burden of proof. However, there are two weaknesses with this argument. First, if the state's case is at all strong, the defense will need witnesses to answer the state's points. Second, the defense can call character witnesses, whereas the state cannot.

Sones, 1992: 3). Of those who do not, three out of four lose at trial anyway (ibid: 6). Having credible witnesses can even affect the sentence imposed. In Georgia, a significant factor in predicting the imposition of the death penalty in homicide cases, even after controlling for some 230 other variables, is whether the prosecution's principal witness is a police officer or a citizen with no credibility problems (Baldus, Woodworth, and Pulaski, 1990: 625).[17]

## WITNESSES FOR INDIVIDUALS

Individuals also differ among themselves in their ability to attract high-quality evidence. Since research shows that "people develop relations with people like themselves" (Burt, 1992: 12), high-status people will tend to have high-status family members and friends who may be of assistance when disputes arise. Wealthy people convicted of white-collar crimes, for instance, can usually evoke character and other mitigating testimony from affluent and law-abiding colleagues and associates (Mann, 1985: 204, 220–222). But even without a prior relationship, their strong gravitational attraction makes their cases more appealing, enabling them to mobilize high-status and relationally distant partisans, such as respected attorneys and experienced expert witnesses.

These advantages will not be available in the ordinary course of things to, say, an unemployed manual worker. The pool of potential witnesses available to this litigant will typically be considerably less effective in fighting legal battles. Many of them are likely to be handicapped by low-status characteristics, such as poverty and low levels of education. Some may themselves be unemployed or tainted by a criminal record. Even if they are of high status, they are unlikely to "go to bat" for the litigant to the same degree as they would for a more socially exalted friend. The result is that in a factual dispute with a high-status adversary the chance that this litigant will prevail is low; his version of events will almost invariably appear less convincing.[18]

A Georgia case illustrates some of these patterns. The defendant, a wealthy businessman well-known in his community, was charged with child molestation. He called 10 character witnesses. They included an assistant district attorney, a clergyman, a school administrator, a businessman, a police officer, a school teacher, a librarian, and an elderly neighbor with deep roots in the community. Though low-

[17]Similarly, the typical civil case in the United States involves an organizational plaintiff and an individual defendant (Wanner, 1974), a case structure that should work to the advantage of the plaintiff in attracting evidence and thereby help to explain the greater success rate in civil litigation of organizations (Wanner, 1975).

[18]Wealthy and respectable individuals are not only able to attract high-quality witnesses to their cause, they can also rely on their own intrinsic credibility. Analogous to the Matthew effect in science under which eminent scientists get disproportionate recognition for their achievements (Merton, 1968), a double advantage operates in these situations when the testimony of those viewed as influential is reinforced by the influential testimony of others. (The Matthew effect is named after a passage in Saint Matthew's gospel: "For unto every one that hath shall be given, and he shall have abundance: but from he that hath not shall be taken away even that which he hath.")

status defendants can sometimes attract the support of one, or maybe two, high-status individuals, support of this standing and volume is largely confined to those who enjoy the twin advantages of high social stature and many strong connections.

Another benefit individuals may have, independent of social status, is an extensive network of more distant social relationships consisting of acquaintances and associates. As argued above, people with a wide circle of family and friends have a reservoir of support from which they can draw, and this can be extremely effective in fighting legal battles. But because intimate witnesses carry less weight than distant witnesses, it also pays litigants to have less intimate ties. These relationships are valuable for a number of reasons. However tenuous and indirect they might appear, they can make the difference between the witness appearing and not appearing; they seem, as noted above, to have subtle but advantageous effects on the partisanship of testimony; and they generate inherently convincing evidence because of the greater relational distance involved. Most important, though, distant relationships may create a bridge to individuals outside the party's immediate circle, such as those in specialized fields of knowledge or even strangers (Granovetter, 1973). To have lots of contacts, however superficial, is itself an advantage in the evidentiary process.[19]

When both parties are wealthy, respectable, and connected to distant others, they can each attract evidence from elevated and distant regions of social space. Under these circumstances, cases tend to become more complex as each side tenders large quantities of plausible evidence. Experts or other high-quality witnesses present credible but conflicting testimony on different issues for each party. For example, in the von Bulow case—described earlier—the defendant and his wife were each of very high social status. After the defendant was charged with the attempted murder of his spouse, eminent doctors appeared for both the prosecution and the defense to support sharply conflicting medical theories of the facts (Dershowitz, 1986: 225–229, 234–237). Cases such as this demonstrate that the complexity of the evidence is not simply a product of the events in dispute but is also a function of the social characteristics of the parties (see also McBarnet, 1981: 147–148; Green, 1989: 114).

## CONCLUSION

Evidence is the currency in which legal cases are transacted. The amount and quality of evidence helps to determine whether crimes will be cleared, prosecutions brought, the gravity of the charges levied, the decision to plead or go to trial, the likelihood of a conviction, and the length of any sentence imposed. The same is true of civil cases: Issues of evidence are central to the making and winning of complaints at all stages of the process. Despite its importance, surprising-

---

[19]One resource lawyers bring to cases are their own ties. These ties can prove useful in attracting relationally distant evidence to their clients' cases (e.g., Dees, 1991: 171, 174).

ly little is known about the social origins of evidence. I have attempted to address this lacuna, citing data from a number of sources indicating that people have varying capacities to mount a strong evidentiary case. Thus, individuals possessing the advantages of high status and strong social ties tend to generate more supporting evidence. Furthermore, high status parties and those with extensive weak ties have the additional advantage of being able to attract more credible supporting evidence. More specifically, it can be said that holding constant the disputed behavior, in legal cases *the quantity of supporting evidence increases with the principal parties' social status and the number of intimate ties they have*, and *the quality of supporting evidence increases with the principal parties' social status and the number of distant ties they have.*[20]

These propositions, themselves implied by Black's more general theory of partisanship, do not assume that evidence is wholly social. But neither do they exhaust the range of social patterns in the production of evidence. For example, membership in large and dispersed professional groups often generates strong partisanship, even though the individual members are relationally distant from one another.[21] Likewise, nonintimate dependent relationships (e.g., suspect-prosecutor) are often a source of highly partisan testimony. More tellingly, the poor and socially isolated are not always disadvantaged. Sometimes they act (to borrow a term from chaos theory; see Gleick, 1987: 119–154) as "strange attractors" obtaining support from high-status individuals or organizations. Quirks of witness mobilization may therefore explain why low-status parties sometimes prevail against high-status parties (Baumgartner, 1992: 148–149). These are among the many areas in which more information is needed.

Though they are far from being the final word, the propositions nonetheless indicate the weakness of the distinction sometimes drawn between the legal and the social dimension of cases (see, e.g., Hagan, 1974; Lizotte, 1978; Nagel, 1983). Useful though this dichotomy may have been in establishing the legitimacy of sociological analyses of legal phenomena, it assigns too modest a role to sociological factors. The diverse data presented here, unsystematic though they are, combine to demonstrate that the evidence in a case is not a straightforward reflection of what happened but is mediated by the parties' relationships and social standing. Consequently, quantitative analyses of legal decisions that apportion legal outcomes to the strength of the evidence or the seriousness of the defendant's conduct, on the one hand, and the social characteristics of the parties, on the other, systematically underestimate the social dimension of law. Evidentiary strength and offense seriousness are themselves at least partially explained by the social composition of the case. Legal cases do not have an asocial legal core.

[20]Since these propositions require the underlying events to be held constant, they are best tested experimentally, although other methods may also be appropriate.

[21]To cite one example: In a modern English case, a baby born with Down's syndrome, not wanted by its parents, died as a result of overdosing with an analgesic drug and subsequent contraction of bronchopneumonia (Smith, 1989: 81–84). The pediatrician treating the baby was charged with murder, but acquitted after the prosecutor "found every specialist pediatric facility in Britain closed to inquiries, and that no pediatrician was prepared to appear as a prosecution expert witness" (ibid: 82).

The propositions suggest as well that the relationship between evidence and the outcome of cases based on the social characteristics of the litigants ("discrimination") requires reevaluation. As O'Barr (1982) and others have shown, the credibility of testimony depends not just on what is alleged but also on who alleges it. I have argued that whether and how evidence is presented in the first place is itself a function of the status and ties of the parties. Together, these two lines of attack suggest that far from eliminating the role of social variables, as is traditionally believed, evidence provides the medium through which these variables permeate the factual center of legal disputes. This is not to deny that evidence may reduce discrimination in this sense. A legal system that paid much less attention to evidence might be a lot more concerned with who the parties are (though there are no data on the point). Even so, the idea that evidence is external to any discrimination in legal decisionmaking is insupportable. The relationship between the two is more complex and subtle than is conventionally allowed. In important ways, evidence facilitates legal discrimination.

One explanation of why relatively little attention has been devoted to the discriminatory role of evidence is that its social bases are often difficult to detect, especially after the case has concluded. There is a dearth of first-hand information about the early stages of legal disputes. And the official documents on which researchers often rely rarely reveal that a case was not investigated in much depth, that important witnesses did not come forward, or that crucial testimony might have been presented in a very different manner. Thus, some partisan effects operate before the empirical events harden into legal facts; others take root beyond the gaze of legal officials; many leave no trace. Evidence is therefore something of a veiled source of discrimination for particular categories of litigants. Legal sociologists have long been aware of the principal social mechanisms by which the "haves come out ahead": they are repeat players, have better lawyers, can exploit institutional passivity, and because the rules favor them (Galanter, 1974). But if the two propositions presented here are correct, high-status and well-connected litigants in addition enjoy the considerable advantage of being able to put together a convincing story. They shape legal reality itself.

## REFERENCES

Adams, Randall, William Hoffer, and Marilyn Mona Hoffer. 1991. *Adams v. Texas*. New York: St. Martin's Press.

Allen, John. 1977. *Assault with a Deadly Weapon: The Autobiography of a Street Criminal*. New York: McGraw-Hill.

Baldus, David C., George Woodworth, and Charles A. Pulaski Jr., 1990. *Equal Justice and the Death Penalty: A Legal and Empirical Analysis*. Boston: Northeastern University Press.

Bartlett, Robert. 1986. *Trial by Fire and Water: The Medieval Judicial Ordeal*. Oxford: Clarendon Press.

Barton, R. F. 1919. *Ifugao Law*. Berkeley: University of California Press, 1969.

Baumgartner, M.P. 1992. "The myth of discretion." In *The Uses of Discretion,* edited by Keith Hawkins. Oxford: Clarendon Press.

————. 1993. "Violent networks: the origins and management of domestic conflict." In *Violence and Aggression: The Social Interactionist Perspective,* edited by Richard B. Felson and James Tedeschi. Washington: American Psychological Association.

Beckstrom, John H. 1989. *Evolutionary Jurisprudence: Prospects and Limitations on the Use of Modern Darwinism Throughout the Legal Process.* Urbana: University of Illinois Press.

Bentham, Jeremy. 1827. *Rationale of Judicial Evidence.* New York: Garland, 1978.

Black, Donald. 1971. "The social organization of arrest." *Stanford Law Review* 23: 1087–1111.

————. 1976. *The Behavior of Law.* New York: Academic Press.

————. 1979. "A strategy of pure sociology." In *Theoretical Perspectives in Sociology,* edited by Scott McNall. New York: St. Martin's Press.

————. 1980. *The Manners and Customs of the Police.* New York: Academic Press.

————. 1983a."Crime as social control." *American Sociological Review* 48: 34–45.

————. 1983b. Lecture in "Sociology of Law" course. Harvard Law School, Spring semester.

————. 1989. *Sociological Justice.* New York: Oxford University Press.

————. 1993. "Taking sides." Chapter 7 in *The Social Structure of Right and Wrong,* by Donald Black. San Diego: Academic Press.

Black, Donald, and M.P. Baumgartner. 1983. "Toward a theory of the third party." In *Empirical Theories about Courts,* edited by Keith O. Boyum and Lynn Mather. New York: Longman.

Bohannan, Paul. 1957. *Justice and Judgment among the Tiv.* London: Oxford University Press.

Boland, Barbara, Paul Mahanna, and Ronald Sones. 1992. *The Prosecution of Felony Arrests, 1988.* Washington: U.S. Department of Justice.

Brown, Peter. 1975. "Society and the supernatural: a medieval change." *Daedalus* 104: 133–151.

Burt, Ronald S. 1992. *Structural Holes: The Social Structure of Competition.* Cambridge: Harvard University Press.

Caenegem, R. C. van. 1991. "Methods of proof in Western medieval law." In *Legal History: A European Perspective.* London: Hambledon Press.

Calder, Bobby J., Chester A. Insko, and Ben Yandell. 1974. "The relation of cognitive and memorial processes to persuasion in a simulated jury trial." *Journal of Applied Social Psychology* 4: 62–93.

Caplow, Theodore. 1968. *Two against One: Coalition in Triads.* Engelwood Cliffs: Prentice-Hall.

Carlin, Jerome E., and Jan Howard. 1965. "Legal representation and class justice." *UCLA Law Review* 12: 381–437.

Carlson, Ronald L., Edward J. Imwinkelreid, and Edward J. Kionka. 1991. *Evidence in the Nineties: Cases, Materials and Problems for an Age of Science and Statutes.* Charlottesville: Michie.

Chevigny, Paul. 1969. *Police Power: Police Abuses in New York City.* New York: Vintage Press.

Cicourel, Aaron V. 1968. *The Social Organization of Juvenile Justice.* New York: John Wiley and Sons.

Cohen, L. Jonathan. 1977. *The Probable and the Provable.* Oxford: Clarendon Press.

Colson, Elizabeth. 1953. "Social control and vengeance in Plateau Tonga society." *Africa* 23: 199–212.

Cooney, Mark. 1988. The Social Control of Homicide: A Cross-Cultural Study. Unpublished S.J.D. dissertation, Harvard Law School.

————. 1991. Law, Morality, and Conscience: The Social Control of Homicide in Modern America. Unpublished doctoral dissertation, Department of Sociology, University of Virginia.

Coyle, Marcia, Fred Strasser, and Marianne Lavelle. 1990. "Fatal defense." *National Law Journal* (June 11): 30–44.

Daly, Kathleen. 1987. "Discrimination in the criminal courts: family, gender, and the problem of equal treatment." *Social Forces* 66: 152–175.

Dees, Morris (with Steve Fiffer). 1991. *A Season For Justice: The Life and Times of Civil Rights Lawyer Morris Dees.* New York: Simon and Schuster.

Dershowitz, Alan M. 1986. *Reversal of Fortune: Inside the von Bulow Case.* New York: Pocket Books.

Eckhoff, Torstein. 1967. "The mediator, the judge and the administrator in conflict resolution." *Acta Sociologica* 10: 148–172.

Eggleston, Richard. 1983. *Evidence, Proof and Probability.* London: Widenfield and Nicolson.

Engel, David M. 1984. "The oven bird's song: insiders, outsiders, and personal injuries in an American community." *Law and Society Review* 18: 551–582.

Ericson, Richard V. 1981. *Making Crime: A Study of Detective Work*. Toronto: Butterworths.

————. 1982. *Reproducing Order: A Study of Police Patrol Work*. Toronto: University of Toronto Press.

Ericson, Richard V., and Patricia M. Baranek. 1982. *The Ordering of Justice: A Study of Accused Persons as Dependents in the Criminal Process*. Toronto: University of Toronto Press.

Evans-Pritchard. E.E. 1940. *The Nuer: A Description of the Modes of Livelihood and Political Institutions of a Nilotic People*. New York: Oxford University Press.

Farrell, Ronald A., and Victoria Lynn Swigert. 1978. "Legal dispositions of intra-group and inter-group homicides." *Sociological Quarterly* 19: 565–576.

Feynman, Richard B. 1985. *"Surely You're Joking, Mr. Feynman!": Adventures of a Curious Character*. New York: W.W. Norton.

Frank, Jerome. 1949. *Courts on Trial: Myth and Reality in American Justice*. Princeton: Princeton University Press.

Galanter, Marc. 1974. "Why the 'haves' come out ahead: speculations on the limits of legal change." *Law and Society Review* 9: 95–160.

Geertz, Clifford. 1983. "Local knowledge: fact and law in comparative perspective." In *Local Knowledge: Further Essays in Interpretive Anthropology*. New York: Basic Books.

Ginat, Joseph. 1987. *Blood Disputes among Bedouin and Rural Arabs in Israel: Revenge, Mediation, Outcasting, and Family Honor*. Pittsburgh: University of Pittsburgh Press.

Gleick, James. 1987. *Chaos: Making a New Science*. New York: Viking.

Gluckman, Max. 1967. *The Judicial Process among the Barotse of Northern Rhodesia*. Manchester: Manchester University Press.

Graham, Michael H. 1985. *Witness Intimidation: The Law's Response*. Westport: Quorum Books.

Granovetter, Mark. 1973. "The strength of weak ties." *American Journal of Sociology* 78: 1360–1380.

Green, Jeremy. 1989. "Industrial ill health, expertise, and the law." In *Expert Evidence: Interpreting Science in the Law*, edited by Roger Smith and Brian Wynne. London: Routledge.

Gronfors, Maarti. 1986. "Social control and law in the Finnish gypsy community: blood feuding as a system of justice." *Journal of Legal Pluralism and Unofficial Law* 24: 101–125.

Gulson, J.R. 1905. *The Philosophy of Proof and its Relation to the English Law of Judicial Evidence*. Littleton: Fred B. Rothman, 1990.

Hagan, John. 1974. "Extra-legal attributes and criminal sentencing: an assessment of a sociological viewpoint." *Law and Society Review* 8: 357–383.

Haward, Lionel R.C. 1982. "Establishing the probity of testimony through experimental psychology." In *Reconstructing the Past: The Role of Psychologists in Criminal Trials*, edited by Arne Trankell. Deventer, The Netherlands: Kluwer.

Holmstrom, Lynda Lytle, and Ann Wolbert Burgess. 1983. *The Victim of Rape: Institutional Reactions*. New Bunswick: Transaction Press.

Hood, Roger (in collaboration with Graça Cordovil). 1992. *Race and Sentencing: A Study in the Crown Court*. A Report for the Commission for Racial Equality. Oxford: Clarendon Press.

Hunt, Jennifer, and Peter Manning. 1991. "The social context of police lying." *Symbolic Interaction* 14: 51–70.

Jeans, James W., Sr. 1992. *Litigation*. Three Volumes. Charlottesville: Michie.

Just, Peter. 1986. "Let the evidence fit the crime: evidence, law and 'sociological truth' among the Dou Donggo." *American Ethnologist* 13: 43–61.

Kalven, Harry Jr., and Hans Zeisel. 1966. *The American Jury*. Boston: Little, Brown.

Kaplan, John, Jon R. Waltz, and Roger C. Park. 1992. *Cases and Materials on Evidence*. Westbury: Foundation Press.

Kassin, Saul M., and Lawrence S. Wrightsman. 1985. *The Psychology of Evidence and Trial Procedure*. Beverly Hills: Sage Publications.

LaFree, Gary D. 1989. *Rape and Criminal Justice: The Social Construction of Sexual Assault*. Belmont: Wadsworth.

Langbein, John H. 1977. *Torture and the Law of Proof*. Chicago: University of Chicago Press.

Lea, Henry Charles. 1892. *Superstition and Force: Essays on The Wager of Law, The Wager of Battle, The Ordeal, Torture*. New York: B. Blom, 1971.

Lewicki, Roy J., Stephen Weiss, and David Lewin. 1992. "Models of conflict, negotiation and third-party intervention: a review and synthesis." *Journal of Organizational Behavior* 13: 209–252.

Lizotte, Alan J. 1978. "Extra-legal factors in Chicago's criminal courts: testing the conflict model of criminal justice." *Social Problems* 25: 564–580.

Loftus, Elizabeth. 1979. *Eyewitness Testimony*. Cambridge: Harvard University Press.

Lundsgaarde, Henry P. 1977. *Murder In Space City: A Cultural Analysis of Houston Homicide Patterns*. New York: Oxford University Press.

McAlary, Mike. 1990. *Cop Shot: The True Story of a Murder that Shocked a Nation*. New York: Jove Books.

McBarnet, Doreen. 1981. *Conviction: Law, the State and the Construction of Justice*. London: Macmillan.

McConville, Mike, Andrew Sanders, and Roger Leng. 1991. *The Case for the Prosecution*. London: Routledge.

MacCormack, Geoffrey. 1990. *Traditional Chinese Penal Law*. Edinburgh: Edinburgh University Press.

Mann, Kenneth. 1985. *Defending White-Collar Crime: A Portrait of Attorneys at Work*. New Haven: Yale University Press.

Matthiessen, Peter. 1983. *In the Spirit of Crazy Horse*. New York: Viking, 1991.

Merry, Sally Engle. 1982. "The social organization of mediation in nonindustrial societies: implications for informal community justice in America." In *The Politics of Informal Justice*, Volume 2: *Comparative Studies*, edited by Richard L. Abel. New York: Academic Press.

Merton, Robert K. 1968. "The Matthew effect in science." *Science* 159: 55–63.

Moore, Sally Falk. 1992. "Treating law as knowledge: telling colonial officers what to say to Africans about running 'their own' native courts." *Law and Society Review* 26: 11–46.

Morrill, Calvin, and Peter C. Facciola. 1992. "The power of language in adjudication and mediation: institutional context as predictors of social evaluation." *Law and Social Inquiry* 17: 191–212.

Myers, Martha A., and John Hagan. 1979. "Private and public trouble: prosecutors and the allocation of court resources." *Social Problems* 26: 439–459.

Nader, Laura. 1969. "Styles of court procedure: to make the balance." In *Law in Culture and Society*, edited by Laura Nader. Chicago: Aldine.

Nagel, Ilene H. 1983. "The legal/extra-legal controversy: judicial decisions in pretrial release." *Law and Society Review* 17: 481–515.

Nash, June. 1967. "Death as a way of life: the increasing resort to homicide in a Mayan Indian community." *American Anthropologist* 69: 455–470.

O'Barr, William M. 1982. *Linguistic Evidence: Language, Power, and Strategy in the Courtroom*. New York: Academic Press.

Piliavin, Irving M., and Scott Briar. 1964. "Police encounters with juveniles." *American Journal of Sociology* 70: 206–214.

Pollock, Frederick, and Frederic William Maitland. 1898. *The History of English Law: Before the Time of Edward 1*. Two volumes. Cambridge: Cambridge University Press, 1968.

Porter, Bruce. 1982. "California prison gangs: the price of control." *Corrections Magazine* 6: 6–19.

Posner, Richard A. 1990. *The Problems of Jurisprudence*. Cambridge: Harvard University Press.

Pospisil, Leopold. 1971. *Anthropology of Law: A Comparative Theory*. New York: Harper and Row.

Reskin, Barbara A., and Christy A. Visher. 1986. "The impact of evidence and extralegal factors in jurors' decisions." *Law and Society Review* 20: 423–438.

Roberts, John M. 1965. "Oaths, autonomic ordeals, and power." *American Anthropologist* 67 (Special Publication on The Ethnography of Law, edited by Laura Nader): 186–212.

Rosen, Lawrence. 1980–81. "Equity and discretion in a modern Islamic legal system." *Law and Society Review* 15: 217–245.

———. 1989. *The Anthropology of Justice: Law as Culture in Islamic Society*. Cambridge: Cambridge University Press.

Rubinstein, Jonathan. 1973. *City Police*. New York: Ballantine Books.

Sanders, Andrew. 1987. "Constructing the case for the prosecution." *Journal of Law and Society* 14: 229–253.

Sanders, William B. 1977. *Detective Work: A Study of Criminal Investigations*. New York: Free Press.

Scheppele, Kim Lane. 1988. *Legal Secrets: Equality and Efficiency in the Common Law*. Chicago: University of Chicago Press.

———. 1991. "Facing facts in legal interpretation." In *Law and the Order of Culture*, edited by Robert Post. Berkeley: University of California Press.

Senechal de la Roche, Roberta. 1990. *The Sociogenesis of a Race Riot: Springfield, Illinois in 1908*. Urbana: University of Illinois Press.

Shakur, Sanyika. 1993. *Monster: The Autobiography of an L.A. Gang Member*. New York: Penguin.

Sheppard, Blair H., and Neil Vidmar. 1980. "Adversary pretrial procedures and testimonial evidence: effects of lawyers's role and Machiavellianism." *Journal of Personality and Social Psychology* 39: 320–332.

Simon, David. 1991. *Homicide: A Year on the Killing Streets*. New York: Fawcett Columbine.

Skolnick, Jerome H. 1966. *Justice without Trial: Law Enforcement in Democratic Society*. New York: John Wiley and Sons.

Smith, Roger. 1989. "Forensic pathology, scientific expertise, and the criminal law." In *Expert Evidence: Interpreting Science in the Law*, edited by Roger Smith and Brian Wynne. London: Routledge.

Smith, David J., and Jeremy Gray. 1985. *Police and People in London: The PSI Report*. Aldershot: Gower.

Stanko, Elizabeth Anne. 1981–82. "The impact of victim assessment on prosecutors' screening decisions: the case of the New York County District Attorney's Office." *Law and Society Review* 16: 225–239.

Stanton, Bill. 1992. *Klanwatch: Bringing the Ku Klux Klan to Justice*. New York: Mentor.

Tillers, Peter, and Eric D. Green. 1988. *Probability and Inference in the Law of Evidence: The Uses and Limits of Bayesianism*. Dordrecht, The Netherlands: Kluwer Academic Publishers.

Twining, William (editor). 1983. *Facts in Law*. Wiesbaden, Germany: Franz Steiner Verlag.

Twining, William, and Alex Stein (editors). 1992. *Evidence and Proof*. New York: New York University Press.

Vera Institute of Justice. 1977. *Felony Arrests: Their Prosecution and Disposition in New York City's Courts*. New York: Vera Institute of Justice.

Waegel, William B. 1981. "Case routinization in investigative police work." *Social Problems* 28: 263–275.

Wanner, Craig. 1974. "The public ordering of private relations. Part one: initiating civil cases in urban trial courts." *Law and Society Review* 8: 421–440.

———. 1975. "The public ordering of private relations. Part two: winning civil court cases." *Law and Society Review* 9: 293–306.

Wells, Gary L., and Elizabeth Loftus (editors). 1984. *Eyewitness Testimony:Psychological Perspectives*. Cambridge: Cambridge University Press.

Williams, Kipling D., Elizabeth F. Loftus, and Kenneth A. Deffenbacher. 1992. "Eyewitness evidence and identification." In *Handbook of Psychology and Law*, edited by D.K. Kagehiro and W.S. Laufer. New York: Springer-Verlag.

Wolf, Saron, and Albert M. Bugaj. 1990. "The social impact of courtroom witnesses." *Social Behaviour* 5: 1–13.

# 9

# STRUCTURE AND PRACTICE OF FAMILIAL-BASED JUSTICE IN A CRIMINAL COURT*

## KATHLEEN DALY

### INTRODUCTION

A variety of theories have been advanced to explain gender differences in criminal court outcomes. They include court paternalism (e.g., Nagel and Weitzman, 1971; Moulds, 1980; Curran, 1983); gender differences in informal social control (Hagan *et al.,* 1979; Kruttschnitt, 1982; 1984; extending upon Black, 1976); sociostructural "typescripts" by which men exercise institutional hegemony by maintaining women's familial labor (Harris, 1977); and multifactor explanations that include court chivalry, attributions of male and female criminality, and the practical problems of jailing women with children (Simon, 1975; Steffensmeier, 1980). Each attempts to explain a body of statistical evidence showing that women are sentenced more leniently than men (see Parisi, 1982; Nagel and Hagan, 1983; Chesney-Lind, 1986).

These theories all evince a common problem: None has been grounded in a systematic study of the decisionmaking processes of court officials. For example, those who have found significant sex effects favoring women say these differences arise from "court paternalism." Yet how do we know that paternalism structures court officials' reactions to men and women? How do we know that other interpretations of officials' reasoning are more accurate? Although sentencing studies may reveal more lenient outcomes for women, they tell us little about how court officials arrive at these decisions.[1]

*This research was supported by a fellowship grant from the National Institute of Justice. My thanks to Aida Rodriguez for her encouragement, research assistance, and friendship.

[1]As Maynard (1982) suggests in his critique of "variable analysis," this problem obtains generally

Concerned with the paucity of qualitative evidence on how gender enters into the "commonsense reasoning practices" and "conceptions of justice" (Feeley, 1979: 284; Maynard, 1982: 347) of court personnel, I observed court proceedings and interviewed court officials (prosecutors, defense attorneys, probation officers, and judges) in a western Massachusetts courthouse from October 1981 through January 1982. Reported here are the results from my interviews with 35 officials concerning their considerations in sentencing men and women. The interviews reveal a pattern of responses not adequately explained by existing theory but instead consistent with a model I call *familial paternalism*. Before illustrating how this familial-based logic is used in the adjudication process and how it affects the court's response to men and women, I shall review extant theory.

## THEORETICAL REVIEW

Current theoretical explanations for the more lenient treatment of female defendants are court paternalism toward women, multifactor explanations, and social control arguments.

### PATERNALISM

The most frequent explanation in the literature is that judges and other court officials try to protect women as the "weaker sex," from the stigma of a criminal record or the harshness of jail.[2] Precisely why such a notion might arise in the criminal courts and how officials justify this gender-based disparity have not, however, received empirical attention. Typically, researchers either interpret statistics indicating that women are favored as evidence of judicial paternalistic attitudes (e.g., Nagel and Weitzman, 1971; Moulds, 1980; Curran, 1983), or conclude that "widespread conviction" (Martin, 1934: 58) and "popular beliefs" (Baab and Furgeson, 1967: 497) offer convincing proof. Feminist critiques of the paternalism thesis include Klein's (1973) argument that only a few women before the court (white and middle class) may be subject to court protection, Moulds's (1980) concern that the protection of women as the "weaker sex" reflects unequal power relations between men and women, and Chesney-Lind's (1978) and Edwards's (1984) conclusions that paternalistic treatment can promote more harsh outcomes for women.

---

for American criminal court research and is not specific to research on gender differences. Although Kruttschnitt (1984) and Kruttschnitt and Green (1984) present evidence of probation officers' evaluations of female defendants, and Simon (1975: 108–110) refers to her interviews with 30 midwestern judges and prosecutors, the kind of qualitative research on gender in the criminal courts conducted by British scholars (e.g., Eaton, 1983; 1985; Edwards, 1984) has yet to be seriously entertained by their counterparts in the United States (but see Lipetz, 1984).

[2]Like Nagel and Hagan (1983), I will consider chivalrous and paternalistic treatment to be synonymous, though Moulds's (1980) discussion of their differing meanings is useful. Note that paternalism is rarely defined precisely and can even by defined differently by the same author (compare, e.g., Nagel, 1969, with Nagel and Weitzman, 1971).

Although scholars continue to debate whether paternalism generates more lenient or more harsh treatment of women (Nagel and Hagan, 1983: 115), the concept is so entrenched in the literature that few have raised the more fundamental and more critical question: Do court officials use paternalistic reasoning, that is, are they in fact concerned with protecting women?

## MULTIFACTOR EXPLANATIONS

Simon (1975) and Steffensmeier (1980) identify several factors in addition to paternalism that bear on gender differences in court outcomes. Both emphasize the difficulty judges have in jailing women with children. Steffensmeier also suggests that court officials hold differing gender-based conceptions of the seriousness of criminality (men are perceived as more dangerous) and of the potential for reform (women are viewed as more easily directed to law-abiding behavior). In addition to assessing the merits of the paternalism thesis, another aim of my interviews was to determine whether judges find it difficult to jail women with children and, if so, why. I also wanted to see if court personnel believed that women had greater potential for reform than men.

## SOCIAL CONTROL ARGUMENTS

Kruttschnitt (1982;1984) and Kruttschnitt and Green (1984) use social control arguments to explain gender differences in the treatment of defendants, and Hagan et al. (1979) use them to explain gender differences in juvenile offending rates. Their arguments center on the impact of an inverse relationship between informal and formal social controls for the criminal involvement, arrest, and sanctioning of men and women.

As applied to criminal court practices, a social control explanation takes the following form: The more tied a person is to others (e.g., family members), the more that person is subject to informal social control; thus, the chances for future law-abiding behavior are greater, and the need for formal social control (especially penal sanctions) is reduced. To explain gender differences in criminal court outcomes, Kruttschnitt (1982: 496–498) and Kruttschnitt and Green (1984: 542–543) suggest that the differences in the amount of informal (i.e., familial) social control in the lives of men and women promote differences in the degree to which they will be subject to formal control. Further, they argue that informal social control is greater in women's than men's lives because women are more likely to be economically dependent on others (e.g., a spouse or the state). Their interpretation of why women are less likely to be subject to formal social control differs from the view of Harris (1977). He theorizes that women are less likely to be incarcerated than men not because women are more dependent on others, but because men have an interest in maintaining women's familial labor in the home.

Does social control reasoning operate in criminal court decision making? Does it explain differences in the court's treatment of men and women? I explore these questions, together with the different ways in which Kruttschnitt and Harris explain why women are less likely subject to jail time than men. Does leniency arise because women are more likely than men to be dependent on others, or because men are dependent on women's familial labor?

## JURISDICTION, OBSERVATIONS, AND INTERVIEWS

I conducted the research in the Springfield, Massachusetts, Hall of Justice, a building housing both the lower (District) and the upper (Superior) criminal courts. Located in a city of some 152,000 residents, the Springfield court's annual case-load ranks third to that in the Boston and Worcester area courts. In comparison to the Springfield population, defendants appearing before the court are more likely to be young, members of minority groups, and male—a profile typical in state criminal court samples.[3] My observational study of the lower court's routines and dispositions showed patterns similar to those in other jurisdictions: Most cases are disposed of by guilty plea, a minority of defendants receive jail sentences (Feeley, 1979), and the individualized decisionmaking model is utilized (Hogarth, 1971; Gaylin, 1974; Rossett and Cressey, 1986; Heumann, 1978; Mann et al., 1980; Maynard, 1982).[4]

Although observations of courtroom discourse can reveal how justice is constructed in a public forum, I was interested in how court personnel themselves describe their decisionmaking processes. Specifically, how do they reach the sentencing decision? How, if at all, might this process vary depending on the sex of the defendant? The 35 court officials interviewed worked in the upper and lower courts, and included 11 judges, 9 court probation officers, 6 prosecutors, and 9 defense attorneys (see Table 1).[5] Interviews lasted from 1 to 2 hours, and the responses were recorded by shorthand.

[3]In 1980 the Springfield population was 75% white, 16% black, and 9% Hispanic. During the 25 days of observation in the lower court, 60% of the defendants whose cases were disposed were white, 20% were black, and 20% were Hispanic; 80% were male.

[4]The results of the observational study (Daly, 1983) are remarkably similar to Eaton's (1983) study of a British magistrate's court. Both of us find that: (1) sentences in the lower court were similar for men and women, a result attributed to the typically routine and low-stakes nature of cases disposed (i.e., few jail sentences); and (2) the defendant's work and familial situation was the major biographical element used by defense attorneys to explain the incident and justify a sentence.

[5]The number of judges includes all those sitting on the bench during December 1981 and January 1982. Among prosecutors, I selected the more senior, full-time, individuals. I chose 4 of the 8 lower court probation officers who worked in the courtroom, together with the head of the District Court's probation department; in Superior Court, I chose the probation officers based on varying years of experience and differing viewpoints. Of the 9 defense lawyers, 5 were public defenders; the remainder were private attorneys working daily in the upper and lower courts. I oversampled women in comparison to their proportions as court personnel to see if there were gender differences in court officials' perceptions of the handling of male and female defendants. Although some differences were found, male and female court workers' conceptions of justice were quite similar.

TABLE 1    Court Personnel Interviewed

|  | District Court | Superior Court | Total | N Female |
|---|---|---|---|---|
| Judges | 5 | 6 | 11 | 3 |
| Probation officers | 5 | 4 | 9 | 3 |
| Prosecutors | 3 | 3 | 6 | 2 |
| Defense attorneys | (worked in both courts) | | 9 | 2 |
| Total | 13 | 13 | 35 | 10 |

I tailored the interview to the specific concerns of each of the four groups of court officials. For example, I asked judges, "What specifically do you want to know about a defendant's background before sentencing?" while the corresponding question of prosecutors was, "In what ways do background characteristics of defendants have a bearing on making deals with defense counsel?"

Other items centered on the relations between the four groups of court workers. For example, I asked court probation officers whether judges typically heeded their recommendations or those of prosecutors, and I queried defense attorneys about their power to influence judges' decisions in comparison to that of prosecutors and court probation officers. Some questions were directed to judges only, including their response to a hypothetical sentencing situation and their reaction to the paternalism thesis. I also obtained information on the court workers' legal background. All the questions were open-ended, and the interview ended with several general questions, including "Are there things I should know about your role as _____ that I've overlooked?" and "Are there other things about the handling of male and female defendants that you think I should know?" While most interview questions centered on the identification of the factors influencing the sanctioning process and whether these varied for men and women, broader questions helped me obtain a comprehensive picture of the experience and concerns of the court personnel.

## ANALYSIS OF INTERVIEWS

To understand the context of the interview responses, it is important to know the ways in which court officials oriented themselves to the questions. Two predictable response sets emerged when I asked them what they considered in sentencing: All immediately focused on the "in-out" decision, and all emphasized case individualization.

All interpreted "the sentencing decision" to mean whether a defendant should receive jail time or probation. Thus, when contemplating the exercise of discretionary power, they reflected on the decision that poses dilemmas for them and has the greatest consequences for defendants. Wheeler *et al.* (1982) suggest that the in-out decision is the "first and hardest" for federal judges, and this holds true for these state court officials as well. The interview analysis focuses on their considerations for this particular decision, although the same types of concerns are evident for the pretrial release decision.

Case individualization was stressed by all court personnel, reflecting their emphasis on rehabilitation as a primary aim of punishment.[6] Indeed, initial reactions to the question "What factors are important to you in sentencing?" were radically individualistic, and included responses such as, "Each case is unique," "Every crime has a different set of facts," or "Defendants are all individual human beings so it is hard to say." But as Maynard (1982) and Mann *et al.* (1980) show, case individualization is patterned, even if specific selected elements of the defendant's biography and the incident are complexly interwoven. Springfield court personnel repeatedly mentioned three factors in characterizing cases: the defendant's prior record; the specific aspects of the incident, including the circumstances that gave rise to it and the defendant's motivation; and the defendant's work and family situation.

## WORK, FAMILY, AND DIFFERENTIAL TREATMENT

Court officials consistently drew on the categories of work and family in explaining why some defendants deserved leniency. The following comments serve to illustrate the major themes in a reasoning process widely shared by all court personnel.

One theme is that defendants who provide economic support or care for others deserve more lenient treatment than those without such responsibilities. I shall refer to these defendants as "familied" and "nonfamilied," respectively.[7] When identifying the factors important in sentencing, one judge said:

> Is he or she employed and what is the employment history? If you have a defendant who has worked at the same job for 5 years, has a wife and 2 children, I would be less inclined to put him in jail than one who is not working and doesn't have a wife. Otherwise, you may be short-changing the pound of flesh. You have got to think of the good for society. You try to balance equities.

Leniency toward the familied defendants is thus justified on the grounds that these defendants are more stable and have more to lose by getting into trouble again, as one prosecutor put it:

---

[6]While court workers generally emphasized rehabilitation rather than general deterrence or retribution as primary punishment goals, prosecutors and judges who had worked as prosecutors were more likely to defend the latter.

[7]A "familied man" or "familied woman" can connote different meanings, although having dependents is common to both. A familied man is married, with or without children; whereas a familied woman has children, with or without a spouse. These different connotations reveal a specific gender structure of presumed dependencies in family life.

I look at it this way. People with family responsibilities are being given a break. You can't say that singles are being treated more harshly; it's that people with dependents are being treated more leniently. There's the maxim: "There's more stability in these defendants because they have a family." The fact of being hit with incarceration, the kids being taken away from you—the chances are more likely that they won't get in trouble again.

The prosecutor's comment reveals a second theme: Leniency toward familied defendants is legitimate and just because these defendants have more informal social control in their lives and have a greater stake in normative social adulthood. Although such social control reasoning is apparent in the court's risk-taking calculus of those thought to be deserving of leniency, court officials typically justify leniency in other ways. They would repeatedly refer to the negative consequences for families and society if familied defendants were jailed. When the judge above says, "You have got to think of the good for society," he is concerned with the potential social cost of a broken family. And, as the defense attorney argues below, when familied defendants are jailed, the defendant's dependents are also punished. This attorney likes to "stress the family situation" in defense summations because if the defendant is

supporting the household and a couple of kids, you are trying to show the judge that he will be hurting other people. He should pay for it, but not other people. . . . Who is going to pay the price if we send them away? Does he pay the price, or does the family? Do the kids pay the price?

This concern with the negative consequences of jailing familied defendants anticipates a third theme: Familied women deserve greater leniency than familied men. This probation officer alludes to the "special consequences for the family unit" if women with children are jailed:

I am looking for support. Are there small children that would be better with parents? Will they need social services? Is the person employable? Is he supportive of the family? Will the incident happen again with the same family situation? For women with children, there may be special consequences for the family unit. I'm afraid to continue the defendant's problems if children are there.

The most succinct statement about what influences sentencing was made by another probation officer, who said simply, "Prior record and the intangibles." If, as all court officials said, prior record and the nature of the offense strongly inform their sentencing decisions, "the intangibles" hinge on how much informal social control features in defendants' lives, whether defendants are responsible for the welfare of others, and whether society or families can or should pay the costs that result from removing the sources of the families' economic support or care.

## FAMILY AND SOCIAL CONTROL

The general proposition of an inverse relationship between informal and formal social control rings true in the way Springfield court personnel describe their decisionmaking. A defendant's particular familial situation is a diagnostic tool that allows the court officials to weigh an appropriate sanction. However, positing this informal-formal social control relation begs the question, *why* and *how* is this diagnosis made?

For example, why is "being embedded in a family" or having "strong family ties" salient to the court? Although a complete answer to this question is beyond the scope of this chapter,[8] I highlight two related causes. First, the state does not have the resources to impose penal sanctions or intensive probation on all those found guilty; second, the state must therefore rely on others—family members or perhaps employers—to inculcate law-abiding behavior. Using the family to do the state's work can be rationalized as a more humane method of rehabilitation; as a defense attorney stated, "There is no way a state can do what a family can do better." This rationalization, however, stems from the inability of the state to implement prescribed sanctions or, perhaps alternatively, to devise less punitive sanctions.

How court officials apply social control reasoning is contingent on the nature of a defendant's familial situation. The strength and locus of informal social control vary depending upon whether the defendant has dependents or is dependent on others. As one prosecutor said:

> The characteristics that are important are: Responsibilities—who are the people dependent on the defendant? Family contact—do they have concern from parents and siblings? If concern is shown, then the defendant will be on double probation. . . . The responsibilities of family is what is important for female defendants: Will the children be the victims? Other family ties are very important, and family support is important: Will someone be at home to keep an eye on the defendant?

For familied defendants, the locus of social control comes from family members who are dependent on the defendant; but for nonfamilied defendants, social control emanates from those upon whom the defendant is dependent, or as the prosecutor suggests, "someone [who will] be at home at keep an eye on the defendant."

## Nonfamilied Defendants

Judges spoke of the positive impression created by the presence of "concerned" family members of defendants in the courtroom. They felt it was easier to be lenient toward such defendants because of the expectation that kin could provide daily supervision and rehabilitation (in essence, "familial probation") that the state could not. As one judge expressed, "Many kids feel parents give worse punishment than the court." Another judge was quite specific in describing the kind of family relation he could count on to provide informal social control for the nonfamilied man: "Sometimes you see him with his mother present, and you may say to yourself that he has been conning her for 25 years and *this* is a con. The family I like to see for men is their father or uncle, an older responsible male." In a string of characteristics describing a "17 year old male in need of maximum [rather than

---

[8]This would require a historical analysis of family–state relations and their articulation with psychological theory, penal philosophies, and the economics of institutionalization.

minimum or moderate] probation supervision," a probation officer recited the following: "10th grader, unemployed, from a broken home, living with an elderly grandma, no means of support. . . ." Thus, mothers and "elderly grandmas" may not be considered effective sources of informal social control in the lives of nonfamilied men. Whether the same notion obtains for nonfamilied women is uncertain because court officials rarely spoke of differences in informal social controls between nonfamilied men and women.

The salient factors that may differentiate treatment among the nonfamilied men and women are the presence of an active familial authority figure in the household and the defendant's employment-job training-educational situation. I say "*may* differentiate" because court personnel routinely learn that nonfamilied men and women are "living with parents" or "trying to get a job," but they are not convinced this translates into informal social control. Indeed, one judge said:

> Such things as, "He has a part-time job and lives at home with his mother and father, and he's 19 years old, etc. etc.," doesn't interest me. But if you tell me that this guy works for a children's group or other sort of helping group, that would have an effect.

What would impress this judge is whether the nonfamilied defendant is helping others. With familied defendants, however, it is evident that they are in some way helping others via their economic support or caretaking labor.

## Familied Defendants

It is assumed by court officials that familied defendants have greater informal social control in their lives than nonfamilied defendants. In the words of one judge, familied defendants are "already conforming" and "showing some responsibility":

> I am more loathe to incarcerate the family man and woman. It is harder to send someone off to jail who has family responsibilities. They are already conforming to society and the norms that we have at this time in society. They are showing some responsibility.

In their summations before sentencing, defense attorneys said they like to impress upon the court that their clients "have a lot of family support" or "care for others."[9] Recalling the pretrial advice given to a male client, a defense attorney said:

> I told my guy to get married, have a kid, settle down. You usually know what the judges want. I could say to the judge, "Look, this kid has been trying, so give him a break." If he were single and unemployed, he'd be in jail now.

If getting married and settling down is "what the judges want," does this imply that the court is rewarding familied defendants for conforming to norms of social adulthood—for being "good" fathers, husbands, wives, or mothers? In part, yes. However, court officials gave another set of reasons for being lenient to familied de-

---

[9]In some situations defense attorneys will not introduce information about their clients' familial relations. For example, they will not say that a male client is providing economic support to families when that man's family is receiving Aid to Families with Dependent Children (AFDC), nor will they emphasize that a woman charged with prostitution has children since this may jeopardize her custody of the children.

fendants: They pointed to the differing social and economic consequences of jailing familied and nonfamilied defendants, which I call the social costs of punishment.

## FAMILIED DEFENDANTS AND SOCIAL COSTS
## OF PUNISHMENT

The following comments reveal judicial concern with the consequences of sentencing for families and society. Note how each judge wants to learn what the defendant is doing for others; once they obtain this information, they try to predict the impact of their sentences.

> If a woman has children, that affects me. The kind we usually get has two children. If she is supporting them and if she is doing a crime for the benefit of others, compared to drugs, then that counts positively. For women, if a woman has children, but she in fact has no child care responsibilities, that won't impress me.

> Now you look at the record, Is this the first time? What were the circumstances? What are the defendant's living conditions? Is the defendant supporting children or family members? What effect will the disposition have on other family members? Are they a breadwinner? Are you taking a father or a mother away from a family? Are you punishing a victim? Is the society in danger?

Judges are concerned with fitting the punishment not only to the the crime and the defendant's background but also to those to whom the defendant might be tied. The second judge above asks if the sentence might be "punishing a victim" and if jail is necessary because "society [is] in danger." The first judge above is not impressed by the mere fact that a woman has children but whether she is caring for them. This judge also said, "If [the sentence] has a side effect on innocent people, you have to take it into account. If it's not a violent crime, then leniency is called for. You don't hurt a group because of just one guy." Court officials face a set of constraints in sanctioning familied defendants that are not present for nonfamilied defendants. By removing economic or caretaking responsibilities from families, they may cause the dissolution of these fragile units of social order. Moreover, they may punish victims or other innocents—those dependent on the defendant—in the process.

### Family and Gender Divisions

Court personnel assume gender divisions in the work and family responsibilities of familied men and women. In fact, such assumptions are so ingrained that one judge, when asked about these differing responsibilities, replied impatiently:

> Male and female, mother and father. Are you following through on that responsibility? There are different responsibilities depending on whether you are male or female. . . . The responsibilities they assume when they bring children into the world are different. Are they fulfilling those responsibilities? For men, I want to know: Is he holding the home together as best he can? Does he contribute to the support of the family? A woman has a different function. Is she fulfilling her obligations as a mother?

Differences in the expected responsibilities of familied men and women, combined with the family profiles of defendants, foster discrepancies in the treatment of familied men and familied women. As one probation officer said, "The treatment of males and females balances out. If the guy is working, you try to help him keep his job; and with a female, you try to keep her with the kids." Although this official believes that the treatment of male and female defendants "balances out," note his asymmetrical reasoning: Being a male is qualified by "if the guy is working," while being a female contains the unqualified assumption that she has children.

The presumed gender divisions in work and family life can make it difficult, one lawyer said, to persuade the court that familied men do care for their children. Coming directly from bail arguments to the interview, this lawyer recounted with exasperation his inability to secure pretrial release of his client, who was caring for his children while his wife was about to be hospitalized:

> The man was charged with A & B [assault and battery]. He has a wife going into the hospital, and he has two kids. They wanted $1000 bail. There is no prior, and there doesn't seem to be any reason for the high bail. There is a presumption that he is going to leave town. How can he leave, with a wife and two children? He's not going anywhere. If it were a woman, she would have been ROR'd [released on recognizance].

## Familied Men and Women

Three features of the differential response to men and women can be analytically distinguished, although they overlap in the minds of court personnel:

1. Women are more likely to have dependent children than men.
2. Familied women fulfill their familial obligations more responsibly than familied men.
3. Child care is more important than breadwinning in the maintenance of families.

With respect to the first, more familied women than familied men appear in court; indeed, court officials characterized most female defendants as having children. Although this typification is not wholly inaccurate, it activates a reasoning pattern, exemplified by the above statement from the probation officer, that conceptualizes the differential treatment of men and women as the response to *all* men and *familied* women.

Among the familied men and women, court officials see more "good" mothers than "good" fathers. Although many familied men are biological fathers, they may not be providing economically for families. Furthermore, from the court's viewpoint, men's affective support for families is not sufficient to define social fatherhood, which rests on being a breadwinner. Familied women, in contrast, are viewed as fulfilling their familial responsibilities more often, as a probation officer expressed,

> If a female is a mother of a child, we overlook certain weaknesses she may have in a lot of areas. A lot of girls get jammed up in serious offenses, but if she is a good mother of small children, this is very, very important. It has a neutralizing effect on seriousness. You do more harm to the community by locking them up. A lot of female defendants are good mothers, but not many male defendants are good fathers. For male defendants, we see them after they have failed in school and in the marketplace. In every area, including family, he is a total

failure. You check probate, and you know he is not doing his duty as a father—though they often cry about how they have to support kids.

Note the officer's concern that greater harm will accrue to the community by jailing mothers. Mann *et al.* (1980) discovered similar concerns in their analysis of judicial considerations in sentencing male white-collar offenders; but unlike these defendants, male common crime defendants have "failed in school and in the marketplace" and are less likely to be "good" fathers. Indeed, some court officials acknowledged that minority group men may have more difficulty presenting themselves as "good family men" because this status is contingent on having a job; according to a judge, "A person with a job and supporting a family is less likely to go to jail than someone who isn't. Having a job is a negative factor to putting someone in jail. Of course, this works against minority groups who have more difficulty getting employed."

Finally, differences emerge in the treatment of familied men and women because child care is considered more essential than economic support in maintaining families. This attitude is revealed by a defense attorney's description of how a defendant's familial relations evoke the "same reaction" but have a "different impact" for the familied man and woman: "The [court's] reaction is the same if the man has a family. It helps, but the impact is different than if it's a mother." Judges do have difficulty jailing a woman with children, and they also find this more difficult than jailing a familied man. When I asked judges if they considered different factors when sentencing men and women, they replied that women may have an advantage not as a consequence of sex but of differences in men's and women's work for families:

> Family responsibility is something you have to recognize. It weighs against incarceration or the difference between a long versus a short incarceration. Women are more likely to have kids and dependents than men. It is more difficult to send a woman with a kid to prison than a man. But if the man was taking care of a child, it would be the same thing, but this has never happened to me in the court.

As this and other judges report, familied men would be treated like the familied women, if they were caring for children.

Women's care for children is often cited in the literature as a reason for their more lenient sentences (e.g., Simon, 1975; Steffensmeier, 1980). However, it is not self-evident why judges and other court officials believe that child care is more important than economic support for maintaining families. Without this distinction, familied men and women might be treated equally. Like gender divisions in work and family life, the privileging of child care over economic support is simply assumed by court officials, and few tried to explain the basis of this presupposition. One judge, however, provides a clue:

> For [the woman with children], it is a two-fold consideration. First, financial, by putting the mother in jail, are we going to throw the children on society as a burden? No, we're not going to do that. Second, for the female defendants, how much do the children need the mother, or the aunt, or the grandmother?

The judicial reference to financial reasons suggests that there are different economic consequences to the state of removing breadwinning and child-care responsibilities from families. Father surrogates exist in the form of welfare benefits and other state supports (for example, Aid to Families with Dependent Children, housing allowances, and food stamps), but mother surrogates in the form of foster or institutional care of children are more rare and expensive.[10] Thus, the loss of breadwinning is more easily replaced by state supports than is the loss of parental care. This asymmetry is at the heart of the "practicality problem": Extending on Harris (1977), both men's and the state's interests are jeopardized by removing women's familial labor.

The consequences of gender divisions in work and family life take an ironic twist in the criminal courts. The differential value placed on men's and women's labor in the wider society, where women's unpaid familial labor has "no price" and is not socially recognized as work, is reversed in the context of contemplating its removal from families. Parental labor, based on a model of personalized motherhood, becomes socially recognized as invaluable, priceless, and nonreplaceable while breadwinning does not.

## FEMALE VERSUS FAMILIAL PATERNALISM

The interviews show that although a form of paternalism exists in the court, it does not center on the protection of women. Rather, its ideological emphasis is on protecting the social institution of the family, specifically: (1) keeping families together; (2) maintaining familied defendants' labor for families, and especially women's caretaking labor; and (3) protecting those dependent on a defendant's economic support or care. These results challenge the commonly held notion that the court protects women (female paternalism), and reveal instead that the real object of court protection is families (familial paternalism). This distinction between female and familial paternalism is illustrated by the following judicial discussion of whether a woman who cared for children should be jailed:

> A lot will depend on what will happen to the children. Chances are that if there is no one to take care of the children, I won't punish the children. I feel no sympathy toward her, but I do feel that the children are entitled to sympathy.

In extending sympathy toward children and in trying to keep families together, court officials respond to both men and women using a familial paternalistic logic.[11] While familied defendants are generally thought to deserve greater leniency

[10]In addition to the emerging ideology of personalized motherhood, "economic efficiency" was cited by advocates of mothers' pensions when, during the early 20th century in the United States, public and private provision for the care of children shifted from institutional care to "mother's subsidies," the forerunner of AFDC (Vandepol, 1982).

[11]The concept of familial paternalism can be applied to other criminal justice practices, such as the reaction to domestic violence (Vera Institute of Justice, 1977; Stanko, 1982; New York Task Force, 1986), and it may help to reconcile competing interpretations of the effect of paternalism on the treatment of females in juvenile and criminal courts (see, e.g., Chesney-Lind, 1977; 1978; 1986).

than nonfamilied defendants, familied women may be treated more leniently than familied men for two reasons: (1) gender divisions of labor define women, not men, as the primary caregivers; and (2) the court attaches more importance to caregiving than breadwinning in maintaining family life. Thus, those engaged in caregiving (predominantly women) are thought to be most deserving of leniency.[12]

Although court officials' reasoning is infused with familial paternalism, they frequently conflate "female" and "being familied" by assuming that all women have children. This conflation may explain a contradiction that emerges from the interviews of the nonjudicial court workers. On the one hand, they make their decisions along familial paternalistic lines, but on the other, they say that women are sentenced more leniently than men because of judicial female paternalism.

I asked the 24 prosecutors, defense lawyers, and probation officers, "Do you think that judges are more lenient to women than men?," and 20 replied "yes." The most frequent set of reasons they gave for judicial leniency was "sexism," "paternalistic attitudes," or a view of women as "the weaker sex" ($N = 14$).[13] Thus, the courthouse lore is that judges engage in female paternalism.

Do judges actually use female paternalistic reasoning, or are the nonjudicial court workers' characterizations simply inaccurate? The interviews suggest that judges, like the other court workers, invariably employ familial paternalism to justify leniency for some defendants. To examine female paternalism further, I asked judges if a certain statement from the literature, which was the paternalism thesis but was not identified as such, applied to their decisionmaking.[14] The judicial reaction to the statement was mixed. Although most judges said it did not apply to them, three believed it might have some applicability to their decisionmaking. Thus, although judicial thinking is not completely devoid of female paternalism, the processes structuring an apparent judicial leniency toward women are rooted in a family-based paternalism that is practiced by all court workers.

[12]Some might argue that the caregiving/breadwinning hierarchy exists because women, not men, are the primary caregivers and thus this reflects female paternalism. I would say that this hierarchy is a consequence of the distinctive qualities of caregiving and wage earning in industrialized societies. The personalized, nonreplaceable nature of parental care in comparison to the depersonalized, more replaceable nature of economic support for families makes it more difficult for court officials to remove caregivers from families. This asymmetry is in turn built into and reinforced by state policies in the support of families.

[13]Additional or other reasons they gave were judges find it hard to think of women as evil or bad ($N = 7$), women's child-care responsibilities ($N = 6$), and women are thought to be more easily reformed than men ($N = 4$).

[14]The statement was as follows (modified from Simon, 1975: 49): "Judges treat female defendants more kindly or protectively than they do male defendants because female defendants remind them of their daughters, or wives and sisters—women close to them. Or just in general, judges find it hard to be as tough on a woman as a man." Not surprisingly, all the female judges prefaced their responses by pointing out the male bias of the statement. Note that Simon's definition of judicial paternalism also includes "the practicality problem" of jailing women with young children. Because I distinguish the notion of protecting *women* (female paternalism) from the concern of maintaining women's *labor* for families (familial paternalism), the "practicality problem" was excluded in the statement.

## QUALIFYING CONCERNS

Some caveats about familial paternalistic practices are in order to present a balanced and fair view of its expression and impact.

### "Hiding Behind the Children" and "Bad Mothers"

Women's caregiving may mitigate against but certainly does not prevent incarceration.[15] Both the quality and indispensability of women's parental care were considered by Springfield court personnel in a manner similar to the diagnosis of men as "good" or "bad" fathers. Of all court officials, prosecutors were most likely to question whether familied women were "good" mothers. They were skeptical of defense attorneys who "used the mother situation," criticizing it as a means for female defendants to "hide behind the children":

> Women can use children as an excuse. There are a lot of women who are not good mothers. If I could prove that she was a lousy mother, then I would prove it. You have to think of the welfare of the children.

> Defense lawyers do use the tactic of women with children to prevent incarceration of the defendant or holding before trial. But in some cases, it is really just a tactic. For example, I saw a woman brought in for stealing hubcaps at 3 a.m. with her boyfriend. Her lawyer said she needed to care for a 1-month old baby at home. Well, I really wondered why she was out at 3 a.m. if she had to care for an infant.

The standards for being classified as a "good" mother were never made explicit but rather couched in vague terms of "taking responsibility" for the welfare of children, much in the same way that the criteria for being a "good" father rested on notions of "taking responsibility" for the economic welfare of the family unit. Thus, having children is necessary but not sufficient for social motherhood for female defendants in the same way that having a family is not sufficient for social fatherhood for male defendants.

### Gender, Family Responsibilities, and Offenses Charged

The interviews reveal that gender, family responsibilities, and offenses charged interact in different ways. First, the offense and the defendant's prior record can eclipse both gender and familial relations in determining sentencing (or pretrial release) decisions. Court personnel said that familied defendants were as likely to be jailed as nonfamilied defendants if previously convicted of serious or violent offenses (e.g., murder, sexual assault, major drug dealing, and robbery). However, sentence length and type (e.g., weekend sentences) may vary by the familial situation of those incarcerated.

---

[15]Baunach (1982) shows that 40% to 50% of women in American jails and prisons had children at home at the time of arrest and that care for children of incarcerated mothers is normally provided by relatives (75%) rather than foster care (10%). Court officials often want to know if there are female kin to care for children in a mother's absence, and thus, defense attorneys will emphasize the indispensability of a familied woman's parental care by "never mentioning that there is an aunt or grandma also in the household," as one such lawyer explained.

Second, some offenses themselves indicate that familied men and women may be "bad" parents and thus not deserving of court mercy. The offense provoking the strongest reaction against familied men and women was sexual abuse of children. Concern was frequently voiced for this type of familial violence but not for spouse abuse—a predictable (Vera Institute of Justice, 1977; McNulty, 1980; Stanko, 1982) but no less troubling finding.

Familied women charged with prostitution are *a priori* considered "bad" mothers as prosecutors rhetorically ask, "Who's taking care of the children while she's out at night?" These women are as likely to be jailed as nonfamilied women. Springfield court personnel disagreed, however, over how these cases should be handled. A probation officer and defense lawyer described the visceral reaction of judges by saying, respectively, "Some judges hate prostitutes," and "They treat prostitutes ridiculously." Three judges said they thought of prostitutes more as victims than offenders, and they stressed that they did not consider prostitution to be as serious as other judges did.

Finally, a defendant's familial situation can interact with the motivation for criminal involvement and affect the degree of blameworthiness attributed to a defendant's behavior. For example, in the sentencing vignette given to judges, which involved a person convicted of larceny, one judge wanted to know, "Was there a need for the family or not?" while another said, "If it's stealing milk for the children, I wouldn't send the person to jail." Their responses suggest that more leniency may be given to those who commit crimes intended to help family members, that is, those motivated by need rather than self-interest or greed.[16] Familied defendants may more often conform to this "Robin Hood" image, particularly for property-related offenses.

## Punishment and Potential for Reform

Perceptions of the reform potential of men and women, independent of their familial situation, may be another basis for differential treatment. Some probation officers thought that women—both familied and nonfamilied—were "more easily reformed than men" and that men did not "want to help themselves," one even saying that "Females are easier to intimidate. I guarantee her jail if she is not clean. Females are impressed with this more than males." Thus, Steffensmeier's (1980) ideas on the reform potential of men and women receive some support from these interviews, although this "potential" is related to job segregation by sex. For example, when describing the relative success of men and women on probation, a probation officer reported, "It's easier for women to find jobs," adding that the reason is that men have a "masculine image" to protect and thus "are hesitant to go into the Skills Center if they can't get a masculine job. They will drive a regular bus, but not a school bus." It is in fact no easier for women to find paid jobs, but so-called feminine jobs, which often pay less, are not acceptable to men.

In contrast to the three other groups of court workers, probation officers more

[16]Mann *et al.* (1980) and Eaton (1985) also discuss this phenomenon.

often spoke of a gender-based substantive justice that was independent of a woman's familial situation. The logic of this substantive justice is that the "equal punishment" of men and women is not necessary to achieve "equal outcomes" (i.e., identical rehabilitation or deterrent effects). We need additional research to determine the distribution and extent of this reasoning pattern; perhaps this type of thinking is more common among court workers and jurisdictions taking a forward-looking (rehabilitation) rather than backward-looking (retribution or "just deserts") stance in sanctioning (see, e.g., von Hirsch, 1985).

## SUMMARY

Family-based conceptions of justice dominate the reasoning of Springfield court officials when they describe and justify their sanctioning decisions. The court's interest in protecting family life and those dependent on the defendant promote two axes of variation in treatment—between familied and nonfamilied defendants and between familied men and familied women. Court officials think of this differential treatment not as discrimination but rather as legitimate and pragmatic justice. Because of their concern with the *consequences* of their sanctioning decisions for families and society, they rationalize leniency for familied defendants in the following ways: If familied men or women are jailed, social disorder may increase, bonds of economic and affective responsibilities to others may be severed, and victims, particularly children, may be punished. Differences in the treatment of familied men and women arise because familied women are thought to be "more responsible" than familied men and child care is considered more important than economic support to maintain family life.

The ideological emphasis given to defendants' familial relations by Springfield court officials has also been documented by Eaton (1983; 1984; 1985) for an English lower court. While I agree with Eaton that traditional and gendered conceptions of work and family life are reproduced in criminal court decisionmaking, I would add that this ideological stance also appears to be structured by economic considerations. The state pays both economically and socially for imposing equal punishments on defendants whose obligations for the care and economic support of others are unequal and differ by gender. For example, more families may be placed on welfare (see Maynard, 1982) and foster care for children may be required (see Daly, 1986). These economic costs form part of the decisionmaking calculus in court workers' conceptions of justice.

Based on the interviews, Kruttschnitt's (1982; 1984) and Kruttschnitt and Green's (1984) social control arguments need to be modified. With respect to the locus of social control, the presence of dependents is what court officials consider, for as a prosecutor said, "As long as there are dependents in the picture, they will help men as well as women." Being dependent on others is less important to court workers and primarily affects the treatment of nonfamilied defendants. In jailing familied men and women, the differing social costs arising from separating them from their families seem to be more significant than differences in informal social control.

I have described the kinds of decisionmaking processes that promote gender differences in criminal court outcomes, but the skeptical reader may require more statistical evidence. I have conducted multivariate analyses of court outcomes in two other states—a lower court in New York City and an upper court in Seattle—to test hypotheses on the differential treatment of familied and nonfamilied defendants and of familied men and women in sentencing and other court decisions (Daly, 1983; 1987). Both analyses showed strong family effects mitigating against pretrial detention and jail sentences. In addition, I found family effects in nonjail sentencing outcomes, suggesting that familial paternalism may spill over to other court decisionmaking contexts. Thus, although the familial paternalistic logic is most vividly revealed in the in-out decision, it may also be applied in other, less dramatic contexts. Future research might investigate this possibility and, more generally, whether the kinds of family-based reasoning patterns employed by Springfield court officials exist elsewhere. The statistical analyses suggest that such patterns are not confined to just one medium-sized city courthouse in one state.[17]

For too long theories of gender differences in the criminal court sanctioning process have suffered from a lack of empirical attention to the ways in which court officials construct justice and rationalize their decisions. Rather than continuing to speculate and make inferences about their reasoning processes from analyses of large court data sets, we may do better by observing and interpreting these processes firsthand.

## REFERENCES

Baab, George W., and William Furgeson. 1967. "Texas sentencing practices: a statistical study." *Texas Law Review* 45:471–503.

Baunach, Phyllis Jo. 1982. "You can't be a mother and be in prison . . . can you?: impacts of the mother-child separation." In *The Criminal Justice System and Women,* edited by Barbara Price and Nancy Sokoloff. New York: Clark Boardman.

Black, Donald. 1976. *The Behavior of Law.* New York: Academic Press.

Chesney-Lind, Meda. 1977. "Judicial paternalism and the female status offender: training women to know their place." *Crime and Delinquency* 23: 121–130.

———. 1978. "Young women in the arms of the law" and "Chivalry re-examined: women and the criminal justice system." In *Women, Crime, and the Criminal Justice System,* edited by Lee Bowker. Lexington: Lexington Books.

———. 1987. "Female offenders: paternalism re-examined. " In *Women, the Courts, and Equality,* edited by Barbara Crites and Winifred Hepperly. Beverly Hills: Sage.

[17]The racial minority representation in the Seattle sample (32%) was similar to that for Springfield; however, the New York City sample was almost entirely composed of black (48%) and Hispanic (40%) defendants. The statistical studies show that family-based justice is applied across race and ethnic groups, although more research is needed to explore how gender, familial relations, and race/ethnicity interact.

Curran, Debra A. 1983. "Judicial discretion and defendant's sex." *Criminology* 21:41–58.

Daly, Kathleen. 1983. Order in the Court: Gender and Justice. Unpublished doctoral dissertation, Department of Sociology, University of Massachusetts-Amherst.

———. 1986. "Gender in the adjudication process: are judges *really* paternalistic to women?" Revised version of a paper presented at the Annual Meeting of the American Society of Criminology, 1985.

———. 1987. "Discrimination in the criminal courts: family, gender and the problem of equal treatment." *Social Forces* 66: 152–175.

Eaton, Mary. 1983. "Mitigating circumstances: familiar rhetoric." *International Journal of the Sociology of Law* 11:385–400.

———. 1984. Familial Ideology and Summary Justice: Women Defendants before a Suburban Magistrates' Court. Unpublished doctoral dissertation, Department of Sociology, University of London.

———. 1985. "Documenting the defendant: placing women in social inquiry reports." In *Women-in-Law: Explorations in Law, Family, and Sexuality,* edited by T. Brophy and C. Smart. Boston: Routledge and Kegan Paul.

Edwards, Susan S. M. 1984. *Women on Trial.* Manchester: Manchester University Press.

Feeley, Malcolm M. 1979. *The Process is the Punishment: Handling Cases in a Lower Criminal Court.* New York: Russell Sage.

Gaylin, Willard. 1974. *Partial Justice.* New York: Knopf.

Hagan, John, John H. Simpson, and A. R. Gillis. 1979. "The sexual stratification of social control: a gender-based perspective on crime and delinquency." *British Journal of Sociology* 30: 25–38.

Harris, Anthony R. 1977. "Sex and theories of deviance: toward a functional theory of deviant typescripts." *American Sociological Review* 42:3–16.

Heumann, Milton. 1978. *Plea Bargaining.* Chicago. University of Chicago Press.

Hogarth, John. 1971. *Sentencing as a Human Process.* Toronto: University of Toronto Press.

Klein, Dorie. 1973. "The etiology of female crime: a review of the literature." *Issues in Criminology* 8:3–30.

Kruttschnitt, Candace. 1982. "Women, crime, and dependency." *Criminology* 19:495–518.

———. 1984. "Sex and criminal court dispositions: the unresolved controversy." *Journal of Research in Crime and Delinquency* 21:213–232.

Kruttschnitt, Candace, and Donald Green. 1984. "The sex-sanctioning issue: is it history?" *American Sociological Review* 49: 541–551.

Lipetz, Marcia J. 1984. *Routine Justice: Processing Cases in Women's Court.* New Brunswick: Transaction Books.

McNulty, Faith. 1980. *The Burning Bed.* New York: Harcourt, Brace Jovanovich.

Mann, Kenneth, Stanton Wheeler, and Austin Sarat. 1980. "Sentencing the white-collar offender." *American Criminal Law Review* 17:479–500.

Martin, Roscoe. 1934. *The Defendant and Criminal Justice.* University of Texas Bulletin No. 3437. Bureau of Research in the Social Sciences, University of Texas, Austin.

Maynard, Douglas W. 1982. "Defendant attributes in plea bargaining: notes on the modeling of sentencing decisions." *Social Problems* 29:347–360.

Moulds, Elizabeth F. 1980. "Chivalry and paternalism: disparities of treatment in the criminal justice system." In *Women, Crime, and Justice,* edited by Susan Datesman and Frank Scarpitti. New York: Oxford University Press.

Nagel, Ilene, and John Hagan. 1983. "Gender and crime: offense patterns and criminal court sanctions." In *Crime and Justice: An Annual Review of Research,* edited by Michael Tonry and Norval Morris. Chicago: University of Chicago Press.

Nagel, Stuart. 1969. *The Legal Process from a Behavioral Perspective.* Homewood: Dorsey Press.

Nagel, Stuart, and Lenore Weitzman. 1971. "Women as litigants." *Hastings Law Journal* 23:171–181.

New York Task Force on Women in the Courts. 1986. *Report of the New York Task Force on Women in the Courts.* New York: Office of Court Administration, Unified Court System.

Parisi, Nicolette. 1982. "Are females treated differently?: a review of the theories and evidence on sentencing and parole decisions." In *Judge, Lawyer, Victim, Thief,* edited by Nicole Hahn Rafter and Elizabeth Stanko. Boston: Northeastern University Press.

Rosett, Arthur, and Donald R. Cressey. 1986. *Justice by Consent.* Philadephia: J.B. Lippincott.

Simon, Rita J. 1975. *Women and Crime.* Lexington: Lexington Books.

Stanko, Elizabeth. 1982. "Would you believe this woman?: prosecutorial screening for 'credible' witnesses and a problem of justice." In *Judge, Lawyer, Victim, Thief,* edited by Nicole Hahn Rafter and Elizabeth Stanko. Boston: Northeastern University Press.

Steffensmeier, Darrell. 1980. "Assessing the impact of the women's movement on sex-based differences in the handling of adult criminal defendants." *Crime and Delinquency* 26:344–357.

Vandepol, Ann. 1982. "Dependent children, child custody, and the mothers' pensions: the transformation of state-family relations in the early 20th century." *Social Problems* 29:221–235.

Vera Institute of Justice. 1977. *Felony Arrests: Their Prosecution and Disposition in New York City's Courts.* New York: Vera Institute of Justice.

von Hirsch, Andrew. 1985. *Past or Future Crimes.* New Brunswick: Rutgers University Press.

Wheeler, Stanton, David Weisburd, and Nancy Bode. 1982. "Sentencing the white-collar offender: rhetoric and reality." *American Sociological Review* 47:641–656.

# LAW AND CULTURE

# 10

# DEVIANCE AND RESPECTABILITY: AN OBSERVATIONAL STUDY OF REACTIONS TO SHOPLIFTING*

DARRELL J. STEFFENSMEIER
ROBERT M. TERRY

The interactionist-labeling perspective in deviance asserts that audience responses to deviant acts are crucial to the understanding of deviant behavior. Furthermore, to understand audience responses—reactions toward various types of deviance—investigators need to discover the meaning these behaviors have for potential reactors. These meanings may vary with the deviant's other social identities, with situational factors such as social support and social setting, and with the characteristics of potential reactors. Although some research relates these variables to audience reactions, few studies have manipulated such variables within a field setting.

A growing body of observational field studies treats the reactions of official control agents such as the police (e.g., Black, 1970; Piliavin and Briar, 1964) and courts to deviant actors (Emerson, 1969). But such research has generally lacked the kind of control that allows for experimental manipulation of variables and the systematic examination of posited relationships. In addition, studies examining the reactions of the general public have been largely ignored. With few exceptions (e.g., Darley and Latané, 1968; Denner, 1968; Freed *et al.,* 1955; Lefkowitz *et al.,*

*The authors are grateful for financial assistance provided by the Center for Research in Interpersonal Behavior and the Graduate College of the University of Iowa. We would also like to thank Renee Steffensmeier for critical readings of earlier drafts of this paper and Larry Rhoades for helpful suggestions regarding final editing.

1955), there is a dearth of experimental field research that systematically examines posited relationships between reactions of the general public and deviant behavior.

Current thinking in sociology indicates that the study of deviant behavior must overcome problems in the validity of official statistics (see especially, Douglas, 1971a; Kitsuse and Cicourel, 1963; Wheeler, 1967), must recognize that while official control agents are important it is the general public that usually initiates responses to deviant behavior (e.g., Black, 1970), and must study deviance in its natural setting rather than as mediated through the official reports and actions of formal control agents (e.g., Douglas, 1971b; Humphreys, 1970).

This research attempts to shed some light on the nature and basis of reactions to a particular kind of deviance and, in doing so, tries to overcome the aforementioned problems by (1) using field research methods; (2) ascertaining responses of the general public to instances of deviant behavior in real life situations; and (3) making direct observations of behavior of members of the social audience. Specifically, appearance and sex of the deviant are varied systematically in order to assess their effects upon the responses of the general public to observed instances of shoplifting.[1]

There is much theoretical support for the notion that the actor's social identity is a crucial determinant of reactions to deviant behavior (Douglas, 1970; Goffman, 1963; Lemert, 1951; Lofland, 1969). Two important aspects of social identity considered in this research are those of appearance and sex, both of which can be subsumed under the more abstract rubric of respectability.

Much of the literature in the interactionist-labeling perspective has argued that differential treatment is accorded persons with poor social backgrounds, less than perfect social identities, or "bad" reputations. Many analyses of deviant categories are founded on the assumption that particular classes of people are more likely to perform deviant acts and to be particular types of deviant persons (Hughes, 1945; Kitsuse, 1962; Lofland, 1969; Scheff, 1966; Simmons, 1965; Sudnow, 1965). Such studies are highly consistent in arguing that respectability decreases the likelihood of deviant imputations, whereas "unrespectability" has the opposite effect.

In this research, appearance and sex are used as indicators of respectability. Reports by Ball (1970) and Cameron (1964) have noted that a respectable appearance serves as a buffer against a deviant imputation. Lefkowitz *et al.* (1955) found that a respectable appearance was influential in inducing others to engage in deviant behavior (jaywalking). In a field experiment, Bickman (1971) found that per-

---

[1]Theoretically the choice of shoplifting is predicated on the assumption that it is a form of deviant behavior which elicits variable social reactions that are usually mild to moderate. Moreover, shoplifting is a sufficiently problematic form of deviance to allow for other deviant identities to influence reactions to it. Several practical considerations also determined the selection of shoplifting as the object of investigation. It was a behavior around which a field experiment could readily be constructed and that in turn allowed for the observation of a large number of subjects within a limited time period and simultaneously permitted the control and manipulation of the independent variables.

sons who appeared to be of low status were treated more dishonestly by experimental subjects than were those of apparently higher status. It has been noted that one's appearance (kinds of clothing, hair style, and the like) is part and parcel of being a particular kind of person and also indicates, in a general sense, an individual's attitude toward community norms (Carey, 1968; Stone, 1962). In the current scene (early 1970s), commonsense distinctions between hippie and straight appearances are especially noteworthy.

Another of an actor's social identities thought to affect reactions to deviance is one's sex. Consistent research findings show that females are less severely dealt with by formal control agents than are males and some evidence exists to support the notion that public attitudes and reactions toward the sexes tend to favor females (Pollak, 1961; Reckless, 1961; Ward and Kassebaum, 1965). Schur (1969) has argued that the greater attitude of protectiveness taken toward women in our society and more generally the nature of their social roles and situations permit women to exploit their sex for criminal purposes and to engage in various kinds of criminal behavior with relatively little fear of detection or prosecution.

The effect of sex status on deviant imputation can be fitted into Goffman's discussion of social identities and more specifically into the rubric of respectability. Goffman (1963) argues that an individual's biography is composed of both past and present events and characteristics which function so as to establish an individual's social identity. The latter refers to those attributes others can observe, providing thereby a basis for classifying an actor as a particular kind of person. Such attributes as age and sex are of primary importance in making such categorizations. Although none of these variables is inherently bound to the notion of respectability, the deviant behavior literature rather clearly indicates that being a male tends to be viewed as an unfavorable attribute by social control agents and increases a person's vulnerability to the imputation of deviance.

Our third independent variable, sex of subject, is ambiguously grounded in research that generally indicates that females are less tolerant of deviance than are males (Phillips, 1964; Westie and Martin, 1959; Williams, 1964), although there is conflicting evidence (Whatley, 1959). Traditional sex role differences, theoretically at least, have emphasized more support of stability and the ongoing system among females than among males. Thus, females should be less accepting of nonconforming behavior than males (Parsons and Bales, 1955) and therefore should be more likely to report deviant acts.

## HYPOTHESES

On the basis of the foregoing, the following hypotheses are targets of inquiry:

(1) Store customers will be more likely to report a shoplifting incident when the shoplifter has a hippie rather than a straight appearance.

(2) Store customers will be more likely to report a shoplifting incident when the shoplifter is male rather than female.

(3) Female store customers will be more likely to report a shoplifting incident than male store customers.

## METHODS

This research sought to discover factors related to reactions to shoplifting. "Reactions" was defined in terms of variations in the willingness of store customers to report behavior (shoplifting) which was blatantly illegal and deviant. In order to observe the reactions of a wide variety of subjects and simultaneously maintain some degree of control over the frequency of occurrence and consistency of the deviant behavior, a natural field experiment was designed. While this approach assured a rather high degree of external validity it presented some difficulties in settling on the variables determining societal reactions, for the experimental situation allowed us to investigate only those independent variables that were amenable to immediate observation in fleeting encounters: hence, sex and appearance.

The study was conducted in three preselected stores in a midwestern university city of 50,000. The experiment can best be described as a rigged shoplifting incident—that is, its occurrence was prearranged. The store's manager and personnel had complete knowledge of the experiment and the researchers had their full cooperation in staging the shoplifting incidents.

## SHOPLIFTING SEQUENCE

The main concern of this research was the extent to which customers were willing to report shoplifting to store personnel. In order to control the frequency and consistency of the shoplifting situation three accomplices were employed. One accomplice played the part of a shoplifter and two more accomplices played the parts of store employees. The experimental procedure is best understood through a discussion of the roles played by the accomplices.

The first accomplice played the part of a shoplifter. This accomplice was to place himself under the direct observation of a customer (the subject), and then steal some item of merchandise in an obvious and deliberate manner.[2] Having done his shoplifting, the first accomplice moved to another location where he remained out of hearing distance but within eyesight of the subject. This procedure avoided the possible intimidation of the subject and simultaneously eased identification of the shoplifter if the subject showed a willingness to report the incident. The appearance and sex of the shoplifter were varied systematically.

The second and third research accomplices played the parts of store employ-

---

[2]In the course of pretesting, we found that for subjects to be aware of the shoplifting as well as for them to be reasonably certain that it was shoplifting, our shoplifters had to be quite blatant and aggressive in their shoplifting. At least one member of the research team had to be reasonably certain that the subject saw the shoplifting.

ees.[3] The principal task of the second accomplice or first store employee was to make himself readily available should the subject wish to report the shoplifting incident. As soon as the shoplifter moved away to another location (after he had shoplifted) the first store employee had instructions to move into the immediate vicinity of the subject and act as though he were arranging merchandise on the shelves or counters. The accomplice remained in the area for a brief period of time in order to allow the subject ample opportunity to report. If the subject reported, then the store employee was instructed to "apprehend" the shoplifter and both of them moved backstage.[4] If the subject did not report the shoplifting, the accomplice left the area and signaled to a third accomplice to intervene.

The third accomplice played the part of a second store employee. He was instructed to act more directly and vigorously in order to increase the likelihood of reporting. He asked the subject for assistance in identifying a possible shoplifter by prompting the subject in two different ways. The first prompting was as follows: "Good afternoon (evening), sir (madam), we have been watching so-and-so (identifying description) for shoplifting. Did you happen to see anything?" If, in response to this first prompting the subject reported the shoplifter, then the employee "apprehended" him and they moved backstage. If the subject did not respond to the first prompting, the same store employee was instructed to intervene more forcefully to elicit reporting from the subject. The second prompting was as follows: "Gee, I was quite sure I saw him (her) take something (specify item) and put it down his coat. You didn't happen to see anything suspicious, did you?" If the subject still did not report, the accomplice left the vicinity and there was no further prompting of the subject.

After the experiment was completed each subject was immediately debriefed by another research assistant. Every conceivable effort was made to clarify to the subject the nature and the purpose of the deception. In addition, an attempt was made to interview the subject briefly as to his perception of and reaction to the experiment.[5]

---

[3]The research accomplices who were assigned the roles of store employees were all males who appeared to be between 25 and 30 years old. To give as much credibility as possible to the experiment, these accomplices wore the same apparel as the regular store employees. In Stores A and B, long white aprons made the accomplices easily identifiable. However in Store C regular employees were less well differentiated and thus some minor modifications were introduced in our accomplices in order to ensure their proper identification by subjects. These modifications did not seem to create any noticeable differences in the experimental situation that would affect our interpretation of the data.

[4]Backstage refers to an area of the store reserved for store personnel where the researcher and his associates were able to record each event as it happened and plan for the next event without being observed by subjects.

[5]Studying behavior in the natural environment raises ethical questions about the deception of subjects and the invasion of their privacy. Should people be used in a social-psychological experiment without their permission or awareness? The question is difficult to answer. We feel that in the case of this study the permission of the subjects was not crucial. None of the subjects expressed hostility toward the experiment and most were highly cooperative. Note, for example, that 178 of the 191 adult subjects completed the postexperimental interview, and 171 of these 178 consented either to a mailed questionnaire or home interview. Careful and thorough pretesting enabled us to avoid numerous problems.

## OPERATIONALIZATION OF THE DEPENDENT
## VARIABLE

The dependent variable in this research is willingness to report a shoplifting incident. On a higher theoretical level we are getting at the willingness of potential reactors to impute a deviant label to presumably deviant actors. The use of prompting as a device to obtain variation in the dependent variable was suggested by the previous research of Latané and Darley (1969) and Denner (1968). As operationalized in this research, willingness to report could achieve four possible values:

1. If the subject reported the shoplifting incident to the first store employee this response was assigned a value of *high* willingness to report. As will be recalled, the first store employee took a passive stance toward the subject and made no direct attempt to encourage reporting. No prompting was used at this point.

2. If the subject reported the shoplifting incident to the second store employee in response to the first prompting, this behavior was held to indicate *medium high* willingness to report.

3. If the subject reported the shoplifting incident to the second store employee in response to the second prompting, this behavior was assigned a value of *medium low* willingness to report.

4. The category of *low* willingness to report consisted of all subjects who did not report the shoplifting incident.

Table 1 gives the distributions obtained for the sample on the dependent variable, willingness to report. As can be seen, we got good variance in type of response. A good deal of reporting took place even without prompting.

### RESEARCH SITES

Stores were selected on the basis of several criteria. We thought it important to use stores of differing size and degree of bureaucratization.[6] Also, the stores had to retail merchandise that would be easy and obvious to steal. We also sought stores that had customers who represented the nonstudent population of a university-dominated city.

After considering these matters, we approached several store managers to determine their willingness to participate in the project. Some were encouraging and enthusiastic. Out of necessity, then, the stores finally selected as research sites were those at which the most cooperation was offered. Fortunately, these stores varied along the relevant dimensions of size and bureaucratization. In addition, each store had certain unique features.

Store A was a small, older chain grocery store, located close to the downtown area. Patrons consisted largely of persons living in the immediate neighborhood,

---

[6]Subsequent reports will deal with the effects on reporting levels of size of store and degree of bureaucratization of the store. In general, these variables had little effect on reporting levels and did not affect the relationships between reporting levels and the three variables discussed in this article.

TABLE 1  Frequency Distribution of Respondent
Reporting Levels

| Reporting | Total sample (n = 212) | Adults (n = 191) | Students (n = 21) |
|---|---|---|---|
| High | 62 (29.2) | 61 (31.9) | 1 (4.8) |
| Medium high | 73 (34.4) | 71 (37.2) | 2 (9.5) |
| Medium low | 28 (13.2) | 25 (13.1) | 3 (14.3) |
| Low | 49 (23.1) | 34 (17.8) | 15 (71.4) |

older people, and university students. Store B was a relatively new, large chain grocery store located in a fringe area shopping center. The patrons consisted chiefly of housewives. Store C was a very large discount department store located on the edge of the city. For a number of reasons (location, prices, variety of merchandise, store hours, etc.) this store was more likely to attract out-of-town customers than the other stores.[7]

We tried to get approximately equal numbers of subjects in each store. Except for persons later identified as college students, this aim was achieved, with 67 subjects exposed to shoplifting in Store A, 69 in Store B, and 55 in Store C. Since the stores differed in size and therefore in the number of customers during any given time period, trial runs were conducted on four separate occasions in Store A, on two separate occasions in Store B, and on one occasion in Store C. In addition, Store A was used to conduct all pretests for the experiment.

## EXPERIMENTAL DESIGN

A primary justification for the study of contrived rather than real shoplifting is the greater ability to manipulate the independent variables. Two identities of the shoplifters were systematically varied—appearance and sex. In addition, sex of the subject (shopper) was also varied across experimental events. Each variable is dichotomized, resulting in an overall research design of the 2 × 2 × 2 variety. Figure 1 illustrates the eight comparison groups produced by this design. Approximately 25 subjects are represented in each cell, with a total sample size of 212. Each subject was exposed to only one combination of the independent variables, sex of shoplifter and appearance of shoplifter. We tried to include proportionate numbers of male and female subjects from various age categories and backgrounds and to exclude persons who appeared to be college students. Of the total of 212

[7]Since two of the stores studied were grocery stores, most things stolen were food items. The remainder consisted of articles of clothing, small appliances, cosmetics, etc. The items shoplifted were of relatively small value, most retailing for less than $3.00.

FIGURE 1     Representation of the Research Design

| | Sex of Shoplifter | | | |
| --- | --- | --- | --- | --- |
| | Male | | Female | |
| | Appearance of Shoplifter | | Appearance of Shoplifter | |
| Sex of Subject | Hippie | Straight | Hippie | Straight |
| Male | | | | |
| Female | | | | |

subjects, 191 were classifiable as nonstudent adults. All future tabulations of experimental data are based on these 191 subjects.[8]

## OPERATIONALIZING THE INDEPENDENT VARIABLES

The major independent variables in this research were appearance and sex. Appearance was varied: hippie vs. straight. Sex was varied by using male and female
shoplifters. Attributes of the shoplifter presentation types are as follows:

### Hippie Shoplifter

(a) *Male:* He wore soiled patched blue jeans, blue workman's shirt, and blue
   denim jacket; well-worn scuffed shoes with no socks. He had long and unruly hair with a ribbon tied around his forehead. He was unshaven and had
   a small beard.

(b) *Female:* She wore soiled patched blue jeans, blue workman's shirt, and
   dirty blue denim jacket; well-worn ragged tennis shoes with no socks. She
   had long unruly and ratted hair. She wore no makeup.

### Straight Shoplifter

(a) *Male:* He wore neatly pressed dress slacks, sport shirt and tie, sport jacket, shined shoes. He had short, trimly cut hair and was clean shaven.

(b) *Female:* She wore a dress, shined shoes or boots, a fur coat. Her hair was
   well-styled. She wore makeup and was well groomed.

Other than the induced differences of grooming and dress, the shoplifters were
about the same age, same height and build, and attractiveness.

---

[8]A subject was operationally defined as a student if he/she indicated that he/she attended the university full- or part-time and was less than 26 years old. Pretesting indicated that students were highly unlikely to report, irrespective of prompting.

## RESULTS

Tables 2 and 3 analyze the effects on reporting levels of our three independent variables. Table 2 also shows the interaction effects among our three independent variables. The tests of hypotheses, which are treated separately below, are derived from the information presented in Tables 2 and 3.

## APPEARANCE AND REPORTING

Our hypothesis predicts that the level of reporting of a shoplifting incident will be higher for the hippie than for the straight shoplifter. The hypothesis is clearly supported in that the relationship ($r = .465$) is large and in the expected direction and the $F$-test results are highly significant. In line with previous arguments, the shoplifter's appearance provides the potential reactor with information that enables him to locate the actor on a high-low evaluative continuum. Apparently a hippie appearance constitutes a negative identity that results in a greater willingness on the part of subjects to report the hippie over the straight shoplifter and, by extension, a greater willingness to impute a deviant label to a hippie rather than a straight actor. The effect of shoplifter's appearance on reporting levels is discussed in greater detail following presentation of other results.

## SEX OF SHOPLIFTER AND REPORTING

Our hypothesis as to the effect of shoplifter's sex on reporting levels is not supported in the data. The relationship ($r = .012$) is in the expected direction but is so small as to be nonexistent. In addition, $F$ test results are not significant.

Explanations for this finding are easy to come by, although such explanations are speculative. First, the findings may be limited to shoplifting and may not be generalizable to other deviance. Also, the trend toward sexual equality may be narrowing sex differentials in attitudes and actions toward offenders and the protectiveness argument may be no longer feasible. Finally, findings of differential reactions to offenders on the basis of sex have focused upon the reactions of formal control agents rather than the general public. It may be that control agents discriminate whereas the public does not.

## SEX OF SUBJECT AND REPORTING LEVELS

Our hypothesis asserts that females will be more likely to report than will males. The data offer little support for the hypothesis. As indicated in Tables 2 and 3, the relationship ($r = .096$) is in the expected direction, but it is so small that we reject the hypothesis. In addition, $F$-test results are not significant. Again, it is possible that changing cultural definitions of female social roles and the increasing equalitarianism of women in general has had the effect of narrowing sexual differentials in reactions to deviance. Williams (1964) has argued that this is occurring with

**TABLE 2** Three-way Analysis of Variance of Reporting Levels and Tests for Interaction Effects for Appearance of Shoplifter, Sex of Shoplifter, and Sex of Subject*

| Source | SS | DF[†] | MS | F | Prob. |
|---|---|---|---|---|---|
| Total | 235.1296 | $(npqr - 1) = 190$ | | | |
| Main effects | | | | | |
| Appearance of shoplifter (A) | 46.9782 | $(q - 1) = 1$ | 46.9782 | 48.1186 | <.001 |
| Sex of shoplifter (B) | .0048 | $(p - 1) = 1$ | .0048 | .0049 | >.05 N.S. |
| Sex of subject (C) | 2.7066 | $(r - 1) = 1$ | 2.7066 | 2.7723 | >.05 N.S. |
| Interactions | | | | | |
| AB interaction | .1688 | $(q - 1)(p - 1) = 1$ | .1688 | .1728 | >.05 N.S. |
| AC interaction | .5145 | $(q - 1)(r - 1) = 1$ | .5145 | .5269 | >.05 N.S. |
| BC interaction | 4.6232 | $(p - 1)(r - 1) = 1$ | 4.6232 | 4.7354 | .01 < p < .05 |
| ABC interaction | 1.4594 | $(q - 1)(p - 1)(r - 1) = 1$ | 1.4594 | 1.4948 | >.05 N.S. |
| Error | | | | | |
| Error SS (W. cell) | 178.6741 | $pqr(\bar{n} - 1) = 183$ | .9763 | | |

*The analysis of variance procedures used in Table 2 were based on the "method of expected equal frequencies." According to this procedure, if cell $N$s do not differ markedly, a fairly simple weighting procedure can be used to estimate what the cell sums and sums of squared scores would be if all $N$s had been the same. (See Kohout, 1974; Schuessler, 1971, for cogent discussions of the procedure involved.)

[†]In computing the degrees of freedom, $q$ = levels of A, $p$ = levels of B, $r$ = levels of C, and $\bar{n}$ = the average cell frequency.

TABLE 3   Summary Correlation Table*

| Zero-order | First-order | Second-order |
|---|---|---|
| $r_{wy} = .465$ | $r_{wy,x} = .465$ | $r_{wy,xz} = .471$ |
| (appearance of shoplifter) | $r_{wy,z} = .471$ | |
| $r_{xy} = .012$ | $r_{xy,w} = .016$ | $r_{xy,wz} = .018$ |
| (sex of shoplifter) | $r_{xy,z} = .014$ | |
| $r_{zy} = .096$ | $r_{zy,w} = .127$ | $r_{zy,wx} = .127$ |
| (sex of subject) | $r_{zy,x} = .096$ | |

*The measure of association reported is Pearson's coefficient of correlation.

$z$ = sex of subject
$x$ = sex of shoplifter
$w$ = appearance of shoplifter
$y$ = reporting level

racial prejudice and discrimination, and a similar process might have produced these results with respect to deviance.

## INTERACTION EFFECTS

Table 2 shows the interaction effects on reporting levels of various combinations of our independent variables. Only the interaction effect between sex of shoplifter and sex of subject proved to be significant (*BC* Interaction: $.01 < p < .05$). This interaction effect can be explained ex post facto by means of further analyses. The cell means for combinations of the independent variables were used to rank-order reporting levels for various categories of shoplifters and subjects. In addition, a new variable was derived by combining the sex of subject and sex of shoplifter. The derived variable yields a dichotomy—opposite sex vs. same sex reporting. The results are presented in Table 4, a table that neatly summarizes the results of this research.

First, the appearance of the shoplifter has the strongest and most clear-cut effect on reporting levels. Hippie shoplifters are always more likely to be reported than straight shoplifters. Second, for hippie shoplifters, female subjects report more than male subjects, irrespective of sex of shoplifter. For straight shoplifters, subject's willingness to report is greater when the shoplifter is of the opposite, rather than the same sex. According to these rank orders, straight shoplifters who are the same sex as the subject-witness are the least likely of all shoplifters to be reported.

Within categories of shoplifter's appearance we have a case of specification. For the hippie shoplifter, sex of subject has an independent effect on reporting: females report more often than males. In the case of the straight shoplifter, the interaction of sex of subject and sex of shoplifter clearly affects the level of report-

**TABLE 4** Mean Reporting Levels for Combinations of Independent Variables

| Rank order | Sex of subject | Sex of shoplifter | Sex of subject and Sex of shoplifter | Appearance of shoplifter | Mean reporting level |
|---|---|---|---|---|---|
| 1 | Female | Male | Opposite | Hippie | 1.4347 |
| 2 | Female | Female | Same | Hippie | 1.5217 |
| 3 | Male | Female | Opposite | Hippie | 1.7173 |
| 4 | Male | Male | Same | Hippie | 1.9130 |
| 5 | Female | Male | Opposite | Straight | 2.2962 |
| 6 | Male | Female | Opposite | Straight | 2.5000 |
| 7 | Female | Female | Same | Straight | 2.8518 |
| 8 | Male | Male | Same | Straight | 2.9166 |

ing. The simple finding of interaction between these two independent variables becomes more complicated than it at first appeared to be in Table 2.

This specification of different levels of reporting requires us to try to explain the results for each category, separately. For straight shoplifters, same-sex reporting may be less than opposite-sex reporting because subjects are more able to empathize with persons of the same sex. Another possibility is that subjects are more likely to report a member of the opposite sex because they feel less threatened. That is, subjects may feel that they are less likely to be attacked (physically or verbally) in a highly visible public situation by a member of the opposite sex than by a member of the same sex.

On the other hand, female subjects are more likely than male subjects to report the shoplifter who is a hippie because they are probably more offended by the overt violation of community norms and are more threatened by such attacks on the social order of the community. Females therefore are more likely than males to sanction persons with a nonrespectable appearance. The possibility that female subjects are more concerned with the appearance of respectability and with maintenance of social order explains the differential in reporting between male and female subjects when the shoplifter is a hippie.

## DISCUSSION

The major results of this research are that sex of shoplifter and sex of subject had little effect on reporting levels, whereas appearance of shoplifter exerted a major independent effect on reporting levels. The importance of appearance merits further discussion: How to account for its significance?

The evidence presented clearly indicates that a hippie appearance constituted a highly salient basis for social differentiation. From the perspective of "middle class" America, hippies and other beatnik types are viewed as basically unstable, as lacking in ambition and ability, and as marginal contributors to the social system. By the mere fact of being a hippie the person has demonstrated his lack of moral worth, his unrespectability, from the dominant cultural perspective. As such, a hippie label represents a stigma, an extreme negative identity. Such an identity has been variously dealt with as a "master status" by Becker (1963), a "pivotal category" by Lofland (1969), or a "central trait" by Asch (1946). All of these concepts refer to a similar phenomenon: an extreme negative identity can exercise a disproportionate influence in structuring perceptions and behaviors and, in terms of this research, the reactions to shoplifting. A hippie identity or label constitutes, for many subjects in this research, a master status, a pivotal category, or a central trait, which greatly increases the individual's vulnerability to stigmatization as a deviant.[9]

[9]Related notions have been dealt with in exchange theory wherein perceived statuses or identities are characterized in terms of positive and negative credits. In dealing with reactions to deviance the reasoning is as follows: the higher the perceived status of an individual the greater his "stock" of es-

Some anecdotal observations illustrate these notions. These observations also depict the less conscious, less deliberate reactions of the subjects to the hippie identity than to the straight identity. In general, most subjects appeared to be inclined *not* to report the shoplifting incident and to avoid getting involved. When they witnessed the incident and the shoplifter gave off no other negative cues or stimuli they were apt to hesitate. Hesitation of this sort was likely to result in disengagement and failure to report.

Subjects were more likely to hesitate when the shoplifter was straight rather than hippie. A number of subjects, for instance, indicated that they considered reporting the straight shoplifter but thought twice or hesitated before proceeding with a course of action. This "thinking twice" or hesitating then often resulted in their deciding simply to ignore the incident.

But in the case of hippie shoplifters, this hesitation was less likely to occur. That is, when witnessing a hippie shoplifting the subject was not only more likely to consider reporting but he was also less likely to think twice about it and thus in reality he was more likely to proceed to report. The hippie appearance seemed to tip the scales in the direction of increased reporting.

Further support for the importance of appearance comes from the level of enthusiasm in reporting. In reporting the hippie shoplifter some subjects were very excited—even enthusiastic. Although not true of all subjects, reporting of hippie shoplifters (without prompting) frequently included such comments as "That hippie thing took a package of lunchmeat," or "That son of a bitch hippie over there just stuffed a banana down his coat." For these subjects, the high levels of reporting of hippie shoplifters must be viewed within a particular situational context wherein his undoing was not simply a result of his being a shoplifter, but because he was both shoplifter *and* hippie.

## CONCLUSIONS

Via the use of field research techniques combined with an experimental design we have provided clear support for the basic interactionist-labeling contention that the imputation of deviance resides not only in the *fact* of deviance per se; it also depends heavily on the meanings that the audience attach to the behavior and the actor. Willingness to report deviant acts can be assumed to depend on the "de-

---

teem, or accumulation of credits. Being involved in visibly deviant behaviors, such as shoplifting, reduces the absolute level of these accumulated credits. However, if a high- (straight-appearing actor) and low- (hippie-appearing actor) status individual commit the same deviant act the high-status person can retain some level of positive credits while the low-status person can go to zero or minus quantity of credits (Alvarez, 1968; Hollander, 1958; Homans, 1961). Thus having a high-status or respectable identity serves to "protect" the actor from being reported for shoplifting whereas having a low-status or less-than-respectable identity increases the likelihood of being reported. That is, a hippie appearance reduces an actor's level of positive credits to a considerable degree, with the effect that when such an actor engages in deviant behavior, more positive credits are lost and his chances for being reported are greatly increased.

viant's" other social identities, a significant clue to identity being provided by his appearance.

At the same time, however, some other identities that may seem to be important at first glance may actually prove to be unimportant aspects of the interpersonal relationships between offender and audience. This seemed to be the case with sex of shoplifter and sex of subject, although it is apparent that the complexity of the relationships involved necessitates additional research. Further research should also focus upon other aspects of the social identities of the offender, the situational contexts in which deviant acts occur, and the backgrounds and relevant identities of members of the social audience. At the very least we have demonstrated that in order to get at such problems it is possible and fruitful to utilize experimental field research techniques.

## REFERENCES

Alvarez, R. 1968. "Informal reactions to deviance in simulated work organizations: a laboratory experiment." *American Sociological Review* 33: 895–911.

Asch, S. E. 1946. "Forming impressions of personality." *Journal of Abnormal and Social Psychology* 41:258–290.

Ball, D. W. 1970. "The problematics of respectability." In *Respectability and Deviance,* edited by Jack Douglas. New York: Basic Books.

Becker, Howard S. 1963. *Outsiders: Studies in the Sociology of Deviance.* New York: Free Press.

Bickman, L. 1971. "The effect of social class on the honesty of others." *Journal of Social Psychology* 85: 87–92.

Black, Donald J. 1970. "Production of crime rates." *American Sociological Review* 35: 733–748.

Black, Donald J., and Albert J. Reiss, Jr. 1970. "Police control of juveniles." *American Sociological Review* 35: 63–77.

Cameron, Mary O. 1964. *The Booster and the Snitch.* Glencoe: Free Press.

Carey, James T. 1968. *The College Drug Scene.* Englewood Cliffs: Prentice-Hall.

Darley, J. M., and B. Latané. 1968. "Bystander intervention in emergencies: diffusion of responsibility." *Journal of Personality and Social Psychology* 8: 377–383.

Denner, B. 1968. "Did a crime occur? Should I inform anyone? A study of deception." *Journal of Personality* 36: 454–468.

Douglas, Jack (editor). 1970. *Respectability and Deviance.* New York: Basic Books.

————. 1971a. *American Social Order.* New York: Free Press.

———— (editor). 1971b. *Research on Deviance.* New York: Random House.

Emerson, Robert M. 1969. *Judging Delinquents.* Chicago: Aldine.

Freed, A., P. J. Chandler, R. R. Blake, and J. S. Mouton. 1955. "Stimulus and background factors in sign violation." *Journal of Personality* 23: 499.

Goffman, Erving. 1963. *Stigma: Notes on the Management of Spoiled Identity.* Englewood Cliffs: Spectrum Books.

Hollander, E. P. 1958. "Conformity, status, and idiosyncrasy credit." *Psychological Review* 65: 117–127.

Homans, George C. 1961. *Social Behavior: Its Elementary Forms.* New York: Harcourt, Brace and World.

Hughes, E. C. 1945. "Dilemmas and contradictions of status." *American Journal of Sociology* 50: 353–359.

Humphreys, Laud. 1970. *Tearoom Trade.* Chicago: Aldine.

Kitsuse, J. I. 1962. "Societal reaction to deviant behavior: problems of theory and method." *Social Problems* 9: 247–256.

Kitsuse, J. I., and A. Cicourel. 1963. "A note on the uses of official statistics." *Social Problems* 11: 131–139.

Kohout, Frank J. 1974. *Statistics for Social Scientists: A Coordinated Learning System.* New York: Wiley.

Latané, B., and J. Darley. 1969. "Bystander apathy." *American Scientist* 57: 244–268.

Lefkowitz, M., R. R. Blake, and J. S. Mouton. 1955. "Status factors in pedestrian violation of traffic signals." *Journal of Abnormal and Social Psychology* 51: 704–705.

Lemert, Edwin. 1951. *Social Pathology.* New York: McGraw-Hill.

Lofland, John. 1969. *Deviance and Identity.* Englewood Cliffs: Prentice-Hall.

Parsons, Talcott, and Robert F. Bales. 1955. *Family Socialization and Interaction Process.* Glencoe: Free Press.

Phillips, D. L. 1964. "Rejection of the mentally ill: the influence of behavior and sex." *American Sociological Review* 29: 679–687.

Piliavin, I., and S. Briar. 1964. "Police encounters with juveniles." *American Journal of Sociology* 70: 206–214.

Pollak, Otto. 1961. *The Criminality of Women.* New York: Perpetua Books.

Reckless, Walter. 1961. *The Crime Problem.* New York: Appleton-Century-Crofts.

Scheff, Thomas J. 1966. *Being Mentally Ill: A Sociological Theory.* Chicago: Aldine.

Schuessler, Karl. 1971. *Analyzing Social Data.* Boston: Houghton Mifflin.

Schur, E. M. 1969. "Reactions to deviance: a critical assessment." *American Journal of Sociology* 75: 309–322.

Simmons, J. L. 1965. "Public stereotypes of deviants." *Social Problems* 13: 223–232.

Stone, G. P. 1962. "Appearance and the self." In *Human Behavior and Social Processes,* edited by Arnold Rose. Boston: Houghton Mifflin.

Sudnow, D. 1965. "Normal crimes: sociological features of the penal code in a public defender office." *Social Problems* 12: 255–276.

Ward, David A., and Gene Kassebaum. 1965. *Women's Prison: Sex and Social Structure.* Chicago: Aldine.

Westie, F. R., and J. C. Martin. 1959. "The tolerant personality." *American Sociological Review* 24: 521–528.

Whatley, C. D. 1959. "Social attitudes toward discharged mental patients." *Social Problems* 6: 313–320.

Wheeler. S. 1967. "Criminal statistics: a reformulation of the problem." *Journal of Criminal Law, Criminology, and Police Science* 58: 317–324.

Williams, Robin M., Jr. 1964. *Strangers Next Door.* Englewood Cliffs: Prentice-Hall.

# 11

# LEGAL CONTROL OF MUSIC: THE CASE OF ROCK AND RAP

## NANCY A. HEITZEG

*"If one were permitted to make all the ballads, one need not care
who should make the laws . . . "*
*—Andrew Fletcher, Scottish Parliament, 1704*

Across history and cultures, many have recognized, and often feared, the power of music to effect social change. Music, it is argued, is not merely entertainment, but a potent force that may influence individual attitudes and actions, encourage deviant behavior, spark social movements, and threaten the very foundations of the social order.

As a result, music deemed to be socially disruptive is often socially or legally regulated, and, in some cases, banned. The music of ancient China, India, and Greece, for example, was closely monitored by rulers and philosophers. Confucius warned that "coarse and sensual" music could lead to moral degradation (Tame, 1984:19), and Plato, in *The Republic,* contended that deviations in musical style could have far-reaching sociopolitical consequences: "Any musical innovation is full of danger to the whole state and ought to be prohibited. . . . When the mode of the music changes, the walls of the city will shake . . . " (Plato, 1945).

Legal control of music is certainly not limited to the ancients. A variety of European monarchies legislated against ballads that did not reflect their religious beliefs, and more contemporary political regimes have legally prohibited certain types of music. The political suppression of reggae in Jamaica, soca/calypso in Trinidad and Grenada, Rara in Haiti, Salsa in Cuba, freedom songs in South Africa, and Western rock in the former USSR are cases in point (Denisoff, 1982:19; Bergman, 1985; Seeger, 1992:113–143).

The United States is no exception. Music, as a cultural product, has frequently been linked with deviance. This is particularly true when it is associated with unconventional groups, or expresses unconventional values and beliefs (Black, 1976:67–80; Denisoff, 1972; Hebdige, 1980; Brake, 1985; Weinstein, 1991; Rose, 1994; Sexton, 1995; Heitzeg, 1987; Heitzeg, 1996:397–430).

Further, social control is magnified when the music in question is linked with subcultures that are already vulnerable due to their position in the system of stratification (e.g., youth, racial/ethnic minorities, the poor and economically disenfranchised) (Denisoff, 1972; Black, 1976:13–36; Hebdige, 1980; Brake, 1985; Heitzeg, 1987; Weinstein, 1991; Gaines, 1992; Rose, 1994; Sexton, 1995; Heitzeg, 1996:397–430). It is not surprising, then, that the most extreme reactions to music have been reserved for jazz, folk, rock, and rap. All have been legally controlled in a variety of ways, primarily as a result of their unconventionality and association with marginal social groups.

## TWENTIETH CENTURY PRECEDENTS: JAZZ, FOLK, AND FORMAL DEVIANCE

Throughout U.S. history, a variety of styles of music have been directly or indirectly subject to legal control. In the early 20th century, jazz and folk caused widespread concern and negative societal reaction on a number of levels.

Primarily due to its association with African-Americans, jazz was targeted for a media smear campaign. As jazz historian Frank Tirro notes, "Jazz became the symbol of crime, feeblemindedness, insanity, and sex . . . " (Tirro, 1979:42). It was later associated with marijuana and heroin use, illicit alcohol use, and organized crime during Prohibition, along with African-American "insolence" and integration and generalized "moral decay." A Chicago newspaper of the 1920s reported as follows: "Moral disaster is coming to hundreds of young American girls through the pathological, nerve-irritating, sex-exciting music of jazz orchestras . . . " (Tame, 1984:193–194). Ironically, the spread of jazz to Chicago and elsewhere was precipitated by a legal crackdown on the music in New Orleans. In 1917, the U.S. Secretary of the Navy ordered the bars and brothels of the Storeyville section there closed (Tirro, 1979:46). Jazz, sex, violence, and dissipation were cited as the reasons. Later, from 1943 to 1948, Harry Anslinger, head of the Federal Bureau of Narcotics (now the DEA), ordered his agents to conduct surveillance and keep files on virtually all jazz and swing musicians (Herer, 1991:66).

Folk music of the early 1900s met with similar opposition. The burgeoning labor movement of the period relied heavily on folk protest songs as a means of persuasion and a way to promote solidarity. Although labor unions are part of mainstream politics today, they were widely opposed in the early 1900s. The early labor movement in the United States also adhered to leftist political ideologies (i.e., socialist, communist, anarchist) (Runkle, 1972:23–40).

Political repression of the union movement, and, later, the leftists, simultaneously meant suppression of folk protest music and its disseminators. The Industrial Workers of the World (IWW or Wobblies) were largely eradicated through a series of events taking place between 1914 and 1920 (Greenway, 1953; IWW, 1992; Seeger, 1992:87–90). The IWW, founded in 1905, used the protest songs of Joe Hill (contained in *The Little Red Songbook*) to further the union movement. As a result of his ability to translate familiar tunes and hymns into union anthems, Joe Hill became an influential and subsequently feared union organizer. He was arrested in 1914 for killing a shopkeeper in Utah. Many, then and now, believe he was framed. Nonetheless, he was executed by firing squad in 1915, almost ensuring legendary status. His last letter contains the admonition, "Don't mourn; organize," which has become an almost universal reformist slogan (Seeger, 1992:88). Joe Hill became the subject of a folk song, most notably sung by Joan Baez at the Woodstock music festival in 1969. The death of Joe Hill, however, and further political suppression of the IWW in the Palmer raids of 1919 and 1920 effectively eliminated the influence of the IWW (Runkle, 1972:29).

Folk songs were also used by the Communist Party of the United States of America (CPUSA) from the 1920s until the "Red Scare" of the 1950s. The Party, and the political left in general, were promoted by protest songs from the Almanac Singers, Woody Guthrie, Pete Seeger and the Weavers, and others. The folk music of this era is characterized by a wide variety of political themes: pro-labor, pro-union, anticapitalist, and antiwar sentiments (Denisoff, 1972:63–69). Folk musicians came under attack during the McCarthy era of the mid-1950s, when anti-Communist sentiment was rampant. Although no one suffered as extreme a fate as Joe Hill, many folk singers were blacklisted, denied record contracts and radio play, and at least one—Pete Seeger—was blacklisted from television until 1967. The music, however simple, was treated as threatening to the prevailing political order (Seeger, 1992).

In more recent times, jazz and folk have become generally accepted and only minimally regulated styles of music. They are no longer seen to present the danger many once felt they did, and are performed without negative media coverage, public outrage, or legal intervention. Perhaps it is because time has tempered them, and the artists and audiences are older and more respectable now. Or, perhaps they have been supplanted by musical genres deemed to be far more inflammatory. Indeed, for the past 40 years, the public, the media, lawmakers, and law enforcement officials have been preoccupied with the regulation of first, rock music, and most recently, rap.

## ROCK, RAP, AND INFORMAL DEVIANCE

The association of rock and rap with deviance may be attributed to two key factors. First, rock and rap are the musics of choice for many youth. Youth, particularly males and minorities, are already more vulnerable to all types of social control: informal, medical, and legal. They are politically disenfranchised and economically marginalized, and thus serve as convenient scapegoats for a host of social ills including alcohol and drug use, illegitimate births, and violence (Gaines, 1992; Grossberg, 1995:25–46; Weinstein, 1995:67–86; Males, 1996). Since nearly every aspect of youthful lives is regulated, it is not surprising that the music of youth should come under special scrutiny as well.

The second factor that contributes to the social control of rock and rap is the unconventionality of these genres. Both types of music represent a series of informal deviations from the prevailing norms of musical sound, style, and statement.

At the outset, rock and rap, in their subcultural manifestations, represent deviations from popular Top 40 music, as well as classical and country music (Garofalo, 1997:395–440; Hebdige, 1980; Brake, 1985; Weinstein, 1991; Heitzeg, 1996:399–401). The music of both rock and rap is harder, louder, faster, more minimal and less melodic, more grating and unpredictable than pop melodies. The sound is often described by nonfans as harsh, noisy, and annoying. The singers scream and talk over loud and fast instrumentation, intended and interpreted as an audio assault.

In addition, the styles favored by performers and participants deviate from accepted informal norms of appearance with respect to attire, hair, make-up, tattoos, and body decoration. The multitude of rock genres that have appeared since the mid-1950s have twisted conventional style norms in a number of specific ways. Metal, for example, features long-haired males in black leather, silver-studded gear, and spandex. Punk rock has multicolored mohawks and shredded clothing. Grunge is associated with dirty matted hair, unkempt clothing, and body/facial piercings. Glam rock became infamous for its gender-bending style and the use of make-up by androgynous male performers. Rap, too, draws on styles that reflect the street rather than conventional society. Rappers and their audiences favor oversized baggy pants, tattoos, shaved heads, faded haircuts or dreadlocks, pierced ears or noses; in general, the look that has been widely associated with inner-city black youth in general and gangs in particular (Garofalo, 1997:395–440; Hebdige, 1980; Brake, 1985; Weinstein, 1991; Heitzeg, 1996:399–401).

The statements of rock and rap also deviate from the standard pop themes of love and romance. Rock music has always included lyrical discussions of forbidden topics, including sex of all sorts (i.e., gay/straight/bisexual relations, promiscuity, rape, bondage, and domination), alcohol and other drug use, violence, suicide, homicide, revolution, rejection of all types of authority, and extreme individualism (Hebdige, 1980:100–118; Weinstein, 1991:93–107; Heitzeg, 1996:428–429).

Rap also features lyrical themes that deviate from conventional norms. These include life on the street, crime, alcohol and other drugs, sex, homicide, rape, black nationalism, militarism, police brutality, violence against the police, economic inequality, and racism (Spencer, 1991; Rose, 1994; Sexton, 1995; Shomari, 1995).

The sound, style, and statement deviations of both rock and rap combine to produce an explicit social commentary that, in different ways, is highly critical of the prevailing social order. In rock music, the criticism is leveled at pressures to conform, the constricting effect of the nine-to-five life, and a myriad of rules and regulations perceived to be mindless and needless. Fundamentally, rock is about the freedom to be yourself, however different that may be (Hebdige, 1980:100–118; Heitzeg, 1996:428–429).

The cumulative social statement of rap is directed toward describing, and often condemning, a social reality rife with classism, racism, blocked opportunity, gang violence, police brutality, and crack cocaine. It is a rage against injustice and inequality, as well as a depiction of their consequences. Already stigmatized as outsiders, due to race and social class, rappers and their audiences are unconcerned about the right to be different. Rap is simply about the right to be (Spencer, 1991; Rose, 1994:99–140; Sexton, 1995).

The sounds, styles, and statements of rock and rap clearly deviate from conventional social norms. Few, including performers and participants, would dispute this. Most certainly, these forms of music and their adherents have been informally defined and controlled as deviant on the interpersonal and organizational levels by a variety of conventional groups.

Opposition to rock and rap has historically been associated with particular groups. Parents, whether through intrafamilial confrontations with their own children or through organizational efforts (e.g., PTA, Parents of Punkers, Back in Control, and the Parents' Music Resource Center) have been a major impetus behind efforts to define and control rock and rap music. Their concerns have spilled over into other social arenas, and, as a result, parents' interests are frequently supported by other social subgroups. School officials and academicians, often in conjunction with parents, have expressed disapproval, either on an isolated case-by-case administrative basis, through academic research and speculation, or on a large-scale organizational level. Such is also the case with religious leaders and groups. Opposition to rock and rap has come from leaders of various Christian and Jewish sects, and has ranged from individual commentary to entire antimusic movements. The Christian Crusade, the Rally for Decency, and, most currently, the St. Paul Ministry of the Reverends John, Steve, and Dan Peters have built careers around the denunciation of rock and its attendant implications, while the Reverend Jesse Jackson's Rainbow Coalition and the Reverend Calvin Butts have recently been at the fore of critical attacks against rap (Denisoff, 1982, 1986; Peters and Peters, 1984; Sexton, 1995:75–77, 81–96; Garofalo, 1997:438).

The efforts of parents, academicians, and religious organizations have frequently received the support of the mass media (e.g., television, radio, newspapers, and magazines). Indeed, the media represent another essential special interest that has historically played an integral role in the informal definition and control of rock and rap. The media, with their pervasive influence in our society, have become implicated in these efforts primarily via selective coverage and negative stereotyping. Rock and rap music have received almost exclusively negative coverage from the media. At times, fans are the focus, at other times the performers; occasionally, entire genres are targeted. Almost every possible type of deviance has been presented by the media as the result of rock and rap music: sexual perversions and promiscuity, violence, alcohol and drug abuse, political extremism, satanism, antisocial behavior, suicide, murder, and gang activity. Exceptional or occasional occurrences involving such behavior are almost always presented as the rule, and positive coverage of rock and rap is very rare (Sanchez, 1979; Hebdige, 1980; Herman, 1982; Stallings, 1984; Brake, 1985; Vermore and Vermore, 1985; Balfour, 1986; Davis, 1986; Des Barres, 1986; Duncan, 1986; Weinstein, 1991; Dotter, 1995:87–114; Sexton, 1995:136–216; Garofalo, 1997:395–439).

Much of the informal social control of rock and rap has a very specific focus. The goal is redefinition of the informal deviance expressed in rock and rap as deviance of a more serious legal sort. The argument presented is that rock and rap, already deviant in themselves, also contribute to other kinds of deviance. The unconventional sound, style, and statement are alleged to incite law-breaking behavior in already suspect youth and to call for control by law rather than merely by convention. Because the sanctions available under the informal model are comparatively minimal, opponents of rock music prefer to redefine it as a problem for formal control. In fact, rock and rap music have been and continue to be the subject of extensive control by administrative, civil, and criminal law. Further, participants in the rock and rap subcultures have been disproportionately accused of a wide variety of acts that come under the purview of formal social control: for example, sexual deviance (homosexuality, bestiality, necrophilia, and indecent exposure), substance use (underage consumption of alcohol and use of illicit drugs), vandalism, and violence (suicide and interpersonal violence such as rape, gang activity, aggravated assault, and murder) (Garofalo, 1997:395–439; Sanchez, 1979; Hebdige, 1980; Herman, 1982; Stallings, 1984; Brake, 1985; Vermore and Vermore, 1985; Balfour, 1986; Davis, 1986; DesBarres, 1986; Duncan, 1986; Weinstein, 1991; Dotter, 1995:87–114; Sexton, 1995:136–216).

### ROCK, RAP, AND LAW

Much like jazz and folk in preceding eras, rock and rap have been controlled by the law. Legal control is, in part, directed at subcultural participants; at times, however, it is directed toward the music itself. The legal control of these forms of music is multilayered, involving criminal, civil, and administrative laws and sanctions. The law has been used to control rock and rap and their subcultural participants via two distinct approaches: indirect legal control, and direct legal control. Each is examined in turn.

### INDIRECT LEGAL CONTROL

Performers and fans in rock and rap music subcultures have long been subject to indirect legal control—that is, they have been subject to far more legal scrutiny than the average citizen, and are more likely to be controlled by laws that are

not directly related to their music. As Black notes, "Any person who is unconventional in dress, speech, manner, ideas or anything else, is more vulnerable to
law of every kind" (Black, 1976:71). The most frequent legal violations for which
people associated with rock and rap are put under surveillance include illicit drug
use, vandalism, violence, the underage consumption of alcohol, sexual deviance,
weapons possession, and gang activity (Herman, 1979; Brake, 1985; Heitzeg,
1987; Weinstein, 1991; Rose, 1994:120–139; Garofalo, 1997:436–438). Legal
agents tend to assume that rock and rap foster all these violations, a belief fueled
in part by media stereotyping.

It is important to note in this regard that there is no evidence to suggest that participants in rock and rap subcultures are more criminally deviant than youth in general, or adults for that matter. Law-violating behavior is widely distributed across
economic, racial/ethnic, and age groups (Samaha, 1997). Further, evidence indicates that the greatest economic and physical harms are due to the legal violations
of the wealthy and the corporate (Reiman, 1994; Friederichs, 1996; Simon, 1996).
Nonetheless, it is the young, particularly the poor, the male and minority who are
disproportionately subject to stringent legal control, with unconventional youth
facing the greatest risks of all (Cohen, 1980; Hebdige, 1980; Brake, 1985; Heitzeg,
1987; Gaines, 1992; Weinstein, 1992:250–270; Grossberg, 1995:25–46; Heitzeg,
1996:427–430; Males, 1996). As a result, rock and rap fans and performers have
a long history of arrests and civil suits that occur both in conjunction with performances and within the context of everyday life.

Many arrests occur on the occasion of concert or club performances; this is true
for both fans and performers. Since 1952, when Alan Freed's first concert promotion resulted in five arrests, rock concerts have been a focal point for law. Rock
and rap history is replete with fan arrests for alcohol, drug, and weapons violations. The late 1960s festival movement was stereotyped as providing havens for
drug use, and, consequently, police enforcement of drug laws was frequently directed at such events. Police still use extensive search and seizure methods to attempt to curtail concert-related drug use, particularly at heavy metal events. In addition to police presence, concerts are monitored by private security agencies that
"in many respects, have more authority than a police officer. They are working as
an agent for the show and they can establish any rules they wish. If you break the
rules, you don't get a jury trial. They just throw you out." As a result, few such
concerts transpire without at least a few arrests for drug or alcohol violations or
disorderly conduct (Peterson, 1973; Cohen, 1980; Denisoff, 1982, 1986; Lewis,
1995). Such is also the case with rap concerts.

Rock and rap performers, like their fans, are also especially vulnerable to legal
control exercised by police during concerts. Many of the alleged violations have
been related to overt sexuality such as "indecent exposure," or the use of "obscene
language." Other arrests have been for encouraging crowd activity, such as by urging the audience to ignore security restrictions and stand or dance in the aisles. The
long list of rock and rap stars arrested for such on-stage behavior includes Jim Mor-
rison of the Doors, Wendy O. Williams of the Plasmatics, Devo, Einstruzende

Neubauten, Sebastian Bach of Skid Row, Alex Rose of Guns N' Roses, the Beastie Boys, NWA, Bobby Brown, and 2 Live Crew (Peterson, 1973:170; Herman, 1982; Heitzeg, 1987; Weinstein, 1991; Rose, 1994:128–129; Sexton, 1995:136–164).

Police control of rock and rap performers and participants extends beyond the concert setting. In many instances, arrests are not directly linked to a musical context, yet the deviance in question is often associated with musical subcultures. The police react differentially to identifiable members of the rock subculture. Due to their self-presentation as "outsiders" via stylistic deviations, participants in rock music subcultures usually have set themselves apart. Their unconventional appearance identifies them to the police as symbolic assailants, and thus as potential criminals to be watched, followed, stopped, frisked, and arrested. Indeed, participants in rock music subcultures are likely to be harassed and arrested for activities that are not related to rock music; historically, this has been the case in both Great Britain and the United States. Research has shown that participants in rock music subcultures have high arrest rates for a variety of offenses. When compared with nonparticipants, it becomes apparent that rock music fans are arrested more often because they are under closer police scrutiny; it is not due only to a different volume of deviance.

One study, for example, found that participants in rock subcultures were more likely to be arrested for a variety of offenses than were nonparticipants, despite similar rates of self-reported criminality. Since the two groups were comparable in regard to other social characteristics (i.e., SES, race, gender, age, and education), unconventional appearance is the essential factor in explaining differential arrest rates for subcultural participants. Further, participants in rock subcultures indicated that police were likely to stop and question them without apparent justification; many felt that their unconventional appearance was a contributor to increased police encounters (Heitzeg, 1987). Other research on rock subcultural participants, including mods and rockers, punks, skinheads, and heavy metal fans has found a similar pattern of escalated police surveillance, and, subsequently, higher rates of arrest (Cohen, 1980; Hebdige, 1980; Knight, 1982; Brake, 1985; Baron, 1989:207–237; Gaines, 1992; Weinstein, 1991; Grossberg, 1995:25–46; Heitzeg, 1996:417–427).

Current police concern over juvenile gangs has served to increase the monitoring of rock subcultures and their participants. Many law enforcement agencies now define heavy metal fans and punk rockers as gang members. Drawing on information from school officials and juvenile justice personnel, police now consider youth who dress in punk or metal attire as gang participants who are inclined to violence, anarchism, and the occult. Several California police departments use the training manual, *Punk Rock and Heavy Metal: The Problem/One Solution,* which lists dangerous bands and advocates surveillance of their fans and censorship of their music. Further, the probation department in Orange County, California, has defined involvement in certain kinds of rock music as delinquent behavior. As part of the rules of probation, juveniles are forbidden to listen to any heavy metal or punk groups, to hang the groups' posters on the walls, to wear T-shirts with the groups' names, to go to their concerts, and to dress like their fans. An Orange County organization called Back in Control conducts training sessions for the probation department on the allegedly nefarious effects of punk and heavy metal music (Marsh, 1989; Minnesota Police and Peace Officers, 1990:110–132; Garofalo, 1997:433).

Undoubtedly, participants in rap music are already targets of disproportionate police surveillance. By virtue of being mostly young, black, and male, they are under more police scrutiny than any other category of U.S. citizen, a fact substantiated by a large body of sociological research (e.g., Bridges and Meyers, 1994; Reiman, 1994; Walker, Spohn, and Delone, 1996; Samaha, 1997). (Ironically, this very point is stressed anecdotally in much rap music. As KRS-ONE so aptly put it: "You were put here to protect us, but who protects us from you?" [KRS-ONE, 1989]) The situation is compounded by a number of factors including the conflict between law enforcement and various rap artists, the critique of the police leveled by much rap music, and the rise of west coast "gangsta rap" which is linked to gang activity via lyrics as well as alleged artist affiliations. Young black males were already the most likely "symbolic assailants" prior to rap; now police have additional reasons to target this group, and evidence suggests that they do. As already noted, rap concerts and movies with rap themes draw additional police scrutiny (Harig, 1989:1; Costello and Wallace, 1990; Rose, 1994). Further, the attire of rap and gang have become nearly synonymous to law enforcement officials, thus subjecting rap fans to an added risk of police encounters (Skolnick, 1975; Costello and Wallace, 1990; Marsh, 1989:6; Minnesota Police and Peace Officers, 1990; Rose, 1994; Majors and Billson, 1992; Spohn and Delone, 1996).

Rock and rap performers, like their fans, are often arrested for activities that occur outside a musical context. From the 1950s to the present, the arrest of rock performers for sexual offenses, drug use, income tax violations, and property damage have made headlines. Certain performers have been subject to much publicized legal attention. Chuck Berry (tax evasion), Paul McCartney (possession of marijuana), Iggy Pop (possession of drugs), Jerry Lee Lewis (income tax evasion), Donovan (possession of marijuana), the Rolling Stones (public urination and innumerable international drug arrests characterized by extensive trials in 1967 and 1977), John Lennon and Yoko Ono (possession of marijuana), Ron Wood (possession of cocaine), the Stranglers (possession of heroin, cocaine, and marijuana, and theft), the Sex Pistols (possession of amphetamines), Gregg Allman (possession of heroin and reckless driving), Joe Cocker (possession of marijuana and illegal entry), Eric Clapton (alcohol violations), Sid Vicious (murder), David Crosby (possession of cocaine and weapons), Motley Crue member Vince Neill (vehicular homicide), Jello Biafra (distributing material harmful to minors), Boy George (possession of heroin), Kurt Cobain and wife Courtney Love (possession of heroin shortly before Cobain's 1994 suicide, and child endangerment due to Courtney's alleged use of heroin during pregnancy) are but a few cases in point (Herman, 1982; Marsh and Stein, 1987; Azerrad, 1994; News Service, 1994:1A).

The list of arrests for rap stars is comparable. Notable examples include Flavor Flav of Public Enemy (attempted murder and criminal possession of a firearm), Slick Rick (manslaughter), and Snoop Doggy Dogg (murder) (Nelson, 1993:32; Roberts, 1996:69; Samuels and Leland, 1996:66–70; Garofalo, 1997:436–438). Perhaps the most notorious cases of late involve the late Tupac Shakur and the head of Death Row Records, Marion "Suge" Knight. During the last 3 years of his life, Tupac was involved in an escalating series of legal conflicts. There were several allegations of assault, and an arrest in 1993 on charges of shooting two off-duty police officers in Atlanta. Due to lack of evidence, this case never made it to a grand jury. Also in 1993, Tupac was arrested for sexual assault and later convicted, serving 8 months of a four-and-a-half-year sentence. In total, Tupac was arrested eight times, although he noted that "I never had a record until I made a record" (Powell, 1996:40).

In addition to the criminal law, civil suits against rock and rap artists are an increasingly common method of legal control. The initial precedents involved rock music. One of the first cases was brought by the parents of 11 young people who were crushed and trampled to death at a Who concert in Cincinnati. The parents sued the band for $11 million (Herman, 1982:141; Lewis, 1995:251–282). In recent years, more suits have been filed, most of which are filed under civil statutes related to wrongful death or consumer product safety. Two notable cases, involving Ozzy Osbourne and Judas Priest, were brought by parents of suicide victims. Both cases raise First Amendment issues and revive a debate over the existence and effects of subliminal messages in popular music.

Ozzy Osbourne and CBS Records were sued by a California couple whose 19-year-old son shot himself with his father's rifle after listening to the song "Suicide Solution." The civil suit was based on a California law "prohibiting assistance or encouragement of suicide." The teen, a high school dropout who had problems with the law, reportedly listened to a steady diet of heavy metal. After the suit was dismissed, new evidence alleged that a 28-second instrumental interval on "Suicide Solution" contains masked lyrics that induced the suicide. Steve Wilhauson of the Institute for Bio-Acoustic Research discovered the following lyrics after playing the song at one-and-one-half times the rate of normal speech. "Ah know people, you really know where it's at. You got it. Why try, why try? Get the gun and try it. Shoot, shoot, shoot" (Weinstein, 1991:250–256).

A similar suit was filed against Judas Priest and CBS Records in Washoe County, Nevada. The lawsuit claimed that Judas Priest's music caused two Reno youths, James Vance and Ray Belnap, to shoot themselves. "The suggestive lyrics, combined with the continuous beat and rhythmic non-changing connotation of the music combined to induce . . . and otherwise mesmerize the plaintiff into believing the answer to life was death" (Peterson, 1990:1E; Garofalo, 1997:250–252). The case was allowed to proceed due to the presiding judge's ruling that subliminal messages were not protected by the First Amendment. Judas Priest won the lawsuit when the judge found that no clear-cut proof of subliminals or malicious intent could be established.

Most recently, civil suits have been brought against rap artists. Tupac Shakur and his previous label, Interscope Records, settled a 1992 case out of court. The suit was brought by the mother of a 6-year-old boy killed at a Marin City rap festival. The boy was killed when one of Tupac's crew fired at another group of festivalgoers. Two other civil suits were already pending at the time of Tupac's death. Lawyers defending a man accused of killing a Texas state trooper in 1992 claimed that their client had been influenced by Tupac's first solo album, *2 Pacalypse Now*. The trooper's widow then filed a multimillion dollar lawsuit against the rapper, Interscope Records, and Time Warner, which was then the label's parent company. Most recently, a suit was brought by a woman who was left partly paralyzed after being shot at a Tupac concert in 1995. Her case claims that the rapper worked the crowd into a riotous frenzy, which resulted in the shooting (Powell, 1996:45–46).

## DIRECT LEGAL CONTROL

As we have seen, legal control has been exercised against both fans and performers for a variety of alleged infractions in and out of the concert setting. Legal control of rock and rap can, however, be extended to yet another level: the official adoption of criminal, civil, and administrative laws regulating the content and performance of the music itself. This has taken four major forms: threats of legal control, administrative control through the Federal Communications Commission (FCC), concert restrictions, and legislation focusing on alleged pornography in the music.

### Threats of Legal Control

Sometimes the mere threat of legal action is sufficient to persuade record companies, radio and television stations, and recording industry trade associations to censor themselves. The groundwork is often laid in antirock or rap campaigns led by various interest groups, perhaps with the support of politicians or other public figures. The threat of legal control may invoke the prospect of more stringent Federal Communications Commission (FCC) regulations or penalties. It may also involve the possibility of state and/or federal legislation providing for civil remedies or criminal sanctions.

Such threats have been used to control rock music from the outset. Individual politicians, including President Richard Nixon, Vice President Spiro Agnew, former Alabama Governor George Wallace, and President Ronald Reagan, have openly attacked rock music and supported more rigid legal control. So have a multitude of conservative political groups, including the John Birch Society, the Decency Movement, Citizens for Conservative Action, Constructive Action Inc., and the Young Republicans. On occasion, congressional hearings investigating rock music have been held. The response of the rock recording industry in the face of such threats has been self-censorship (Denisoff, 1982; Malone, 1985; U.S. Senate, 1985; Denisoff, 1986; Gore, 1988; Marsh, 1989). Record companies, radio stations, and television networks perform a gatekeeper function, determining through record contracts, releases, and air play which types of music and which performers will be presented to the public (Hesbacher, 1973, 1976; Frith, 1987; Rothenbuler, 1985:209–232). Major labels have historically avoided the marketing of the most unconventional and subcultural rock, forcing such groups to rely on small independent labels for exposure. Thus, in the process of deciding which groups to sign and promote, record companies implicitly engage in a subtle form of self-censorship. Radio stations serve a similar function, deciding which records to add to play lists and which to put into heavy rotation. Once again, the most unconventional groups rarely have access to the airwaves, and even Top 40 groups may experience restricted exposure. Television, too, can censor before and after the fact. Current examples of media gatekeeping abound on MTV, a network devoted primarily to the airing of music videos. All of these outlets—record companies, radio and television—are extremely sensitive to threats of increased legal intervention.

The most comprehensive example of the threat of increased legal control can be seen in the Senate Commerce Committee hearing held on September 19, 1985, at the urging of the Parents' Music Resource Center, a coalition founded by well-connected Washington wives. Headed by Senator John Danforth (a Republican from Missouri), the committee heard lengthy testimony on "porn rock," listened to lyrics, and examined videos and album covers. What transpired was a 5-hour excursion into "sex, violence, incest, rape, sadomasochism, suicide, and Satanism," according to Danforth, which "shocked the sensibilities" of those in attendance (U.S. Senate, 1985). The congressional critique of rock's corruptive efforts was further bolstered by President Reagan in a press conference on October 9, 1985. When questioned about rock's themes and the movement to suppress them, Reagan "implied that the violent and the malevolent should not be protected by the First Amendment" (Weinstein, 1991:249). Reagan also complained that movie and rock stars make drug use "look attractive and friendly" (Denisoff, 1986:423). The Senate hearing and presidential remarks added new credibility to the attacks on rock that have existed as long as the music.

The result of the hearing was more industry self-censorship, as recommended by the Recording Industry of America. The RIAA, the recording industry's trade association, agreed to encourage its members to place warning stickers on albums with "explicit lyrics" (Garofalo, 1997:428). This self-censorship was largely an effort to prevent more direct methods of industry censorship from being mandated by government: The Senate Commerce Committee had warned the industry to "clean up your act" or face formal regulation (Marsh, 1989).

The growing popularity of rap throughout the 1980s meant that it, too, would be threatened with increased legal action. Although the FBI had never before adopted an official policy on any record (or work of art for that matter), it felt compelled to do so in 1989. Milt Attlerich, an assistant FBI director, wrote a vaguely threatening official letter condemning the rap group NWA's "Fuck the Police," a song that appeared on their debut album, *Straight Outta Compton*. The letter, which was sent to the group's record company, Priority Records, as well as to law enforcement agencies nationwide, expressed concern over violence and antipolice sentiment in the song's lyrics (Marsh and Pollack, 1989:33–37). NWA steadfastly maintained that the song was an expression of inner-city frustration with police harassment of minorities: "Fuck the police/Comin' straight from the underground/A young nigga got it bad/'cause I'm brown/And not the other color/So police think/They have the authority to/Kill a minority" (NWA, 1988). Nonetheless, the FBI's letter did have a chilling effect on NWA's concert tour that summer. Several concerts were disrupted when the group was detained by police, and, apparently as a result, NWA chose not to perform the song in several venues (Rose, 1994:128–129).

A comparable controversy erupted over Ice-T's "Cop Killer" in 1992. The song appeared on *Body Count,* a hard-rock crossover recording. It was technically a rock recording, but added to the mounting controversy over rap music due to Ice-T's status as a west coast rapper. "Cop Killer," like "Fuck the Police," expressed the anger many people feel about police brutality and racism. In light of the Rodney King verdict and ensuing Los Angeles riots, the lyrics were particularly chilling: "I'm about to bust some shots off. I'm about to dust some cops off" (Ice-T, 1992).

The song had been performed for over a year before it came to the attention of law enforcement officials and high-ranking politicians, who expressed immediate outrage. Over 60 congressmen, the Fraternal Order of Police, dozens of local law enforcement agencies, President George Bush, Vice President Dan Quayle, and congressional candidate Oliver North called for a boycott of Warner Brothers records and all products, movies, and amusement parks owned and operated by the label's parent company, Time Warner (Rose, 1994:130; Sexton, 1995:173–88; Garofalo, 1997:436). Ironically, the boycott was not supported by the National Black Police Association, which noted that " 'Cop Killer' did not happen in a vacuum. People have always expressed their feelings and opinions through songs, and they are talking about how African-American people have been victimized by police brutality; and that is very real. Where were those organizations when Rodney King was beat up and that verdict came in?" (Orr, 1992:79). In spite of this limited support, the pressure to remove "Cop Killer" from future pressings of the record was too great, and Ice-T and Warner Brothers agreed to do so (Rose, 1994:130).

Pressure toward control of the rap industry continued to mount throughout the 1990s. In December, 1993, the National Political Congress of Black Women (NPCBW), led by Dr. C. Delores Tucker, staged demonstrations against two Washington, D.C., record stores. At issue was the alleged violence, gang imagery, and sexism found in some rap music. The demonstrations were supported by the National Council of Negro Women, the NAACP, and the Reverend Jesse Jackson's Rainbow Coalition. The NPCBW advocated a governmental investigation of rap, which took place in February, 1994 (Holland, 1994:10). Both the House and Senate held hearings reminiscent of those sparked by the PMRC in 1985. Rating systems were again proposed, even though the RIAA warnings accompanied rap records as well as rock (Garofalo, 1997:440–441). The result was similar, as well. Several black radio stations banned violence and profanity from the airwaves,

Black Entertainment Television (BET) instituted a no guns policy for videos, MTV curtailed its airing of rap videos, and The Box, a pay-per-view video channel, instated a "guns suck" ad campaign. And, tired of the controversy, Time Warner sold back its 50% share of its rap distributor, Interscope Records, to the label's founders (Stark, 1993:141; Powell, 1996:46). Most recently, Hollywood Records was ordered by its parent company, Disney, to drop the Detroit rap duo, Insane Clown Posse, from its roster. Insiders feel that Disney was responding to pressure from a boycott by the Southern Baptist Convention. Already under attack for what the Convention terms an "immoral, reprehensible, and anti-family" agenda, Disney may have caved in to the pressure by pulling the album (Boehlert, 1997: 29).

## FCC Regulations

Created in 1934, the Federal Communications Commission regulates interstate and foreign commerce in commercialization by wire and radio. As an administrative agency, it creates, investigates, and enforces laws regarding communication over the airwaves. Its primary sanction is the fine. Although the FCC is prohibited by law from engaging in prior censorship, it does "expect radio and television to address the 'problems, needs and interests' of the community which it services." Failure to do so may result in fines or, in more serious situations, failure to obtain a license renewal. Aside from this vague stipulation, the FCC has few objective guidelines regarding lyrical or visual content, and this "very amorphous and uncertain policy" provides the basis of the Commission's control of radio and television. Controversy over the use of airwaves to present "deviant" themes did not arise until the early 1960s. The first case of FCC concern arose in 1963 in regard to the Kingsmen's hit, "Louie, Louie." The slurred delivery led to rumors that the song had explicit sexual content, and an extended FCC investigation was undertaken. It concluded that the song was unintelligible at any speed (Denisoff, 1982:402–418; Dotter, 1995:87–114). Aside from this incident, the FCC took limited action in regulating lyrical content until more serious concerns developed in the late 1960s and early 1970s.

After the advent of so-called protest songs, and an increase in the inclusion of lyrical drug references, the FCC became more involved in policing the content of popular music. Following the 1970 condemnation of drug lyrics by then-Vice President Spiro Agnew, the FCC issued a public notice warning stations about the array of allegedly pro-drug songs. It expressed similar concern about songs with explicit sexual or political references. The FCC threatened to levy strict fines if radio stations failed to comply. Not surprisingly, the stations preferred to avoid the fines, and a number of them removed questionable songs from their playlists. Examples include "Let It Bleed," "Lucy in the Sky With Diamonds," "Needle and Spoon," "White Rabbit," "Monkey Man," "One Toke Over the Line," "Eight Miles High," and "D.O.A," all banned for alleged obscenity or drug references. Recently, stations have refused to air even some decidedly Top 40 material, claiming that explicit sexual references and the alleged promotion of homosexuality were violations of FCC guidelines. Similarly, MTV has written guidelines on sex and violence designed to meet FCC standards. "Videos containing gratuitous violence are unacceptable. . . . Exceptional care must be taken in instances where women and children are victims of, or are threatened by, acts of violence." MTV has returned several videos for reediting, complaining about "unacceptable visuals," and officially banned Madonna's "Justifying Love" video (Weinstein, 1991:162; Garofalo, 1997:433).

While it is very rare for the FCC actually to levy fines or pull licenses, its ability to do so is an incentive for many radio and television stations to be extremely cautious. As a result of previous FCC warnings about rock and rap music, even Top 40 material is occasionally denied air play because of its potential for controversy. More underground themes of rock and rap are rarely, if ever, given mass exposure for the very same reasons. All of this is fueled by fear of closer FCC scrutiny and the sanctions the agency has at its disposal.

**Concert Regulation**

Much regulation has been directed toward rock and rap concerts. These efforts date to in the late 1960s, and are designed either to restrict or to curtail concert performances. They include injunctions prohibiting concerts, zoning restrictions, regulations pertaining to seating arrangements, and regulations regarding sanitation and suppliers, all legal approaches taken to thwart concerts (Peterson, 1973:170; Haring, 1989:1; Weinstein, 1991; Rose, 1994:133; Lewis, 1995:251–282).

Occasionally, city councils have specifically denied concert permission to certain performers, including Ozzy Osbourne, Metallica, Public Enemy, NWA, and 2 Live Crew. Some cities have passed local ordinances that require concerts to be rated much as movies are. The city council of San Antonio passed a law barring unescorted children, age 13 and under, from attending performances by groups whose songs or acts depict sadistic or masochistic sex, child molestation, exhibitionism, rape, incest, or anal copulation. Under this law, concert promoters are required to determine which performances are obscene, and are subsequently required to screen out underage youth. The city council of Corpus Christi, Texas, is considering a measure that calls for concerts to limit sound volume and to ban persons under fourteen years of age from attending (Weinstein, 1991:268–270; Garofalo, 1997:435).

Several states (e.g., Wisconsin, New York, Washington, New Jersey, and Georgia) have established statewide boards to evaluate potential concerts on a case-by-case basis. These boards can and do set facility requirements and ask promoters to post sizable money bonds to ensure compliance. Social control of this kind uses legal suppression to curtail subcultural activities by controlling concerts in a variety of ways.

**Pornography/Obscenity**

In direct response to the recommendations of the Parents Music Resource Center (PMRC) and other groups, several states have passed legislation regulating phonograph records, magnetic tapes, and compact discs by extending existing laws that prohibit the sale, advertisement, and possession of pornography. In various forms, bills outlawing "porn rock and rap"—either for offensive lyrics or packaging judged to be obscene—are under consideration in 35 other states. Several key cases involve the use of pornography laws on the local level, as well (Greenfield and Wright, 1988:72–73; Graham, 1990:1D; Garofalo, 1997:434–435).

On April 15, 1986, an attempt to enforce existing pornography ordinances took place in San Francisco. Six police officers, accompanied by three members of the Los Angeles Police Department, raided the offices of the independent record label, Alternative Tentacle. Officers seized posters inserted into the Dead Kennedy's *Frankenchrist* LP; the H. R. Giger poster entitled "Penis Landscape" was deemed obscene. As a result, lead singer Jello Biafra and four others were charged with distributing harmful material to minors, an offense that carries a maximum penalty of one year in jail and a $2000 fine. Owners of a Michigan record store were also arrested after displaying a poster from the rock group Jane's Addiction's new LP *Ritual delo Habitual*. They were charged with displaying obscene material (Lifeline, 1990:1D; Garofalo, 1997:434). While all parties were eventually acquitted, this was only after great legal expense. Further, the acquittals did not seem to stymie enforcement efforts. Many record stores nationwide now require identification with purchases to verify that customers are over the age of 18.

The landmark cases here involved 2 Live Crew. Their legal troubles began in June, 1988, when an Alabama record store owner was arrested on obscenity charges for selling the group's LP *Move Something* to an adult undercover police officer. At trial, the judge declared the album obscene and fined the store owner $500. The case was later overturned on appeal, but the legal confrontations over 2 Live Crew's music were only beginning (Garofalo, 1997:434–435).

In 1989, the Broward County, Florida sheriff's office submitted a partial transcript of the group's *Nasty as They Wanna Be* recording to a circuit court. The court found probable cause to hold the material obscene under Florida law, and ordered all Broward County sales of the record to cease. 2 Live Crew sought an injunction in federal district court. The presiding judge, Jose A. Gonsalez, declared the recording obscene, making *Nasty as They Wanna Be* the first recording to be legally deemed obscene at the federal level. More arrests of record store owners followed (*Skyywalker Records v. Navarro*, 1990).

2 Live Crew appealed, citing First Amendment protections and racism in the application of the obscenity test. Drawing on the expert testimony of African-American scholar Henry Gates, Jr., the group contended that the risque lyrics were part of long-standing African-American word games and, as such, were not "offensive as judged by community standards" (Gates, 1990:A23). The appellate court overturned the original obscenity ruling in May, 1993, and the Supreme Court refused to review the case (Garofalo, 1997:435).

While the foregoing actions originated at the state and local levels, rock and rap are also subject to federal legislation that restricts pornography and obscenity. Since 1980, members of Congress have been regularly petitioned by a variety of religious organizations to regulate the content of rock songs at the federal level. In 1988, Congress responded by amending existing antipornography law, expanding its scope to include record sales and providing for the seizure of property related to profits as a sanction for violation. The bill, the Child Protection and Obscenity Enforcement Act, is directed at the producers and distributors of child pornography, including rock and rap music if found pornographic by the government (Greenfield and Wright, 1988). The law also provides for prosecution under the auspices of the federal Racketeer Influenced and Corrupt Organization Act (RICO). RICO, which states that any business engaging in "immoral commerce" can be closed down and have its assets seized, also is linked to the record labeling laws (Greenfield and Wright, 1988:72–73). The end result is potentially devastating for the record industry. For example, a store that sells an "obscene" record to a minor might have its entire inventory confiscated; the associated record label producer might find its complete profits and property seized; and any and all individuals involved would be subject to federal prosecution on felony charges.

Currently, the legal control of "offensive" rock and rap has moved in a new direction. The focus is now on funding. In June 1997, Texas passed a law that prohibits the administration of state employment pension funds from investing in record companies whose music "explicitly describes, glamorizes, or advocates" violence, bestiality, gang activity, or the debasement of women. The Texas law closely resembles a Maryland measure that failed early in 1997 (Boehlert, 1997:32).

Relying on a similar approach, the Florida State Senate withheld over $100,000 in funding from public radio station WMNF. Their budget was cut due to what Senator John Grant cited as inappropriate programming, including praise for Kurt Cobain, a song that referred to "back-seat sex," and a folk protest song criticizing the wages of business executives. Both actions are facing legal challenges on First Amendment grounds (Boehlert, 1997:32).

## THE REDEFINITION OF ROCK AND RAP: LEGAL CONTROL OF THE MESSAGE AND THE MESSENGERS

What started as informal deviance of sound, style, and statement has attracted the full array of legal control. This is the current status of rock and rap, much like that of jazz and folk music before them. The fundamental question, of course, is why? Why are rock and rap so tightly regulated when comparable themes of sex, violence, and drug consumption are so prevalent in other types of music, indeed throughout much popular culture? Why are the opera songs of suicide and murder, the country songs of drinking and cheating, the violence of sports and popular movies not similarly controlled? What is it about rock and rap music that warrants such extensive measures of legal control?

The answer is twofold. First, it is not the sex, the violence, the alcohol and drug consumption that is really so troubling to agencies of the law. Past and present, our popular culture—music, television, movies, and sports—is steeped in such themes. The real issue with rock and rap is their fundamental criticism of the prevailing social order. The other themes are mere sidebars to the bottom line: society is flawed, society is unfair. The rules, the rulemakers, the enforcers, the entire social order are suspect. It is this statement, this questioning, this criticism of the existing social arrangements that distinguishes rock and rap (Heitzeg, 1987; Weinstein, 1991; Sexton, 1995; Heitzeg, 1996:428–429). It is an essential element of their perceived threat, and a key component in the escalation of social control.

Second, and perhaps most importantly, rock and rap are the music forms of the young, the economically and politically disenfranchised, the minority, and the male—the social groups already deemed the most dangerous, the most subject to all types of social control (Parenti, 1992; Reiman, 1994; Males, 1996; Walker, Spohn and Delone, 1996; Samaha, 1997). It is the young, poor male that is portrayed by the media as the delinquent, the street criminal, and the gang member. It is the young, poor male that is the subject of an undue amount of police surveillance and arrest. It is the young, poor male who fills our prisons and populates our death rows (Bridges and Meyers, 1994; Walker, Spohn, and Delone, 1996; Samaha, 1997).

The legal control of rock and rap, then, provides an additional method of controlling those already defined as a dangerous, criminal class. It reflects and simultaneously reinforces a criminal justice policy that largely ignores the wrongdoing of the older, the wealthy, and the corporate, at the expense of the young and the poor (Reiman, 1994; Friedrichs, 1996; Simon, 1996). If the opposite were true, we might expect extensive formal control of country and classical music, and, not surprisingly, we might also expect these forms of music to express more anger, more alienation, and more dissatisfaction with the status quo.

Legal control of rock and rap is directed toward both the message and the messengers. In a sad and ironic twist, the expressed anger of the disaffected is used as an additional weapon against them. Their participation in the unconventionality of rock and rap subcultures increases their legal vulnerability and their risk. Rock and rap music, to the extent that they articulate the anger and outsider status of the young, the male, the minority, and the poor, also are targeted for formal legal control. Indeed, to paraphrase Andrew Fletcher, if the lawmakers are not permitted to make the ballads, then they can certainly control the ballads, and, in fact, the balladeers, with law.

## REFERENCES

Azerrad, Michael. 1994. *Come As You Are: The Story of Nirvana*. New York: Doubleday.
Balfour, Victoria. 1986. *Rock Wives*. New York: Beech Tree Books.
Baron, Stephen W. 1989."Resistance and its consequences: the street culture of punks." *Youth and Society* 21:207–237.
Bergman, Billy. 1985. *Reggae and Latin Pop: Hot Sauces*. New York: Quarto.

Black, Donald. 1976. *The Behavior of Law*. New York: Academic Press.

Boehlert, Eric. 1997. "Culture skirmishes." *Rolling Stone* (August 21):29–32.

Brake, Michael. 1985. *Comparative Youth Culture*. London: Routledge and Kegan Paul.

Bridges, George S., and Martha A. Meyers (editors). 1994. *Inequality, Crime and Social Control*. Boulder: Westview Press.

Cohen, Stanley. 1980. *Folk Devils and Moral Panics: The Creation of Mods and Rockers* (2nd edition). New York: St. Martin's Press.

Costello, Mark, and David Foster Wallace. 1990. *Signifying Rappers: Rap and Race in the Urban Present*. New York: Ecco Press.

Davis, Stephen. 1986. *Hammer of the Gods: The Led Zeppelin Saga*. New York: Ballantine Books.

Denisoff, R. Serge. 1972. *Sing a Song of Social Significance*. Bowling Green: Bowling Green University Popular Press.

———. 1982. *Solid Gold* (2nd edition). New Brunswick: Transaction Books.

———. 1986. *Tarnished Gold*. New Brunswick: Transaction Books.

DesBarres, Pamela. 1986. *I'm With the Band: Confessions of a Groupie*. New York: Jove Books.

Dotter, Daniel. 1995. "Rock and roll is here to stray." In *Adolescents and Their Music: If It's Too Loud, You're Too Old,* edited by Jonathan S. Epstein. New York: Garland.

Duncan, Robert. 1986. *The Rock 'n' Roll Book of the Dead: Only the Good Die Young*. New York: Harmony Books.

Friedrichs, David O. 1996. *Trusted Criminals: White-Collar Crime in Contemporary Society*. Belmont: Wadsworth.

Frith, Simon. 1987. *Sound Effects: Youth, Leisure and the Politics of Rock 'n Roll*. New York: Pantheon Books.

Gaines, Donna. 1992. *Teenage Wasteland: Suburbia's Deadend Kids*. New York: Pantheon.

Garofalo, Reebee. 1997. *Rockin' Out: Popular Music in the USA*. Boston: Allyn and Bacon.

Gates, Henry Louis Jr. 1990. "2 Live Crew decoded." *New York Times* (June 9):A23.

Gore, Tipper. 1988. *Raising PG Kids in an X-Rated World*. Nashville: Abbington Press.

Graham, Jefferson. 1990. "Lyrics face a legal rap." *USA Today* (March 20):1D.

Grand Upright Music. 1991. LTD v. Warner Brothers Records, Inc., 91 Civ. 7648 (KTD) (Dec. 16).

Greenfield, Adam, and Christian Logan Wright. 1988. "Music under siege." *Spin* (November):72–73.

Greenway, John. 1953. *American Folksongs of Protest*. Philadelphia: University of Pennsylvania Press.

Grossberg, Lawrence. 1995. "The political status of youth and youth culture." In *Adolescents and Their Music: If It's Too Loud, You're Too Old,* edited by Jonathan S. Epstein. New York: Garland.

Harig, Bruce. 1989. "Lyrics concerns escalate." *Billboard* (November 11):1.

Hebdige, Dick. 1980. *Subculture: The Meaning of Style*. New York: Methuen.

Heitzeg, Nancy A. 1987. The Solidarity of Self: Rock Music Subcultures and Societal Reaction. Unpublished doctoral dissertation, University of Minnesota.

———. 1996. *Deviance: Rulemakers and Rulebreakers*. St. Paul: West.

Herer, Jack. 1991. *Hemp and the Marijuana Conspiracy: The Emperor Wears No Clothes* (7th edition). Van Nuys, CA: Hemp Publishing.

Herman, Gary. 1982. *Rock 'n' Roll Babylon*. New York: Perigee Books.

Hesbacher, Peter. 1973. "Sound exposure in radio: the misleading nature of the station playlist." *Popular Culture and Society* 2:297–310.

———. 1976. "Radio format strategies." *Journal of Communication* 26:110–119.

Holland, Bill. 1994. "Senate hearing examines gangsta lyrics." *Billboard* (March 5):10.

Ice-T. 1992. "Cop Killer." *Body Count*. Warner.

IWW. 1992. *The Little Red Songbook*. Chicago: International Workers of the World.

Knight, Nick. 1982. *Skinhead*. London: Omnibus Press.

KRS-ONE. 1989. "Who Protects Us from You?" *Ghetto Music: The Blueprint of Hip Hop*. Jive/Zomba Records.

Lewis, Jerry M. 1995. "Crowd crushes at two concerts: a value-added analysis." In *Adolescents and Their Music: If It's Too Loud, You're Too Old,* edited by Jonathan S. Epstein. New York: Garland.

Lifeline. 1990. "Poster Problem." *USA Today* (August 22):1D.

Males, Mike A. 1996. *Scapegoat Generation: The War on America's Adolescents.* Monroe: Common Courage Press.

Malone, Julia. 1985. "Washington wives use influence to target sex, drugs in rock music." *Christian Science Monitor* (August 23):1A.

Marsh, Dave. 1989. *You've Got a Right to Rock: Don't Let Them Take It Away.* Long Beach: Duke and Duchess Ventures.

Marsh, Dave, and Kevin Stein. 1987. *The Book of Rock Lists.* New York: Dell.

Marsh, Dave, and Phyllis Pollack. 1989. "Wanted for attitude." *Village Voice* (October 10):33–37.

Majors, Richard, and Janet Mancini Billson. 1991. *Cool Pose: The Dilemmas of Black Manhood in America.* New York: Touchstone.

Minnesota Police and Peace Officers. 1990. *Street Drugs/Gang Violence.* Minneapolis: Stuart-Bradley Productions.

Nelson, Havelock. 1993. "Music and violence: does crime pay?" *Billboard* (November 13):32.

News Service. 1994. "Nirvana's Kurt Cobain is found dead." *Star Tribune* (April 9):1A.

NWA. 1988. "Fuck the Police." *Straight Outta Compton.* Priority.

Orr, Charlene. 1992. "Texas police pursue 'Cop Killer.'" *Billboard* (June 27):1.

Parenti, Michael J. 1992. *Make-Believe Media: The Politics of Entertainment.* New York: St. Martin's Press.

Peters, Dan, and Steve Peters. 1984. *Why Knock Rock?* Minneapolis: Bethany House Publishers.

Peterson, Anne M. 1990. "Judas Priest won't alter its time." *Star Tribune* (November 27):1E.

Peterson, Richard. 1973. "The unnatural history of rock festivals: an instance of media facilitation." *Popular Music and Society* 2:163–174.

Plato. 1945. *The Republic,* translated by Francis MacDonald Cornford. New York: Oxford University Press.

Powell, Kevin. 1996. "The short life and violent death of Tupac Shakur: bury me like a G." *Rolling Stone* (October 31):46.

Reiman, Jeffrey R. 1994. *The Rich Get Richer and the Poor Get Prison: Ideology, Class and Criminal Justice* (4th edition). New York: Macmillan.

Roberts, Johnnie L. 1996. "Blood on the record biz." *Newsweek* (September 23):69.

Rose, Tricia. 1994. *Black Noise: Rap Music and Culture in Contemporary America.* Hanover: Wesleyan University Press.

Rothenbuler, Eric W. 1985. "Programming decision making in popular music radio." *Communication Research* 12:209–232.

Runkle, Gerald. 1972. *Anarchism: Old and New.* New York: Delta.

Samaha, Joel. 1997. *Criminal Justice* (4th edition). St. Paul: West.

Samuels, Allison, and John Leland. 1996. "Trouble man." *Newsweek* (September 23):66–70.

Sanchez, Tony. 1979. *Up and Down with the Rolling Stones.* New York: Signet.

Seeger, Pete. 1992. *The Incomplete Folksinger.* Lincoln: University of Nebraska Press.

Sexton, Adam (editor). 1995. *Rap on Rap: Straight Up Talk on Hip-Hop Culture.* New York: Delta.

Shomari, Hashim A. 1995. *From the Underground: Hip Hop Culture as an Agent of Social Change.* Fanwood, NJ: X-Factor Publications.

Simon, David R. 1996. *Elite Deviance* (5th edition). Boston: Allyn and Bacon.

Skolnick, Jerome K. 1975. *Justice Without Trial: Law Enforcement in Democratic Society* (2nd edition). New York: John Wiley and Sons.

*Skyywalker Records Inc. v. Navarro,* DC SFIA, No. 90–6220-CIV-JAG (June 6, 1990).

Spencer, Jon Michael (editor). 1991. *The Emergency of Black and the Emergence of Rap.* Durham: Duke University Press.

Stallings, Penny. 1984. *Rock 'n' Roll Confidential.* Boston: Little, Brown.

Stark, Phyllis. 1993. "Gangsta rap under the gun." *Billboard* (December 18):141.

Tame, David. 1984. *The Secret Power of Music.* New York: Destiny Books.

Tirro, Frank. 1979. *Jazz: A History.* New York: J.M. Dent and Sons.

U.S. Senate. 1985. *Record Labeling (Senate Hearing 99–529): Hearing Before the Committee on Commerce, Science and Transportation* (United States Senate, Ninety-Ninth Congress, First Session on Contents of Music and the Lyrics of Records). Washington, DC: U.S. Government Printing Office.

Vermore, Fred, and Judy Vermore. 1985. *Stardust: The Secret Fantasies of Fans*. London: Comet Books.

Walker, Samuel, Cassia Spohn, and Miriam DeLone. 1996. *The Color of Justice: Race, Ethnicity and Crime in America*. Belmont: Wadsworth.

Weinstein, Deena. 1991. *Heavy Metal: A Cultural Sociology*. New York: Lexington Books.

———. 1995. "Expendable youth: the rise and fall of youth culture." In *Adolescents and Their Music: If It's Too Loud, You're Too Old,* edited by Jonathan S. Epstein. New York: Garland.

# 12

# JUSTICE, CHINESE STYLE

## ROGER GRACE

The place is a parking lot in San Francisco. . . . A young man arrives to claim his car and becomes involved in a dispute with the attendant. Tempers flare. The attendant swings at the patron, misses, and receives a blow that leaves him with a bloodied nose and a stained suit.

This is a case involving a battery. The attendant demands compensation, and the youth—relying on a right of self-defense—refuses. Similar cases are heard by the courts everyday.

This matter, however, was not litigated. No lawyer was ever consulted. It happened that both parties were members of the Chinese community—and to them, the proper means of resolving their conflict was the process called "tiewo."

### TIEWO

Tiewo is conciliation. It is conducted by the wise and respected "elders" of family associations and tongs. They are not lawyers, for the most part, and they rely on no written law; they simply seek to "do justice" as their consciences direct them. Tiewo is but one example of the elders' role in adjusting matters within the community, obviating the need to resort to courts.

This particular dispute was brought by the injured party to the attention of his tong. (The tongs were formed on the West Coast by the early Chinese immigrants as "protective associations." They were lawless and often engaged in open combat—but today bear more resemblance to YMCAs.) The elders of the tong conferred with elders of the young man's family association (such associations go back thousands of years in China), but no agreement was reached. The controversy was finally resolved by the Chinese Consolidated Benevolent Association in San Francisco—each of the leaders chipped in a few dollars to pay for the attendant's stained suit.

But such instances of tiewo are diminishing. The proceedings are traditionally conducted in Chinese, and this eliminates from participation many of the younger members of the community—who are probably too Westernized to have an interest, anyway. But this custom—and the elders' involvement in other areas—persist in the large communities (such as New York, Chicago, Boston, and Los Angeles) for several reasons. For one, there is the matter of "keeping face": a Chinese would feel disgraced to have the other members of the community know he was being sued. Also, there is somewhat of a lingering distrust of American courts, which were initially less than cordial to the Chinese immigrants. (*People v. Hall,* decided by the California Supreme Court in 1859, serves as an illustration of the courts' attitude. In that case, the Chinese were labeled as "Indians" and were said to constitute "a race of people whom nature has marked as inferior, and who are incapable of progress or intellectual development past a certain point as their history has shown.")

## COMMUNITY CONTROL OF CRIME

Minor criminal matters, too, are often handled within the community. There is a general reluctance to report crimes to the police because of the feeling that the actions of one Chinese reflect on all Chinese. So, if one member of the community strikes another and causes serious injury, the incident probably will go unreported if the offender assures the elders that he will make restitution for all medical expenses. Similarly, if a youth is caught shoplifting (although juvenile delinquency is notably rare among Orientals), a Chinese shopkeeper will probably make his report to the parents, rather than the police. Eager to keep the matter "hushed up," the parents can be counted on to make ready restitution.

## ELDERS AS ATTORNEYS

Another area where the elders take the place of attorneys is in the administration of estates. Few Chinese have written wills and the family associations take full charge of disbursing assets. Recipients are often not those persons whom American courts would denominate as heirs, but all this is in keeping with the decedent's expectations as to how his estate would be handled.

Too, the elders concern themselves with domestic affairs. One case was that of a Chinese who came to the United States and wed—failing to bring to mind the slight matter of having left a wife back in China. The wife followed him to the United States and took shelter in the family association headquarters. It happened that some of the woman's habits—such as breaking windows and employing abusive language—proved rather annoying to those who worked at the headquarters, and letters were sent to the husband beseeching him to provide support for his "Number One Wife." There was no response. The elders then decreed that the husband's obligations would have to be enforced—and resort was made to a subtle, but effective method. The family association placed an advertisement in a local Chinese newspaper demanding of the husband a recognition of his duties. The husband then faced constant ostracism within the community until he complied.

Advertisements of a similar nature are not infrequent. (Redress for invasion of privacy does not occur.) The moral obligations involved are often not legally enforceable, but there is full expectation within the community that they will be lived up to. Bankruptcy, for example, is not recognized by the Chinese: when the debtor is able to pay—even years hence—he is expected to do so. Nor is any cognizance taken of the statutes of limitation on monetary obligations. (The Wong family in the District of Columbia recently paid off on a debt that had simply been overlooked for 20 years. The creditor, a man in his 80s, proffered the bill and was paid in full.)

As business contacts outside of the community have increased, the Chinese have found the necessity of familiarizing themselves with some of the American law.

Because of the growing volume of "outside" commercial transactions, Chinese are growing accustomed to new rules of business conduct. These tend to carry over to dealings of the Chinese among themselves. Also, television and other Westernizing influences acquaint them with new ways. Many of the old customs, such as tiewo, are withering away and the status of the elders is diminishing.

Somehow it seems a shame that this simple community system of justice—predicated on honor—is being displaced. Perhaps before it vanishes, we of the larger community might take a look at it, and learn some lessons.

# 13

# RACIAL AND EVIDENTIAL FACTORS IN JUROR ATTRIBUTION OF LEGAL RESPONSIBILITY*

DENIS CHIMAEZE E. UGWUEGBU

The type of research most commonly carried out by social scientists interested in legal decisionmaking is juror research. Most of this research has been concerned, implicitly or explicitly, with the problem of assessing the extent to which the juror is indeed "the trier of the facts" of the case.

A recent comprehensive review of the literature on jurors and juries (Davis, Bray, and Holt, 1977) outlined two classes of "guilt irrelevant" variables that tend to bias juror decisionmaking. One class of such biasing variables includes those associated with characteristics of the defendant such as race, attractiveness, and juror-defendant attitude similarity. A second class of biasing variables includes characteristics of the juror, such as demographic factors (e.g., race, sex), attitudes, and values.

Two guilt-irrelevant variables that have received much attention are the race of the defendant and the race of the victim. Kalven and Zeisel (1966) indicated that black defendants tend to arouse negative sentiments before jurors (p. 210). Greenberg (1959) observed that in the South a black person accused of interracial criminal behavior was the most likely to suffer the death penalty. Bullock (1961) studied 3644 white and black inmates of the Huntsville (Texas) State Prison who were committed for various offences of burglary, rape, or murder. The results of the sur-

*This article is based on a dissertation submitted to the Department of Psychology of Kent State University in partial fulfilment of the requirements for the Ph.D. degree. The author would like to express deep appreciation to Clyde Hendrick for continued guidance and assistance as dissertation advisor. In addition, the assistance of Cassandra Taylor, who ran all the white subjects, and of the entire staff of the African-American Affairs Institute at Kent State who aided me in different ways are gratefully acknowledged.

vey showed racial bias in jury sentencing. It has been suggested, however, that Bullock's data must be interpreted with caution because of the post hoc nature of the analysis (Davis, Bray, and Holt, 1977; Ugwuegbu, 1973).

Influenced by Rose and Prell (1955), Mayer (1972) investigated the relationship between the perceived seriousness of a criminal act and the race of the offender. Mayer (1972) presented one-sentence descriptions of 14 minor felony cases to college students for judgments. The results showed that juror estimates of perceived seriousness of a criminal behavior depended marginally on the race of the offender. The data further indicated that it was more serious for black than for white offenders to commit property crimes, but slightly more serious for white than for black offenders to commit crimes against the person.

Johnson (1941) emphasized the possible biasing effects of the race of both the defendant and the victim. Johnson suggested that instead of two categories of offenders, black and white, there should be four: black defendant versus white victim (B-W), white defendant versus white victim (W-W), black defendant versus black victim (B-B), and white defendant versus black victim (W-B). Johnson predicted that the perceived seriousness of a criminal behavior and the severity of punishment imposed on the offender would follow in that order. Johnson's survey data showed trends indicating some confirmation of the prediction.

Many of these studies were surveys or archival investigations. However, these data generally indicate that the race of the defendant and the victim may influence juror judgment.

The effects of race on juror behavior are predictable from the results of research on interpersonal attraction indicating that attraction toward other people is influenced by the degree of attitudinal similarity (e.g., Byrne, 1971); similarity of belief systems (Rokeach, Smith, and Evans, 1960); perceived racial identity (Hendrick, Bixenstine, and Hawkins, 1971); ideological similarity (Mitchell and Byrne, 1973); and the attractiveness of the victim and the defendant (Landy and Aronson, 1969). Generally, the similarity-attraction position is that given a situation where other things are held constant, any demographic or attitudinal similarity between the juror and the defendant will bias the juror evaluation of the defendant in a favorable direction.

Of course, the juror does not rely entirely on his heart in making his judgments, but is subject to some reality constraints. One of the most important of these is likely to be the evidence in the case. Unfortunately very few studies of jurors have explicitly varied the strength of the evidence. Broeder (1958) reported that a civil case with clear evidence produced more damage awards than a case with somewhat doubtful evidence, not surprisingly. Heimbach (1970) reported that legally strong evidence resulted in significantly more guilty verdicts than did weak evidence. Sue, Smith, and Caldwell (1973) presented subjects with either strong or weak evidence about a murder case. The jurors received other information ruled as admissible or inadmissible by the presiding judge. The results of the study showed that inadmissible evidence was influential only when the evidence for the case was weak.

Kalven and Zeisel (1966) advanced a major hypothesis about evidence. They suggested that the primary role of evidence was to "liberate" the juror to follow affective preferences when there was doubt about the evidence. This hypothesis has not been empirically evaluated probably because of Kalven and Zeisel's failure to give more elaboration to the theory. The present research permits examination of the combined influence of evidence and race in juror ascription of culpability. It was expected that ambiguous evidence would activate affective preferences along racial lines, more than evidence beyond reasonable doubt.

The experiments to be reported here were simulated juror evaluations of a rape case in which the racial identities of the victim and the defendant and the amount of evidence presented to the jurors were varied. As stated above one expectation was that the amount of evidence for ascription of culpability would interact with race in activating juror biases and prejudices, especially in instances involving an interracial forcible rape. The specific hypotheses that were tested in the study were:

1. The crime of rape arouses more negative affect for females than males; consequently, female jurors are more negative and harsher in their attitude toward a defendant in a rape case than male jurors.

2. A racially dissimilar defendant is accorded more negative and harsher evaluation than a similar defendant, irrespective of the race of the victim.

3. The victim of a forcible rape arouses more positive affect in a racially similar juror than does a dissimilar victim, and therefore, more punitiveness toward the rapist.

4. The greater the amount of evidence, the greater the tendency of the juror to convict a defendant.

5. Interracial rape will be more punitively punished than intraracial rape when the victim is of the same race as the juror.

6. When the evidence is ambiguous, the difference in punitiveness between racially similar and racially dissimilar defendants will be especially strong.

7. A three-way interaction effect of the victim's race, the defendant's race and strength of evidence was predicted. The interaction was expected to be due to the juror's overascription of culpability when evaluating marginal evidence, dissimilar defendant, and similar victim.

## EXPERiMENT 1

### METHOD

#### Subjects

The subjects were 256 white undergraduates from introductory psychology classes at a midwestern university. The subjects were run in five different sessions of nearly equal numbers of males and females. All the experimental conditions were run simultaneously in each session. Twelve subjects were deleted from the data analysis for various reasons. One subject was a policeman who indicated that he could not serve as a juror, six had poor scores on the retention and recall test, and five were minors. The final analysis for the study included 244 (120 male and 124 female) subjects who met the legal requirements for service as jurors, as determined by the Summit County, Ohio, jury selection questionnaire. There were about 10 or 11 subjects in each experimental cell.

## Pretesting

Prior to the main experiment the evidence to be used in the actual experiments was rated by 72 male and female undergraduates. The pilot study differed from the main experiment in that the case briefs were presented to the subjects without racial identities of the victim and the defendant. Each subject read one of the scripts and rated the following item: "I feel that the evidence in this case is extremely (insufficient, weak, sufficient) for a conviction." The results indicated significant main effects of sex $F(1,66) = 4.3, p < .04$ with the male subjects rating the evidence as less sufficient than the females, and strength of evidence $F(2,66) = 53.8$, $p < .001$. The mean values on a 9-point scale for the near zero ($\bar{x} = 0.7$), marginal ($\bar{x} = 3.7$), and strong ($\bar{x} = 7.3$) evidence differed significantly from the other two means by the Neuman-Keuls test. There were no other significant effects.

## Procedure

When the subjects arrived at the experimental room, the experimenter randomly distributed a booklet to them. On the first page of the booklet, entitled "Personal Inventory," were 16 questions. Some items among these questions determined whether each subject met the eligibility requirements for serving as a juror in Summit County, Ohio. The rest of the questions dealt with background factors that might affect the judgment of a subject on the case.

On page 2 of the booklet, entitled "A Jury Trial: A Case Study," the subjects were instructed thus:

> On the following pages you will read a condensed case description of a jury trial concerning an aggravated rape case. The criminal suit was brought against Ken S. Williams by the State of Illinois on behalf of Miss Mary R. Brown. Mr. Williams was indicted and tried before a jury of 12 people (6 men and 6 women), who deliberated on the case and reached a verdict. The purpose of this project is to find out how well the judgments of average students agree with the jury's decision when the students can study the case objectively.
>
> Please read the case description carefully, and on the basis of the information presented, answer the rating questions. Your judgments here may possibly influence judicial decision-making as to the ability of college students to render judicial decisions based on the principles of the law.
>
> As you very well know, the jury decision-making is a two-stage process. First, each juror considers the evidence and reaches a private decision. This is the predeliberation stage. Second, all the jurors gather in a private room, discuss the case and try to reach a verdict: This is the deliberation stage.
>
> The first part of this project requires you to read the transcript very carefully and make predeliberation judgment based on the evidence. The second part will require subjects to come in groups of 12 to deliberate on the case. It is expected that you will be able to participate in both parts of this project. The deliberation part will be arranged to suit your con-

venience. [Subjects completed and dropped into a basket before leaving the experimental room an envelope they believed would be used to arrange for them to participate in the deliberation stage of the juror case.]

Once again, please take time to read the case transcript very carefully and based on the evidence provided indicate your personal judgment by rating the questions.

After reading the written instructions, the subjects read a transcript of a simulated rape case that occurred on the campus of a midwestern university. The transcript contained a case number, the name of the defendant (Ken S. Williams) and the name of the victim of the rape (Miss Mary R. Brown).

The transcript began with a brief statement within which the defendant and the victim's racial identities were varied:

The defendant, a 21-year-old black (white) male was indicted and charged with aggravated and forcible rape of Mary R. Brown, a 19-year-old white (black) girl in September 1971.

Following that, the prosecuting attorney presented the state's position and called Mary Brown to testify. Mary was cross-examined by the defense attorney. A prosecution eyewitness and the arresting officer testified. A consistent procedure was maintained in the presentation of the testimonies for all the treatment conditions.

For the first level of evidence, subjects read the script that presented minimum testimony that the defendant committed the crime for which he was being tried. This experimental condition was designated "near-zero probability." In this condition the victim was not sure whether it was Williams (the accused) who assaulted her, the prosecution eyewitness testified that it was *not* the defendant that he saw assaulting the victim, and the arresting officer was quoted as saying that he arrested the defendant because of his suspicious presence near the scene of the crime.[1]

Another group of subjects read a script which presented strong evidence in favor of conviction. This condition was designated the "strong-evidence condition." For this condition the script indicated that Mary (the victim) was able to identify Williams as the assailant. It was also indicated that according to the police report the defendant had previously admitted to the crime before the police, when he claimed that the victim "asked for it." The prosecution eyewitness had no difficulty identifying Williams from among the people in the court room as the man he saw assaulting the victim.

A third condition, called the "marginal condition," presented the subjects with doubtful evidence that was achieved by pitting the victim's identification of the defendant against the defendant's denial of any responsibility for the crime. Also the evidence presented by the prosecution eyewitness and the arresting officer was ambiguous.

---

[1]In a strict legal procedure if the evidence was as minimal as in our near-zero condition the district attorney probably would not prosecute. However, cases do exist where the mere presence of a black at the scene of a crime, or his known association with a criminal resulted in arrest and trial. The famous Angela Davis case is a recent example.

The design of the experiment, therefore, included 3 levels of evidence (near-zero, marginal, strong) × 2 defendant's race (black versus white) × 2 victim's race (black versus white) × 2 subject's sex (male versus female).

The dependent variables included the following questionnaire items:

1. I feel that the defendant's *intention* was to cause the victim, Miss Brown: (No harm at all, some harm, extreme harm.)

2. To what extent was Mr. Williams, the defendant, *responsible* for the rape?: (Not at all responsible, moderately responsible, very much responsible.)

3. With respect to my *verdict,* I feel the defendant is guilty as charged: (Not guilty of any crime, moderately guilty as charged, exactly guilty as charged.)

4. Based on the evidence, I feel I would recommend for the defendant as punishment: (No punishment at all; suspended sentence; 1–5 years in the state prison; 5–9 years; 10–14 years; 15–20 years; over 20 years but not life; life imprisonment; death penalty.)

All of the items incorporated 9-point rating scales and were scored from 1 to 9. The extremes and midpoints of items 1, 2, and 3 were verbally anchored with 1 indicating no culpability, 5 average, and 9 strong culpability, respectively. Item 4 was rated on a scale of nine alternatives. In each case the higher the number the more punitive the judgment.

On indication by the subject that the first booklet was completed, the booklet was collected by the experimenter who handed the subject a second booklet and an envelope. The second booklet contained a 10-item true-false retention and recall test of the case transcripts. The subjects also rated another item that measured whether the subjects thought the evidence easy, difficult, or very difficult.

After the subjects completed the second booklet, the experiment terminated with each subject completing a self-addressed envelope that he expected would be used to arrange for the deliberation part of the jury trial project. However, the envelopes were used to mail the subjects a description of the purposes and the results of the study.

## RESULTS

The subject's responses to each of the items in the questionnaire, and the 10-item recall and retention test, were subjected to a 2 × 2 × 2 × 3 analysis of variance (Kim and Kohout, 1975). The Duncan Multiple-Range test was used as a further test for the significant $F$-ratios.

### Control Measures

An item was included and used to measure how well the subjects understood the evidence presented in the case brief which the subjects read. A retention and recall test was also included. Variance analyses of the subjects' ratings of these variables indicated no significant main or interaction effects.

## Deriving the Culpability Measure

The rating data from all four items were correlated, using all subjects and ignoring experimental conditions. The items were significantly correlated with a range of $r = .67$ to $r = .92$. The items were then factor analyzed by the principal component method. As expected, one factor emerged with the following loadings on the items: verdict .96, responsibility .92, intention .83, and punishment .79.

Based on the intercorrelations and the factor loadings, these four items were summed for each subject to derive a total score. The summed scores were considered as a general measure of juror ascription of culpability. Scores on this measure could range between 4 and 36.

## Analysis of Culpability Attribution

The culpability sum scores were subjected to a 3 (levels of evidence) × 2 (defendants' race) × 2 (victims' race) × 2 (sex of subject) analysis of variance. Hypotheses 1, 2, 3, and 4 were supported by the results. The female subjects rated the defendant as more culpable ($\bar{x} = 15.9$) than the male subjects ($\bar{x} = 13.8$), $F(1,220) = 7.3, p < .01$. The main effect of the defendant's race was also significant, $F(1,220) = 8.5, p < .01$. The mean values for the race effect indicated that a black defendant was rated more culpable ($\bar{x} = 15.9$) than a white defendant ($\bar{x} = 13.8$). When the rape involved a white victim, the subjects rated the offense as more culpable ($\bar{x} = 15.7$ versus 14.0) than when it involved a black victim, $F(1,220) = 4.1$, $p < .04$. The data from the main effect of the victim's race supported the expectation that a racially dissimilar victim would arouse negative affect in a juror while a similar victim would arouse positive affect. The significant main effect of the amount of evidence, $F(2,220) = 160.1, p < .001$ indicated that the defendant was rated as most culpable when the evidence against him was strong ($\bar{x} = 23.1$) as against when the evidence was marginal ($\bar{x} = 15.1$) or near-zero ($\bar{x} = 6.4$).

The data also indicated two first order interaction effects of the Victims' Race × Defendants' Race, $F(2,220) = 3.1, p < .05$, and the Defendants' Race × Evidence, $F(2,220) = 3.2, p < .04$. The mean values for the interaction effect of the Victims' Race × Defendants' Race are displayed in Table 1. The means indicate that a black defendant who committed interracial forcible rape was rated as most culpable ($\bar{x} = 17.2$) when compared to a white defendant who committed interracial rape ($\bar{x}$ 13.6) and a black or white defendant who committed intraracial forcible rape ($\bar{x} = 14.5$ versus $\bar{x} = 13.8$), respectively. The data thus supported Hypothesis 5.

Table 2 represents the mean ratings for the Evidence × Defendants' Race interaction effect. The data are in conformity with Hypothesis 6. When the evidence was strong or near zero the subjects rated the defendants, irrespective of race, as equally culpable. However, when the evidence was marginal a black defendant was rated significantly more culpable by the subject-jurors than was a white defendant. In other words when the evidence is not strong enough for conviction a

TABLE 1   Mean Ratings of Culpability (White Subjects)
Race of Victim × Race of Defendant

|         | Defendant |         |
|---------|-----------|---------|
|         | White     | Black   |
| Victim  |           |         |
| White   | $13.8^a$  | $17.2^b$ |
|         | (60)      | (62)    |
| Black   | $13.6^a$  | $14.5^{ab}$ |
|         | (60)      | (62)    |

*Note.* Mean values with different superscripts differ from each other at the .05 level or better by the Duncan Multiple-Range test. Numbers in parentheses indicate the number of subjects in each experimental group.

white juror gives the benefit of the doubt to a white defendant but not to a black defendant. No other effect was significant.

## DISCUSSION

The results of Experiment 1 appear to confirm six out of seven hypotheses made in the present study. As noted above, black interracial rape was more punitively punished by white jurors than white interracial or black intraracial rape. Secondly, when evidence was ambiguous a black defendant received more culpable evaluation than a white defendant. In other words, a white defendant was more likely to be given the benefit of the doubt by a white juror when the evidence in a rape case is not straightforward than a black.

TABLE 2   Mean Ratings of Culpability (White Subjects)
Race × Amount of Evidence

|       | Evidence  |          |          |
|-------|-----------|----------|----------|
| Race  | Near-zero | Marginal | Strong   |
| Black | $7.2^a$   | $17.1^c$ | $24.4^d$ |
|       | (41)      | (41)     | (40)     |
| White | $6.5^a$   | $12.9^b$ | $21.7^d$ |
|       | (40)      | (41)     | (41)     |

*Note.* Means with different superscripts differ from each other at the .05 level or better by the Duncan Multiple-Range test. Numbers in parentheses indicate the number of subjects in each experimental group.

Whether one can generalize from these data to a black population remains an open question. For years research on race relations has supported the hypothesis that blacks identify with the values and social attitudes of whites, thereby contributing to their own self-rejection (Banks, 1970; Bayton, 1965; Steckler, 1957). Based on this hypothesis one would expect black people to be prejudiced more against black than they are against white offenders.

On the other hand, the decade from 1963 through 1973 was a period of black awareness in most black communities in America. Black awareness was popularized by slogans such as "Black is beautiful," and the creation of Black Studies Centers in most American universities. One of the objectives of the slogans and the Black Studies Centers was to arouse some level of identity and identification with that which is black among black people. With this type of stimulation, it was expected that in the present study black jurors' attitudes toward a racially similar defendant involved in an interracial forcible rape would parallel the attitudes of white jurors toward own-race offender. This expectation was investigated in the next study.

## EXPERIMENT 2

The second experiment examined the other side of the question which was whether a black juror in an interracial case would be as prejudiced as a white juror in a similar case.

## SUBJECTS

The subjects were 196 black undergraduates who were taking various classes from the African-American Affairs Institute. Ten subjects' responses were excluded because they failed to meet the legal requirements for jury participation or they had poor scores on the retention and recall test. Data were analyzed for 186 (88 male and 98 female) subjects, with about seven or eight subjects in each experimental cell. The procedure was identical to that in Experiment 1.

## RESULTS

The range of the correlations among the measures (intention, responsibility, verdict, and punishment) for the black subjects was $r = .68$ to $r = .90$. Factor analysis yielded a single culpability factor with the following loadings: verdict .96, responsibility .92, intention .88, and punishment .76.

### Analysis of Attribution of Culpability

Variance analysis for the subjects showed significant main effects which paralleled the results obtained for the white subjects. Detailed analysis of the mean values for the main effects showed that the female subjects evaluated the defendant as more culpable ($\bar{x} = 17.8$ versus 13.2) than the males, $F (1,162) = 23.6, p <$ .001. The main effect of the race of the defendant $F (1,162) = 29.0, p < .001$, indicated that a black defendant was rated as less culpable ($\bar{x} = 13.2$) than a white defendant ($\bar{x} = 18.0$). When the victim of the rape was white the subjects rated the offense as less culpable ($\bar{x} = 13.6$ versus 17.6) than when the victim was black, $F (1,162) = 17.9, p < .001$. The amount of evidence $F (2,162) = 71.5, p < .001$ was directly related to the level of culpability ascribed to a defendant. When the evidence was strong ($\bar{x} = 22.2$) the defendant was held more culpable than when the evidence was near-zero ($\bar{x} = 8.7$), or marginal ($\bar{x} = 16.2$). The data obtained for the sex effect, the main effects of race and evidence were in conformity with the expectations of the first four hypotheses.

The results also indicated two significant interaction effects of Sex of Subject × Evidence, $F (2,162) = 6.7, p < .002$, and the Defendants' Race × Evidence, $F (2,162) = 3.2, p < .04$. The mean values for the interaction effects are displayed in Tables 3 and 4, respectively. Table 3 shows a tendency for female jurors to disregard the marginality of evidence and to hold the rapist culpable under ambiguous evidence. The mean values for the Defendants' Race × Evidence are displayed in Table 4. The expectation that a juror would hold a racially dissimilar defendant more culpable than a similar defendant in the marginal evidence condition was confirmed. The result was consistent with the data for the white subjects. Unlike the white subjects, however, the blacks also judged a dissimilar defendant significantly more harshly, $p < .05$, than a similar defendant in the *strong* evidence condition. In other words, the black subjects tended to grant the black defendant the benefit of the doubt not only when the evidence is doubtful but even when there was strong evidence against him.

The final significant effect was the three-way interaction, $F (2,162) = 2.7, p <$ .059. The nature of this interaction is indicated by the pattern of means shown in

TABLE 3   Mean Ratings of Culpability (Black Subjects)
Sex × Evidence

|        | Evidence | | |
| --- | --- | --- | --- |
| Sex | Near-zero | Marginal | Strong |
| Male | $7.4^a$ | $11.4^b$ | $21.6^c$ |
|      | (30) | (30) | (28) |
| Female | $10.0^{ab}$ | $20.7^c$ | $22.9^c$ |
|        | (33) | (33) | (32) |

*Note.* Mean values with different superscripts differ from each other at the .05 level or better by the Duncan Multiple-Range test. Numbers in parentheses indicate the number of subjects in each experimental group.

TABLE 4    Mean Ratings of Culpability (Black Subjects)
Defendant's Race × Evidence

| | Evidence | | |
|---|---|---|---|
| Race | Near-zero | Marginal | Strong |
| Black | $8.8^a$ | $12.6^b$ | $19.1^c$ |
| | (31) | (32) | (31) |
| White | $9.6^a$ | $19.5^c$ | $25.2^d$ |
| | (32) | (31) | (29) |

*Note.* Mean values with different superscripts differ from each other at the .05 level or better by the Duncan Multiple-Range test. Numbers in parentheses indicate the number of subjects in each experimental condition.

Table 5. Inspection of Table 5 indicates that ascription of culpability was strong for white interracial rape and weak for black interracial rape. Generally the effect was marginally significant but the mean values (averaged across evidence) showed a significant trend with the white defendant versus black victim (W-B), and white versus white (W-W) rated more punitively than black versus black (B-B) and black versus white (B-W) rape, in that order.

TABLE 5    Mean Ratings of Culpability (Black Subjects)
Defendant × Victim × Evidence

| | Defendant | | | |
|---|---|---|---|---|
| | Black | | White | |
| Victim | Black | White | Black | White |
| Evidence | | | | |
| Near-zero | $8.2^a$ | $7.6^a$ | $11.8^b$ | $7.2^a$ |
| | (16) | (15) | (15) | (17) |
| Marginal | $16.3^c$ | $8.9^{ab}$ | $20.0^d$ | $19.0^{cd}$ |
| | (16) | (16) | (15) | (16) |
| Strong | $22.1^{de}$ | $16.4^c$ | $26.9^d$ | $23.7^{de}$ |
| | (14) | (17) | (16) | (13) |
| Mean | 15.5 | 11.0 | 19.6 | 16.3 |

*Note.* Mean values with different superscripts differ from each other at the .05 level or better by the Duncan Multiple-Range test. Numbers in parentheses indicate the number of subjects in each experimental condition.

## DISCUSSION

The main purpose of the experiment was to determine the conditions under which racial similarity of a juror to the victim or the defendant influenced the juror's evaluation of a defendant in a case involving interracial forcible rape. Six of the seven hypotheses made in the present study were supported by the data for the white and black subjects. The data for the black subjects paralleled the data for the white subjects fairly closely. The results showed very convincingly that the race of the defendant and the race of the victim inappropriately influenced the level of culpability the jurors ascribed to the defendant.

The results further showed that under marginal-evidence conditions the jurors judged a defendant of a dissimilar race more harshly than a racially similar defendant. Black subjects, but not white subjects, showed a significant bias in favor of own-race defendant in the strong evidence condition.

The bias effects found for the marginal evidence are particularly very significant because it is exactly these middling cases that get to the courts. Cases where the evidence is weak are likely to be dropped by the prosecution, while cases where the evidence is very strong are likely to be plea-bargained by the defense. Kalven and Zeisel (1966) noted the bias effect of middling cases in their field work. They concluded that when there was doubt as to evidence the juror was liberated from factual constraints and as a result more likely to be influenced by affective factors. The present data supported Kalven and Zeisel's liberation hypothesis. Beyond the liberation hypothesis, our data showed that although race is a cue to biased juror ascription of culpability, in some cases the implementation of biased judgment due to race is most accentuated when the evidence is marginal.

Broeder (1965) and Simon (1967) found that black jurors tend to express sympathy for the underdog and are more prone to acquit than whites. The present data showed that black jurors were more likely to acquit a black defendant even when the evidence for a conviction is very strong. In other words black subjects are more likely to grant a black rapist the benefit of the doubt even when there is evidence beyond reasonable doubt against the rapist.

The genesis of the benefit of the doubt for a black defendant by blacks could be the result of black experiences with the law. In the past a white woman could frame any black man for rape and have him brought to trial before the law. Second, blacks distrust the legal system and its enforcement agencies. The legal system and its enforcement agencies are perceived as instruments of white oppression and as lacking in legitimacy for black defendants (Greenberg, 1959). Consequently, strong evidence against a black rapist may be less convincing for black jurors than evidence brought against a white rapist.

Another plausible explanation for the black subjects' tendency to minimize a black defendant's culpability in the strong evidence condition could be a direct result of the black university students' change in attitude to black and white ideologies. In the last 15 years, there has been a decrease in the extent to which black students accept antiblack attitudes and an increase in their acceptance of antiwhite ideologies (Banks, 1970). The harsher judgments of white than black defendants in an interracial rape could be due to the newfound awareness among blacks, and identification with that which is *black* among the black university population. The generality of the black leniency to the black defendant may be limited, therefore, since black consciousness was probably higher on campuses than in the general community.

The strong tendency for the female jurors to evaluate the rapist more punitively than male jurors probably reflects the women's strong negative feelings about the high incidence of rape on university campuses at that particular period, the spread of the women's liberation ideology, and the general tendency to identify with a similar victim.

The finding that when a black defendant raped a white female, white jurors rated it more punitively than when a black female was raped, is in conformity with the widely held opinion among the blacks that whites are anxious to protect the white woman from the black man, and that the white man's prejudice and discrimination against blacks are meant to consolidate the protection for the white woman.

The absence of voir dire examination and the simulation procedure used in the studies may limit the generality of the data. However, there is no strong a priori reason to believe that real jurors would be able to set aside these biases, especially if the jurors are less sophisticated than university students.

The present studies provide substantial laboratory support for the liberation hypothesis by showing that ambiguity in the facts of a case serves to liberate the juror to respond to racial prejudices and biases. Davis, Bray, and Holt (1977) indicated that demographic variables may be more important than personality factors in predicting juror verdict preferences. The present data show that the accurate prediction of juror verdict preferences increases with knowledge of demographic variables and the evidence factor.

## REFERENCES

Banks, W. M. 1970. "The changing attitudes of black students." *Personnel and Guidance Journal* 48: 739–745.

Bayton, J. 1965. "Negro perception of negro and white personality traits." *Journal of Personality and Social Psychology* 1: 250–253.

Broeder, D. W. 1958. "The University of Chicago jury project." *Nebraska Law Review* 38: 744–761.

————. 1965. "The negro in court." *Duke Law Journal* 19: 19–31.

Bullock, H. A. 1961. "Significance of the racial factor in the length of prison sentences." *The Journal of Criminal Law, Criminology and Police Science* 52: 411–417.

Byrne, D. 1971. *The Attraction Paradigm.* New York: Academic Press.

Davis, J. H., R. M. Bray, and R. W. Holt. 1977. "The empirical study of decision processes in juries." In *Law, Justice, and the Individual in Society: Psychological and Legal Issues,* edited by J. Tapp and F. Levine. New York: Holt, Rinehart, and Winston.

Greenberg, J. 1959. "Race relations and American law." Cited in: "The case for black juries." *Yale Law Journal* 79:531–550.

Heimbach, J. T. 1970. "Social psychology in the jury room: the effects of evidence, confession, and group interaction in sentencing." Paper presented at the Annual Meeting of the Midwestern Psychological Association.

Hendrick, C., V. E. Bixenstine, and T. Hawkins. 1971. "Race versus belief similarity as determinants of attraction: a search for a fair test." *Journal of Personality and Social Psychology* 17: 250–258.

Johnson, G. B. 1941. "The negro and crime." *The Annals of the American Academy of Political and Social Science* 217: 93–104.

Kalven, H., Jr., and H. Zeisel. 1966. *The American Jury.* Boston: Little, Brown.

Kim, J., and F. J. Kohout. 1975. "Analysis of variance and covariance: subprograms ANOVA and oneway." In *Statistical Package for the Social Sciences* (2nd edition) edited by Norman H. Nie *et al..* New York: McGraw-Hill. [The SPSS subprogram ANOVA was used in the present analysis.]

Landy, D., and E. Aronson. 1969. "The influence of the character of the criminal and victim on the decisions of simulated jurors." *Journal of Experimental Social Psychology* 5: 141–152.

Mayer, S. E. 1972. "Does the punishment fit the crime?: a replication after 18 years, plus a study of present-day race differences." Paper presented at the Annual Meeting of the Midwestern Psychological Association.

Mitchell, H. E., and D. Byrne. 1973. "The defendant's dilemma: effects of jurors attitudes and authoritarianism on judicial decisions." *Journal of Personality and Social Psychology* 25: 123–129.

Rokeach, M., P. Smith, and R. Evans. 1960. "Two kinds of prejudice or one?" In *The Open and Closed Mind,* edited by M. Rokeach. New York: Basic Books.

Rose, A. M., and A. E. Prell. 1955–1956. "Does the punishment fit the crime?: a study in social evaluation." *American Journal of Sociology* 61: 247–259.

Simon, Rita J. 1967. *The Jury and the Defense of Insanity.* Boston: Little, Brown.

Steckler, G. 1957. "Authoritarian ideology in Negro college students." *Journal of Abnormal and Social Psychology* 54: 396–399.

Sue, S., R. E. Smith, and C. Caldwell. 1973. "Effects of inadmissable evidence on the decision of simulated jurors: a moral dilemma." *Journal of Applied Social Psychology* 3: 344–353.

Ugwuegbu, D. C. E. 1973. "Attribution of responsibility in the law and social psychology." Area paper, Kent State University.

Wyer, R. S., Jr. 1973. "Category ratings as 'subjective expected values': implications for attitude formation and change." *Psychological Review* 80: 446–467.

# 14

# WHY WERE THE EARLY CHRISTIANS PERSECUTED?*

## G. E. M. DE STE. CROIX

The presecution of the Christians in the Roman Empire has attracted the attention of scholars of many different kinds. The enormous volume of literature on the subject is partly due to the fact that it can be approached from many different directions: it offers a challenge to historians of the Roman Empire (especially of its public administration), to Roman lawyers, to ecclesiastical historians, to Christian theologians, and to students of Roman religion and Greek religion. In fact all these approaches are relevant, and they must all be used together.

The question I have taken as a title needs to be broken down in two quite different ways. One is to distinguish between the general population of the Greco-Roman world and what I am going to call for convenience "the government": I mean of course the emperor, the senate, the central officials and the provincial governors, the key figures for our purposes being the emperor and even more the provincial governors. In this case we ask first, "For what reasons did ordinary pagans demand persecution?" and secondly, "Why did the government prosecute?" The second way of dividing up our general question is to distinguish the reasons which brought about persecution from the purely legal basis of persecution—the juridical principles and institutions invoked by those who had already made up their minds to take action.

But let us not look at the persecutions entirely from the top, so to speak—from

*This article is a revised version of a paper read to the Joint Meeting of the Hellenic and Roman Societies and the Classical Association at Oxford on 12 August 1961. As I am engaged in a book on the persecutions, in which the matters discussed here will be treated in greater detail, I have not attempted to supply complete documentation and bibliographies; but I have added a certain number of references. Except when otherwise stated the Passions of the martyrs to which I have referred here can be found in Krüger and Ruhbach, 1965.

the point of view of the persecutors. Scholars who have dealt with this subject, Roman historians in particular, have with few exceptions paid too little attention to what I might call the underside of the process: persecution as seen by the Christians—in a word, martyrdom, a concept that played a vitally important part in the life of the early Church (see Frend, 1954; 1958; 1959).

We cannot be certain how and when the government began to take action [against Christians]; but, like many other people, I believe it was in the persecution by Nero at Rome which followed the great fire in A.D. 64. The much discussed passage in Tacitus[1] that is our only informative source leaves many problems unsolved, but I can do no more here than summarize my own views, which agree closely with those expressed by Professor Beaujeu in his admirable recent monograph on this persecution (Beaujeu, 1960).[2] In order to kill the widely believed rumor that he himself was responsible for starting the fire, Nero falsely accused and savagely punished the Christians. First, those who admitted being Christians[3] were prosecuted, and then, on information provided by them (doubtless under torture), a great multitude were convicted, not so much (according to Tacitus) of the crime of incendiarism as because of their hatred of the human race ("odio humani generis").[4] Tacitus, like his friend Pliny and their contemporary Suetonius,[5] detested the Christians; and although he did not believe they caused the fire,[6] he does say they were "hated for their abominations" ("flagitia") and he calls them "criminals deserving exemplary punishment."[7] The Christians were picked on as scapegoats, then, because they were already believed by the populace to be capable of horrid crimes, *flagitia*: that is worth noticing. (Had not the Empress Poppaea Sabina been particularly sympathetic toward the Jews,[8] they might well have been chosen as the most appropriate scapegoats.) And once the first batch of Nero's Christian victims had been condemned, whether on a charge of organized incendiarism or for a wider "complex of guilt" (Momigliano, 1934: 725–726, 887–888), there would be nothing to prevent the magistrate conducting the trials (probably the *Praefectus Urbi*) from condemning the rest on the charge familiar to us in the second century, of simply "being a Christian"—a status that now necessarily involved, by definition, membership of an antisocial and potentially criminal conspiracy.

I now want to begin examining the attitude of the government toward the persecution of the Christians. I propose to consider mainly the legal problems first,

---

[1]Tacitus, *Annals,* xv.44.3–8.

[2]The other sources are discussed and quoted by Canfield, 1913: 43ff., 141ff. A good selective bibliography up to 1934 will be found in Cook, Adcock, and Charlesworth, 1934: 982–983.

[3]The imperfect tense, "qui fatebantur," shows that the confession was one of Christianity and not of incendiarism.

[4]Tacitus, *Annals,* xv.44.5. See also Tacitus, *Historiae,* v. 5; Tertullian, *Apologeticus,* 37.8; Cicero, *Tusculanae disputationes,* iv. 25, 27; Diodorus Siculus, *Bibliotheca,* xxxiv.1.1.

[5]Suetonius, *De vita Caesarum: Nero,* 16.2.

[6]His words "abolendo rumori Nero *subdidit* reos"(44.3) prove that.

[7]Tacitus, *Annals,* xv.44.4,8.

[8]Josephus, *Antiquitates Judaicae,* xx.8.11; see also Josephus, *Vita* 3. Josephus describes Poppaea as "God-fearing." See also Canfield, 1913: 47–49.

because although they involve some highly technical questions of Roman public law, the more important ones can, I believe, be completely solved, and we shall then be in a very much better position to understand the reasons that prompted the government to persecute; although before we can finally clarify these, we shall have to consider the other side of our problem: the reasons for the hatred felt toward Christianity by the mass of pagans.

The legal problems,[9] from which a certain number of nonlegal issues can hardly be separated, may be grouped under three heads. First, what was the nature of the official charge or charges? Second, before whom, and according to what form of legal process, if any, were Christians tried? And third, what was the legal foundation of the charges? (For example, was it a *lex,* or a *senatusconsultum,* or an imperial edict specifically directed against Christianity, or some more general edict, or an imperial rescript or series of rescripts?) I will deal with the first question now, and then the other two together.

First, then, the nature of the charges against the Christians. Here I am going to be dogmatic and say that from at least 112 onward (perhaps, as we have seen, from 64) the normal charge against Christians was simply "being Christians": they are punished, that is to say, "for the Name," the *nomen Christianum.* This is quite certain, from what the Christian Apologists say in the second and early third centuries,[10] from several accounts of martyrdoms,[11] and from the technical language used by Pliny and Trajan in their celebrated exchange of letters, probably at about the end of 112,[12] concerning the persecution conducted by Pliny in his province of Bithynia et Pontus.[13] Pliny speaks of the Christians he had executed as "those who were charged before me *with being Christians*" ("qui ad me tamquam Christiani deferebantur") and the only question he says he asked these confessors was whether they admitted this charge ("interrogavi ipsos, an essent Christiani")[14]; and Trajan in his reply speaks of "those who had been charged before you *as Christians*" ("qui Christiani as te delati fuerant"), and goes on to say that anyone "who *denies he is a Christian*" ("qui negaverit se Christianum esse") and proves it "by offering prayers to our gods" can go free.[15] With the other evidence, this settles the matter. Now the *delatores* [private citizens acting as prosecutors] who first accused the Christians as such before Pliny could not be sure (as we shall see) that Pliny would take cognizance of the matter at all, let alone inflict the death penal-

[9]The modern literature is vast and much of it is worthless. All the works that anyone could wish to consult today are given by Krüger and Ruhbach, 1929: vi–ix, 130–144 and the bibliographies for individual Passions; Sherwin-White, 1952; Monachino, 1953; Wlosok, 1959).

[10]E.g., Justin, *I Apologia,* 4; *II Apologia,* 2; Athenagorus, *Legatio.,* 1–2; Tertullian, *Apologeticus,* 1–3 etc.; Tertullian, *Ad Nationes* I.3; and many similar passages.

[11]Eusebius, *Ecclesiastical History,* iv.15.25 and the Passions of Polycarp, the Scillitans, and Apollonius (respectively, 12.1; 10, 14; and 1ff.).

[12]But perhaps a year or even two years earlier; see Syme, 1958: i, p. 81 and ii, p. 659 (App. 20).

[13]Pliny, *Epistulae* (Letters), x. 96–97. It is a pleasure to be able to welcome at last a really good English translation of Pliny's *Letters,* by Betty Radice (1963).

[14]Pliny, *Epistulae,* 96. 2–3.

[15]Pliny, *Epistulae,* 97.1, 2.

ty. Since they thought it was worth "trying it on," they evidently knew that in the past other officials had been prepared to punish Christians as such. And in fact Pliny now did so,[16] although later he had second thoughts and consulted the emperor, saying he was doubtful on what charge and to what extent he should investigate and punish, and in particular whether he should take the age of the accused into account, whether he should grant pardon to anyone who was prepared to apostatize, and whether he should punish for the Name alone or for the abominable crimes associated with being a Christian (the "flagitia cohaerentia nomini"). Trajan explicitly refused to lay down any general or definite rules and was very selective in his answers to Pliny's questions. In two passages which do him great credit he instructs Pliny that Christians must not be sought out ("conquirendi non sunt"), and that anonymous denunciations are to be ignored, "for they create the worst sort of precedent and are quite out of keeping with the spirit of our age." Christians who are accused as such, in due form (by a private prosecutor, *delator*), and are convicted must be punished, but anyone who denies he is a Christian, and proves it "by offering prayers to our gods," is to receive "pardon on the score of his repentance" and be set free. In my opinion, Pliny could justifiably take this to mean that punishment was to be for the Name alone.

One often hears it said that the Christians were martyred "for refusing to worship the emperor."[17] In fact, emperor worship is a factor of almost no independent importance in the persecution of the Christians.[18] It is true that among our records of martyrdoms emperor worship does crop up occasionally;[19] but far more often it is a matter of sacrificing *to the gods*[20]—as a rule, not even specifically to "the gods *of the Romans.*" And when the cult act involved does concern the emperor, it is usually an oath by his Genius[21] or a sacrifice to the gods on his behalf.[22] Very characteristic is the statement of Vigellius Saturninus, proconsul of Africa in 180, to the Scillitan martyrs: "We too are religious, and our religion is simple, and we swear by the Genius of our lord the emperor, and we pray for his welfare, as you also ought to do."[23] This is also the situation which is reflected in the Apologists. Tertullian, addressing himself in 197 to the Roman governing class in the *Apologeticus,* examines at great length the charges against the Christians: "You don't

[16]Pliny, *Epistulae,* 96.3.

[17]See Syme, 1958, ii., p. 469: "an invincible spirit that denied allegiance to Rome when allegiance meant worship of Caesar."

[18]That this is just as true of the third century as of the second has recently been demonstrated by Andreotti, 1956. It is particularly significant that Cyprian never mentions the imperial cult. And "the cult of the emperors plays a very subordinate part in the last great persecution" (Baynes, 1939: 659).

[19]As in Pliny, *Epistulae,* x. 96.5 (contrast 97.1: "dis nostris"); Eusebius, *Ecclesiastical History,* vii.15.2.

[20]As e.g. in Pliny, *Epistulae,* x .97.1, and the Passions of Justin, Carpi *et al.,* the Fructuosi, and Canonicus.

[21]As e.g. in Eusebius, *Ecclesiastical History,* iv. 15.18, 20, 21, and the Passions of Polycarp, the Scillitans, and Apollonius. Contrast Tertullian, *Apologeticus,* 10.1; 28.2, etc.

[22]As e.g. in the Passions of the Scillitans, 3.5; the Passions of the Perpet., vi.2; and other sources.

[23]The Passions of the Scillitans, 3.

worship the gods, and you don't offer sacrifice for the emperors."[24] And there is ample evidence to show that the situation remained substantially the same right through the third and early fourth centuries, even during the general persecutions.[25]

I now turn to the nature of the judicial process against the Christians. (In considering this, I shall go beyond the strictly legal sphere from time to time, and look at some of the reasons why persecution took place.)

The procedure against Christians was in every case that used for the vast majority of criminal trials under the Principate: *cognitio extra ordinem* (or *extraordinaria*), which I shall discuss in a moment. Capital trials under this process in the provinces took place before the provincial governor and no one else. In Rome, the only trials of Christians about which we have good evidence were before the Praefectus Urbi[26] or a Praefectus Praetorio;[27] none of the known cases was important enough to come directly before the emperor himself, or the senate,[28] although in the early Principate appeals by Roman citizens first accused elsewhere may have gone to the emperor's court.

In making use of *cognitio extra ordinem* the magistrate concerned had a very wide discretion (the "arbitrium iudicantis," on which see de Robertis, 1939)— even more so, of course, in criminal trials than in civil actions, just because of the relative vagueness of the criminal law. This discretion extended not only to fixing penalties, but even to deciding which cases the magistrate would recognize as criminal and which—like Gallio when appealed to by the Jews of Corinth against St. Paul[29]—he would refuse even to consider.

It is important to remember that the standard procedure in punishing Christians was "accusatory" and not "inquisitorial": a governor would not normally take action until a formal denunciation was issued by a *delator,* a man who was prepared not merely to inform but actually to conduct the prosecution in person, and to take the risk of being himself arraigned on a charge of *calumnia,* malicious prosecution, if he failed to make out a sufficient case.[30] Trajan, as we have seen, forbade the seeking out of Christians. This principle, however, could be and sometimes was disregarded. The best attested example comes from the savage persecution at Lyons and Vienne in 177, when the governor did order a search to be made for

---

[24]Tertullian, *Apologeticus,* 10.1; and see, for discussion of the two charges separately, 10.2–28.1 and 28. 2–35. Tertullian goes on (10.1) to sum up the two charges against the Christians as *sacrilegium* and *maiestas,* but he is hardly using either word in its technical sense (see Mommsen, 1899: 760ff).

[25]See note 18 above.

[26]Justin, *II Apologia,* 1–2 (Ptolemaeus, Lucius, and another); Passion of Justin, I.

[27]Early in the reign of Commodus, Apollonius was tried and sentenced by the Praetorian Prefect Perennis; but the surviving versions of the Passion, and the narrative by Eusebius (*Ecclesiastical History,* v. 21) are confused, notably with regard to the role played by the senate, which has been much discussed. A confident explanation is hardly possible; the best so far produced seems to me that of Griffe, 1952; see also Monachino, 1953.

[28]See the preceding note.

[29]Acts of the Apostles 18: 12–17.

[30]See Eusebius, *Ecclesiastical History,* iv.9. 3.

Christians[31]—and incidentally seems to have punished apostates for what Pliny had called the "flagitia cohaerentia nomini," the shocking crimes of which Christians were supposed to be guilty, and that had been alleged against them by their pagan slaves.[32]

Christian propaganda from at least the middle of the second century onwards tried to make out that it was only the "bad emperors" who persecuted, and that the "good emperors" protected the Christians,[33] but there is no truth in this at all. We know, for example, of quite a number of martyrdoms under the first two Antonines in widely separated parts of the empire, and even at Rome itself.[34] In reality, persecution went on automatically, if sporadically, whoever the emperor might be; and until the third century at any rate it is better not to think of persecutions primarily in terms of emperors. It was the provincial governor in each case who played the more significant role—and even his attitude might be less important than what I must call "public opinion." If the state of local feeling was such that no one particularly wanted to take upon himself the onus of prosecuting Christians, very few governors would have any desire to instigate a persecution. If, on the other hand, public opinion was inflamed against the Christians (as we shall see it often was, down to the middle of the third century), then delators would not be lacking, and Christians would be put on trial; and few governors would have any motive for resisting strong local feeling demonstrated in this perfectly permissible way, especially if some of the more influential men in the area were leading in the agitation, as they often would be. Imperial instructions (*mandata*) given to provincial governors bade them take care to rid their provinces of "bad men" (*mali homines*),[35] and Ulpian said it was characteristic of a good and serious-minded governor that he kept his province "settled and orderly" ("pacata atque quieta"), adding that he would have no difficulty in securing this end if he diligently saw to it that the province was cleared of "mali homines"—and sought them out accordingly.[36] The governor was advised by a first-century jurist to consider not so much what was the practice at Rome as what the circumstances required;[37] and the principle that in the exercise of his criminal jurisdiction the governor should act according to the circumstances existing in his particular province was well recognized.[38] Probably the main reason why some martyrdoms—perhaps many martyrdoms—took place was that they were thought to be necessary if the province

[31]Eusebius, *Ecclesiastical History*, v.1.14.

[32]Eusebius, *Ecclesiastical History*, 33, see also 14.

[33]The first writer we know to have asserted this is Melito of Sardis; see Eusebius, *Ecclesiastical History* iv.26.9. It soon became "common form"; see Tertullian, *Apologeticus*, 5, etc.

[34]E.g., those of Polycarp, of the Christians of Lyons, of the Scillitans, and, at Rome, of Ptolemaeus and Lucius, of Justin and his companions, and of Apollonius—to name only a few of whom we possess reasonably reliable records.

[35]Paulus, in the *Digest*, i.18.3; see also *Sententiae Pauli*, v.22.1.

[36]*Digest.*, i.18.13.pr.

[37]Proculus, in the *Digest.*, i.18.12.

[38]See, e.g., Ulpian, in the *Digest*, xlvii.11.9, 10 (see also 14.1.pr); Saturninus, in the *Digest*, xlviii. 19.16.9.

were to be kept "pacata atque quieta."[39] Most governors were doubtless only too willing to take action against men who were strongly disapproved of by "all right-thinking people," and who tended to become the center of disturbances. Everyone will remember how Pilate yielded to the vociferous demands of the local notables and their followers for the crucifixion of Jesus.[40] If a governor, indeed, refused to do what was expected of him in this way, not only would he become unpopular: the general indignation against the Christians would be only too likely to vent itself in riots and lynching, as we have evidence that it did on occasion;[41] and once violence began, anything might happen.

Christians might also be suspect, as *mali homines,* in the eyes of some governors, because they worshipped a man who had admittedly been crucified by a governor of Judaea, as a political criminal,[42] who thought of himself as "king of the Jews."[43] Their loyalty to the state, whatever they might say, could well appear doubtful, if only because they refused even to swear an oath by the emperor's Genius.[44] They were always talking about the imminent end of the world; and one of their books spoke with bitter hatred of Rome, thinly disguised under the name of Babylon, and prophesied its utter ruin.[45] And furthermore the secrecy of their rites might well seem a cover for political conspiracy, or at any rate antisocial behavior. A governor who had such considerations in mind when trying Christians might even decide to find them guilty of *maiestes* (treason): this would account for various statements by Tertullian about Christians being accused of that crime[46]—although I would not take these pieces of rhetoric very seriously myself. In any event, the factors I have just been mentioning would have less and less weight as time went on, and it became clear that Christians had no political objectives whatever and few particularly antisocial habits.

Sometimes a Christian who was in danger of being put on trial might be able to escape altogether by bribing the intending delator or the authorities. There is evidence that this was happening in Africa by the early third century at the latest:[47] not merely individuals but whole churches had purchased immunity, to the disgust of Tertullian,[48] who believed that during persecution Christians must stand their ground and neither take to flight nor buy themselves off. This rigorist attitude was only partly shared by the churches of the West, and in the East it seems to have been generally repudiated: flight or concealment during persecution was official-

[39]Ronconi (1956: 628) gives great emphasis to the need to satisfy "public opinion" as a cause of persecution.

[40]Gospel of Mark 15: 1–15 and parallel passages; and especially the Gospel of John 19: 12, 15.

[41]See, e.g., Eusebius, *Ecclesiastical History,* v. Praef. 1; 1.7; vi. 41. 1–9.

[42]See Minucius Felix, *Octavius,* 9.4.

[43]Gospel of Mark 15: 2, 9, 12, 26 (and parallel passages); Gospel of Luke 23: 2; Gospel of John 19: 12, 15.

[44]See note 21 above.

[45]Book of Revelations 14: 8; 16: 19; 17–18.

[46]Tertullian, *Apologeticus,* 10.1; 28.3ff., etc.

[47]Tertullian, *De Fuga,* 5.5; 12–14 (written c. 212, during Tertullian's Montanist period).

[48]Tertullian, *De Fuga,* 13.5.

ly approved everywhere (except insofar as leading clergy might incur disapproval for deserting their flocks); but in the West, though apparently not in the East, the purchase of immunity, at any rate in a form which might give the impression of apostasy, was regarded as a sin, if not a particularly grave one (see de Ste. Croix, 1954). Our evidence comes mainly from Africa, Spain, and Rome during the Decian persecution, when certificates of compliance with the imperial order to sacrifice to the gods were purchased wholesale by the less steadfast members of the Christian community (de Ste. Croix, 1954).

Although we have not yet disposed of all the legal issues, we have at least reached a point from which we can see that the last of my three questions of a legal nature, "What was the legal foundation for the charges against the Christians?" has answered itself, because under the *cognitio* process no foundation was necessary, other than a prosecutor, a charge of Christianity, and a governor willing to punish on that charge. Theories that the Christian churches could be legally regarded as *collegia illicita,* unlawful associations, either in the sense of being irremediably illegal (so that their members were at all times liable to criminal punishment), or merely because they were unlicensed (and liable to be prosecuted if they failed to obey an order to disband), have been strongly attacked in recent years by specialists in Roman public law (see especially de Robertis, 1938; Bovini, 1949; Sherwin-White, 1952; but contrast Duff, 1938: 169–170); and in spite of some texts which suggest there may have been some technical irregularity,[49] I am convinced that this issue can have had no real importance: we never hear that any Christian was ever prosecuted as a member of a *collegium illicitum.*

My next point concerns what I call the "sacrifice test," used by Pliny in order to give those who denied being Christians a chance to prove their sincerity.[50] The earliest example we have of the use of such a test in the Roman world, as far as I know, is at Antioch early in the year 67, when it was used during a pogrom by the Greeks of that city, to distinguish between Jews and non-Jews.[51] The character of the sacrifice test changed when judicial torture, which until the second century had been used (except in very special circumstances) only on slaves, came to be regularly applied to all those members of the lower classes (the vast majority of the population of the empire) who became involved in criminal trials, whether they were Roman citizens or not.[52] Once judicial torture had become a standard practice, the sacrifice test naturally tended to lose its original character as a privilege, and to become something that was enforced, usually with the aid of torture. But the essential aim was to make apostates, not martyrs. One could say without exaggeration that a governor who really wanted to execute Christians would be care-

[49]Notably Origen, *Contra Celsum,* I.1; see also Pliny, *Epistulae,* x. 96.7 (with 33.3; 34.1); Tertullian, *Apologeticus,* 38. 1–2; 39 (especially sections 20–21); Tertullian, *De Ieiunio,* 13. But for the third century see *Scr. Hist. Aug., Sev. Alex.,* 49.6; Eusebius, *Ecclesiastical History,* vii. 13: 30, 19.

[50]Pliny, *Epistulae,* x. 96.5.

[51]Josephus, *Bellum Judaicum,* vii. 3.3, sections 50–51. For the date, see section 46.

[52]The practice seems to have been well established by the reign of Marcus Aurelius (161–180); see the references in de Ste. Croix, 1954: 80, n. 29.

ful to avoid torturing them, lest they should apostatize and go free. For there is no doubt that with few exceptions an accused who was prepared to perform the prescribed cult acts was immediately released without punishment. Tertullian, of course, in his barrister's way, makes much of this as evidence that the authorities did not really regard the Christians as criminals at all. "Others, who plead not guilty," he cries, "you torture to make them confess, the Christians alone to make them deny."[53] This was perfectly true, and it must surely count as a lonely anomaly in the Roman legal system. The explanation is that the only punishable offense was *being* a Christian, up to the very moment sentence was pronounced, not *having been* one. I certainly know of no parallel to this in Roman criminal law. Tertullian ridicules the situation. What is the use of a forced and insincere denial, he asks scornfully. What is to prevent a Christian who has given such a denial and been acquitted from "laughing at your efforts, a Christian once more?"[54]

I need not spend much time on the question of the supposed abominations (*flagitio*) with which the Christians were charged, meaning of course cannibalism and incest.[55] It is hard to say how seriously these charges were taken by the government. The Christian Apologists of the second and early third centuries devote a good deal of attention to rebutting such accusations, which were evidently believed by the populace in both the eastern and the western parts of the empire. After the first half of the third century, however, they seem to have died out, although we know from Eusebius that a Roman military commander in Syria in 312, under the bitterly anti-Christian emperor Maximin, did try to fake charges of immoral behavior against the Christians of Damascus, in order to inflame public opinion against them.[56] The behavior of the ordinary pagan during the Great Persecution suggests that he no longer believed such slanders. Moreover, even for the early period, when these accusations were generally credited, one may feel that a more fundamental interpretation is necessary. As Macaulay said over a hundred years ago, "There never was a religious persecution in which some odious crime was not, justly or unjustly, said to be obviously deducible from the doctrines of the persecuted party" (see Last, 1937: 89, n.63). The reproaches of *flagitia* seem to have been essentially appendages of some more real complaint. Unfortunately, these charges were given some color by by the fact that orthodox Christians and heretics tended to fling them at each other, a fact upon which Gibbon severely remarks, "A pagan magistrate . . . might easily have imagined that their mutual animosity had extorted the discovery of their common guilt" (Gibbon, 1776: Chapter 16: 80–81).[57]

[53]Tertullian, *Apologeticus,* 2 (especially section 10); see also Tertullian, *Ad Scapulam,* 4.2; Cyprian, *Ad Demetrian.,* 13; Minucius Felix, *Octavius,* 28. 3–5.

[54]Tertullian, *Apologeticus,* 2.17.

[55]Eusebius, *Ecclesiastical History,* v. 1.14; Athenagorus, *Legatio,* 3, 31; see also Eusebius, *Ecclesiastical History,* iv. 7.11; v. 1.26; ix. 5.2; Justin, *I Apologia,* 26; *II Apologia,* 12; *Dialogus c. Trypho,* 10; Tertullian, *Apologeticus,* 6. 11–7.2 etc.; Minucius Felix, *Octavius,* 8–9, 28, 30–31; Origen, *Contra Celsum,* vi. 27, 40.

[56]Eusebius, *Ecclesiastical History,* ix. 5.2.

[57]For examples, see Justin, *I Apologia,* 26; Irenaeus, *Adversus Haereses,* I. 6.3–4; 24.5; 25.3–5

Before I come to the final stage of this investigation, I want to take a brief glance at a long series of events that may have given pagans rather more ground for their active antagonism to Christianity than we tend to suppose: I refer to what I have called "voluntary martyrdom."[58] Examination of it will require us to look at persecution, for once, mainly from the receiving end.

It is a significant fact, as yet not generally appreciated, that a very large number of sources (Passions as well as literary texts) show intrepid Christians going far beyond what their churches officially required of them, often indeed offering themselves up to the authorities of their own accord, and occasionally acting in a provocative manner, smashing images and so forth. After making a detailed study of the evidence for these "voluntary martyrs," I would claim that the part they played in the history of the persecutions was much more important than has yet been realized. It seems to me impossible to doubt that the prevalence of voluntary martyrdom was a factor that, for obvious reasons, both contributed to the outbreak of persecution and tended to intensify it when already in being. Contrary to what is usually said, voluntary martyrdom was by no means confined mainly to heretical or schismatic sects such as Montanists and Donatists, but was a good deal more common among the orthodox than is generally admitted. The heads of the churches, sensibly enough, forbade voluntary martyrdom again and again, and were inclined to refuse to these zealots the very name of martyr—passages to this effect could be cited from a dozen different sources, including Clement of Alexandria, Origen, and Lactantius, at least three bishops (Cyprian and Mensurius of Carthage, and Peter of Alexandria), the Passion of Polycarp, and the Canons of the Council of Elvira (for some of these references, see de Ste. Croix, 1954: 83, n.40). Nevertheless, we do hear of an astonishingly large number of volunteers, most of whom, whatever the bishops might say, were given full honor as martyrs, the general body of the faithful apparently regarding them with great respect.

One of the most fascinating of the Passions of the Great Persecution is that of Euplus, who suffered at Catana in Sicily. It begins:

> In the consulship of our lords Diocletian (for the ninth time) and Maximian (for the eighth time) [that is, in 304], on the 29th of April, in the most famous city of Catana, in the courtroom, in front of the curtain, Euplus shouted out, "I wish to die, for I am a Christian." His excellency Calvisianus the *corrector* said, "Come in, whoever shouted." And the Blessed Euplus entered the courtroom, bearing the immaculate Gospels—

and he achieved the end he had sought.[59]

In the next year, 305, while a festival was being celebrated at Caesarea in Palestine, a false rumor began to spread that certain Christians would be given to the beasts as part of the joyful celebrations. While the governor was on his way to the amphitheater, six young men suddenly presented themselves before him with their

---

(and see Eusebius, *Ecclesiastical History,* iv. 7.9–11); Clement of Alexandria, *Stromateis* iii, especially 2, 4, 5; Tertullian, *De Ieiunio,* 17; Philaster, *De Heres.,* 29, 57.

[58]For some remarks on this phenomenon, see de Ste. Croix, 1954: 83, 93, 101–103. I shall give the very considerable body of evidence for voluntary martyrdom in a forthcoming article.

[59]Passion of Euplus, I.

hands bound behind them, crying out that they were Christians and demanding to be thrown to the beasts with their brethren. We can well believe Eusebius when he adds that the governor and his entire suite were reduced to a condition of no ordinary amazement. The young men were arrested and imprisoned, but instead of giving them to the beasts as they had demanded, the merciless pagan condemned them to a speedy death by decapitation.[60]

These are but two of a large number of similar examples. Sometimes the fact that certain martyrs were volunteers, and were not sought out by the authorities, may alter our whole picture of a persecution. For example, the many Christians Eusebius says he himself saw condemned to death in a single day in the Thebaid in Upper Egypt during the Great Persecution are described by him in terms that show that they were volunteers, who, after sentence had been pronounced upon one of their brethren, "leapt up before the judgment seat from this side and from that, confessing themselves to be Christians."[61] The seeking out of Christians in this area, therefore, need not have been nearly as vigorous as we might otherwise have assumed from the evidently large number of victims.

Now voluntary martyrdom was not just a late phenomenon, which appeared only in the general persecutions: we have examples from the second century too—indeed, from the very earliest period at which we have any detailed records of martyrdoms at all: that is to say, from the 150s onward, including one on quite a large scale from about the year 185, recorded in Tertullian's *Ad Scapulam*. When Arrius Antoninus, proconsul of Asia, was holding his periodic assize in one of the towns of his province, a whole crowd of Christians presented themselves in a body before him, demanding the privilege of martyrdom—all the Christians of that town, says Tertullian, but we must allow for his customary exaggeration. The astonished proconsul ordered a few off to execution, but contemptuously dismissed the remainder, saying to them, "If you want to die, you wretches, you can use ropes or precipices."[62]

The positive evidence for voluntary martyrdom begins in the Antonine period, about 150. Conceivably, I suppose, it could have been a Montanist practice in origin. But I should like to suggest, with all the reserve necessitated by lack of direct evidence, that in fact it is likely to have begun much earlier, and that the reason why we do not hear of it before the middle of the second century is simply that we have too little specific evidence of any sort about persecution or martyrdom before that time. Here the Jewish background of Christianity, above all the Jewish martyr literature, is a very material factor. As far back as the Maccabaean period, as Professor Baron has put it, there was born "that great exaltation of religious martyrdom which was to dominate the minds of Jews and Christians for countless generations" (Baron, 1952: 230). We have examples of voluntary martyrdom on the part of Jews even before the Christian era, notably the incident in 4 B.C., described by Josephus, when two pious rabbis instigated their followers to cut down the golden

---

[60]Eusebius, *The Martyrs of Palestine*, 3.2–4 (in both Rescensions).

[61]Eusebius, *Ecclesiastical History*, viii. 9.5.

[62]Tertullian, *Ad Scapulam*, 5.1, quoting the proconsul's words in the original Greek.

eagle set up by Herod over the great gate of the Temple: about 40 men were executed, the rabbis and the actual perpetrators of the deed being burnt alive.[63] Now the two most fervent works of Jewish martyr literature, the Second and Fourth Books of Maccabees, with their unrestrained sensationalism and gruesome depictions of tortures, both formed part of the Septuagint, and must therefore have been well known to the early Church. And indeed a detailed linguistic study by Dr. Perler has shown it to be very likely that IV Maccabees exerted an important influence on the thought and writings of Ignatius (Perler, 1949), whose martyrdom must have taken place during the first quarter of the second century. Although there is no evidence of any value that Ignatius himself was actually a voluntary martyr,[64] we may, I think, see him as the precursor of the whole series; for in his letter to the Church of Rome, written while he was being taken from Antioch to the capital for persecution, he displays what has often been called a pathological yearning for martyrdom. He describes himself as "lusting for death,"[65] and he admonishes the Roman Christians not to try to do anything to save him. The eager way in which he speaks of the tortures confronting him—"Come fire and cross and encounters with beasts, incisions and dissections, wrenching of bones, hacking of limbs, crushing of the whole body"[66]—shows an abnormal mentality. It is difficult to believe that Ignatius was an isolated case, even in his own day. If even a few Christians of the late first and early second centuries had a similar craving for martyrdom (as so many others certainly did later), and gave practical expression to it, especially if they did so by insulting pagan cults, it would be even easier to understand how persecution quickly became endemic in many parts of the Roman world.

We are in a position at last to attempt to answer the question confronting us, which, it will be remembered, is twofold: "Why did the government persecute?" and "Why did the mass of pagans often demand and initiate persecution?" I propose to take the second question first.

The answer is clear: it is given to us over and over again in the sources. It was not so much the positive beliefs and practices of the Christians that aroused pagan hostility, but above all the negative element in their religion: their total refusal to worship any god but their own. The monotheistic exclusiveness of the Christians was believed to alienate the goodwill of the gods, to endanger what the Romans called the *pax deorum* (the right harmonious relationship between gods and men),[67] and to be responsible for disasters which overtook the community. I shall

---

[63]Josephus, *Bellum Judaicum,* I. 33.2–4, sections 648–655 (see also ii. 1. 2–3); *Antiquitates Judaicae,* xvii. 6.2–4, sections 149–167.

[64]John Malalas (*Chronographia,* xi) speaks of Trajan as "exasperated against Ignatius because he reviled him," but this hardly makes Ignatius a volunteer, and is entirely unreliable anyway; see also Lightfoot, 1889: ii. 2: 363ff., 383–391, 436ff., 480–481ff., 575–576.

[65]Ignatius, *Epistula ad Romani,* 7.2.

[66]Ignatius, *Epistula ad Romani,* 4.1–2; 5.2–3.

[67]This subject has been discussed in innumerable works, of which I will mention here only Fowler, 1911: 169ff., 272ff.

call this exclusiveness, for convenience, by the name the Greeks gave to it, "atheism";[68] characteristically, the Latin writers refer to the same phenomenon by more concrete expressions having no philosophical overtones, such as "deos non colere" (not paying cult to the gods): the word *atheus* first appears in Latin in Christian writers of the early fourth century, Arnobius and Lactantius (see Harnack, 1905).[69]

Whatever view we may hold about the mentality of educated, upper-class intellectuals, we must admit that the great mass of the population of the Roman Empire, in both East and West, were at least what we should call deeply superstitious; and I see not the least reason why we should deny them genuine religious feeling, provided we remember the essential differences between their kind of religion and that with which we are familiar. By far the most important of these was that pagan religion was a matter of performing cult acts rather than of belief, or ethics. No positive and publicly enforceable obligation, however, rested upon any private individual, whether a Roman citizen or not, or upon a common soldier,[70] to participate in any particular acts of cult (see Mommsen, 1899; Nock, 1952: esp. 189–192, 212–213), although magistrates and senators of Rome itself,[71] and magistrates (and perhaps senators) of individual Greek and Roman towns,[72] might be legally obliged to do so; and of course great social pressure might be brought to bear upon individuals who refused (on adopting Christianity or Judaism, for instance) to take part in family or other observances. No compulsion was necessary, because until the advent of Christianity no one ever had any reason for refusing to take part in the ceremonies that others observed—except of course the Jews, and they were a special case, a unique exception. Much as the Jews were detested by the bulk of the Roman governing class, as well as by many humbler Romans and Greeks, it was admitted (by the educated, at any rate) that their religious rites were ancestral, and very ancient. All men were expected piously to preserve the religious customs of their ancestors. And so even Tacitus, who strongly disliked Judaism, could say

---

[68]Among the texts are the *Epistula ad Diognetus,* 2.6; the Passion of Polycarp, iii. 2; ix. 2; see also xii.2 (Eusebius, *Ecclesiastical History,* iv. 15. 6, 18–19, see also 26); Eusebius, *Ecclesiastical History,* v. 1.9; Justin, *I Apologia,* 5–6, 13; Athenagorus, *Legatio,* 3, 4–30; Clement of Alexandria, *Stromateis,* vii. 1.1.1; Tertullian, *Apologeticus,* 6.10 (note "in quo principaliter reos transgressionis Christianos destinatis"); 10.1–28.2 (especially 24.1, 9); Arnobius, *Adversus Gentes,* I.29; iii. 28; v.30; vi.27.

[69]Arnobius, as cited in the preceding note, each time referring to pagan charges against Christians. Lactantius (*Epitome,* 63.2; *De Ira Dei,* 9.7) uses the word of pagan philosophers only. Cicero (*De Natura Deorum,* i.63) has the Greek word (applied to Diagoras), and Minucius Felix (*Octavius,* 8.2) transliterates ("atheon").

[70]See Tertullian, *De Idolatria,* 19: for a man serving in a "[militia] caligata vel inferior quaeque" there is no "necessitas immolationum."

[71]For Roman senators, see e.g. S.C. *ap Edict. Augusti ad Cyren.,* 135–136 (in the *Fontes Iuris Romani Anteiustiniani,* edited by Riccobono, 1941); Suetonius, *De Vita Caesarum: Divus Augustus,* 35.3. If Eusebius, *Ecclesiastical History,* viii. 11.2, is to be believed, some Christian officials in the provinces in the late 3rd century will have been given an imperial dispensation from religious duties. (These men . . . will hardly have been provincial *governors:* see *Ecclesiastical History,* viii.9.7; 11.2).

[72]If only to take oaths when required: see e.g. the *Lex Municipalis Salpensana,* xxvi (in the *Fontes Iuris Romani Anteiustininani,* edited by Riccobono, 1941). The Severi gave Jews holding municipal *honores* exemption from religious acts offensive to them: *Digest* l. 2.3.3.

that the religious rites of the Jews "have the recommendation of being ancient."[73] The gods would forgive the inexplicable monotheism of the Jews, who were, so to speak, licensed atheists.[74] The Jews of course would not sacrifice to the emperor or his gods, but they were quite willing, while the Temple still stood, to sacrifice to their own god for the well-being of the emperor; and Augustus, if we may believe Philo,[75] by a happy compromise not only accepted this but himself paid for the sacrifices. Matters were very different with the Christians, who had *ex hypothesi* abandoned their ancestral religions. Gibbon expressed the contrast perfectly when he wrote, "The Jews were a people which followed, the Christians a sect which deserted, the religion of their fathers" (Gibbon, 1776: Chapter 16: 74).

The Christians asserted openly either that the pagan gods did not exist at all or that they were malevolent demons. Not only did they themselves refuse to take part in pagan religious rites; they would not even recognize that others ought to do so. As a result, because a large part of Greek religion and the whole of the Roman state religion was very much a community affair, the mass of pagans were naturally apprehensive that the gods would vent their wrath at this dishonour not upon the Christians alone but upon the whole community; and when disasters did occur, they were only too likely to fasten the blame on to the Christians. That the Christians were indeed hated for precisely this reason above all others appears from many passages in the sources, from the mid-second century right down to the fifth. Tertullian sums it all up in a brilliant and famous sentence in the *Apologeticus:* the pagans, he says, "suppose that the Christians are the cause of every public disaster, every misfortune that happens to the people. If the Tiber overflows or the Nile doesn't, if there is a drought or an earthquake, a famine or a pestilence, at once the cry goes up, 'The Christians to the lion'."[76]

The essential point I want to make is that this superstitious feeling on the part of the pagans was due above all to the Christians' "atheism," their refusal to acknowledge the gods and give them their due by paying them cult. The Christian Apologists have much to say in reply to this charge[77]—and, by the way, they are addressing themselves to the educated class, sometimes in theory to the emperors themselves. The earliest surviving Apologists are of the mid-second century, but there is no reason to think the situation was different earlier.

We must not confuse the kind of atheism charged against the Christians with

[73]Tacitus, *Historiae,* v.5: "antiquitate defenduntur." See also Origen, *Contra Celsum,* v.25ff. And the fact that Jewish cult was aniconic seems to have appealed to some Romans, e.g. Varro (Augustine, *De Civitate Dei,* iv.31).

[74]For pagans calling Jews "atheists," see Juster, 1914: i., p.45 n. 1.

[75]Philo, *De Legatione ad Gaium,* 157, 317. Contrast Josephus, *Contra Apionem,* ii.6, section 77 (and see also *Bellum Judaicum,* ii. 10.4, section 197).

[76]Tertullian, *Apologeticus* 40. 1–2 (with 37.2); see also Tertullian *Ad Nationes,* I.9; also Firmilian, *ap.* Cyprian, *Epistulae,* lxxv. 10; Cyprian, *Ad Demetrian.,* especially 2–5; Arnobius, *Adversus Nationes* i.,1ff (especially 13, 16, 26) and *passim;* Augustine, *De Civitate Dei,* ii.3 (proverb: "No rain, because of the Christians") etc.; Origin, *Contra Celsum,* iii. 15; Comm.ser in Matt., 39; Maximin Daia, in Eusebius, *Ecclesiastical History,* ix. 7. 3–14 (esp. 8–9); 8.3.

[77]See note 68 above.

philosophical scepticism. Tertullian pretends to be very indignant because philosophers are permitted openly to attack pagan superstitions, while Christians are not. "They openly demolish your gods and also attack your superstitions in their writings, and you applaud them for it," he exclaims.[78] The vital difference was, of course, that the philosophers, whatever they might believe, and even write down for circulation among educated folk, would have been perfectly willing to perform any cult act required of them—and that was what mattered.

That the religious misbehavior of certain individuals should be thought of by pagans as likely to bring unselective divine punishment may seem less strange to us when we remember that similar views were held by Jews and Christians. Orthodox Christians felt toward heretics much as pagans felt toward them. The martyred bishop Polycarp, who (it was said) had actually known the Apostles personally, used to tell how the Apostle John, entering the baths at Ephesus, rushed out again when he saw the heresiarch Cerinthus inside, crying, "Away, lest the very baths collapse, for within is Cerinthus the enemy of the truth."[79]

About the middle of the third century, however, the attitude of the general run of pagans toward the Christians began to undergo a distinct change. Whereas until then the initiative in persecution seems to have come from below, from 250 onward persecution comes from above, from the government, and is initiated by imperial edict, with little or no sign of persecuting zeal among the mass of pagans. The beginning of the change seems to me to come with the Decian persecution. The last two recorded major outbreaks of popular fury against the Christians that I know of were those in Cappadocia and Pontus in 235[80] and at Alexandria in 249.[81] The change has gone quite far by the time of the Great Persecution, when the majority of pagans (except in a few places, like Gaza)[82] seem to be at least indifferent, some even sympathetic to the Christians,[83] and few provincial governors display any enthusiasm for the task. "The government had outrun pagan animosity" (Baynes, 1939: 677). The reason for the change, I take it, is that Christianity had by now spread widely and lost its secretive character, and pagans had come to realize that Christians were not so different from themselves, and just as religious.

I have ignored minor reasons for popular dislike of the Christians; but no doubt some people might feel a grudge against them on simple economic grounds: we may remember how these are said to have been responsible for arousing opposition to apostolic preaching at Philippi and Ephesus.[84]

---

[78]Tertullian, *Apologeticus*, 46.4.

[79]Irenaeus, *Adversus Haereses*, iii. 3.4.; Eusebius, *Ecclesiastical History*, iii. 28.6; iv. 14.6. The same mentality can be found among the Christian emperors: see, e.g., Constantine's letter to Aelafius, of 313–314 (Optatus, *Appendix* iii, f. 30b); *Codex Theodosianus*, xvi. 5.40.1 (A.D. 407); *Novellae Theodosianus*, iii. pr., and above all 8 (A.D. 438).

[80]Firmilian, as cited in note 76 above.

[81]Dionysius of Alexandria, *ap.* Eusebius, *Ecclesiastical History*, vi. 41.1–9. The cause of this outbreak is not given.

[82]See Eusebius, *The Martyrs of Palestine*, 3.1 (Long Rescension).

[83]See especially Athanasius, *History of the Arian Heresy*, 64.

[84]Acts of the Apostles 16: 16–24. (For the trade in images, see Philostratus, *Vita Appolon.*, v.20.)

Finally, we can try to analyze the attitude of the government. For once it is of little avail to ransack earlier Roman history for precedents, in the hope of discovering the principles on which Rome treated foreign religions,[85] because the great problem posed by Christianity, its exclusiveness, was something Rome had never encountered before—except under very different conditions, in the Jewish national religion.[86]

I do not myself believe that there is a single solution to our problem. I believe that different members of the governing class may have been actuated by different motives, and I think that each one of us must decide for himself how much weight he would attach to each. I have already mentioned some minor factors, which may in some cases have played an important and even a decisive part: the need to pacify public opinion; and suspicion of the Christians as a conspiratorial body, or at least as undesirables, *mali homines*. But for my own part I believe that the main motives of the government, in the long run, were essentially religious in character, according to the ancient conception of religion. These religious motives appear in two rather different forms, which some people might prefer to call "superstitious" and "political," respectively, thereby avoiding the term "religious" altogether. Some of the governing class, in the third century at any rate (and I believe from the first), were undoubtedly inspired by the very motives I have described as characteristic of their subjects. Among the persecuting emperors, we must certainly place Galerius in this category (on the contemporary evidence of Lactantius),[87] and also Diocletian, who seems to have been a thoroughly religious man.[88] About Decius and Valerian I would reserve my opinion. It is true that after the Severan period we find many soldier-emperors of little or no education, whom we might suspect of the grosser forms of superstition; and of course among the higher officials such as provincial governors there will have been a greater proportion of uneducated men. But, as it happens, Decius cannot be called a man of that sort, and conspicuously not Valerian. I would concede that even in the third century, and to a far greater extent in the second, especially in the early second, there may have been a significant number of members of the governing class who did not share the superstitious horror felt for the Christians by the masses. But even such people, I believe, were impelled to persecute—perhaps as vigorously as their

---

See also Tertullian, *Apologeticus,* 42–43. And see also Pliny, *Epistulae,* x. 96.10—perhaps in a case such as this the butchers might be aggrieved!

[85]The article by Last (1937) is nevertheless useful for its detailed examination of earlier acts of interference in religious matters by the Romans.

[86]It was perhaps a failure to realize the importance of this factor that led Nock (1952: 217) to make a generalization about the policy of the Roman government in religious matters which seems to me mistaken in regard to Christianity: "To sum up, the state interfered not because the Roman gods were failing to get their due but because particular practices or groups were held to be unsuitable or subversive or demoralizing. That is in substance true of official action against the Christians prior to Decius."

[87]Lactantius, *De Mortibus Persecutorum,* 9ff., especially 10.6; 11.1–4, 8. Galerius seems to have been the chief instigator of the Great Persecution (see de Ste. Croix, 1954: 109).

[88]See, e.g., Eusebius, *Vita Constantine,* ii 51. See also Lactantius, *De Mortibus Persecutorum,* 11.6.

less emancipated brethren—by motives I think we are justified in calling religious,[89] in that their aim also was primarily to break down the Christian refusal to worship the pagan gods, even if the basis from which they proceeded was different.

I want to stress two vital pieces of evidence that I do not see how we can explain away. First, there is the fact that except to a limited extent in the time of Valerian, and more seriously under Diocletian, what I have called the positive side of Christianity is never officially attacked: persecution did not extend to any aspect of the Christian religion other than its refusal to acknowledge other gods. No attempt was ever made, even in the general persecutions, to prohibit Christians from worshipping their own god in private, although Valerian[90] and Diocletian[91] (but not Decius) forbade them to assemble for common worship, and Diocletian also ordered the destruction of churches and the confiscation of sacred books and church property (see de Ste. Croix, 1954: 75, n. 1-3). As the deputy prefect of Egypt said to Bishop Dionysius of Alexandria in 257, "Who prevents you from worshipping your own god also, if he is a god, along with the natural gods?"[92] And of course the sacrifice test continues to be used, and if the Christian complies with it he goes free, even in the general persecutions.

Secondly, there is what I believe to have been the complete immunity from persecution of most of the Gnostic sects. Some of these professed doctrines of a recognizably Christian character (heretical in varying degrees as they were) and called themselves Christian. Yet in Roman eyes there was evidently a fundamental difference between Gnostics and orthodox Christians, if Gnostics were not persecuted. Why? The reason can only be that the Gnostics did not think it necessary to be exclusive, like the orthodox, and refuse to pay outward respect to the pagan gods when the necessity arose. We are told by orthodox Christian sources that Basilides, perhaps the most important of all the Gnostic heresiarchs, permitted his followers to eat meat that had been offered to idols, and in time of persecution "casually to deny the faith," doubtless by accepting the sacrifice test.[93] It appears, then, that although the tenets of the Gnostics must have appeared to the Roman governing class to be very similar to those of the orthodox, the Gnostics escaped persecution precisely because they consented to take part in pagan religious ceremonies on demand, when the orthodox refused to do so.

What then was the attitude of the more enlightened pagans among the governing class? Why did they too persecute?

Here I think it may be helpful if I retell a story told by Henry Crabb Robinson about the reception by Lord Thurlow, Lord Chancellor of England, of a deputation

---

[89]In general, I warmly agree with the views expressed by Vogt, 1962.

[90]See the Passion of Cyprian, I.7; Eusebius, *Ecclesiastical History,* vii.11. 10-11.

[91]See Eusebius, *Ecclesiastical History,* ix.10.8; the *Passio Saturnini et al., Abitin.,* especially 1, 2, 5-14, and the *Passio Philippi Heracl.,* 4 (in Ruinart, 1859: 414ff., 441).

[92]Eusebius, *Ecclesiastical History,* vii.11.9.

[93]Agrippa Castor, *ap.* Eusebius, *Ecclesiastical History,* iv.7.7; see also Irenaeus, *Adversus Haereses,* I.19.3; iii.19.4; iv.54; Tertullian, *Scorpiace,* especially 1, 15; Clement of Alexandria, *Stromateis,* iv.4.16.3-17.3; 9.71.1-72.4; 12.81-8. And see Frend, 1954.

that waited upon him in 1788 to secure his support in their efforts to bring about the repeal of the Corporation and Test Acts. Lord Thurlow "heard them very civilly, and then said, 'Gentlemen, I'm against you, by God. I am for the Established Church, damme! Not that I have any more regard for the Established Church than for any other church, but because *it is* established. And if you can get your damned religion established, I'll be for that too' "(Robinson, 1872: 197).

Lord Thurlow may not have been exactly what we should call today a religious man, but his attitude may help us to understand that of some members of the Roman governing class of the late Republic and early Principate—though of course I am not saying it is the same. Religion, for such Romans, was above all the *ius divinum,* the body of state law relating to sacred matters, which preserved the *pax deorum* by means of the appropriate ceremonial.[94] It derived its great value, as Cicero repeatedly affirms, mainly from the fact that it rested upon the *auctoritas maiorum,*[95] the force of ancestral tradition. As Dr. Weinstock has pointed out (Weinstock, 1961),[96] St. Augustine was very much in the Ciceronian tradition when he declared that he would not believe the very Gospel itself, did it not rest upon the *auctoritas* of the Catholic Church[97]—a point of view still held today by some Christian churches. Cicero, legislating in the *De Legibus* for his ideal commonwealth, begins with *ius divinum.*[98] In the *De Natura Deorum* he makes his more sceptical speaker, Cotta, open his case in Book i by proclaiming that he is himself a *pontifex,* who believes that "religious rites and ceremonies ought to be maintained with the utmost reverence,"[99] and much more to the same effect. He makes his Stoic speaker, Balbus, echo sentiments he had expounded himself in his speech to the senate, *De Haruspicum Responsis,* to the effect that the Romans, "in religion, that is the cult of the gods, are far superior to other nations."[100] Such passages could be multiplied. It seems to me entirely beside the point (though doubtless true enough) to object that Cicero rarely if ever shows any unmistakable sign of "personal religion," as we should call it. And when Professor Latte, in his great history of Roman religion, says that one finds in Cicero's philosophical works no "inward participation" (Latte, 1960: 285), I feel as if I were being invited to note the absence of color in a black-and-white drawing. The Roman state religion con-

---

[94]See the remark by Caecilius, the pagan speaker in Minucius Felix's *Octavius,* 7.2: all religious ceremonies were invented "vel ut remuneraretur divina indulgentia, vel ut averteretur imminens ira aut iam tumens et saeviens placaretur."

[95]Cicero, *De Natura Deorum,* iii. 5–9 is perhaps the most illuminating passage. See also Cicero's *De Divinatione,* ii, 148 etc.

[96]I am grateful to Dr. Weinstock for allowing me, before the delivery of the paper on which this article is based, to read the manuscript of his very impressive discussion, then not yet published. I found his paragraph 3, pages 208–210, particularly helpful.

[97]Augustine, *Contra Epistolam Manichaei,* 5.

[98]Cicero, *De Legibus,* ii, 18–22.

[99]Cicero, *De Natura Deorum,* i.61.

[100]Cicero, *De Natura Deorum,* ii. 8; see also his *De Haruspicum Responsis,* 19. Among many similar passages in other authors, see Val. Max., I.1, especially sections 8, 9; Tertullian, *Apologeticus,* 25.2. Other texts are cited in Pease's edition of the *De Natura Deorum,* 1958: 567.

tained nothing that was personal to the individual. And as for *rational* belief (or disbelief) in the gods—did it ever figure in the thoughts of Cicero and his kind except when they were playing the Greek game of philosophical disputation? Contrast the *instinctive* belief that Cotta in the *De Natura Deorum,* speaking to Balbus, proclaims in the words, "From you, a philosopher, I am bound to ask for a rational account of religion. Our ancestors I must *believe,* even in the absence of rational explanation."[101] These people had a deep emotional feeling for Roman religion, as the *ius divinum,* the "foundation of our state,"[102] an essential part of the whole Roman way of life. One can still hold this to be true, even if, taking perhaps an uncharitable view (as I would myself), one holds that quite a large part of that religion was above all an instrument by which the governing class hoped to keep the reins of power in its own hands.[103] In the *De Legibus,* Cicero, himself an augur, glorifies that office because past augurs have been able to annul laws passed by reforming tribunes, to which Cicero refuses the very name of law.[104] But such deep-seated expressions of his own interests and those of his class are far from making his conception of Roman religion "insincere" or "cynical"—indeed, the reverse is true.

I have appealed to Cicero because I suppose most people would agree that the author of the *De Divinatione* may well be considered one of the least superstitious men in an age that was distinctly less superstitious than the age of the persecutions. For Cicero's spiritual descendants of the early Principate, Roman religion was part of the very stuff of Roman life and Roman greatness; and they were prepared to extend their protection also to the cults of the peoples of their empire, whose devotion to their ancestral religions seemed to their rulers only right and proper. Can we imagine that such men, however intellectually emancipated from the superstitions of the vulgar, would have had any compunction about executing the devotees of a new-fangled sect which threatened almost every element of Roman religion, and indeed of all the traditional cults conducted by the inhabitants of the Roman world? I would be prepared to speak of persecution so motivated as being conducted for religious reasons, though I realize that other people might prefer to use another word—political, perhaps.

[101]Cicero, *De Natura Deorum,* iii.6.

[102]Cicero, *De Natura Deorum,* iii.5.

[103]For . . . "fear of the supernatural" as the very cement of the Roman constitution, see Polybius, vi. 56.7–12. Varro, the greatest authority on Roman religion, thought it expedient, as did Scaevola before him, that "states should be deceived in matters of religion": Augustine, *De Civitate Dei,* iv. 27, see also 31, 32. See, in addition, Augustine's attack on Seneca (based on his lost work on Superstition) in *De Civitate Dei,* vi.10; also Livy, i.19.4–5; Dio Cassius, lii. 36.1–3.

[104]Cicero, *De Legibus,* ii. 14, 31. In the face of conflicting opinions among the experts whether divination really had a supernatural basis or was simply a political expedient ("ad utilitatem . . . republicae composita"), Cicero proceeds (*De Legibus,* 32–3) to declare his belief in the divine origin of augury, while lamenting its present decline. In the later *De Divinatione,* however, he makes it perfectly clear that he had no belief in the reality of divination (ii, especially 28–150), although in public he would keep up a pretense of taking it seriously, as a useful buttress of the constitution and the state religion (ii. 28, 70–1).

I shall end by quoting what seems to me the most illuminating single text in all the ancient sources, for the understanding of the persecutions. Paternus, proconsul of Africa, is speaking to Cyprian at his first trial in 257, and telling him what the emperors have just decreed. This, it is true, is a special edict, making it incumbent upon the Christian clergy, on pain of exile, to perform certain acts which ordinary folk would not normally be obliged to carry out; but what is enjoined is something any accused Christian might be ordered to perform, and this gives the text general significance. The decree is: "Eos qui Romanam religionem non colunt debere Romanas caerimonias recognoscere."[105] I think the sense is brought out best by translating the main clause negatively: "Those who do not profess the Roman religion"—it is admitted that there are such people—"must not refuse to take part in Roman religious ceremonies."

## REFERENCES

Andreotti, R. 1956. "Religione ufficiole e culto dell'imperatore nei 'Libelli' di Decio." In *Studi in Onore di A. Calderini e R. Paribeni,* 1. Milan: Ceschina.

Baron, S. W. 1952. *A Social and Religious History of the Jews* (2nd edition). New York: Jewish Publication Society of America.

Baynes, N. H. 1939. "The great persecution." In *The Cambridge Ancient History,* Volume 12: *The Imperial Crisis and Recovery, A.D.193–324,* edited by S. A. Cook, F. E. Adcock, M. P. Charlesworth, and N. H. Baynes. Cambridge: Cambridge University Press.

Beaujeu, J. 1960. *L'Incendie de Rome en 64 et les Chretiens.* Bruxelles-Berchem: Coll. Latomus 49.

Bovini, G. 1949. *La Proprieta Ecclesiastica e la Condizione Guirdica della Chiesa in eta Precostantiniana.* Milan: A. Giuffre.

Canfield, L. H. 1913. *The Early Persecutions of the Christians.* New York: Columbia University Studies in History, Economics and Public Law.

Cook, S. A., F. E. Adcock, and M. P. Charlesworth (editors). 1934. *The Cambridge Ancient History,* Volume 10: *The Augustan Empire, 44 B.C.–A.D. 70.* Cambridge: Cambridge University Press.

de Robertis, F. M. 1938. *Il Divitto Associativo Romano.* Bare.

———. 1939. "Arbitrium iudicantis e statuizioni imperiali." *Zeitschrift der Savigny-Stiftung fur Rechtsgeschicte* 59, Rom. Abt.: 219–260.

de Ste. Croix, G. E. M. 1954. "Aspects of the 'great' persecution." *Harvard Theological Review* 47: 75–129.

Duff, P. W. 1938. *Personality in Roman Private Law.* Cambridge: Cambridge University Press.

Fowler, W. Warde. 1911. *The Religious Experience of the Roman People.* London: Macmillan.

Frend, W. H. C. 1954. "The Gnostic sects and the Roman empire." *Journal of Ecclesiastical History* 5: 25–37.

———. 1958. "The persecutions: some links between Judaism and the Early Church." *Journal of Ecclesiastical History* 9: 141–158.

———. 1959. "The failure of the persecutions in the Roman empire." *Past and Present* No. 16: 10–30.

Gibbon, E. 1776. *The History of the Decline and Fall of the Roman Empire,* edited by J. B. Bury. London: Methuen, 1909.

Griffe, E. 1952. "Les actes du martyr Appolonius." *Bulletin de Litterature Ecclesiastique* 50: 65–76.

Harnack, A. 1905. *Der Vorwurf des Atheismus in den drei ersten Jahr, Texte u. Untersuch* 28 (N.F.13), 4.

---

[105]Passion of Cyprian, I.1.

Juster, J. 1914. *Les Juifs dans l'Empire Romain.* Paris: Paul Geuthner.

Krüger, G., and G. Ruhbach. 1965. *Ausgewählte Martyrerakten* (4th edition). Tubingen: Mohr.

Last, H. 1937. "The study of the 'persecutions.'"*Journal of Roman Studies* 27: 80–92.

Latte, K. 1960. *Römische Religionsgeschiete* (2nd edition). Munich: C. H. Beck'sche Verlagsbuchhandlung.

Lightfoot, J. B. (editor). 1889. *The Apostolic Fathers* (2nd edition). London: Macmillan.

Momigliano, A. 1934. "Nero." In *The Cambridge Ancient History,* Volume 10: *The Augustan Empire, 44 B.C.–A.D. 70,* edited by S. A. Cook, F. E. Adcock, and M. P. Charlesworth. Cambridge: Cambridge University Press.

Mommsen, T. 1899. *Römisches Strafrecht.* Leipzig: Duncker and Humblot.

Monachino, V. 1953. "Il fondamento della persecuzioni mei primi die secoli." *La Scuda Cattolica* 81: 33–39.

Nock, A. D. 1952. "The Roman army and the religious year." *Harvard Theological Review* 45: 187–277.

Perler, O. 1949. "Das vierte Makkabaerbuch, Ignat. v Antiochien u. die altesten Martyreiberichte." *Rivista di Archaeologia Christiana* 25: 47–72.

Radice, Betty (translator). 1963. *Pliny's Letters.* London: Penguin Books.

Riccobono, S. (editor). 1941. *Fontes Iuris Romani Anteiustiniani* (2nd edition). Florence: S. a. G. Barbera.

Robinson, Henry Crabb. 1872. *Diary, Reminiscences, and Correspondence of Henry Crabb Robinson* (3rd edition), edited by T. Sandler. London: Fields, Osgood.

Ronconi, A. 1956. "Tacito, Plinio, e i christiani." In *Studi in onore di U. E. Paoli.* Florence: F. Le Monnier.

Ruinart, Th. 1859 edition. *Acta Martyrum.* Regensburg: G. Joseph Manz.

Sherwin-White, A. N. 1952. "The early persecutions and Roman law again." *Journal of Theological Studies* 3 (new series): 199–213.

Syme, R. 1958. *Tacitus.* Oxford: Oxford University Press.

Vogt, J. 1962. *Zur Religiositat der Christenverfolger im Römische Reich (Sb. Akad. Heidelberg),* Phil-Hist. Klasse. Heidelberg: C. Winter.

Weinstock, S. 1961. "Review of *Romische Religionsgeschicte.*"*Journal of Roman Studies* 51: 206–215.

Wlosok, A. 1959. "Die Rechtsgrundlagen der Christenverfolgungen der ersten zwei Jahr." *Gymnasium* 66: 14–32.

# Law and Organization

# 15

# THE PUBLIC ORDERING
# OF PRIVATE RELATIONS:
# WINNING CIVIL
# COURT CASES*

CRAIG WANNER

## INTRODUCTION AND METHODOLOGY

This chapter analyzes who wins and loses in the civil trial courts in Baltimore, Cleveland, and Milwaukee. Research was conducted during 1971 and 1972 when a total of 7800 civil court cases were examined and summarized from the case folders and dockets of courts of first instance with general jurisdiction in Baltimore, Cleveland, and Milwaukee. Cases were selected randomly, sampling without replacement, from the 1965 and 1970 records of cases filed from those court records that were open to public inspection (records of paternity suits and adoptions, for instance, were not available). Cases were coded by: (1) the type of legal action initiated; (2) the outcome; (3) the names and addresses of all litigants; (4) the names of law firms and attorneys; (5) the date of filing; (6) the date of last recorded docket entry; (7) the number of court proceedings docketed; (8) the amount of money in dispute; (9) the amount of money awarded as damages; and (10) the census tract of each litigant.

The first part of this report (Wanner, 1974) demonstrated that, far from being exposed to all the kinds of conflict which occur in their society, these courts resolve a relatively narrow range of disputes. Of the vast number of legal actions and remedies available, only 31 were found in this large sample of three cities. Of these, only 10 types of action were litigated frequently.[1] Of the 10, suits to secure

---

*Part One of this report, "The Public Ordering of Private Relations: Winning Civil Court Cases," appeared in Volume 8, Number 3 of *Law and Society Review,* 1974, pages 421–440.
[1]The 10 types include: (1) summary petitions to collect delinquent debts, such as cognovit notes,

---

the collection of delinquent debts (rather than personal injury torts) were the type of case most often initiated.

Only some kinds of litigants, it was found, frequently initiated lawsuits.[2] National and local organizations (mostly business) initiated about 50% of all the cases in this sample. Of the 25 types of organizational plaintiffs catalogued, 10 failed to file as many as 38 of the 7800 cases studied in this sample. All groups that might be described as "public regarding" were among these 10. Banks, credit lenders, hospitals, and home construction/maintenance businesses, on the other hand, were the most frequent organizational plaintiffs and together accounted for 50% of all organizational litigation. These groups, and organizations in general, were preoccupied with suits to collect delinquent debts. Individuals initiated litigation less frequently than organizations, initiated a far wider range of lawsuits than organizations, and did not concentrate in collection of debts.

Finally, the burden of defense was shown to fall unevenly on litigants. Most defendants were individuals, not organizations or government. When organizations did appear as defendants, they were often nominal defendants; that is, they were parties of record suffering no jeopardy, as did individual defendants.

## FINDINGS

For this chapter, winning and losing of court cases are defined in terms of the success of the plaintiff, the party bringing a claim to court. The data were searched for types of case outcomes. Twenty-seven types of outcomes were located and their

---

consent judgments, *scirie facias,* replevin, garnishment, and *fi-fa* (aids to execution); (2) money damage contracts, all suits to collect money damages for breach of an agreement; (3) liens, hospital, tax and mechanic's liens; (4) divorce-related actions such as annulments, divorce *a mensa et thoro,* divorce *a vinculo,* alimony, visitation privileges, custody, *capias* to compel support, reciprocal support proceedings, and petitions for permission to remarry; (5) personal injury and property damage torts; (6) foreclosures, all tax, mortgage, land contract, and chattels foreclosures; (7) evictions, including ejectments, and actions for unlawful detainer and for tenant holding over; (8) administrative agency appeals, all appeals from local workmen's compensation commission, from zoning boards, from condemnation boards, from tax court and from liquor license boards; (9) habeas corpus petitions, for bail, postconviction review, and for sanity hearings and child custody; (10) injunctions, all injunctions, and mandamus.

[2]The litigants were categorized as individual men, individual women, married couples, unrelated individuals, local organizations, national organizations, and government. When several individuals appeared who did not share a surname, each was coded as an unrelated individual. Organizations include businesses, voluntary associations, and appearances of individuals in their occupational roles. National organizations are organizations for which branches outside of the three cities could be located. Twenty-four organizations were uncovered in this sample. They are: (1) banks and other commercial lenders; (2) hospitals; (3) home construction and maintenance companies; (4) service industry; (5) department stores; (6) insurance; (7) realtors; (8) furniture stores; (9) manufacturers; (10) attorneys; (11) MDs, DDSs, RNs; (12) clothiers; (13) auto sales; (14) food stores; (15) entertainment; (16) apartments; (17) utilities; (18) gasoline stations; (19) private schools; (20) mass transit; (21) religious groups; (22) mass media; (23) civil improvement groups; and (24) charities. Service industry includes businesses such as television repair shops, small appliance dealers, and watch repair shops.

TABLE 1  Case Outcomes for the Ten Most Frequent Types of Cases

| Type | Frequency | Percentage of the total |
|---|---|---|
| 1. Plaintiff wins judgment or verdict | 2205 | 30.4 |
| 2. Case is not resolved beyond the filing of the complaint or the call for depositions | 1973 | 27.2 |
| 3. Case is formally settled | 1193 | 16.5 |
| 4. Plaintiff's petition is quashed | 550 | 7.6 |
| 5. Plaintiff's satisfaction is docketed | 439 | 6.1 |
| 6. Case is dismissed for *nolle prosequi* | 239 | 3.3 |
| 7. Case is dismissed because the defendant is *non est* | 174 | 2.4 |
| 8. Defendant wins judgment or verdict | 114 | 1.6 |
| 9. Residual outcomes | (361) | 5.0 |
| a. appeal | 2 | |
| b. default *pro* plaintiff | 28 | |
| c. judgment is certified | 19 | |
| d. dismissal for lack of jurisdiction or demurrer by plaintiff | 13 | |
| e. *ne re* | 1 | |
| f. *ne re* overruled | 3 | |
| g. vacated judgment or order to strike a previous order | 17 | |
| h. *nulla bona* or *failure* of a *fi-fa* | 105 | |
| i. transfer to another court | 44 | |
| j. remand of a case to a government agency | 4 | |
| k. *fi-fa* | 5 | |
| l. *capias* for contempt | 8 | |
| m. ratification of sale of property | 3 | |
| n. restitution of premises | 1 | |
| o. money report of a property guardian | 1 | |
| p. amendment of a nar | 14 | |
| q. new trial ordered | 4 | |
| r. a litigant dies | 6 | |
| s. unencodeable outcomes | 83 | |
| *n* | 7248 | 100.0 |

frequency for each type of case noted. Table 1 shows the frequency distribution of the 27 types of outcomes found.

The decision was made to analyze the sample in terms of major types of outcomes and to ignore the residual outcomes. To distinguish primary from residual outcomes a twofold test was devised. If an outcome appeared in one percent or more of the sample of cases and if that outcome appeared at least one time in 5 of the 10 most frequent types of cases, then that outcome was designated a major outcome. All other types of outcomes were classified as residual outcomes.

Applying this test, 8 of the 27 types of outcomes in the data were classified as major outcomes. These 8 types of outcomes were sorted into 5 sets according to the level of success of the plaintiff. The 5 sets were then combined to form a 5-point ordinal scale that measured the degree of plaintiff's success. The scale was ordered from least to most success; the points on the scale were coded from 1 to 5.

(1) The first point on the scale represents the least desirable outcome for a plaintiff. This point includes judgments or verdicts in favor of the defendant or the quashing of a plaintiff's petition. When 1 of these 3 outcomes occurs, the plaintiff receives neither legal ratification of his claim nor any money award even though he has expended resources to initiate a legal proceeding.

(2) Somewhat less undesirable for a plaintiff is the outcome coded as the second point on the scale. This included cases dismissed because the defendant cannot be found (*non est*). In these cases, the plaintiff's claim is not denied even though he receives no judgment or verdict or money award, and plaintiff is likely to have spent little on such cases. Some of these outcomes are only preliminary and not the final resolutions of the disputes at hand. In all three of these jurisdictions, there is a "two *non est*" rule for certain types of cases. According to this rule, if a plaintiff's petition is twice dismissed because the defendant cannot be found, the court summarily awards a judgment in favor of the plaintiff. The fact that these judgments are not among the judgments most likely to be collected is another reason for coding *non est* cases low on the scale.

(3) We considered that a greater degree of success is present when (a) a case is dismissed for lack of prosecution by the plaintiff (*nolle prosequi*) or (b) a case is not resolved beyond the filing of a complaint or beyond the call for depositions and interrogatories. In these cases, a plaintiff has willingly abandoned his claim even though it has received no overt, positive sanction from the court, and the defendant has not conceded a formal settlement. Plaintiff's claims are not contradicted despite the fact that they are not established as legal fact. We know from interviews that credit reporting companies and commercial lenders generally perceive this type of case as a legitimate claim against the defendant.[3] The possibility also exists in these cases that the plaintiff has unofficially received some inducement to settle or withdraw his claim. Perhaps the defendant has capitulated merely because of the notification that he is being sued. On the average, plaintiffs in these cases reported gaining 13.9% of the amount originally claimed as money damages. Hence, these are more successful case outcomes for plaintiffs than those represented in the first or second points of the scale.

(4) A still greater degree of success is represented by notation of settlement in

[3]The source for this assertion comes from an interview with Ralph Buehler, general manager of First Finance Company, in Baltimore on August 1, 1971.

the court record, which forms the fourth point in the scale. In these cases, the plaintiff, on the one hand, has accepted some inducement to withdraw his claim and has obtained some official recognition as a rightful claimant. The defendant, on the other hand, has acquiesced in being officially labeled as in some degree "at fault," and has agreed to a binding promise to compensate the plaintiff. On the average, plaintiffs in these cases report gaining 50% of the money damages they claim are owed to them. This point of the scale signifies a greater degree of success for plaintiffs than any of the first three points.

(5) Finally, the fifth degree of success is comprised of cases in which the plaintiff wins a judgment or verdict or records his "full satisfaction" of his claim on the court record. These are the most successful plaintiffs. Their claims have been fully ratified by the courts.

Table 2 shows the frequency distribution of the 5 points in this scale. Table 2 reveals that success and failure in litigation are distributed unequally among litigants in such a way that the court generally ratifies the demands made by plaintiffs. In 50% of the cases plaintiffs score the fifth point on the success scale; that is, they win judgments or verdicts or record their "full satisfaction." In only 9.6% of the cases do plaintiffs suffer outright and complete defeat (i.e., the first point on the success scale).

When each of the 10 most frequent types of cases is distributed on the 5-point scale, the pattern of plaintiff victory and defendant defeat can be examined in more detail. Table 3 shows the frequency distribution on the 5-point scale for each of the 10 most frequent types of court cases. In 6 of the 10 categories a clear-cut victory by the plaintiff (fifth point on the scale) is the most frequent outcome for that type of case. Outright success of defendants (first point on the scale) is the most fre-

TABLE 2   The Most Frequent Case Outcomes Arranged into a 5-Point Scale of Plaintiff's Success in Litigation (Ranked from Least to Most Successful)

| Rank | Frequency | Percentage of the total |
|---|---|---|
| First rank (defendant wins judgment or verdict; plaintiff's petition is quashed) | 664 | 9.64 |
| Second rank (dismissal of case bacause the defendant is *non est*) | 174 | 2.53 |
| Third rank (case is not resolved beyond the filing of the complaint or beyond the call for depositions minus uncontested liens; dismissal for *nolle prosequi* | 1372 | 19.82 |
| Fourth rank (formal settlement) | 1193 | 17.42 |
| Fifth rank (plaintiff wins judgment or verdict; plaintiff's satisfaction is docketed) | 3484 | 50.58 |
| *n* | 6887* | 99.99 |

*Six cases were excluded as unencodeable, $n$ = 6893 (6893 + 361 = 7254).

TABLE 3    A Frequency Distribution of Success for Each of the 10 Most Frequent
Types of Cases

| Category of case | First rank n % | Second rank n % | Third rank n % | Fourth rank n % | Fifth rank n % | Total n % |
|---|---|---|---|---|---|---|
| Summary debt actions | 43 2.32 | 60 3.23 | 582 31.34 | 328 17.65 | 844 45.45 | 1857 100. |
| Money damage contracts | 107 7.38 | 75 5.17 | 345 23.79 | 241 16.62 | 682 47.03 | 1450 100. |
| Liens | 2 .17 | 0 0.0 | 2 .17 | 336 28.33 | 846 71.33 | 1186 100. |
| Divorce related actions | 143 18.62 | 11 1.43 | 139 18.11 | 18 2.34 | 457 59.51 | 768 100. |
| Personal injury and property damage torts | 114 16.12 | 19 2.69 | 171 24.19 | 208 29.42 | 195 27.58 | 707 100. |
| Foreclosures | 29 9.48 | 3 .98 | 35 11.44 | 17 5.56 | 222 72.55 | 306 100. |
| Evictions | 15 7.21 | 4 1.92 | 39 18.75 | 7 3.37 | 143 68.75 | 208 100. |
| Administrative agency appeals | 84 49.12 | 1 .58 | 31 18.13 | 32 18.71 | 23 13.45 | 171 100. |
| Habeas corpus petitions | 74 56.92 | 1 .77 | 5 3.85 | 1 .77 | 49 37.69 | 130 100. |
| Injunctions | 53 48.18 | 0 0.0 | 25 22.73 | 7 6.36 | 25 22.73 | 110 100. |
| n | 664 | 174 | 1374 | 1195 | 3486 | 6893 |

quent outcome in only 3 types of cases, and these cases are the least frequent types of the 10 in the sample, and types in which the defendant is almost always an organization, usually the government.

Formal settlement (fourth rank) is far less prominent than one would expect. If the civil trial process is as pervaded by compromise as some suggest (e.g., Jacob, 1973: 121), one would expect little outright success (fifth point) and much formal settlement (fourth point); the court process would not generally lead to ratification of the full demands of plaintiffs. The data here refute this. Outright plaintiff victory is modal not only in relatively simple cases for collection of delinquent debts but in cases which involve more complex issues in which compromise and negotiation are expected to be the norm. For example, only 16.6% of the money damage contract disputes are formally settled. More than three times as many of these contracts are resolved by outright success for the plaintiff (fifth point). Formal settlement is no more prominent as an outcome in money damage contract suits than in summary petitions to collect delinquent debts (16.6% versus 17.7%).

TABLE 4   Variation in Success of Plaintiffs in Each of the Three Cities Studied

| | Mean | Standard deviation | N | Variation |
|---|---|---|---|---|
| Success | 3.967 | 1.293 | 6893 | 1.672 |
| Baltimore | 3.954 | 1.371 | 2203 | 1.879 |
| Cleveland | 3.847 | 1.235 | 2491 | 1.525 |
| Milwaukee | 4.115 | 1.262 | 2199 | 1.592 |

*Analysis of Variance*

| | Mean square | Degrees of freedom | F-test | Significance | Eta |
|---|---|---|---|---|---|
| Among groups | 42.097 | 2 | 25.355 | under .001 | .007 |
| Within groups | 1.660 | 6890 | | | |

*T-Tests with Probabilities Corrected for Degrees of Freedom*

| | Difference | Standard error | Degrees of freedom | t-test |
|---|---|---|---|---|
| Baltimore vs Cleveland | 0.107 | .038 | 4692 | 2.806* |
| Baltimore vs Milwaukee | −.161 | .040 | 4400 | −4.051** |
| Cleveland vs Milwaukee | −.268 | .037 | 4688 | −7.331** |

*Significance is .016.
**Significance is under .001.

Despite the prevalence of settlement in resolving personal injury/property damage claims (Ross, 1969), in this sample of cases only 29.4% of these torts are formally settled. Almost as many (27.6%) of these torts are resolved by a clear-cut victory for the plaintiff. Defendants prevail in only three types of cases (administrative agency appeals, injunctions, and habeas corpus petitions). Even here plaintiff's outright victory is the second most frequent outcome in two of these three types.

The three cities in this sample were examined to see if success is evenly distributed among litigants in these cities. Table 4 shows that there is a small but significant difference in the way success is distributed among these three cities.[4] Plaintiffs in Milwaukee are very slightly more successful than plaintiffs in Baltimore, and plaintiffs in Baltimore are very slightly more successful than litigants in Cleveland. The low value of Eta, however, indicates that a very small percent of the variation in success is caused by differences among Baltimore, Cleveland, and Milwaukee.

[4]Strictly speaking, these t-tests are interdependent, but because of the large n in the sample, the significance levels are compatible with Scheffe corrections.

**TABLE 5**  Variation in Success of Individual, Business, and Governmental Plaintiffs

| | Mean | Standard deviation | N | Variance |
|---|---|---|---|---|
| Success | 3.967 | 1.293 | 6887 | 1.672 |
| Individuals | 3.599 | 1.451 | 2805 | 2.106 |
| Business | 4.174 | 1.126 | 3440 | 1.267 |
| Government | 4.461 | .940 | 642 | .884 |

*Analysis of Variance*

| | Mean square | Degrees of freedom | F-test | Significance | Eta |
|---|---|---|---|---|---|
| Among groups | 341.989 | 2 | 217.324 | under .001 | .059 |
| Within groups | 1.574 | 6884 | | | |

*T-Tests with Probabilities Corrected for Degrees of Freedom*

| | Difference | Standard error | Degrees of freedom | t-test |
|---|---|---|---|---|
| Individuals vs business | −0.575 | .033 | 6243 | −17.630* |
| Individuals vs government | −0.862 | .060 | 3445 | −14.368* |
| Business vs government | −9.287 | .047 | 4080 | −6.068* |

*Significance under .001.

The most striking finding is that organizations are uniformly more successful than individual litigants. Table 5 compares the success of individuals and organizations. When a mean success score is computed for each type of litigant, scores for business and government are considerably higher than the mean score for individuals. The analysis of variance shows a significant difference in the mean success of individuals and organizations. The t-tests show that businesses and government plaintiffs are significantly more successful than individual plaintiffs. Among organizations, government plaintiffs are significantly more successful than businesses.

An analysis of variance was calculated to determine whether or not significant differences existed in the distribution of success for individuals and organizations among the three cities in this sample. Table 6 shows the results of this analysis.

About one third of the t-tests calculated resulted in statistically insignificant scores. Among the t-values that were significant, none was large. The greatest variation was recorded for governmental plaintiffs. This spread may reflect differences in the organization of the city law office. In the Baltimore city solicitor's office which recorded the lowest mean score of success (3.75), there is less professional mobility; lawyers stay for many years. No one could remember a lawyer who

TABLE 6  Variation in Success of Individual and Organizational Plaintiffs
in Each of the Three Cities*

| | Individuals | | | |
| | Mean | Standard deviation | N | Standard error |
| --- | --- | --- | --- | --- |
| Baltimore | 3.5616 | 1.552 | 949 | .050 |
| Cleveland | 3.5065 | 1.418 | 926 | .047 |
| Milwaukee | 3.7301 | 1.369 | 930 | .045 |

| | t-value | Degrees of freedom | Two-tail probability |
| --- | --- | --- | --- |
| Baltimore vs Cleveland | 0.80 | 1873 | 0.422 |
| Baltimore vs Milwaukee | −2.49 | 1877 | 0.013 |
| Cleveland vs Milwaukee | −3.46 | 1854 | 0.001 |

| | Businesses | | | |
| | Mean | Standard deviation | N | Standard error |
| --- | --- | --- | --- | --- |
| Baltimore | 4.2711 | 1.108 | 1206 | .032 |
| Cleveland | 3.9711 | 1.095 | 1279 | .031 |
| Milwaukee | 4.3246 | 1.150 | 955 | .037 |

| | t-value | Degrees of freedom | Two-tail probability |
| --- | --- | --- | --- |
| Baltimore vs Cleveland | 6.79 | 2483 | under .001 |
| Baltimore vs Milwaukee | −1.10 | 2159 | 0.274 |
| Cleveland vs Milwaukee | −7.39 | 2232 | under .001 |

| | Government | | | |
| | Mean | Standard deviation | N | Standard error |
| --- | --- | --- | --- | --- |
| Baltimore | 3.75 | 1.557 | 44 | .235 |
| Cleveland | 4.6186 | 0.878 | 312 | .050 |
| Milwaukee | 4.3986 | 0.822 | 286 | .049 |

| | t-value | Degrees of freedom | Two-tail probability |
| --- | --- | --- | --- |
| Baltimore vs Cleveland | −4.21 | 328 | under .001 |
| Baltimore vs Milwaukee | −5.47 | 354 | under .001 |
| Cleveland vs Milwaukee | −3.16 | 596 | 0.002 |

*Pooled variance estimates.

TABLE 7   Variation in Success by Type of Defendant for Individual
and Organizational Plaintiffs

| | Plaintiff is an individual | | | |
|---|---|---|---|---|
| | Mean | Standard deviation | N | Variance |
| Individual defendant | 3.846 | 1.376 | 1831 | 1.894 |
| Organizational defendant | 3.092 | 1.473 | 935 | 2.169 |
| | Difference | Standard error | Degrees of freedom | t-test | Eta |
| Individuals vs organizations | .754 | .057 | 2764 | 13.302* | .06 |

| | Plaintiff is an organization | | | |
|---|---|---|---|---|
| | Mean | Standard deviation | N | Variance |
| Individual defendant | 4.370 | 1.008 | 2768 | 1.016 |
| Organizational defendant | 3.903 | 1.229 | 1287 | 1.509 |
| | Difference | Standard error | Degrees of freedom | t-test | Eta |
| Individuals vs organizations | .467 | .037 | 4053 | 12.771* | .039 |

*Significance under .001.

had used his appointment to the city solicitor's office as a springboard for an elective career in politics. Practice is highly routinized: the chief solicitor meets his staff each morning to examine current cases. The law library contains a set of model briefs that solicitors are expected to follow when they prepare a case. In Cleveland (which registered the highest mean score), on the other hand, the city law office has a different history. Tenure is considerably shorter than in Baltimore, many Cleveland politicians have been solicitors, and administrative control by the chief solicitor is weaker.

Both individual and organizational plaintiffs are more successful when they oppose individual defendants than when they oppose organizational defendants. Table 7 displays the distribution of success for plaintiffs when both individuals and organizations are defendants. The analyses of variance show that the differences between individual and organizational defendants are significant and large.

Organizations spend less time in court than individuals. The average number of months a court case takes from filing to the last recorded docket entry was calculated for this sample. Table 8 shows the distribution of mean number of months for court cases initiated by individual and organizational plaintiffs. The data indicate that cases begun by organizations are resolved, on the average, more rapidly

TABLE 8   Variation in the Average Lifespan in Months of Cases by Types of Plaintiffs

|  | Mean | Standard deviation | N | Variance |
|---|---|---|---|---|
| Lifespan | 5.622 | 12.522 | 6874* | 156.797 |
| Individuals | 8.421 | 14.572 | 2797 | 212.347 |
| Business | 3.672 | 10.330 | 3435 | 106.711 |
| Government | 3.855 | 11.188 | 642 | 125.171 |

*Analysis of variance*

|  | Mean square | Degrees of freedom | F-test | Significance | Eta |
|---|---|---|---|---|---|
| Among groups | 18488.42 | 2 | 122.048 | under .001 | .034 |
| Within groups | 151.48 | 6871 |  |  |  |

*T-tests with probabilities corrected for degrees of freedom*

|  | Difference | Standard error | Degrees of freedom | t-test |
|---|---|---|---|---|
| Individuals vs business | 4.749 | .316 | 6230 | 15.017** |
| Individuals vs government | 4.566 | .613 | 3437 | 7.449** |
| Business vs government | −0.183 | .450 | 4075 | −0.406*** |

*Nineteen cases were unencodeable (19 + 6874 = 6893).
**Significant under .001.
***Not significant at the .05 level.

than cases begun by individuals. The analyses of variance in Table 8 show these differences in speed are significant.

Since organizations have to spend less time pursuing their interests, court cases are less disruptive for daily routines of organizations than for individuals. Coupled with our findings that organizations are more successful than individuals, and most successful when opposing individuals, this advantage in speed for processing of court cases makes organizations exceptionally successful litigants and formidable opponents in court.

Why are organizations more successful than individual litigants? Several explanations come to mind. First, judicial bias might explain the differential in success and speed between organizations and individuals. But there is no reason to believe that judges consciously dislike individuals and prefer organizations. Perhaps, though, there are subtle ideological biases that incline them to be more favorable to the claims of organizations than to those of individuals. If so, we might expect some of these differences to be connected with differences in (a) political affiliations of judges; (b) their background characteristics (e.g., types of law practiced prior to elevation to the bench); (c) their opinions about issues of legal policy; or (d) their images of the proper role of trial court judges (Nagel, 1961; Ulmer, 1969).

To test these hypotheses, it would be desirable to sort the judges on these lines for each case and break down the case outcomes to see if there are any such differences. Unfortunately, the data do not facilitate such a comparison. In the three jurisdictions covered by this sample of cases, there is no all parts-purpose calendaring of cases; no one judge presides over a case from start to finish. Some judges hear motions, others preside over pretrial discovery, and so on. Although it is not impossible for judges to act out their biases in these cases, the format of decision-making (e.g., the absence of all parts-purpose calendars) for judges makes testing cumbersome and conclusions speculative.

Alternatively, organizations may present stronger claims than individuals. Perhaps organizations, both businesses and government, are better prepared to litigate because they can invest more resources in "preventive law" and in the preparation of each court case that goes to court.[5] A variant of this hypothesis is that organizations concentrate on "easier" types of cases than do individual plaintiffs. By easy cases we mean those like summary debt actions and liens in which the issues are typically simple, the evidence typically consists of written records rather than the testimony of witnesses and there is often little contest offered by the defendant. Table 9[6] indicates that both individuals and organizational plaintiffs do better at such easy cases than they do with cases like personal injury claims, administrative agency appeals and injunction proceedings in which there are likely to be complex issues, disputed evidence and genuine contest. But although the cases litigated by organizations are overwhelmingly concentrated among the easier types, Table 9 also indicates that organizations do better than individuals in some harder types of cases as well as in easier ones. (The only reversal of the pattern is in administrative agency appeals, in which individuals are significantly more successful.)[7] The greater success of organizations as plaintiffs appears to reflect in some measure the make-up of their caseload, but it would not seem to be reducible entirely to this factor.[8] Although a rigorous testing awaits further analysis of the data, it appears that organizational success has additional determinants as well.

[5]Preventive use of the law, i.e., counseling designed to prevent potential disputes from ripening into litigation (and to be better prepared in the event that they do), is to be contrasted with restitutive use.

[6]Habeas corpus petitions and divorce-related cases were not included in Table 9 because no organizational plaintiff appeared in the former and only six in the latter.

[7]Several reasons can be suggested for the greater success of individuals than of organizations in the administrative agency appeals. This type of case is rarely begun by businesses. Given that businesses are more likely to rely on preventive than restitutive legal counseling, we expect businesses generally not to fall victim to unfavorable administrative agency decisions or to at least minimize the impact of these decisions. The businesses most likely to be censured by these agencies are marginal enterprises, those most likely to be engaged in questionable practices, least able to plan, and least able to absorb the penalty of an unfavorable decision. Finally, it should be noted, neither individuals nor organizations are successful at appeal of administrative agency decisions: a score of 2.58 or 1.88 on a scale of 5 is a very poor mark. Although the scores are significantly different in terms of statistical decision-making criteria, the real world impact of both outcomes is devastating.

[8]Surprisingly, neither individuals nor organizations are successful in their attempts to obtain in-

TABLE 9   Variation in Success of Plaintiffs in Types of Cases Litigated by Both Individuals and Organizations

| Case type plaintiff | Mean score of success | Standard deviation | N | t-value | Significance |
|---|---|---|---|---|---|
| *Summary debt actions* | | | | | |
| Individuals | 3.81 | 1.01 | 369 | −3.85 | .001 |
| Organizations | 4.05 | 1.05 | 1486 | | |
| *Money damage contracts* | | | | | |
| Individuals | 3.67 | 1.21 | 610 | −6.21 | .001 |
| Organizations | 4.08 | 1.25 | 840 | | |
| *Liens* | | | | | |
| Individuals | 4.51 | 0.74 | 39 | −2.56 | .011 |
| Organizations | 4.71 | 0.46 | 1147 | | |
| *Personal injury/property damage torts* | | | | | |
| Individuals | 3.43 | 1.35 | 542 | −2.16 | .032 |
| Organizations | 3.69 | 1.30 | 164 | | |
| *Foreclosures* | | | | | |
| Individuals | 4.26 | 1.20 | 38 | −0.21 | n.s. |
| Organizations | 4.31 | 1.29 | 267 | | |
| *Evictions* | | | | | |
| Individuals | 4.21 | 1.23 | 115 | −0.35 | n.s. |
| Organizations | 4.28 | 1.24 | 93 | | |
| *Administrative agency appeals* | | | | | |
| Individuals | 2.58 | 1.51 | 132 | +1.79 | n.s. |
| Organizations | 2.07 | 1.60 | 39 | | |
| *Injunctions* | | | | | |
| Individuals | 2.40 | 1.57 | 69 | −1.19 | n.s. |
| Organizations | 2.80 | 1.74 | 40 | | |

n.s. = Not significant at the .05 level.

junctions. According to conventional wisdom, organizations should file most injunctions and easily obtain these orders. In our sample, however, we find the reverse. Individuals file more injunctions, and neither category of litigant prevails. These low scores dovetail with our categorization of hard and easy cases. Injunctions are defined as hard cases; their successful initiation is relatively difficult. In this sample, injunction suits are the type in which individuals are least successful; for organizations, injunctions are the second most unsuccessful type of suit.

## CONCLUSION

In this chapter, we have demonstrated that (1) success and failure at litigation are unequally distributed among the litigants in such a way that the trial process generally ratifies the demands made by plaintiffs; (2) organizations are more successful than individual litigants; (3) among organizational plaintiffs, government has more success at litigation than business; (4) individual defendants are the least successful defendants; and (5) organizational plaintiffs resolve their cases more rapidly than individuals. This implies that the trial process in these cities is an extractive process in which plaintiffs, and plaintiff organizations in particular, usually win and individuals generally lose. On the whole, courts are vehicles by which organizational plaintiffs gain goods and opportunities at the expense of individual defendants.

## REFERENCES

Jacob, Herbert. 1973. *Urban Justice*. Englewood Cliffs: Prentice-Hall.

Nagel, Stuart. 1961. "Political party affiliation and judges' decisions." *American Political Science Review* 55: 843–850.

Ross, H. Laurence. 1969. *Settled Out of Court: The Social Process of Insurance Claims Adjustment.* Chicago: Aldine Press.

Ulmer, Sidney. 1969. "The discriminant function and a theoretical context for its use in estimating the votes of judges." In *Frontiers of Judicial Research,* edited by Joel Grossman and J. Tananhaus. New York: John Wiley and Sons.

Wanner, Craig. 1973. "A harvest of profits." Paper presented at the 68th Annual Convention of the American Political Science Association at New Orleans.

———. 1974. "The public ordering of private relations. Part one: initiating civil cases in urban trial courts." *Law and Society Review* 8:421–440.

# 16

## WHO WINS ON APPEAL? UPPERDOGS AND UNDERDOGS IN THE UNITED STATES COURTS OF APPEALS*

DONALD R. SONGER
REGINALD S. SHEEHAN

"Who gets what?" has traditionally been viewed as one of the central questions in the study of politics. In the United States, the courts are widely viewed as key institutions for the legitimate settlement of a wide spectrum of conflicts between individuals and groups that have important implications for the distribution of material and symbolic goods. Therefore, understanding who wins in the courts is an essential component of a full appreciation of "the authoritative allocation of values" in society (Easton, 1953). In this chapter we are concerned with the relationship between the relative strength of direct parties (their litigation resources) appearing as litigants in the United States Courts of Appeals and their rates of success in that forum.

Several studies of trial courts have concluded that the "haves" tend to come out ahead in litigation (Galanter, 1974; Owen, 1971; Wanner, 1975). Generally, it has been discovered that governments have been more successful in litigation at the trial level than have businesses or other organizations and that organizations have been more successful than individual litigants. Galanter (1974) suggests that the "haves" will win more frequently both because they are likely to have superior ma-

*This material is based upon work supported by the National Science Foundation under grant no. SES-8712053. While the authors appreciate this support which made the research reported in this paper possible, all findings and conclusions are those of the authors and do not necessarily reflect the views of the National Science Foundation.

terial resources and because a number of advantages accrue to them as a result of their "repeat player" status. Superior resources allow the "haves" to hire the best available legal representation and to incur the expenses of extensive discovery, expert witnesses, and so forth, which may increase the chances of success at trial. In addition, as repeat players, they will reap the benefits of greater litigation experience, case-selecting ability, and the ability to develop and implement a comprehensive litigation strategy that may include forum shopping, informed judgments of their chances to win at trial or appeal, and the capability to accept moderate losses through settlements when the prospects for victory at trial or on appeal are small.

At the appellate level, less support has been found for the proposition that the "haves" come out ahead. Sheehan and Songer (1989) examined the success of 10 categories of parties in the United States Supreme Court over a 36-year period and concluded that there was little evidence that litigant resources had a major impact on success in that forum. Instead, the success of different classes of litigants was closely related to the changing ideological composition of the Court (e.g., unions and poor individuals fared substantially better in liberal courts, and state government was most successful in conservative courts).

In a study of 16 state supreme courts from 1870 to 1970, Wheeler *et al.* (1987) applied the general framework of Galanter's analysis to examine the relative success on appeal of five general classes of litigants. Initially they advance three reasons why one might expect the stronger party to come out ahead and also consider several bases for assuming that there should be no systematic pattern of success that favored any class of litigants.[1] One might expect the stronger party to come out ahead, they speculate, first because there might be a normative tilt of the law toward the stronger interests (e.g., in a market economy the law may be designed to protect business interests, and the law may be designed to protect the authority of democratically elected government). Second, the judges themselves may be biased toward the stronger party. Finally, the stronger party may be expected to have greater litigation resources (both more financial resources and greater experience derived from being a repeat player). Alternatively, one might expect no difference in success rates attributable to party strength because lawyers and the parties they represent are rational actors trying to make sensible predictions about what the courts will do, taking into account all the factors of judicial bias, legal philosophy, and the effects of superior resources. Thus, appeals will be undertaken only when there is a substantial chance of winning.

When Wheeler *et al.* attempted to test hypotheses based on these speculations, they found a general pattern that suggested that the "haves" come out ahead, but the relative advantage of parties with superior litigation resources was modest. Their explanation for the greater success of the presumed stronger parties is consistent with that offered by Galanter. They suggest that "the greater resources of the stronger parties presumably confer advantages beyond hiring better lawyers on

[1]Wheeler *et al.* also discussed several reasons that might be advanced to justify the expectation that the weaker parties would come out ahead, but no support was discovered for these speculations in the empirical data.

appeal. Larger organizations may be more experienced and thus better able to conform their behavior to the letter of the law or to build a better trial court record, matters on which we have no evidence. Experience and wealth also imply the capacity to be more selective in deciding which cases to appeal or defend when the lower court loser appeals" (Wheeler *et al.,* 1987: 441).

Since Wheeler *et al.* had neither direct data on judges' attitudes nor even any indirect indicators of those values, they were unable to determine systematically whether the success of stronger parties was due to judicial bias. However, they speculated that the greater success of large units of government versus small units of government and the greater success of big business against small business made such an interpretation unlikely. Similarly, if there was a tilt in the law toward either government or business, it was not likely a tilt that selectively favored only large government or big business. Thus, greater litigation resources were the most likely explanation of the empirical results.

Nevertheless, Wheeler *et al.* appear to be somewhat ambivalent about the significance of the advantage enjoyed by stronger parties. In most of the comparisons examined, the differences between stronger and weaker parties were statistically significant. Yet the magnitude of the disadvantage of weaker parties was not overwhelming. Most notable was that the net disadvantage of individuals was less than 5% or 6% on most measures. This relatively strong showing by individuals led them to speculate that perhaps "there often was a 'pro-underdog' bias in the normative system or in the minds of supreme court judges that tended to offset, at least in part, individual parties' relative disadvantage in litigational experience and capacity" (1987: 442). Alternatively, one might conclude (although Wheeler *et al.* do not offer this explanation) that these results lend at least some plausibility to the rational actor model.

In this paper we apply a framework similar to that employed by Galanter (1974), Sheehan and Songer (1989), and Wheeler *et al.* (1987) in an attempt to determine the extent to which litigation resources (both financial resources and litigation experience) have an effect on the chances for success in the United States Courts of Appeals. Since the position of the courts of appeals is more similar to that of state supreme courts than it is to either the United States Supreme Court or to the trial courts examined by Galanter, the nature of the analysis employed is designed to parallel as closely as possible[2] the analysis by Wheeler *et al..*

## DATA FOR ANALYSIS

In order to examine the success of stronger and weaker parties in cases decided by the United States Courts of Appeals, we coded the nature of the appellant and respondent, the issue, the party of the judges on each panel, the outcome, and

---

[2]The data employed in this analysis were originally collected for a different project, and as a result the categories of parties are not identical to those used by Wheeler *et al..*

the opinion status (published or unpublished) of all cases terminated by judicial action in calendar year 1986 in the Fourth, Seventh, and Eleventh circuits. The number of cases coded was 4281 (2828 unpublished decisions and 1453 cases with published opinions).

Each of the cases was coded by one of the authors or by a carefully trained research assistant. In order to assess the reliability of the coding, a sample of 500 case was independently coded a second time. The results of this analysis, presented in the Appendix, suggest that the coding was highly reliable.

Most previous analyses of the courts of appeals have restricted their analyses to the published opinions of the courts. But Songer (1988) has demonstrated that such an analysis can produce results that may be seriously distorted and Songer, Smith, and Sheehan (1989) have shown that at least in the Eleventh Circuit there are significant differences in the rates of participation of different classes of appellants in published versus unpublished decisions. Therefore, it was concluded that any analysis of the success of litigants in the courts of appeals must be based on all decisions of the courts rather than just the more readily available published decisions. Unfortunately, collection of data on the unpublished decisions is very expensive. Therefore, resource limitations necessitated the restriction of the analysis to just three circuits.

As Wheeler *et al.* point out, specific information about the wealth of particular parties in a given case or the relative litigation experience of those parties is often not available in court opinions. Since the data for this study, like the data for the Wheeler study, were derived from court opinions, we usually did not have enough information to unambiguously classify one of the parties as having greater litigation resources than its adversary. Consequently, we adopted the strategy of Wheeler *et al.* of assigning litigants to general classes and then making assumptions about which class was usually the stronger party.

For the initial analysis, each appellant and respondent was classified as belonging to one of five major classes: individual litigants, businesses, state and local governments, the United States government, or other. The "other" category included unions; nonprofit organizations; private, nonprofit schools; social, charitable, and fraternal organizations; political parties; and litigants who could not be unambiguously categorized. This "other" category included 2.3% of the appellants and 2.5% of the respondents. They were excluded from analysis because it was thought that they could not be safely categorized in terms of relative litigation resources compared to the other four classes of litigants. If the party listed in the case citation was a specific, named individual, but the person's involvement in the suit was due directly to their role as an official of a government agency or as an officer, partner, or owner of a business, they were coded according to their organizational affiliation and not as an individual. For example, if the president of an insurance company was appealing a conviction for rape, the appellant was coded as an individual. However, if the county sheriff was the subject of a 1983 suit for damages because of an alleged beating of a prisoner, then the defendant would be classified in the local government category. All government agencies, even those that are "independent" of the chief executive, and government corporations were categorized in the appropriate government class (e.g., the Federal Communication Commission and the Tennessee Valley Authority were classified in the federal government class). Like Wheeler *et al.* we assume that individuals usually have fewer resources than either businesses or units of government.[3] When business and government parties contend, we assume that governments will usually be stronger because even when the financial resources of government are no greater than those of the business, the government agency is more likely to be a repeat player (or a more frequent repeat player in the particular issue area involved in the suit).

In a second wave of analysis, Wheeler *et al.* "took four types of business parties that seem especially likely to be repeat players and to have substantial financial and legal resources at their disposal: railroads, banks, manufacturing companies, and insurance companies" (1987: 413). These businesses were considered to be particularly likely to be "haves" relative to individuals and other businesses. The success of these "big businesses" was therefore assessed separately. Following this logic, we created a big business category for use in a follow-up to the initial analysis based on the original four categories. In this big business category, we placed each of the four types of business included in the Wheeler study and added airlines and oil companies.[4] While this big business category undoubtedly omits some of the very largest companies (or some of those who are among the most frequent repeat players), our reading of the cases convinces us that those that are included were virtually always parties that had very substantial resources. Thus, we are confident that in a high proportion of cases pitting a "big business" against either an individual or a business in the residual category, the big business could be assumed to have superior resources available.

While Wheeler *et al.* did not subdivide their individual category, we believed that it would be useful to do so for the second wave of analysis. Therefore, we created a category of "underdog individuals" that included the poor and racial minorities.[5] These litigants were assumed to be weaker on average than even those individuals in the residual category. Since court opinions often have incomplete

---

[3]Whether individuals received substantial support from or were sponsored by organizations or groups was not coded because that information is generally not available in the opinions. It should be noted that neither the Wheeler nor the Sheehan and Songer studies coded such information. To do so would take a mini case study of each decision. However, we are relatively confident that the percentage of individuals in our sample who received such group support is quite small. One indicator of the lack of group involvement is the low rate of amicus participation. Only 1.9% of the cases in our sample had any amicus participation, and most of those participations do not appear to be in support of individuals.

[4]Although Wheeler *et al.* do not discuss why they did not include these categories in their study, we speculate that it may have been because airlines and oil companies were not large companies throughout the 100-year period studied. It should be noted that the oil company category does *not* include retail service stations.

[5]Businesses, even if owned by minorities, were not included in this underdog category.

information in regard to the race or wealth of individual litigants, we adopted a conservative strategy for assigning individuals to the underdog category. Litigants were placed in the underdog category only if the opinion explicitly labeled them as poor, black, and so on, or if there was an explicit indication that they were part of a category of people who could safely be presumed to be poor (e.g., welfare recipients or criminal defendants represented by a public defender). Therefore, there were certainly some litigants who were in fact poor or black who were placed in the residual individual category instead of the underdog category, but we are confident that all who were placed in the underdog category do in fact belong to that category.

Following the approach of Wheeler *et al.*, we defined winners and losers by looking at "who won the appeal in its most immediate sense, without attempting to view the appeal in some larger context" (1987: 415). Thus, for example, if the decision of the district court or the administrative agency was "reversed," "reversed and remanded," "vacated," or "vacated and remanded," the appellant was coded as winning regardless of whether the opinion announced a doctrine that was broad or narrow and regardless of whether that doctrine might be supposed in general to benefit future "haves" or "have nots." Also like Wheeler *et al.*, we excluded from analysis all cases with ambiguous results (e.g., those in which the court affirmed in part and reversed in part).

Finally, it should be emphasized that like Wheeler *et al.* our focus is on whether any relative advantage accrues to those classes of parties with superior litigation resources. Even if the normative ideal of blind justice perfectly described the reality of appeals court decision making, one would not necessarily expect that all categories of litigants would win 50% of the appellate cases in which they participated. Appeals are brought by trial court losers after decisionmakers (judge and jury) at the trial who are also normatively presumed to be impartial have engaged in fact finding and made initial interpretations of the law. Therefore, even if appellate justice is blind and litigation resources are irrelevant, one would expect that respondents would prevail against the majority of appeals. And in fact, it is well known that the courts of appeals usually affirm (Howard, 1981; Davis and Songer, 1988). In the data utilized in the present study, the courts of appeals affirmed 84% of the decisions appealed to them. Therefore, in order to assess whether the hypothesized relative advantage of parties with superior resources exists, it is not enough to know whether the "haves" won more frequently in an absolute sense. Instead, we must also explore whether they "were better able than other parties to buck the basic tendency of appellate courts to affirm" (Wheeler *et al.*, 1987: 407). As a measure of this aspect of relative advantage, Wheeler *et al.* computed an "index of net advantage." This index is computed for each type of litigant by first taking their success rate when they appear as the appellant and from that figure subtracting their opponents' success rate in those cases in which the litigant of interest participates as respondent. This index of advantage is independent of the relative frequency that different classes of litigants appear as appellants versus respondents. In addition, it is also independent of the relative propensity of different courts to affirm and is therefore a better measure to use for the comparison of the analysis of appeals courts and state supreme courts than a simple measure of the proportion of decisions won by a given class of litigants would be.

## APPELLANT SUCCESS AND NET ADVANTAGE

The beginning point of analysis was to examine the appellant success rate for each of the four basic categories of litigants. The data are presented in Table 1. In dramatic contrast to the success rates reported by Wheeler *et al.* for state supreme courts, there were wide disparities in the relative success of different classes of appellants in the courts of appeals. In spite of the general propensity of the courts of appeals to affirm, the federal government was successful on 58.2% of its appeals. At the other end of the spectrum of assumed litigation resources, individuals won only 12.5% of their appeals. Moreover, the rank order of the success rate was exactly the order that would be predicted from the hypothesis that the litigation resources of appellants significantly contributed to their success. Individuals had the lowest rate of success, followed in order by business, state and local government, and the federal government. Expressed slightly differently, the United States was 4.66 times as successful an appellant as individuals and 2.58 times as successful as businesses. In contrast, Wheeler *et al.* found that the most successful appellant in state supreme courts was only 1.25 times as successful as the least successful appellant.

When specific matchups are examined, conclusions drawn from the overall success rates of appellants receive general confirmation. Individuals have low rates of success against all other categories of respondents, while the success rate of the United States as appellant remains high against all other parties.

TABLE 1   Appellant Success Rates against Different Respondents

| | Respondent | | | | |
|---|---|---|---|---|---|
| Appellant | Individual (N) | Business (N) | State & local government (N) | United States government (N) | Total (N) |
| Individual | 18.0% | 16.6% | 10.2% | 12.5% | 12.5% |
| | (150) | (518) | (1,327) | (1,403) | (3,398) |
| Business | 25.2 | 22.2 | 34.4 | 17.9 | 22.6 |
| | (111) | (324) | (32) | (117) | (584) |
| State & local government | 40.8 | 57.9 | 0 | 25.0 | 41.2 |
| | (49) | (19) | (1) | (16) | (85) |
| United States government | 62.5 | 46.8 | 77.8 | 50.0 | 58.2 |
| | (64) | (47) | (9) | (2) | (122) |

TABLE 2    Success Rates by Nature of Party in the Courts of Appeals (In Percentages)

| Type of Party | Success rate as appellant (N) | − | When respondent, opponents' success rate (N) | = | Net advantage | Combined success rate as respondent and appellant |
|---|---|---|---|---|---|---|
| Individual | 12.5 (3,398) | − | 30.7 (374) | = | −18.2 | 18.0 |
| Business | 22.6 (584) | − | 21.0 (908) | = | 1.6 | 56.9 |
| State & local government | 41.2 (85) | − | 11.3 (1,368) | = | 29.9 | 85.9 |
| United States government | 58.2 (122) | − | 13.1 (1,538) | = | 45.1 | 84.8 |

Table 2 displays the net advantage of each type of litigant along with the combined rate of success as both respondent and appellant for each type of litigant. The net advantage index may be a better indicator of litigation success than the raw rate of success because it is unaffected by the relative frequency that a given class of litigant appears as an appellant rather than as a respondent. Thus, if there is a propensity to affirm in the courts of appeals, this propensity will not affect the index of net advantage.

The thesis that the stronger party should prevail receives strong support from the data in Table 2. The rank ordering of the parties according to their net advantage is consistent with the presumed ordering of parties according to strength of litigation resources. The federal government, which won 58.2% of the cases they had appealed, held their adversaries to only a 13.1% success rate in the cases they had appealed (i.e., the federal government won 86.9% of the cases in which they appeared as respondent), giving the United States a net advantage of 45.1%. Next highest were state and local governments which had a net advantage of 29.9% and businesses with a net advantage of 1.6%. At the bottom were individuals whose net advantage was −18.2%, reflecting the fact that those who filed appeals against individuals won more than twice as frequently as individuals did when they appealed.

The relationship between strength of party and success reflected in Table 2 is much stronger than that discovered in a similar analysis of state supreme court litigants by Wheeler et al. (1987). The net advantage for state and local governments noted above is more than twice as great as that found in state supreme courts.[6] At the same time, individuals fared much worse in the courts of appeals. As a result,

[6]The definition of state and local government in the present study is not identical to that employed by Wheeler et al., since they exclude small towns while we do not. But as a result, the average litiga-

TABLE 3   Net Advantage for Different Combinations of Parties

| Combination of parties | | Net advantage | |
|---|---|---|---|
| Individuals | v. business | Business | by 8.6% |
| Individuals | v. state & local government | State & local government | by 30.6% |
| Individuals | v. United States government | United States government | by 50.0% |
| Business | v. state & local government | State & local government | by 23.5% |
| Business | v. United States government | United States government | by 28.9% |
| State & local government | v. United States government | United States government | by 52.8% |
| Appellant success rate for stronger party | = 41.2% ($N = 354$) | | |
| Appellant success rate for weaker party | = 12.6% ($N = 3,558$) | | |
| Net advantage for stronger party | = 28.6% | | |

*Note:* For the two-by-two table that summarizes the total success rate: chi square = 203.43, with a two-tailed probability $P < .001$, gamma = .659.

the difference between the net advantage of state and local governments and and individuals is 48.1% for the courts of appeals compared to 13.3% for state supreme courts.[7] The total range, from the highest to the lowest net advantage index, is 63.3% for the present study compared to 17.2% for the state supreme court data reported by Wheeler *et al.*.

Both the marginal distributions reported in Table 1 and the index of net advantage reported in Table 2 include cases in which a litigant faced another party in the same category. To further explore the advantage that the stronger party appears to have in cases before the courts of appeals, we therefore followed the lead of Wheeler *et al.* and selected only those cases in which parties in different categories confronted each other. These comparisons are presented in Table 3.

From Table 3 it can easily be seen that in every match-up, the party presumed to be stronger enjoyed a substantial net advantage. For example, in the 518 cases in which individuals were appellants against businesses, the individuals won 16.6% of the time. In the 111 cases in which businesses appealed against individuals, businesses won 25.2% of the time for a net advantage of business over individuals of 8.6%. In all other comparisons, the stronger party enjoyed a net advantage over its weaker opponent that was more than two and a half times greater than the advantage of business over individuals.

Overall, the stronger party enjoyed a net advantage of 28.6%, a difference significant at the .001 level.[8] In contrast, Wheeler *et al.* (1987: 420) found an overall

---

tion resources of those they classify as city and state government should be greater than the resources of parties we classify as state and local government. Therefore, the higher rate of success in the present study cannot be attributed to differences in operational definitions.

[7]The difference between individuals and state and city governments in state courts is computed from Table 2 in Wheeler *et al.* (1987: 418).

[8]In all of the individual matchups, chi squares computed for the two-by-two tables were significant at least at the .05 level.

net advantage for the stronger party that was only 5.2%. Moreover, Wheeler *et al.* note that although individuals lost against all other types of parties, most of their losses were under 3% (and the largest was only 8.4%). But in the courts of appeals, individuals lost by 8.6%, 30.6%, and 50.0%, respectively, against businesses, state and local governments, and the federal government. To this point in the analysis, then, the "haves" appear to enjoy considerably greater advantage in the courts of appeals than they did in state supreme courts.

## THE FATE OF BIG BUSINESS AND UNDERDOG INDIVIDUALS

To obtain a more refined assessment of the significance of litigation resources for appellate success, the initial categories of business and individuals were each subdivided. We first examined a subcategory of business litigants who were assumed on average to represent large national corporate enterprises rather than locally based businesses. The success rate for these big businesses is displayed in Table 4.

The analysis of the success of big businesses in the courts of appeals is ambiguous just as it was in state supreme courts. In both forums, big businesses enjoyed a decided advantage over the residual category of businesses but held a very modest advantage over individuals. Overall, the net advantage of big business was 5.9% compared to the 1.6% net advantage for the total business category noted in Table 2.

TABLE 4    Success Rates for Big Businesses versus Other Parties (Percentages of Cases Won by Appellant)

| | Big Business | | |
|---|---|---|---|
| Opponent | As appellant (N) | As respondent (N) | Net advantage for big business |
| Individuals | 22.0 (41) | 20.4 (191) | 1.6 |
| Other businesses | 42.1 (38) | 13.6 (88) | 28.5 |
| State & local government | —[a] | —[a] | —[a] |
| United States government | —[a] | —[a] | —[a] |
| Total[b] | 25.2 (139) | 19.3 (332) | 5.9 |

[a]Too few cases for meaningful comparisons.

[b]Includes success against other big businesses, state and local government, and the United States government.

TABLE 5   Success Rates for Underdog Individuals versus
Other Parties (Percentage of Cases Won by Appellant)

| | Underdog individuals | | |
| Opponent | As appellant (N) | As respondent (N) | Net advantage for underdogs |
| --- | --- | --- | --- |
| Other individuals | 3.6 (55) | —[a] | —[a] |
| Business | 10.3 (87) | 25.0 (8) | −14.7 |
| State & local government | 7.1 (857) | 25.0 (8) | −17.9 |
| United States government | 9.1 (374) | 85.0 (20) | −75.9 |
| Total | 7.7 (1,373) | 57.9 (38) | −50.2 |

[a]Too few cases for meaningful comparisons.

Next, the analysis focused on the success of a subcategory of the individual lit-igant category that we have labeled "underdog individuals." Underdogs are de-fined as those that the opinion of the court indicates are either below the federal poverty line or members of racial minorities (who may be presumed on average to be less wealthy than the residual category of individuals). The success rates for these underdogs are displayed in Table 5.

As predicted from the thesis that the stronger party should come out ahead in the appellate courts, underdog individuals had low rates of success against all oth-er categories of litigants. Their rate of success as appellants was very low: under 11% against every other category; and was lower than the appellant success rate for the total category of individuals against each of the other three categories. While the small number of cases in which they appeared as respondents suggests the need for caution in the interpretation of their index for net advantage versus most specific other categories, their overall net advantage of −50.2 is striking tes-timony to their lack of success in the courts of appeals.

As the final test of the effect of litigant strength on success in the courts of ap-peals before the introduction of control variables to the analysis, we examined the overall rate of appellant success for a summary measure of the relative strength of the parties. Appellants and respondents were each classified on a seven-point scale with the federal government = 7, state government = 6, local government = 5, big business = 4, other business = 3, the residual category of individuals = 2, and underdog individuals = 1. We then computed a measure of relative strength of lit-igants for each case with the formula: relative strength equals appellant minus re-spondent. This computation produces an index of relative strength that ranges from +6 (federal government appellant versus underdog individual) to −6 (underdog ap-

TABLE 6    Appellant Success Rates for Relative Strength of
Appellants and Respondents

| Index of relative strength (Appellant − Respondent) | Appellant wins % | (N) |
|---|---|---|
| −6 | 9.1 | (374) |
| −5 to −3 | 12.1 | (2,510) |
| −2 to −1 | 16.2 | (672) |
| 0 | 23.2 | (297) |
| +1 to +2 | 32.2 | (183) |
| +3 to +5 | 46.0 | (150) |
| +6 | 85.0 | (20) |

Note: For the seven-by-two table for the frequencies used to generate the table above: chi square = 260.17, $df = 6$, $P < .001$, gamma = .385.

pellant and United States respondent). If litigation resources significantly affect outcomes, it should be expected that there will be a linear relationship between the index and the rate of appellant success.

The data displayed in Table 6 provide strong additional support for the thesis that litigation resources affect success in the courts of appeals. The success rates of appellants consistently increase with each incremental increase in their strength relative to the strength of the respondent. While the relationship is not perfectly linear, it is moderately strong and is significant at the .001 level. When the index of relative strength is even marginally positive, the rate of appellant success is approximately twice as great as it is when the index is slightly negative. Appellant success rates for moderately positive index scores are more than three and a half times as great as they are for moderately negative scores, and at the extremes of the scale the ratio is more than nine to one.

## APPELLANT STRENGTH
## IN A MULTIVARIATE ANALYSIS

While the analysis of bivariate relationships presented above produced results that are consistent with the thesis that litigant strength is significantly related to rates of appellant success, the thesis can be accepted only provisionally until the effects of a number of potential intervening variables are examined. For example, the apparent success of the presumptively stronger parties may be due in large part to the number of criminal appeals in the sample. Criminal appeals typically match an individual (especially a poor individual) against some level of government. Since many criminal appeals appear to have very little legal merit, the government usually wins. Or alternatively, since party and region have been found to be related to outcomes in the federal courts (Carp and Rowland, 1983; Goldman, 1975; Tate, 1981), the relative success of upperdogs may be due to the fact that the majority of judges on the courts in 1986 were Republicans and the majority of cases in our sample came from southern circuits.

Wheeler *et al.* attempt to account for the effects of a number of variables that might modify the relationship between litigant resources and appellant success by introducing control variables (areas of law, nature of legal relationship between parties, and the nature of counsel) one at a time in a series of cross-tabulations. We believe that a more adequate picture of the effects of a variety of potentially significant variables can be obtained from a multivariate logistic regression model.

The dependent variable in the model is the success of the appellant, coded as one if the appellant won and coded as zero if the respondent won. Thus, the larger the estimate for the coefficient of an independent variable, the more that variable leads to success for the appellant.

The first independent variable in the model is the 7-point scale of appellant strength described above. Since higher scale values indicate appellants who are presumed to have greater litigation resources available than appellants with lower scale scores, it is expected that this variable will be positively related to the dependent variable. The same 7-point scale is used for respondents. Therefore, it is expected that the coefficients for respondents will be negative.

Next, four dummy variables were created to introduce controls for the issue in the case. Each issue variable was coded as one if the issue was the most important issue in the case and as zero otherwise. Therefore, no case was coded as one on more than one issue. The issues coded were criminal, civil liberties, economic regulation and labor relations, and diversity of citizenship. For published decisions, 224 cases (19.4 % of all published cases) were coded zero on all four issue variables. For unpublished decisions, 1,074 cases (48.7% of all unpublished decisions) were coded zero for all issue categories. These cases were primarily those in which the judges disposed of the appeal on procedural grounds without reaching the merits (e.g., questions of standing, jurisdiction, mootness, the allegation that the appeal was not timely, the imposition of sanctions, or the award of attorney's fees) and petitions for rehearing. Also included in the cases coded as zero on all four issues variables were due process questions, federalism cases, and those involving issues that could not be classified.

The party effect variable was designed to take into account the findings of earlier studies that judges appointed by Democratic presidents were more likely than judges appointed by Republicans to support liberal decisions (Goldman, 1975; Gottschall, 1986). To create this variable, each panel was first coded as having either a Democratic or Republican majority and the decision of the court or administrative agency below was coded as being either liberal or conservative.[9]

---

[9]We followed the definitions of liberal and conservative described by Goldman (1975). According to this definition, the liberal position is best described as (1) for the claims of the defendants or pris-

Since data from only three circuits were included in the analysis, only a partial test of the effect of region could be incorporated. For cases decided in the South (the Fourth and Eleventh circuits), the region variable was coded as zero. For decisions of the Seventh Circuit (a midwestern circuit), region was coded as one.

Rather than run the model described above on all of the decisions of the courts of appeals, it was run separately on the published and the unpublished decisions of the courts. Songer (1988) has shown that rates of reversal (i.e., appellant success) are substantially higher in published decisions than they are in the unpublished decisions of the court. In addition, the rates of appearance of most types of parties as appellants and respondents and the incidence of most of the other independent variables in the model are quite different in published versus unpublished decisions of the courts of appeals. Finally, the criteria for publication, which imply that the unpublished decisions of the courts should be expected to contain many frivolous appeals, suggest the likelihood that the effect of many of our independent variables will be different in published and unpublished decisions. Thus, the effect of appellant strength may be quite different in the two types of decisions, and a combined model might mask important differences.[10]

Overall, the models for both published and unpublished decisions perform adequately. The parameter estimates, except for the dummy variable that represents the diversity of citizenship issue, are in the predicted direction (and in the same direction for both published and unpublished decisions), and the overall model is significant at the .001 level.[11] The coefficients for each variable are displayed in Tables 7 and 8.

The control variables that prior research had suggested might be related to ap-

oners in criminal and prisoner petition cases; (2) for the claims of minorities in racial discrimination cases; (3) for the claims of plaintiffs in other civil liberties cases; (4) for the government in regulation of business and tax cases; (5) for individual workers or unions in disputes with management; (6) for the injured person in tort cases; and (7) for the economic underdog in private economic disputes.

[10]In a preliminary analysis, the model described above was run with the addition of a variable that indicated the publication status of the decision. The variable for publication status had a coefficient of 1.155, the highest of any independent variable in the model, and was significant at the .001 level. The variable that indicated strength of appellant was also significant at the .001 level.

[11]Since no attempt is made in the present analysis to create a general model that will explain all variance in appeals judge voting, the overall reduction of error of the model is not of critical importance. The main purpose of the model is to assess the effect of litigant strength under controls for other variables believed to be significantly related to judicial voting choice. Nevertheless, the low reduction in error may produce some skepticism about the significance of the impact of the litigant variables. We believe, however, that the rather extreme skew of the dependent variable makes reduction in error difficult. As at least a partial test of this hunch, we reran our analysis on a sample of cases that would not have such a heavily skewed dependent variable. Specifically, we created a sample composed of all of the reversals in the original sample plus a random sample of the affirmances in the original sample (a 46% sample of published affirmances and a 10.7% sample of unpublished affirmances). The resulting samples had expected values for the dependent variable of .493 and .519, respectively. When we reran the models on these new samples, the reduction in error was 28.5% for published decisions and 36.0% for the unpublished decisions. Although the precise values of the coefficients were of course different in these models, they were all in the same direction as in the models presented in Tables 7 and 8, and there were no changes in which variables reached statistical significance.

**TABLE 7**   Logit Estimates for Appellant Success
in Published Decisions

| Independent variable | MLE | SE | MLE/SE |
|---|---|---|---|
| Intercept | −0.815 | .342 | −2.38 |
| Appellant | 0.223 | 0.047 | 4.74*** |
| Respondent | −0.081 | 0.041 | −1.98* |
| Economic | −0.217 | 0.203 | −1.07 |
| Criminal | −0.619 | 0.210 | −2.96** |
| Civil liberty | −0.456 | 0.248 | −1.84 |
| Diversity | 0.207 | 0.280 | 0.74 |
| Party effect | 0.432 | 0.139 | 3.11*** |
| Region | −0.488 | 0.150 | −3.25*** |

*Note:* Dependent variable = appellant success, mean = 0.297, model chi square = 108.24, with $df = 8$, $P < .001$, $-2\,LLR = 1,300.01$.
$N = 1,157$.
Proportion predicted correctly = 71.7%.
Reduction in error = 4.9%.
*significant at .05; **significant at .01; ***significant at .001.

pellant success were generally found to have their predicted effects. But even after controlling for these effects of issue, party, and region, the nature of the litigants is still strongly associated with the probability of appellant success.[12] The coefficients for strength of appellant are positive, moderately strong, and significant at the .001 level in the models for both published and unpublished decisions. The coefficients for respondents are smaller, but are negative, as predicted, for both

[12]Knowing that the courts tend to rule against criminal defendants, it might be argued that whether they affirm or reverse a given case will depend on whether the defendant or the state is appealing in criminal cases. Similarly, if the South is more conservative, then whether a given decision is affirmed or reversed may depend in part on the region from which it is appealed. In order to test these speculations, we reran the models in Tables 7 and 8 with two multiplicative terms added. The first multiplicative term, crimtype, was defined as the product of the variables criminal and appellant, and was used to measure the effect of the interaction between the presence or absence of a criminal case and the nature of the appellant. The second term, lowctreg, was defined as the product of the variables lowerct and region, and was used to assess the effect of the interaction of region and the ideological direction of the decision below. When these variables were added to the model for published decisions presented in Table 7, neither was statistically significant, the proportions of decisions predicted correctly was not improved, and there was no improvement in the reduction of error produced by the model. When added to the model for unpublished decisions displayed in Table 8, only lowctreg reached the .05 level of statistical significance. But even though this multiplicative term was significant, the proportion of cases predicted correctly by the revised model increased by only 0.1%, and there was no improvement in the reduction of error. We concluded that the interaction effects produced by these two sets of variables added little of use to our understanding of litigant effects, and therefore we did not include the multiplicative terms in the models presented in Tables 7 and 8.

TABLE 8   Logit Estimates for Appellant Success
in Unpublished Decisions

| Independent variable | MLE | SE | MLE/SE |
|---|---|---|---|
| Intercept | −2.954 | 0.344 | −8.587 |
| Appellant | 0.414 | 0.064 | 6.47*** |
| Respondent | −0.034 | 0.064 | −0.69 |
| Economic | −0.187 | 0.194 | −0.96 |
| Criminal | −1.498 | 0.204 | −7.34*** |
| Civil liberty | −0.711 | 0.275 | −2.59** |
| Diversity | −0.651 | 0.645 | −1.01 |
| Party effect | 0.797 | 0.159 | 5.05*** |
| Region | −0.312 | 0.256 | −1.21 |

*Note:* Dependent variable = appellant success with mean = .097, model chi square = 153.95, with $df = 8$, $P < .001$, $-2$ LLR = 1,245.61.
$N = 2,201$.
Proportion predicted correctly = 90.3%.
Reduction in error = 0.
*significant at .05; **significant at .01; ***significant at .001.

published and unpublished decisions (but are only statistically significant for published decisions). This suggests that the nature of the litigants has an effect on the probability of appellant success in both published and unpublished decisions that is independent of the nature of the issue in the case, regional influences, and the policy preferences of the judges. Moreover, while Wheeler *et al.* did not examine in depth whether the resources of the appellant were more critical than the resources of the respondent, the models for both the published and unpublished decisions suggest that while both make a contribution, appellant resources are more important.

## CONCLUSIONS

In their introduction, Wheeler *et al.* suggest a number of reasons why one might predict that there would be no difference between the success rates of stronger and weaker parties. Prominent in this discussion was a rational actor hypothesis that suggested that litigants would consider carefully whatever biases and advantages existed in the system and "move ahead only in cases in which both parties, as advised by counsel, feel that there is a substantial possibility of winning" (1987: 412). The findings presented above demonstrate clearly and convincingly that such a rational actor model has little or no explanatory power for decisions of the courts of appeals. The parties that may be presumed to have superior litigation resources consistently fared better than their weaker opponents, and the disparity in success rates was greatest when the disparity in strength was greatest. While there was a strong propensity of the courts of appeals to affirm, the greater success of stronger parties was not attributable to the number of times they appeared as respondent rather than appellant.

Of course, the findings noted above for the courts of appeals describe who won and who lost in the courts of appeals in only a single recent year, while Wheeler and associates examined a pattern that persisted for a century. Thus, the two studies are not completely comparable. Nevertheless, Wheeler *et al.* note only modest change over time. Whether there has been a similar maintenance of the patterns of winners and losers in the courts of appeals must await future research.

While it is thus apparent that the "haves" come out ahead in the courts of appeals to an impressive degree, somewhat more tentative answers must be suggested for why they come out ahead. Wheeler *et al.* considered but tentatively rejected the hypothesis that the "haves" came out ahead because of a normative tilt in the law that favored them. If we follow the logic employed by Wheeler *et al.*, we also come to the tentative conclusion that the bias in the law argument is not the most likely explanation for the success of stronger parties in the courts of appeals. Like Wheeler *et al.*, we speculate that while there may be a pro-business bias in the law, it would not explain why big business did so well in cases in which they were pitted against smaller business. Likewise, if there is a progovernment tilt in the law (i.e., law designed to protect the authority of government presumed legitimate because it is democratically elected), it would not explain the greater success of the federal government compared to state and local government against most other parties nor the net advantage the United States enjoyed when pitted directly against state and local governments. Moreover, while the crudeness of the issues categories employed suggests the need for some caution in interpretation, the independence of the appellant and respondent effects from the area of law at issue found in the logistic regression models tends to weaken support for the idea that the success of the stronger parties was due primarily to a tilt in the law in their favor.

The second possibility investigated by Wheeler *et al.* was that the success of stronger parties might be due to judicial attitudes that favored them. Like Wheeler *et al.* we believe that the success of big business relative to other business litigants, the success of the national government relative to state and local government, and the success of the residual category of individuals compared to underdogs makes this interpretation unlikely.[13] Moreover, in the U.S. political system at large, support for business interests against individuals and states versus the federal government is usually related to the differences in the ideological centers of the two major parties. Yet on the courts of appeals, the greater success of the stronger parties was independent of partisan effects.

[13]However, it is possible that judges on the courts of appeals share a more positive orientation toward the federal government than toward state and local government. Howard (1981: 146) reports that judges from all three of the circuits expressed national rather than regional loyalties and saw their job as including an obligation to maintain the national supremacy provided by the Constitution in the face of local pressures.

The most probable explanation for the success of the "haves" in the courts of appeals therefore would appear to be their superior litigation resources. The consistency with which the parties presumed to have greater resources came out ahead when pitted against presumptively weaker parties; the steadily increasing margin of victory for the "haves" as the disparity in resources increased; and the independent effects of the index of appellant strength demonstrated in the logistic regression when controls were added for issues, region, and partisan effects all lend support to this conclusion.

## APPENDIX

Reliability of Coding

| Variable | Fourth Circuit ($N = 200$) | | Eleventh Circuit ($N = 200$) | | Seventh Circuit ($N = 100$) | |
| | Agreement Rate % | Pi | Agreement Rate % | Pi | Agreement Rate % | Pi |
|---|---|---|---|---|---|---|
| Circuit | 100 | 1.00 | 100 | 1.00 | 100 | 1.00 |
| Treatment | 100 | 1.00 | 99.5 | .99 | 100 | 1.00 |
| Appellant | 95.5 | .93 | 87.0 | .83 | 90.0 | .87 |
| Respondent | 94.0 | .93 | 84.0 | .82 | 89.0 | .88 |
| Issue | 87.5 | .86 | 84.0 | .82 | 84.0 | .81 |

## REFERENCES

Carp, Robert A., and C. K. Rowland. 1983. *Policymaking and Politics in the Federal Courts.* Knoxville: University of Tennessee Press.

Davis, Sue, and Donald R. Songer. 1988. "The changing role of the United States Courts of Appeals: the flow of litigation revisited." Paper presented at the Annual Meeting of the Law and Society Association.

Easton, David. 1953. *The Political System: An Inquiry into the State of Political Science.* New York: Knopf.

Galanter, Marc. 1974. "Why the 'haves' come out ahead: speculations on the limits of legal change." *Law and Society Review* 9: 95–160.

Goldman, Sheldon. 1975. "Voting behavior on the United States Courts of Appeals revisited." *American Political Science Review* 69: 491–506.

Gottschall, Jon. 1986. "Reagan's appointments to the U.S. Courts of Appeals: the continuation of a judicial revolution." *Judicature* 48: 48–54.

Howard, J. Woodford. 1981. *Courts of Appeals in the Federal Judicial System: A Study of the Second, Fifth, and District of Columbia Circuits.* Princeton: Princeton University Press.

Owen, Harold J. 1971. The Role of Trial Courts in the Local Political System: A Comparison of Two Georgia Counties. Unpublished doctoral dissertation, University of Georgia.

Sheehan, Reginald S., and Donald R. Songer. 1989. "Supreme Court litigation: an analysis of direct parties before the court." Paper presented at the Annual Meeting of the Southern Political Science Association.

Songer, Donald R. 1988. "Are the unpublished opinions of the U.S. Courts of Appeals legally trivial and politically insignificant?" Paper presented at the Annual Meeting of the Southern Political Science Association.

Songer, Donald R., Danna Smith, and Reginald S. Sheehan. 1989. "Nonpublication in the eleventh circuit: an empirical analysis." *Florida State University Law Review* 16: 963–984.

Tate, C. Neal. 1981. "Personal attribute models of the voting behavior of U.S. Supreme Court justices' liberalism in civil liberties and economics decisions, 1946–1978." *American Political Science Review* 75: 355–367.

Wanner, Craig. 1975. "The public ordering of private relations. Part two: winning civil court cases." *Law and Society Review* 9: 293–306.

Wheeler, Stanton, Bliss Cartwright, Robert Kagan, and Lawrence Friedman. 1987. "Do the 'haves' come out ahead?: winning and losing in state supreme courts, 1870–1970." *Law and Society Review* 21: 403–445.

# 17

# THE CORPORATE ADVANTAGE: A STUDY OF THE INVOLVEMENT OF CORPORATE AND INDIVIDUAL VICTIMS IN A CRIMINAL JUSTICE SYSTEM*

JOHN HAGAN

To the extent that criminologists have talked in recent years about corporate entities and criminal law (e.g., Schrager and Short,1978), they have been most concerned with the illegal and unethical activities of commercial organizations, and with the failure of the criminal law to deal with them (e.g., Ermann and Lundman, 1960). The point of this important and growing body of work is to demonstrate that commercial organizations are ineffectively pursued as criminals. Yet there is another, potentially more important, aspect of this situation. That is that corporate entities are nonetheless very active participants in the criminal justice process, pursuing through the police and courts many individuals who commit crimes against them. In other words, corporate entities not only have successfully avoided large-scale criminal prosecutions, they also have proven themselves effective in using

*Presented at the 1980 Annual Meeting of the American Sociological Association. I wish to express my gratitude to the Ministry of the Solicitor General of Canada for providing financial support for this study. The views expressed in this chapter are my own and are not intended to represent the views of the Solicitor General of Canada.

criminal prosecutions to penalize those who offend them. It is the latter part of this imbalanced situation that we will examine in this report.


## CORPORATE ENTITIES AS JURISTIC PERSONS

We will follow Coleman (1974: 14) in interchangeably using the terms corporate entity and corporate actor to refer not only to what are commonly called corporations, but also to other collective entities such as churches, associations, unions, and schools, all of whom may enlist the criminal law to prosecute and convict individuals who commit crimes against them. These corporate entities are juristic persons who for legal purposes are treated much like natural persons. Indeed, it may be this apparent legal equivalence drawn between juristic and natural persons that has distracted social scientists from considering the distinctive roles these respective parties play in the criminal justice system. Thus, the formal legal assumption is that juristic and natural persons have equal rights and interests in law as a protection against those who offend against them. However, this assumption is a formal legal abstraction that is inconsistent with social and economic inequalities that differentiate corporate and individual entities. In other words, the juristic person is a legal form (Balbus, 1977) that obscures more than it reveals. Coleman states the problem clearly when he notes that ". . . a symmetric allocation of rights between corporations and persons can lead in practice to an asymmetric realization of interests" (1974: 76), and when he concludes that ". . . among the variety of interests that men have, those interests that have been successfully collected to create corporate actors are the interests that dominate the society" (ibid: 49). Our concern in this chapter is with how, and with what consequences, corporate advantages in the criminal justice process may have been achieved. The work of Max Weber is relevant to these issues.


## THE IDEAS AT ISSUE

### THE DOMINATION OF LAW

Weber regarded the law, criminal and civil, as bearing a close correspondence to the economy, and to the corporate entities that comprise it. The connecting link in this system of thought was the notion of logical formalism, or formal rationality. In fact, much of Weber's work on law addressed a fundamental question that ultimately was left unresolved: Did formal rationality in legal thought contribute to the rise of capitalism, or, alternatively, did capitalism contribute to the rise of logical rationality in legal thought? Regardless of the answer given to this question, Weber made the following point quite clear, "The tempo of modern business communication requires a promptly and predictably functioning legal system," or said differently, "The universal predominance of the market consociation requires

. . . a legal system the functioning of which is *calculable* in accordance with rational rules" (Weber, 1969: 40). Thus corporate entities have a generalized interest in formal rational legal processes, and a mainstay of formal rationality is the domination of law.

By domination, Weber means the probability that commands will be followed. *A key form of domination for our purposes involves the probability that corporate victims will be better able than individual victims to get individual offenders convicted.* Weber notes that such forms of domination are sustained in large part by efforts to raise or cultivate their legitimacy. Thus ". . . the continued existence of every domination . . . always has the strongest need of self-justification through appealing to the principles of legitimation" (ibid: 336). Weber concludes that "*Rationally* consociated conduct of a dominational structure finds its typical expression in *bureaucracy,* and therefore the purest type of legal domination is that which is carried on by and through a bureaucratic administrative staff." The effectiveness of bureaucracy in the service of this goal is readily explained:

> Bureaucracy tends toward *formalistic impersonality.* The ideal official administers his office *sine ira et studio,* without hatred or passion, hence also without 'love' or 'enthusiasm'; under the pressure of a plain sense of duty, 'without regard of person' he treats equally all persons who find themselves in factually equal situations (ibid: xliii, emphasis in original).

Thus one key feature of a bureaucratically organized criminal justice system is the presumed capacity to rise above consideration of the extralegal characteristics of the persons it processes. Such a system is expected instead to deal only with legally relevant aspects of offenders' cases. Note that this expectation directly contradicts the instrumental Marxist assumption that discrimination against economic and ethnic minorities is an inevitable product of criminal justice decisionmaking in a capitalist society (Chambliss and Seidman, 1971; Quinney, 1970). In contrast to this expectation, we have argued that corporate entities should have an objective interest in the very feature of formal impersonality that a bureaucratically organized criminal justice system is expected to provide: it is this feature that adds the legitimacy, and in turn the predictability and calculability, that are essential to successful commercial enterprise.

If the above reasoning is correct, in historical as well as cross-sectional data, *we should expect the participation of corporate actors as victims in the criminal justice process to be characterized by an increased formal equality in the treatment of offenders.* However, it is essential to underline the word formal here, because as Balbus suggests, ". . . the systemic application of an equal scale to systemically unequal individuals necessarily tends to reinforce systemic inequalities . . ." (Balbus, 1977: 652). That is, it is important to emphasize that although individual offenders might be treated more equally when corporate victims are involved, collectively, they would still fare worse because, as a *group,* they would experience a higher probability of conviction.

A final implication of the above discussion is that corporate actors will not only be anxious to make use of the criminal justice system, but also that they will more easily coordinate their goals with the organizational priorities of this system. Both organization forms have an interest in the bureaucratic pursuit of the formal rational application of law. Furthermore, as bureaucracies themselves, many corporate actors may be better suited than individuals to work effectively with the criminal justice system. For example, the element of formal impersonality may better equip corporate actors to decide which crimes against them are more promising cases for criminal prosecution. As well, because corporate actors may be more impersonal as well as less involved emotionally in their cases, they may be less likely to intrude on the criminal justice process once a case is under way; or, in the course of a case to indicate a change of preference with regard to the prosecution of it. Thus corporate victims may work more effectively than individual victims with criminal justice organizations, and *corporate actors may therefore be more satisfied than individuals with the results they achieve.* This type of prediction is anticipated by Coleman's observation that corporate actors (including not only corporations but also government agencies like those that constitute the criminal justice system) prefer to work with other corporate actors as compared to individuals. Coleman captures the irony and significance of this situation when he notes that "These preferences are often rationally based: the corporate actor ordinarily stands to gain more from a transaction with another corporate actor than from one with a person. But the rational basis makes the preference no less real in its consequences for persons."

Three testable hypotheses are contained in the above discussion:

1.  That corporate actors will be more successful than individuals in obtaining convictions against offenders;
2.  That equal treatment of offenders will be more likely to accompany corporate than individual victim involvement in the criminal justice system; and
3.  That corporate actors will be more satisfied than individuals with the work of the system.

This report presents a cross-sectional empirical test of these hypotheses. First, however, it will be useful to provide a brief discussion of the changing historical role of victims in the criminal justice system. The thesis of this discussion is that the historical emergence of corporate entities has been associated with significant changes in the role of the crime victim.

## THE ROLE OF THE VICTIM VIEWED HISTORICALLY

If the Weberian picture of corporate participation in the criminal justice process we have provided is correct, it should be possible to identify historical changes in the role of crime victims that correspond to changes in the surrounding economy and society (see Tigar and Levy, 1977). Such changes can be identified. In their broadest outline: a resort to blood feuds directly involved victims in achieving criminal justice as then conceived in tribal societies; a form of private prosecution and compensation continued to involve victims, but with some notable modifications, in feudal societies; and the emergence of modern capitalism found victims of crime replaced by public prosecutors in pursuit of a more impersonal, formal rational form of justice.

Thus, early societies, based on kinship ties and tribal organization, functioned without centralized systems of criminal justice and they assigned a prominent role to presumed victims in resolving criminal disputes through blood feuds. In these societies, victims and their kin were expected to put things right by avenging what they perceived as crimes against them: "All crime was against the family; it was the family that had to atone, or carry out the blood-feud" (Traill, 1899: 5).

Feudalism and Christianity were accompanied by a gradual elimination of blood feuding and an emerging system of compensations. What is significant in this is that as feudalism developed, between 700 and 1066, lords and bishops gradually replaced kinship groups as recipients of the compensatory payments (Hibbert, 1963; Jeffrey, 1957). This was a very significant beginning of the decoupling (Hagan *et al.,* 1980) of victims from an emerging criminal justice system. Gradually, the state began to receive a part of the compensation payments. Schaefer notes that "Before long the injured person's right to restitution began to shrink, and after the Treaty of Verdun divided the Frankish Empire, the fine that went to the state gradually replaced it entirely" (Schaefer, 1977: 14). Thus, it was now the state that was replacing the victim as a central actor in the criminal justice process. Finally, although the proceedings of this period (including oaths and ordeals) could be quite formal, at least from a modern viewpoint, they also were quite irrational (see Maine, 1960; Thayer, 1898).

The transition in England to a more modern form of criminal justice occurred during the reign of Henry II (1154–1189). During this period the feudal system of law disappeared and a system of common law emerged (Jeffrey, 1957). Nonetheless, a system of private prosecutions based on the initiative taken by victims of crime remained in effect in England well into the nineteenth century. In fact, the final decline of the victim's role in the criminal justice system did not begin until the Enlightenment, with the work of Cesare Beccaria. Writing in the eighteenth century, Beccaria applied the "principle of utility" in arguing that criminal law should serve the interests of society rather than the individual victim. What is significant throughout this work is the effort to model a criminal justice system on the same principles of calculation and reason that formed the foundations of modern capitalism (for elaboration of this point, see Halevy, 1960). Thus Balbus is able to note direct parallels between the emergence of modern legal forms and the commodity forms that characterize modern capitalism.

With Beccaria and Bentham, then, the formal rationality that Weber associates with modern capitalism found a very fundamental expression. The most important implication of this was that victims should play no direct role in criminal justice decisions about prosecution and punishment. From the utilitarian viewpoint, the crime is against *society,* and the state must therefore use calculation and reason in pursuing its prosecution and in deterring its repetition. However, as indicated earlier, in England the right and power to accuse, collect evidence and manage prosecutions for the state resided with individual citizens well into the nineteenth century (McDonald, 1976). Indeed this access to the law was regarded as an important right of private citizens, and it was not until the middle of the nineteenth century that the principal inadequacy of this arrangement was acknowledged: namely, that offenders were escaping prosecution because victims could not afford to exercise their legal rights. After several unsuccessful attempts to solve this problem in other ways, the office of the Director of Public Prosecutions was established in England in 1879. The ultimate effect of this change, and those discussed above, was a final loosening of the coupling of the victim to the criminal justice system, and a new autonomy for the state in overseeing victim-offender disputes.

It is clear then that a new kind of criminal justice emerged alongside the rise of the corporate form and the emergence of modern capitalism. It is our argument that this new form of criminal justice is particularly effective in promoting and legitimating use of the criminal law for the protection of corporate property against individuals. Put simply, our argument is that the new autonomy of the state in matters of criminal justice better serves corporate than individual interests. The remainder of this chapter is an empirical exploration of this argument.

## PRIOR RESEARCH

In spite of the importance we have attached in this discussion to corporate victims of crime, very little empirical attention has been given to them. Several victimization surveys involving corporate actors have been conducted as part of the National Crime Survey Program in the United States (U.S. Department of Justice, 1975). However, only two types of commercial crime, robbery and burglary, are considered in this work, and the sampling is restricted almost entirely to commercial establishments. Beyond this, a small collection of articles on crimes against businesses has been brought together in a single volume (Smigel and Ross, 1970); there are several studies of shoplifting and its control (e.g., Cameron, 1965; Hindelang, 1974; Robin, 1967); and the United States government has made some attempt to collect information on the costs of several types of commercial victimization (U.S. Department of Commerce, 1974). Among these sources, it is the victimization research that is most instructive.

Victimization data collected on burglary and robbery in thirteen American cities (U.S. Department of Justice, 1975) are brought together, and weighted to produce population estimates, in Appendices 1 and 2 of this report. These data provide preliminary support for our focus on the corporate influence on criminal law. For example, as might be expected given the opportunities and benefits of crimes against corporate actors, both for burglary and robbery, the per capita rates of victimization of commercial establishments are higher than for individuals and households. Across the 13 cities, on a per capita basis, commercial establishments experience more than three times the burglaries and five times the robberies as households and individuals. Furthermore, in every city, for both burglary and robbery, commercial establishments are more likely than individuals and households to report the victimizations they experience to the police. Across the 13 cities, approximately three-quarters (76.1%) of the commercial burglary victims report their experiences to the police, while about half (51.6%) of the household burglary victims report their experiences to the police. Similarly, 82% of the commercial robberies and 57% of the individual robberies are reported to the police. Undoubtedly, this difference is influenced by the types and amounts of corporate insurance coverage. Nonetheless, it remains significant that on a per capita basis, commercial victims are much more likely than individual victims to require and make use of the system. Of course, individuals and households outnumber commercial organizations, so that when the above findings are weighted back to the population, commercial establishments are reduced in their apparent significance. Even then, however, we find that commercial establishments are very important clients of the criminal justice system. Thus across the 13 American cities, commercial establishments are responsible for more than a third, and in some cities (e.g., Cincinnati in the case of burglary and Miami in the case of robbery) more than half, of both the burglaries and robberies reported to the police. In sum, the representation of commercial victims in the criminal justice process is large and disproportionate.

Some comments should be added to these findings. First, these data deal with burglary and robbery only, while thefts (by employees and customers) are clearly the most frequent crimes experienced by commercial victims. Second, these data consider only commercial establishments, ignoring other kinds of corporate victims. Finally, these data stop at the point where victims indicate that they reported incidents to the police. Thus the picture provided by victimization data is suggestive, but partial. Research reported in the remainder of this paper considers in greater detail the involvement of corporate victims in the criminal justice process, in one Canadian jurisdiction.

## THE CURRENT RESEARCH

The data analyzed in this report consist of cases involving victims of crime for whom an offender is charged in a collection of suburban communities adjacent to Toronto, Canada. The restriction to cases where an offender is charged is deliberate. We have already shown with victimization data that commercial organizations are more likely than individual victims to report crimes against them to the police. We now want to consider the role of these victims in the criminal justice system. Focusing on cases where charges are laid increases the likelihood that the victims we consider have something more than a passing contact with the system.

Several kinds of data are considered. First, a population of 1000 cases drawn from police department files from September 1976 to January 1977 is used to establish parameters for the jurisdiction under study. Then a stratified sample of 400 postdisposition interviews with 200 individual and 200 corporate victims is analyzed. The interviews with the individual victims represent the latter half of a panel design involving before and after court contacts which took place between June 1976 and December 1978; the corporate interviews began in September 1977 and continued until September 1978. Individual victims for whom an offender was charged were eliminated from the sampling frame in three circumstances: if the victim was a juvenile, if the crime was against a person's property and resulted in less than five dollars damage, or if the crime was against a person who could not, or would not, recall it. The panel design involving individual victims began with 305 victims and stopped after 200 of these victims could be reached for the follow-up, postdisposition interview.[1]

In establishing the sampling frame for the corporate interviews, two research decisions had to be made. First, which member of the corporate entity should be interviewed? Our decision was to have the interviewer determine who in the organization was most responsible for making decisions to charge, and other decisions, in the relevant case. In practice, this arrangement seemed to work effectively; however, it also raised the second issue to be faced. That issue was: Which cases involving corporate victims should be considered? Many corporate actors—especially the retail department stores—were victimized repeatedly. It would have made little sense to interview representatives of these organizations repeatedly. Instead we formulated as a sampling criterion that each organization was to be interviewed only once about a crime (involving a charged suspect) which was representative of those experienced. This was done in one of two ways. Working with a listing of all cases involving corporate victims for whom an accused was charged, we first sorted the cases by organization. Again as in the case of individual victims, property crimes involving less than five dollars in losses were not considered. If a modal type of case for a corporate victim was present (e.g., shoplifting for many retail stores), a case for interview was selected among these at random. Alternatively, if no modal type of case existed, a case was selected at random from the larger grouping. The resulting sampling frame was made up of cases involving 334 corporate actors.

The variables and their values included in our analysis are listed in Appendix 3. Our analysis focuses first on a set of court outcomes: whether the defendant was held for a bail hearing, convicted, and the type of sentence received; and second on victims' reactions to these outcomes: the perceived appropriateness of the disposition and the overall satisfaction with the outcome of the case.

There may be initial discomfort with the idea of considering cases involving corporate and individual victims in a single analysis; a discomfort that probably follows from the observation that some types of cases, for example shoplifting, only involve corporate actors. However, it is not at all clear that this fact makes shoplifting cases *qualitatively* different from other offenses committed against corporate actors and individuals. Certainly the law provides no separate offense

---

[1] An examination of the population and sample data revealed no systematic evidence of error or bias in the latter (Hagan, 1980: Chapter 2). The panel design forms the basis for an analysis reported in Hagan (ibid: Chapters 3–4). Only the follow-up interviews are used here.

category for shoplifting (i.e., the charge is typically theft), and we have noted that it treats both corporate and individual victims as "persons." Furthermore, Sellin and Wolfgang (1964) have demonstrated that shoplifting and other types of property crimes can be located, along with a variety of other crimes that cause bodily injury, on a common scale of seriousness. Their point, empirically confirmed, is that in everyday life, and particularly in everyday law enforcement, certain equivalences can and must be formed (ibid: 348). Beyond this, our argument is that differences between cases involving corporate actors and individuals are a matter of degree, not kind, involving such things as the impersonality versus intimacy involved in the victim-accused relationship. Consideration of such variables is a part of our analysis, an analysis that successfully accounts for an important difference in the outcomes of cases involving corporate and individual victims.

A wide range of independent variables are considered in the analysis, some deriving from our theoretical interests, others from the conventions of this kind of criminal justice research (e.g., Hagan *et al.,* 1979). For example, in the first part of the analysis, dealing with court outcomes, we consider a number of characteristics of the victim: whether the victim is an individual or a corporate entity, and if the former, the victim's sex and SES; the seriousness of the victimization as measured by the Sellin-Wolfgang scale; whether property was returned to the victim, the willingness of the victim to accept any responsibility for the crime, whether the victim gave testimony, the intimacy of the victim-accused relationship,[2] and whether the victim is a repeat player in the sense of having experienced the same type of crime previously. If the victim is a corporate actor, we consider whether it is involved in retailing, public or private in its base, local to multinational in scale, the number of employees in the representative's division, the number of organization units, the number of employees in the organization, the centralization of the organization, and the perceived relationship between the organization and its clients. A number of characteristics of the accused were also taken from police files for this part of the analysis, including the marital status, sex, condition at arrest, and employment status of the accused. Information from the files was also used to determine whether a statement was taken from the accused, the police perception of the demeanor of the accused, and the number of prior convictions, the most serious prior disposition, and the number of charges against the accused. Finally, for this first part of the analysis we included from these files information on whether the victim mobilized the police, filed the complaint, whether a warrant was issued, and the initial decision whether to hold the person for a bail hearing. The last variable was included only for the adjudication and sentencing outcomes, to determine if early processing decisions are coupled to those made later.

There is some overlap in the independent variables included in the first and sec-

---

[2]Our measure of the intimacy of the victim-accused relationship is based on ordinally ranked responses to five interview questions: How well did you know the offender? How frequently did you talk to the offender? Did you know the offender's name? Would you say that you generally liked the offender before this incident? Did you feel that the offender generally liked you before this incident? Responses to these items were combined into an additive measure of intimacy.

ond parts of the analysis. The type of victim and crime, seriousness of victimization, return of property to the victim, victim responsibility, the relationship between victim and accused, and whether the victim mobilized the police, filed the complaint and gave testimony, are all considered as before. Similarly, four traits of the accused—employment status, prior convictions, most serious prior disposition, and number of other charges—are included in the same way as before. In addition to these variables, we consider a number of others that come from our interviews and that plausibly influence the response to court outcomes.

The remorse of the accused, as perceived by the victim, is included as measured in a Likert-type scale. We also consider characteristics attributed to the accused by the victim, measured in the form of a summed semantic differential scale that includes evaluations of the accused as honest-dishonest, responsible-irresponsible, kind-cruel, gentle-brutal, safe-dangerous, good-bad, predictable-unpredictable, stable-unstable, mature-immature, friendly-unfriendly. Victim ratings of the importance of five goals of sentencing—reformation, general deterrence, individual deterrence, punishment, and incapacitation—are considered. As well, a summed 5-item law and order scale (see Hagan, 1975) is included. A "citizen responsibility" scale was constructed in the same way from responses to two items: (1) there is not much individual citizens can do to prevent crime, and (2) preventing crime is the job of the police, not the job of the average citizen. Separate consideration is given to the victim's belief in free will ("To what extent do you believe that human beings act on their own free will?") and conceptions of individual responsibility ("Do you feel that human beings should be responsible for their actions?"), both coded as Likert scales. Consideration is also given to whether the victim attended trial and to the victim's knowledge of the disposition. Victims who did not know the disposition were told it before being asked to respond to the case outcomes. The last of the independent variables we include is the disposition of the case. We are interested not only in the direct effect of this variable on the victim's response to the criminal justice process, but also in the effects of statistically holding this variable constant.

Tabular and regression techniques are used to analyze our data. Two of our five dependent variables are binary and violate technical assumptions of homosedasticity. Under these conditions, ordinary least-squares regression may produce inefficient, though unbiased, parameter estimates. We therefore ran weighted least-squares solutions as well as ordinary least-squares regressions when the binary dependent variables were involved. This procedure produced changes in some coefficients, but not alterations in substantive conclusions. To conserve space and maintain consistency, we present only the results of the ordinary least-squares regressions in this paper. Unless otherwise indicated, in the regression phase of the analysis we consider only those effects that are statistically significant at the .10 level,[3] with betas of .10 and larger. Throughout the analysis we focus on those fac-

---

[3]Our decision to use the .10 level is based on the exploratory character of the research.

tors that distinguish the involvement of corporate and individual victims in the criminal justice process.

## THE ANALYSIS

The preliminary part of the analysis compared the population and interview data (see Hagan, 1980: Chapter 2) to determine if any systematic sources of error or bias were present in the latter. Although no important discrepancies were discovered, several findings did stand out. First, we found that nearly two-thirds of the victims in the population were corporate entities ($N = 643$), while just over a third were individuals ($N = 357$). As well, both in the population and in the interviews significantly more corporate (79.5 and 75.0%) than individual victims (65.5 and 62.2%) saw accused persons in their cases convicted. We analyze this relationship between type of victim and likelihood of conviction further in a moment. Meanwhile, we can note that these preliminary findings are certainly consistent with our first hypothesis about corporate influence in the criminal justice process; that is, that corporate actors are more successful than individuals in obtaining convictions against offenders.

Before pursuing our multivariate analysis, several additional bivariate relationships are presented in Table 1. The first two findings in this table reveal that corporate victims are more likely than individual victims to believe they could have prevented the incident and less likely to believe that crime prevention is the job of police. The implication is that corporate victims are well aware of the fact that they present more opportunities for crime than individuals, and that they could, and perhaps should, assume a greater responsibility for the crimes committed against them. As we have indicated, however, the paradox of this situation is that corporate victims are more likely to see accused persons convicted.

Table 1 also establishes several other things: individual victims are significantly more likely to know the accused, attend court, and know the case outcome. These indicators suggest that corporate victims are more detached from the accused, and decoupled from the criminal justice system, than are individual victims. We note these findings here because, as we suggest later, they may make for a more formal rational influence of corporate victims on the criminal justice process.

Finally, there is evidence in Table 1, consistent with our third hypothesis above, that corporate victims respond more positively to the criminal justice experience than do individual victims. Corporate victims are less likely than individual victims to be dissatisfied with the sentences the courts generally impose, and more likely to be satisfied with the competence of the police, the overall outcome of the case, and with the specific sentence imposed in the immediate case. All but the last of these differences is statistically significant. In other words, and perhaps with good reason, corporate victims express a greater satisfaction with the criminal justice system than do individual victims. Since some of this satisfaction may derive

**TABLE 1** Type of Victim by Response to Victimization and Court Experience

| | Perceived ability to prevent incident | Prevention of crime job of police | Knowledge of offender | Attended court | Knowledge of case outcome | Sentences generally too easy | Satisfaction with police competence | Satisfied with sentence | Satisfied with overall outcome |
|---|---|---|---|---|---|---|---|---|---|
| Individual | 10.5% (21) | 18.0% (36) | 40.0% (80) | 57.0% (114) | 50.5% (101) | 64.0% (128) | 79.5% (159) | 43.5% (87) | 53.0% (106) |
| Organization | 26.5 (53) | 9.0 (18) | 18.0 (36) | 21.0 (42) | 26.0 (52) | 53.0 (106) | 88.5 (177) | 46.0 (92) | 66.0 (132) |
| | $x^2 = 11.02$ $p = .001$ | $x^2 = 8.21$ $p = .004$ | $x^2 = 23.51$ $p = .001$ | $x^2 = 55.20$ $p = .001$ | $x^2 = 29.02$ $p = .001$ | $x^2 = 5.25$ $p = .072$ | $x^2 = 5.25$ $p = .014$ | $x^2 = 3.27$ $p = .351$ | $x^2 = 16.35$ $p = .006$ |

TABLE 2   Decomposition of the Effect of Type of Victim on Adjudication ($N = 400$)

|  | (1) | | (2) | | (3) | | (4) | | (5) | |
|---|---|---|---|---|---|---|---|---|---|---|
|  | B | F | B | F | B | F | B | F | B | F |
| 1. Type of victim | .16 | 10.18 | .14 | 7.17 | .12 | 5.63 | .09 | 2.99 | .09 | 3.12 |
| 2. Statement taken |  |  | .22 | 21.15 | .18 | 11.94 | .18 | 11.91 | .17 | 11.63 |
| 3. Accused demeanor |  |  |  |  | −.14 | 6.83 | −.14 | 6.93 | −.13 | 6.68 |
| 4. Victim-accused relationship |  |  |  |  |  |  | −.12 | 5.39 | −.12 | 5.62 |
| 5. Repeat player |  |  |  |  |  |  |  |  | −.07 | 2.21 |
| Mediated effect |  |  | .02 |  | .02 |  | .03 |  | .00 |  |

from the greater success of corporate victims in obtaining convictions, we go on next to a multivariate analysis of this success.

In Table 2 we use a step-wise multiple regression procedure to assess the impact of several variables on the greater success of corporate victims in obtaining convictions. These variables were selected in terms of our expectations about corporate participation in the criminal justice process. Thus the first of the variables is the victim–accused relationship, measured in terms of the intimacy, or conversely, the impersonality, of this relationship. Our expectation is that an impersonal relationship is more likely to allow a sustained prosecution, while intimacy between the victim and accused more often does not. Second, we consider the presence of a statement from the accused. Offenders who make incriminating statements are more easily convicted, and corporate entities may be able to use their resources more selectively in picking cases for prosecution when such statements can be generated. As well, we include the demeanor of the accused. One aspect of good demeanor, as perceived by the police, is an acknowledgment of guilt; again, corporate victims may be better able to generate cases with accused persons who have been reduced to this demeanor. Finally, we consider whether the victim is a repeat player, in the sense of having been a victim previously of a similar crime (Galanter, 1974). Corporate entities are more likely to be repeat players ($r = .53$), and this experience may be expected to improve their prospects for successful prosecutions. The above variables were introduced into regression equations in Table 2 in the order that they increased the explained variance in convictions.

Examination of Table 2 reveals that three of the above four variables are indeed involved in the success of corporations in obtaining convictions. Thus the statistical significance of the type of victim was reduced below the .05 level after the introduction of three of these variables.[4] The largest of the mediated effects (.03) in

[4]Introduction of additional variables reduced the statistical significance of this relationship below the .10 level used elsewhere in this paper; however, the mediating influences of subsequent variables were not sufficiently large to justify substantive discussion.

Table 2 is produced by the introduction of the victim-accused relationship. In other words, the impersonality of corporate actors is a key factor in their higher rate of convictions. Only slightly less important is the apparent ability of corporate victims to select and/or generate accused persons who give statements to the police and who demonstrate cooperative demeanor (both mediated effects = .02). The only variable that does not operate as expected is whether the victim is a repeat player. Apparently this experience does not *directly* account for the success of organizations. Indeed, the correlation between this experience and convictions is only .07. On the other hand, we have found evidence that corporate entities seem more generally to choose cases for prosecution with an eye toward what the courts are most likely to convict. Said differently, corporate entities choose their cases impersonally and strategically, a pattern that would seem to promote the formal rational enforcement of criminal law.

There was no evidence in our data that corporate victims were any more likely than individual victims to see accused persons held for a bail hearing or severely sentenced. However, a comparison in Tables 3 and 5 of factors producing these outcomes in cases of individual and corporate victims reveals some striking differences that are consistent with our earlier discussion. For example, in cases with individual victims (see Table 3), the independent variable that most consistently predicts bail, adjudication and sentencing decisions is the employment status of the accused. In these cases, unemployed accused are more likely to be held for bail ($B = -.14$), convicted ($B = -.23$), and sentenced severely ($B = -.16$). It may be possible to legally justify detention of an unemployed accused for a bail hearing in terms of formal standards for the making of these decisions (see Morden, 1980; Nagel, 1980). However, similar justifications do not exist at conviction and sentencing, and measured against normative expectations about equality before the law, these effects therefore may be extra-legal. In contrast, in Table 5, where cases involving corporate victims are considered, the employment status of the accused does *not* play a significant role at conviction and sentencing. These findings support our second hypothesis that formally equal treatment of offenders increases with corporate involvement in the criminal justice system.

Of related interest is the finding that persons accused of crimes against women are more likely than are persons accused of crimes against men to be held for a bail hearing ($B = -.15$) and to be sentenced severely ($B = -.26$). Interpretation of these effects is complicated by the fact that they only become apparent when other variables are held constant ($r = .07$ and $-.06$). Our concern in offering an interpretation of these effects was with the complicating role that the victim's relationship with the accused might play. To explore this we created two dummy variables representing female victims who *were* and *were not* intimately involved with the accused.[5] The "omitted category" for these dummy variables was *male* victims *un*involved with the accused. The results of substituting these dummy vari-

---

[5]Our measure of the intimacy of the victim's involvement with the accused is the scale discussed in note 2, dichotomized at the mean.

TABLE 3   Correlation and Regression Coefficients for Individual Victims

| Independent variables | Bail (N = 188) | | | | Adjudication (N = 188) | | | | Sentence (N = 130) | | | |
|---|---|---|---|---|---|---|---|---|---|---|---|---|
| | r | b | B | F | r | b | B | F | r | b | B | F |
| Seriousness of victimization | .17 | .02 | .15 | 4.20** | | | | | .31 | .08 | .29 | 11.07** |
| Return of property | | | | | .23 | .18 | .15 | 3.70** | | | | |
| Victim-accused relationship | .20 | .14 | .17 | 5.11** | | | | | -.13 | -.03 | -.15 | 3.02* |
| Accused condition at arrest | -.08 | -.11 | -.14 | 3.85*** | | | | | | | | |
| Accused employment status | .16 | .18 | .22 | 8.59*** | -.30 | -.22 | -.23 | 9.47** | -.16 | -.26 | -.16 | 3.87* |
| Statement taken | .17 | .17 | .19 | 7.05*** | | | | | | | | |
| Accused demeanor | | | | | | | | | | | | |
| Accused most serious disposition | .36 | .11 | .35 | 14.38** | | | | | .38 | .18 | .30 | 6.21 |
| Number of charges against accused | | | | | -.12 | -.06 | -.23 | 7.98** | | | | |
| Complaint | -.15 | -.10 | -.13 | 3.28* | | | | | | | | |
| Warrant | | — | | | -.18 | -.27 | -.19 | 6.52** | | | | |
| Victim's sex | .07 | -.12 | -.15 | 3.67* | | | | | -.06 | -.40 | -.26 | 8.49** |
| | | $R^2 = .29$ | | | | $R^2 = .25$ | | | | $R^2 = .38$ | | |
| | | Intercept = .15 | | | | Intercept = .64 | | | | Intercept = 3.41 | | |

*Significant at the .10 level.
**Significant at the .05 level.

TABLE 4  Results of Dummy Variable Regressions Involving Sex of Victim and Involvement with the Accused

| Dummy Variables | Bail | | | | Adjudication | | | | Sentence | | | |
|---|---|---|---|---|---|---|---|---|---|---|---|---|
| | r | b | B | F | r | b | B | F | r | b | B | F |
| Female victim-involved with accused | -.06 | .08 | .09 | 1.24 | -.14 | -.02 | -.02 | .04 | -.12 | .12 | .06 | .49 |
| Female victim-not involved with accused | -.02 | .12 | .13 | 2.91* | .02 | .03 | .02 | .08 | .18 | .42 | .22 | 6.15** |

*Significant at the .10 level.
**Significant at the .05 level.

TABLE 5  Correlation and Regression Coefficients for Organization Victims

| Independent Variables | Bail (N = 200) | | | | Adjudication (N = 200) | | | | Sentence (N = 157) | | | |
|---|---|---|---|---|---|---|---|---|---|---|---|---|
| | r | b | B | F | r | b | B | F | r | b | B | F |
| Seriousness of victimization | | | | | -.16 | -.12 | -.12 | 3.17* | .32 | .08 | .19 | 7.29** |
| Victim responsibility | | | | | | | | | | | | |
| Victim testimony | | | | | .13 | .07 | .12 | 2.78* | -.06 | -.33 | -.13 | 3.41* |
| Accused marital status | | | | | .06 | .16 | .13 | 3.43* | -.23 | -.23 | -.17 | 4.96* |
| Accused condition at arrest | | | | | | | | | | | | |
| Accused employment status | -.16 | -.14 | -.16 | 4.93** | .26 | .26 | .32 | 16.85** | .26 | .47 | .28 | 11.66** |
| Statement taken | | | | | -.21 | -.12 | -.14 | 3.59* | | | | |
| Accused demeanor | | | | | | | | | | | | |
| Accused prior convictions | .42 | .03 | .29 | 7.44** | | | | | | | | |
| Accused most serious disposition | .39 | .06 | .18 | 2.77* | | | | | | | | |
| Number of charges against accused | | | | | -.04 | -.04 | -.13 | 2.87* | | | | |
| Mobilization | | | | | .15 | .14 | .17 | 6.34** | | | | |
| Bail decision | | | | | .15 | .15 | .15 | 3.94** | .39 | .53 | .27 | 12.39** |
| Number of employees | | | | | .10 | .01 | .14 | 3.32* | | | | |
| | $R^2 = .27$ | | | | $R^2 = .28$ | | | | $R^2 = .47$ | | | |
| | Intercept = .09 | | | | Intercept = 1.11 | | | | Intercept = 2.87 | | | |

*Significant at the .10 level.
**Significant at the .05 level.

ables for their component parts in the regression equations of Table 3 are presented in Table 4. These results reveal two things: (1) offender involvement with female victims lessens the probability of conviction ($r = -.14$), and when conviction occurs, tends to result in more lenient sentencing ($r - .12$); (2) other variables held constant, offenders accused of crimes against female victims with whom they are uninvolved are more likely to be held for bail hearings ($B = .13$) and receive severe sentences ($B = .22$). In other words, female victims who are uninvolved with the offender receive greater protective treatment from the courts than do female victims who are involved with the accused. These results suggest another type of inequality before the law that accompanies disputes between individuals.

Rather different findings emerge in Table 5, where cases involving corporate victims are considered. For example, in addition to the finding pertaining to the employment status of the accused noted above, the two most important determinants of being held for a bail hearing are the number of prior convictions and the most serious prior disposition against the accused. Beyond this, the most consistent influence on adjudication and sentencing is whether the accused was held for a bail hearing ($B = .15$ and $.27$). Overall, then, there is a tendency in cases involving corporate victims to give greater attention to legal variables (or in other words to formal rational considerations), and to prior organization decisions. The former finding supports, again, our second hypothesis; the latter reliance on bail decisions at the later stages of adjudication and sentencing suggests a pattern in which decisionmaking is routinized and reaffirmed as the defendant moves through the criminal justice process. One possible further indication of this routinization is that the largest explained variance in Tables 3 and 4 occurs at the sentencing stage in cases involving corporate victims ($R^2 = .47$). It may be here that the court is most certain of what it is doing. Finally, it is significant to note that at the conviction stage, larger corporate entities are apparently more successful than smaller corporate entities in obtaining convictions (i.e., the Beta for Number of Employees is $.14$). Insofar as size is a reflection of power and resources, this finding is consistent with our focus on the corporate advantage in the criminal justice process. More generally, the findings from this part of the analysis also support the link we have drawn between formal rationality and the involvement of corporate victims in the criminal justice process.

The final part of our analysis deals with the specific reactions of individual and corporate victims to the sentences imposed in their cases, and with their overall satisfaction with the outcomes in these cases. As earlier, there are clear differences in the responses of individual and corporate victims (see Table 6). Among these, the most significant again involves the employment status of the accused. If the accused is unemployed, individual victims are more likely to think the sentence was too lenient ($B = -.16$) and to be dissatisfied ($B = -.15$) with the overall outcome of the case. The reader will recall the earlier finding that in cases with individual victims, unemployed accused were more likely to be held for a bail hearing, convicted and sentenced severely. In this analysis we have held disposition

TABLE 6  Correlation and Regression Coefficients for Perceived Sentence Severity and Satisfaction with Outcome in Cases with Individual and Organizational Victims

| | Perceived sentence severity, individual victims (n = 188) | | | | Satisfaction with case outcome, individual victims (n = 188) | | | | Perceived sentence severity, organizational victims (n = 200) | | | | Satisfaction with case outcome, organizational victims (n = 200) | | | |
|---|---|---|---|---|---|---|---|---|---|---|---|---|---|---|---|---|
| | r | b | B | F | r | b | B | F | r | b | B | F | r | b | B | F |
| Seriousness of victimization | .17 | .03 | .16 | 3.68* | .17 | .14 | .24 | 9.19*** | | | | | | | | |
| Victim responsibility | −.11 | −.15 | −.13 | 2.67* | | | | | | | | | | | | |
| Characteristics attributed to accused | .27 | .01 | .25 | 10.50*** | | | | | | | | | | | | |
| Complainant | | | | | −.14 | −.72 | −.22 | 8.06*** | | | | | −.17 | −.79 | −.20 | 6.65*** |
| General deterrence-victim ranking | | | | | | | | | | | | | | | | |
| Individual deterrence-victim ranking | | | | | | | | | | | | | −.15 | −.19 | −.14 | 2.73* |
| Law and order attitudes | −.17 | −.03 | −.18 | 5.68** | −.18 | −.12 | −.21 | 6.92*** | −.19 | −.09 | −.16 | 3.09* | | | | |
| Individual responsibility | | | | | .02 | .05 | .15 | 3.70* | | | | | | | | |
| Victim testimony | | | | | −.07 | −.50 | −.15 | 3.01* | | | | | | | | |
| Accused employment status | −.12 | −.16 | −.16 | 3.89** | −.08 | −.48 | −.15 | 3.62* | .19 | −.07 | −.19 | 5.50** | | | | |
| Disposition | | | | | −.15 | −.26 | −.25 | 9.25*** | | | | | −.26 | −.25 | −.26 | 11.31*** |
| Trial attendance | | | | | −.00 | .61 | .19 | 3.68* | | | | | .02 | | | |
| Relationship between organization and clients | | | | | | | | | | | | | .16 | .24 | .16 | 4.23** |
| | R² = .25 | | | | R² = .25 | | | | R² = .19 | | | | R² = .23 | | | |
| | Intercept = 2.06 | | | | Intercept = 3.04 | | | | Intercept = 5.15 | | | | Intercept = 3.08 | | | |

*Significant at the .10 level.
**Significant at the .05 level.
***Significant at the .01 level.

constant. *Thus, individual victims apparently want more severe sanctioning for un-employed accused than they already receive.* No similar pattern exists when corporate victims are considered. Again, then, the implication is that corporate victims encourage, or at least facilitate, formal equality in the treatment of accused. However, we again emphasize that this gain is offset by the greater collective likelihood of conviction in these cases.

There is further evidence that individual victims who support a "law and order" orientation think sentences in their cases are too lenient and are dissatisfied with their case outcomes ($B = -.18$ and $-.21$). As well, those individual victims who attribute negative characteristics to the accused also find the sentences in their cases too lenient ($B = .25$).

The reactions of corporate victims to their case outcomes are more narrow or circumscribed in character. While individual victims do not vary in their reactions to court outcomes according to their concerns about deterrence, or for that matter in relation to any other goal of sentencing, corporate victims do. Among corporate victims, a concern with individual deterrence is associated with a perception that the sentence is too lenient ($B = -.16$), and a concern with general deterrence is associated with a dissatisfaction with the overall case outcome ($B = -.14$). The other consistent response of corporate victims is to the actual severity of the disposition in the case. As one might expect, the more lenient the disposition, the more likely the corporate victim is to regard the sentence as too lenient ($B = -.19$) and to be dissatisfied with the overall outcome of the case ($B = -.26$). These findings seem quite consistent with Coleman's observation that insofar as corporate actors come to replace individuals in influencing the allocation of organizational resources, "these decisions . . . are more and more removed from the multiplicity of dampening and modifying interests of which a real person is composed—more and more the resultant of a balance of narrow intense interests of which corporate actors are composed" (Coleman, 1974: 49). The corporate attention here seems narrowly focused on the deterrence of future crimes against them.

## DISCUSSION AND CONCLUSIONS

To date, criminal justice research has not given much attention to the structural contexts in which criminal justice decisions are made (see Hagan and Bumiller, 1982). One source of this astructural attitude is undoubtedly the importance Anglo-American law attaches to individuals. Notions of individual rights permeate our system of criminal law and are reflected in the modern ideal of individualized justice. However, one purpose of this paper is to argue that there is a myth of individualism that is stretched beyond plausibility, for example, by the legal conceptualization of corporate entities as juristic persons who are accorded the same formal status as natural persons. Criminal justice research has accepted uncritically the myth of individualism insofar as it has neglected to explore the consequences of the involvement of these juristic persons as victims in criminal justice decisionmaking. Making the role of corporate entities explicit in this system is one way of adding a structural dimension to work in this domain.

We hypothesized that the involvement of these new juristic persons in the criminal justice system has resulted in a corporate influence in the criminal justice process that is characterized by (a) the greater success of corporate than individual actors in getting individual offenders convicted; (b) a greater likelihood of formal equality in the treatment of individuals prosecuted for crimes against corporate than individual victims; and (c) a greater satisfaction of corporate than individual victims with their experiences in the criminal justice system. We noted that an increase in formal equality in the treatment of individuals prosecuted for crimes against corporate actors (Hypothesis 2) is offset by the possibility that as a group, these individuals may still be more likely to be convicted for crimes against corporate entities (Hypothesis 1). This combination of possibilities may also serve to increase the legitimacy as well as the efficiency with which criminal justice agencies serve corporate actors, and therefore to anticipate the greater satisfaction corporate actors are hypothesized to take from the criminal justice experience (Hypothesis 3). To put all this in Weberian terms, we are suggesting that there is an "elective affinity" between corporate actors and agencies of criminal justice.

There is much in our data that supports the perspective just outlined. Our historical review of victim involvement in criminal justice decisionmaking revealed that it was not until the Enlightenment and the rise of modern capitalism that the role of the state-supported public prosecutor fully emerged, and consequently reduced the involvement of private victims in criminal justice operations. We noted that this new autonomy of the state might better serve the interests of corporate than individual victims. Thus our review of contemporary victimization data from thirteen American cities revealed that as compared to individuals, commercial organizations experience and report crimes to the police in large and disproportionate numbers. While we have no data to indicate precisely when the increased involvement of corporate actors began, it is reasonable to assume that it has paralleled the tremendous growth of commercial retailing in this century. The purpose of the current study has been to examine how the involvement of corporate victims may influence contemporary criminal justice operations. We have explored this issue within a Canadian jurisdiction.

Overall, our data provide support for the perspective outlined above. For example, corporate actors actually outnumber individuals as victims in the jurisdiction studied.[6] As well, corporate actors are more likely than individuals to obtain convictions, and, the larger the organization, the greater is the likelihood of conviction. The greater success of corporate actors as compared to individuals in obtaining convictions is explained by their more impersonal relationships with the

[6]How this suburban Canadian jurisdiction compares to other jurisdictions is, of course, an issue that calls for further research.

accused, and by their selection of accused who give statements to the police and who convey a demeanor that acknowledges their guilt. The picture that emerges is of corporate entities that use their resources in an impersonal, formal, rational, efficient fashion. One of these resources, the use of private security personnel, deserves further study. It is likely that size of organization acts as a proxy in our data for quantity and quality of private security arrangements. Access to private security may well be a crucial part of what we have called the corporate advantage.

We also considered separately factors that lead to bail, conviction and sentencing decisions in cases involving corporate, as contrasted with individual, victims. Measured against legal standards of equality before the law, we found that the involvement of individual victims is associated with the operation of extralegal factors in the decisionmaking process. For example, in cases with individual victims, unemployed accused are more likely to be held for a bail hearing, convicted, and sentenced severely. Furthermore, even when the severity of dispositions in these cases is held constant, individual victims of unemployed accused still express a greater desire for severe sanctions and a dissatisfaction with overall case outcome. The implication is that individual victims are a part (although not as large a part as they might wish) of the differential imposition of the sanctions noted above. A different pattern emerges when corporate victims are involved. More influential here are factors that derive from contact of the accused with criminal justice organizations (e.g., bail decisions, prior convictions and dispositions, and statements given to the police) and corporate concerns about individual and general deterrence. Measured against legal expectations, corporate victims again seem to be part of a more formal rational application of law.

We have argued that the form and content of criminal justice found in modern capitalist societies supports and legitimates the use of criminal law for the protection of corporate property against individuals. That is, we have argued that the modern criminal justice system better serves corporate than individual interests. One consequence of this situation is that criminal justice agencies originally thought to have emerged for the purposes of protecting individuals against individuals today are devoting a substantial share of their resources to the protection of large affluent corporate actors. It is important to note that this may not be the unique fate of modern institutions of criminal justice. For example, the post office has long complained of a related set of pressures generated by the growth of commercial enterprise; and it is interesting to note that in the same way commercial retailers have encouraged the development of private security services to do what the criminal courts will not, similar commercial interests have generated a private mail industry to do what the post office will not. Thus the patterns we have observed probably have parallels and consequences beyond those explored in this chapter. This is another way of saying that the corporate domination of our everyday lives is probably a more pervasive phenomenon than the subject matter of this chapter may unintentionally have implied.

APPENDIX 1  Victimization Data on Burglary in 13 American Cities

| | Boston | Buffalo | Cincinnati | Houston | Miami | Milwaukee | Minneapolis | New Orleans | Oakland | Pittsburgh | San Diego | San Francisco | Washington | 13 Cities |
|---|---|---|---|---|---|---|---|---|---|---|---|---|---|---|
| Burglary incidents per 1,000 population | 149 | 97 | 143 | 164 | 85 | 152 | 177 | 112 | 174 | 93 | 138 | 115 | 75 | 128.7 |
| Percent reported to police | 56% | 50% | 55% | 46% | 58% | 54% | 52% | 47% | 57% | 50% | 50% | 51% | 57% | 51.6% |
| Incidents reported to police weighted to population | 17,360 (56.7%) | 7,200 (60.4%) | 12,375 (48.9%) | 32,016 (70.4%) | 6,090 (50.4%) | 13,926 (76.9%) | 14,768 (74.3%) | 10,199 (62.8%) | 13,224 (56.2%) | 8,100 (66.5%) | 17,650 (74.4%) | 16,932 (64.6%) | 11,229 (62.3%) | 187,069 (64.2%) |
| Burglary incidents per 1,000 establishments | 576 | 319 | 566 | 518 | 292 | 321 | 436 | 448 | 637 | 293 | 358 | 253 | 330 | 411.3 |
| Percent reported to police | 78% | 75% | 84% | 71% | 79% | 82% | 71% | 68% | 77% | 73% | 80% | 72% | 79% | 76.1% |
| Incidents reported to police weighted to population | 13,260 (43.3%) | 4,725 (39.6%) | 12,936 (51.1%) | 13,490 (29.6%) | 6,004 (49.6%) | 5,986 (23.1%) | 5,112 (25.7%) | 6,052 (37.2%) | 10,318 (43.8%) | 4,088 (33.5%) | 6,080 (25.6%) | 9,288 (35.4%) | 6,794 (37.7%) | 104,133 (35.8%) |
| Per capita ratio of commercial to household burglaries | 3.9 | 3.3 | 4.0 | 3.2 | 3.4 | 2.1 | 2.5 | 4.0 | 3.7 | 3.2 | 2.6 | 2.2 | 4.4 | 3.2 |
| Total number of incidents reported to police weighted to population | 30,620 | 11,925 | 25,311 | 45,506 | 12,094 | 25,912 | 19,880 | 16,251 | 23,542 | 12,188 | 23,730 | 26,220 | 18,023 | 291,202 |

APPENDIX 2   Victimization Data on Robbery in 13 American Cities

| | Boston | Buffalo | Cincinnati | Houston | Miami | Milwaukee | Minneapolis | New Orleans | Oakland | Pittsburgh | San Diego | San Francisco | Washington | 13 Cities |
|---|---|---|---|---|---|---|---|---|---|---|---|---|---|---|
| Robbery incidents per 1,000 population | 31 | 16 | 15 | 17 | 10 | 18 | 21 | 18 | 22 | 15 | 11 | 29 | 17 | 18.5 |
| Percent reported to police | 53% | 51% | 51% | 47% | 65% | 51% | 49% | 53% | 53% | 56% | 46% | 44% | 63% | 57% |
| Incidents reported to police weighted to population | 5,989 (64.9%) | 2,295 (73.0%) | 2,091 (54.6%) | 6,157 (60.8%) | 1,430 (43.4%) | 4,182 (80.0%) | 2,793 (67.9%) | 3,392 (54.6%) | 2,650 (52.4%) | 2,744 (65.3%) | 2,438 (74.0%) | 6,160 (66.1%) | 4,914 (70.4%) | 47,235 (63.8%) |
| Robbery incidents per 1,000 establishments | 132 | 56 | 72 | 140 | 104 | 49 | 91 | 173 | 137 | 77 | 49 | 80 | 88 | 96.0 |
| Percent reported to police | 83% | 77% | 87% | 78% | 69% | 95% | 88% | 83% | 83% | 97% | 85% | 77% | 90% | 82% |
| Incidents reported to police weighted to population | 3,237 (35.1%) | 847 (27.0%) | 1,740 (45.4%) | 3,978 (39.2%) | 1,863 (56.6%) | 1,045 (20.0%) | 1,320 (32.1%) | 2,822 (45.4%) | 2,407 (47.6%) | 1,455 (34.7%) | 855 (26.0%) | 3,157 (33.9%) | 2,070 (29.6%) | 26,796 (36.2%) |
| Per capita ratio of commercial to personal robberies | 4.3 | 3.5 | 4.8 | 8.2 | 10.4 | 2.7 | 4.3 | 9.6 | 6.2 | 5.1 | 4.5 | 2.8 | 5.2 | 5.2 |
| Total number of incidents reported to police weighted to population | 9,226 | 9,142 | 3,831 | 10,135 | 3,293 | 5,227 | 4,113 | 6,214 | 5,057 | 4,199 | 3,293 | 9,317 | 6,984 | 74,031 |

APPENDIX 3   Variables, Values, and Descriptive Statistics for Analyses

| | Values | $\bar{x}$ | $s$ |
|---|---|---|---|
| *Independent Variables:* | | | |
| *Individual & Organizations* | | | |
| Type of victim | Individual = 0 | .50 | .50 |
| | Organization = 0 | | |
| Type of crime | Person = 0 | | |
| | Property = 1 | | |
| Seriousness of victimization | Sellin-Wolfgang scale | 3.36 | 2.47 |
| Return of property to victim | Property not returned = 0 | .37 | .48 |
| | Property returned = 1 | | |
| Victim responsibility | Denies responsibility = 0 | 1.26 | .44 |
| | Accepts responsibility = 1 | | |
| Victim testimony | Victim did not testify = 0 | .23 | .43 |
| | Victim testified | | |
| Victim-accused relationship | Intimacy scale | 6.45 | 4.25 |
| Repeat player | No = 0 | | |
| | Yes = 1 | | |
| Accused marital status | Divorced, separated, common law = 0 | 1.05 | .65 |
| | Single = 1 | | |
| | Married, widowed = 2 | | |
| Accused sex | Female = 0 | .88 | .33 |
| | Male = 1 | | |
| Accused condition at arrest | Sober = 0 | .23 | .42 |
| | Intoxicated = 1 | | |
| Accused employment status | Unemployed = 0 | .44 | .50 |
| | Employed = 1 | | |
| Accused demeanor | Good = 0 | .67 | .47 |
| | Bad or indifferent = 1 | | |
| Accused prior convictions | Actual number | 2.98 | 4.80 |
| Accused most serious prior disposition | None = 0 | 1.18 | 1.26 |
| | Fine = 1 | | |
| | Probation = 2 | | |
| | Prison = 3 | | |
| Number of charges | Actual number | .56 | 1.61 |
| Statement taken | No statement = 0 | .39 | .49 |
| | Statement taken = 1 | | |
| Warrant | No warrant = 0 | .14 | .35 |
| | Warrant executed = 1 | | |
| Mobilization | Other than by victim = 0 | .56 | .50 |
| | By victim = 1 | | |
| Complaint | Other than victim = 0 | .27 | .44 |
| | Victim = 1 | | |
| Perceived remorse of accused | Likert scale (high to low) | 2.90 | .75 |
| Characteristics attributed to accused | Summated semantic differential (positive to negative) | 42.53 | 7.93 |
| Reformation-victim ranking | Likert scale (high to low) | 1.56 | .91 |

(*continues*)

APPENDIX 3    *(Continued)*

| | Values | $\bar{x}$ | $s$ |
|---|---|---|---|
| General deterrence-victim ranking | Likert scale (high to low) | 1.92 | 1.03 |
| Individual deterrence-victim ranking | Likert scale (high to low) | 1.64 | .92 |
| Punishment-victim ranking | Likert scale (high to low) | 2.58 | 1.24 |
| Incapacitation-victim ranking | Likert scale (high to low) | 2.46 | 1.17 |
| Law and order attitudes | Summated Likert scale (high to low) | 11.70 | 2.96 |
| Citizen responsibility | Summated Likert scale (high to low) | 7.78 | 1.58 |
| Belief in free will | Likert scale (high to low) | 7.28 | 2.63 |
| Individual responsibility | Likert scale (high to low) | 5.58 | 3.83 |
| Knowledge of disposition | No = 0<br>Yes = 1 | .39 | .49 |
| Disposition | Withdrawn, dismissed or acquitted = 0<br>Absolute discharge = 1<br>Peace bond or fine = 2<br>Probation = 3<br>Prison = 4 | 2.39 | 1.46 |
| Trial | Victim did not attend = 0<br>Victim attended = 1 | .39 | .49 |
| *Independent Variables*<br>*Organizations Only* | | | |
| Type of organization | Retail = 0<br>Other = 1 | .42 | .49 |
| Organizational base | Private = 1<br>Public = 0 | 1.38 | .49 |
| Scale of organization | Local = 1<br>Regional = 2<br>Provincial = 3<br>Interprovincial = 4<br>National = 5<br>Multinational = 6 | 3.20 | 2.04 |
| Number of employees in division | Actual number | 99.76 | 342.85 |
| Number of organizational units | Actual number | 44.18 | 126.41 |
| Number of employees in organization | Actual number | 352,359.91 | 449,393.03 |
| Centralization of organization | Likert scale (decentralized to centralized) | 3.52 | 1.09 |
| Relationship between organization and clients | Likert scale (decentralized to centralized) | 3.90 | .87 |
| *Dependent Variables*<br>*Individuals & Organizations* | | | |
| Bail hearing | Not held for hearing = 0<br>Held for hearing = 1 | .21 | .40 |

*(continues)*

APPENDIX 3 *(Continued)*

| | Values | $\bar{x}$ | $s$ |
|---|---|---|---|
| Adjudication | Not guilty = 0 | .72 | .45 |
| | Guilty = 1 | | |
| Sentence | Absolute discharge = 1 | 2.96 | .83 |
| | Peace bond or fine = 2 | | |
| | Probation = 3 | | |
| | Prison = 4 | | |
| Perceived severity of disposition | Too severe = 1 | 2.45 | .52 |
| | About right = 2 | | |
| | Not severe enough = 3 | | |
| Satisfaction with outcome | Very satisfied = 1 | 2.69 | 1.52 |
| | Satisfied = 2 | | |
| | Neutral = 3 | | |
| | Dissatisfied = 4 | | |
| | Very Dissatisfied = 5 | | |

## REFERENCES

Balbus, Issac. 1977. "Commodity form and legal form: an essay on the 'relative autonomy' of the law." *Law and Society Review* 11: 571–588.

Beccaria, Cesare. 1963. *On Crimes and Punishments* (translated by Henry Paolucci). Indianapolis: Bobbs-Merrill.

Bentham, Jeremy. 1970. *An Introduction to the Principles of Morals and Legislation,* edited by J. H. Burns and H. L. A. Hart. University of London: Athlone Press.

Cameron, Mary O. 1965. *The Booster and the Snitch.* New York: Free Press.

Chambliss, William, and Robert Seidman. 1971. *Law, Order and Power.* Reading: Addison-Wesley.

Coleman, James. 1974. *Power and the Structure of Society.* New York: Norton.

Ermann, M. David, and Richard J. Lundman. 1960. *Corporate Deviance: Toward a Sociology of Deviance, Social Problems and Crime.* New York: Holt, Rinehart and Winston.

Galanter, Marc. 1974. "Why the haves come out ahead." *Law and Society Review* 9: 95–160.

Gower, L. C. B. 1969. *The Principles of Modern Company Law.* London: Stevens.

Hagan, John. 1975. "Law, order, and sentencing: a study of attitude in action." *Sociometry* 38: 374–384.

———. 1980. A Study of Victim Involvement in the Criminal Justice System. Final Report to the Solicitor General of Canada.

Hagan, John, and Kristen Bumiller. 1982. "Making sense of sentencing: a review and critique of sentencing research." In *Research on Sentencing,* edited by Alfred Blumstein. Washington: National Academy of Sciences.

Hagan, John, J. Hewitt, and D. Alwin. 1979. "Ceremonial justice: crime and punishment in a loosely coupled system." *Social Forces* 58: 506–527.

Hagan, John, Ilene Nagel, and Celesta Albonetti. 1980. "The differential sentencing of white collar offenders in ten federal district courts." *American Sociological Review* 45: 802–820.

Halevy, Eli. 1960. *The Growth of Philosophic Radicalism* (translated by Mary Morris). Boston: Beacon Press.

Hibbert, Christopher. 1963. *The Roots of Evil: A Social History of Crime and Punishment.* Boston: Little, Brown.

Hindelang, Michael. 1974. "Decisions of shoplifting victims to invoke the criminal justice process." *Social Problems* 21: 580–593.

Jeffrey, Clarence R. 1957. "The development of crime in early English society." *Journal of Criminal Law, Criminology and Police Science* 47: 647–666.

McDonald, William F. 1976. "Towards a bicentennial revolution in criminal justice: the return of the victim." *American Criminal Law Review* 13: 649–673.

Maine, (Sir) Henry James Summer. 1960. *Ancient Law*. London: Dent.

Morden, Peter. 1980. A Multivariate Analysis of Bail Decisions Involving the Police. Unpublished Masters Thesis, University of Toronto.

Nagel, Ilene. 1980. "The behavior of formal law: a study of bail decisions." Unpublished manuscript.

Quinney, Richard. 1970. *The Social Reality of Crime*. Boston: Little, Brown.

Robin, Gerald D. 1967. "The corporate and judicial disposition of employee thieves." *Wisconsin Law Review* (Summer): 685–702.

Schaefer, Stephen. 1977. *Victimology: The Victim and His Criminal*. Reston, Virginia: Reston.

Schrager, Laura Shill, and James F. Short, Jr. 1978. "Toward a sociology of organizational crime." *Social Problems* 25: 407–419.

Sellin, Thorsten, and Marvin E. Wolfgang. 1964. *The Measurement of Delinquency*. New York: Wiley.

Smigel, Erwin O., and H. Laurence Ross (editors). 1970. *Crimes Against Bureaucracy*. New York: Van Nostrand Reinhold.

Thayer, James Bradley. 1898. *A Preliminary Treatise on Evidence at the Common Law*. Boston: Little, Brown.

Tigar, Michael, and Madeleine Levy. 1977. *Law and the Rise of Capitalism*. New York: Monthly Review Press.

Traill, H. D. 1899. *Social England*. Volume 1. New York: Putnam.

U. S. Department of Commerce. 1974. *The Costs of Crimes Against Business*. Washington: U. S. Government Printing Office.

U. S. Department of Justice. 1975. *Criminal Victimization in Thirteen American Cities*. Washington: U. S. Government Printing Office.

Weber, Max. 1969. *Max Weber on Law in Economy and Society* (translated by Max Rheinstein). Cambridge: Harvard University Press.

# 18

# THE ORGANIZATION
# AND IMPACT OF
# INSPECTOR DISCRETION
# IN A REGULATORY
# BUREAUCRACY*

JOHN LYNXWILER
NEAL SHOVER
DONALD A. CLELLAND

Since approximately 1900, regulatory bureaucracies in the United States have become an expanding, ubiquitous presence in modern economic life. The earliest agencies regulated economic and competitive practices. By the 1950s, these "old-style" regulatory agencies had been attacked by scholars and others for a variety of operational shortcomings (Bernstein, 1955). By the mid-1960s, the thesis that they were prone to "capture" by the industries they were established to regulate gained widespread currency.

In the late 1960s, especially at the federal level, legislators began to create a "new style" of regulatory agency (Lilly and Miller, 1977). In contrast to their predecessors, these agencies are charged with protecting the public welfare from the external costs of industrial activities (e.g., the Environmental Protection Agency). They are "new" in another sense as well. In creating them, legislators devised statutory provisions meant to minimize their potential for capture by industry. This legislative creativity is evident especially in newer provisions for regulatory inspection and enforcement (Bardach and Kagan, 1982). Whereas earlier forms of "economic" regulation emphasized a reactive, flexible inspection and enforcement

*This research was supported by grant 80-IJ-CX-0017 from the National Institute of Justice. Opinions are those of the authors, not the Department of Justice.

*This research was supported by grant 80-IJ-CX-0017 from the National Institute of Justice. Opinions are those of the authors, not the Department of Justice.

*The Social Organization of Law, Second Edition*      371

strategy, the newer emphasis on "social" regulation stresses a proactive, nondiscretionary stance.

In this chapter, we examine the exercise and impact of inspector discretion in one of the new-style regulatory agencies: the federal Office of Surface Mining Reclamation and Enforcement (OSM). Following a brief historical description of surface coal mining and its social and environmental consequences, we discuss the federal legislation enacted in response to the historical legacy of unregulated strip mining. Then we discuss the mandate given to the OSM and its inspection and enforcement program. Finally, we discuss the exercise of discretion at the field-level and some resulting benefits for larger mining corporations.

## BACKGROUND

The United States is underlain with enormous coal deposits, approximately 474.6 billion tons of which is recoverable (U.S. Department of Energy, 1982). U.S. coal has been mined commercially for more than a century. For many decades it was mined almost exclusively by underground methods. In 1920, approximately 98% of U.S. coal was produced in this manner. However, by the late 1950s and early 1960s, surface coal mining methods began to dominate U.S. production (President's Commission on Coal, 1980). By 1980, only 41% of U.S. coal production came from underground mines (U.S. Department of Energy, 1982).

The technical process of surface coal mining can be comprehended easily. When mining is followed by reclamation of the mined area,

> the coal is produced . . . from seams lying fairly close to the earth's surface. The earth and rock above the coal seam—the overburden—are removed and placed to one side; the exposed coal is broken up, loaded into trucks and hauled away. Bulldozers then grade the overburden to the desired shape, the surface is replanted with seeds or young trees, and the land is restored to productive use (National Coal Association, 1976: 11).

This idyllic description ignores the fact that the rapid ascendance of surface coal mining was not matched by advances in, and sound use of, reclamation practices.

Until 1977, the regulation of surface coal mining was left entirely to the states. Excepting a few states, the result was weak, occasionally corrupt, regulation. State laws, regulations, and regulatory agencies suffered from inadequate resources, weak statutes and regulations, and lax enforcement policies.

Deficiencies in state regulation permitted the proliferation of socially and environmentally harmful mining practices. Especially in Appalachia, homes and other property were ruined by mining operations. Streams and wells were polluted by sedimentation and acid water flowing from surface mining sites. On occasion mine operators endangered or destroyed entire communities (Erikson, 1976).

By the 1960s, a spate of published work by popular writers (e.g., Caudill, 1963) and governmental agencies (e.g., U.S. Department of the Interior, 1967) documented and called attention to the social and environmental dangers of surface coal mining. Already, nearly one million acres of land had been disturbed by surface coal mining (U.S. Department of the Interior, 1967).

In the Midwest and in Appalachia, indigenous citizen groups and landowners were becoming more vocal in their call for tough regulation of the surface coal mining industry (Schneider, 1971). When this grass-roots movement met with resistance at the state level, it pressed for federal legislation. After a decade of legislative debate and two presidential vetoes, a bill finally was passed in 1977.

## THE OFFICE OF SURFACE MINING

The Surface Mining Control and Reclamation Act of 1977 (Public Law 95–87; U.S.C. 1202 *et seq.*) created an Office of Surface Mining Reclamation and Enforcement in the Department of the Interior and empowered it to promulgate regulations for the conduct of surface coal mining in the United States. During an interim period (approximately 4 years), the OSM was to enforce these regulations while the states were given the opportunity to submit proposed laws and regulations at least as rigorous for OSM's approval. Those states establishing approved programs would acquire primary regulatory responsibility ("primacy") for surface coal mining within their borders. After the interim period, the OSM would continue to be the primary regulatory authority only in states that failed to submit or to receive approval of their own programs.

## METHODS

The data for this paper were collected during a 30-month study of the Office of Surface Mining Reclamation and Enforcement (Shover *et al.,* 1982). First, we conducted personal interviews with 43 OSM inspectors and former inspectors regarding field-level enforcement of mining regulations.[1] The majority of the interviews were tape-recorded and later transcribed for analysis. Generally, the inspector interviews fall into two categories. Nineteen interviews examined the agency's relationship with state programs, its early inspection and enforcement program, and the impact of the Reagan administration on inspection and enforcement. The remaining 24 interviews focused on the agency's penalty process, the inspecors' daily routines, and their attitudes on discretion, the coal industry, and the OSM's regulatory mandate. This paper relies heavily on the latter interviews.

Second, we used a mail questionnaire to collect comparable data for OSM's en-

[1]We interviewed 154 respondents in the course of the larger research project. OSM respondents ranged from field-level personnel to the highest ranking executives at headquarters. Exclusive of the agency itself, the personal interviews included Congressional staff members and former staff members, former White House personnel, representatives of environmental and other citizens groups, representatives of coal industry trade and lobbying organizations, employees and officers of numerous mining companies, and personnel in several state surface mining regulatory agencies. We also interviewed personnel in the Department of the Interior, including the Solicitor's Office whose attorneys represent the Office of Surface Mining.

tire inspector corps. It was mailed in July 1981 to all 158 OSM inspectors, and we received 126 replies (79.8%).

Finally, we collected and analyzed routine, periodic statistical reports on the agency's inspection and enforcement operations. Also, we selected a sample of 83 coal-mining firms and examined OSM's inspection and enforcement records for all enforcement actions taken against the companies during an 18-month period between 1978 and 1980. Data from the files were coded and analyzed to determine the major variables that affect enforcement activities, especially the magnitude of civil fines imposed on mining companies for regulatory violations.

## THE OSM'S INSPECTION
## AND ENFORCEMENT PROGRAM

Like legislation creating other new regulatory agencies, Public Law 95–87 reflects a concerted effort to eliminate agency discretion through a uniform policy of detailed, legalistic mandates (Shover *et al.,* 1982). Surpassing in stringency nearly all existing state laws, it requires mining corporations to meet 115 environmental performance standards during mining operations. Also, the act imposes rigid, detailed requirements on the OSM and its personnel, especially in the area of inspection and enforcement. It specifically requires that the OSM conduct unannounced, biannual inspections at every permitted coal mining operation in the United States. Further, OSM inspectors are mandated to write a notice of violation (NOV) for every regulatory infraction they observe during an inspection [P.L. 95–87, Sec. 521. (a)(1)]. It also requires them to issue a cessation order (CO: an order to cease all mining) when (1) they observe a violation which causes or creates a threat of significant environmental harm or imminent danger to the health or safety of the public [P.L. 95–87, sec. 521. (a)(2)], or (2) a mine operator fails to comply with an order to abate an earlier violation [P.L. 95–87, sec. 521. (a)(3)].

The act was not the only source of the OSM's drive to minimize regulatory discretion. Executives at the agency's initial headquarters held several values and beliefs which influenced the agency's inspection and enforcement program (Thomas, 1980). Certainly, one of the most strongly held values, not only within the OSM's headquarters but throughout the entire agency, was a desire to protect the environment. Many felt this was the underlying intent of the act. They were aware of the past abuses of surface mining and shared a belief in the ubiquity of environmentally harmful mining practices. Also, agency personnel generally agreed that a rigorous, uniformly applied inspection and enforcement program would deter such practices in the future. As one of the OSM's initial headquarters executives told us: "We were *reformers.*"

Further, the agency's executives and environmental supporters were convinced that many states' inability to regulate surface mining was due to lax enforcement practices (Save Our Cumberland Mountains, 1978). They believed that the coal industry, historically, had operated in a lawless fashion and had become adept at evading the law. Hence, there was a strong desire to "take the rule of law" to the coal fields. As a result, headquarters executives generally favored a "hard line" and advocated an aggressively stringent enforcement program.

One other factor contributed to the OSM's legalistic, nondiscretionary stance. From the beginning, OSM was to be the primary regulatory authority *only* until the states gained primacy. Hence, there was no need to plan for a prolonged system of cooperation with the regulated industry (Bardach and Kagan, 1982). Many respondents at various levels in the agency indicated that they were determined to "shape up" the industry and, at the same time, set an example for the states to follow. The impact of this decision was put succinctly by one regional manager, who told us:

> OSM literally had to lead the way, sort of show that this is what was going to be expected in the future when you [the states] get your turn. . . . And you couldn't very well demand that of them [the states] if you didn't demand it of yourself.

The OSM's interim regulations for the conduct of surface coal mining were issued in December, 1977 (42 *Federal Register* 44920–44957). Generally, they are detailed and rigid, intentionally written to minimize discretion by mining corporations and OSM personnel alike (Shover *et al.,* 1982).

The OSM's headquarters executives tried to employ an inspector corps with values and biases similar to their own. They identified a pool of potential inspectors through contacts with other federal agencies and former state regulatory managers. Another important source of names for this pool came from contacts with an informal network of attorneys and environmentalists who had been active in local and regional programs aimed at curbing mining abuses. Through these contacts, a chain of referrals was established which led to the hiring of the agency's initial inspector corps.

Interviewed inspectors recounted strong feelings of camaraderie and a sense of commitment among the first group of inspectors. Most of them previously had worked for state regulatory programs and had experienced varying degrees of frustration in their jobs. They saw their OSM employment as an opportunity to establish a regulatory program that would be taken seriously by the industry—something that many of them believed had not been true of the state programs in which they had labored. They shared the strong pro-environmental protection philosophy that produced the act and served as a pervasive influence in the promulgation of the regulations.

Throughout the OSM's first 3 years of operation, their determination to promote better reclamation and environmental protection for future generations remained strong. It was an important component of their socialization. Because subsequent groups of inspectors were trained and supervised by this initial group, these beliefs became an enduring part of the agency's inspection and enforcement program.

By May 1978, when the agency first began inspecting mine sites, a combination of circumstances had produced an agency and personnel with a clear, perceived mission to protect the environment by rigorous, nondiscretionary rule enforcement.

## INSPECTORS AND THEIR WORK

### A PROFILE OF OSM INSPECTORS

Based on our questionnaire data, the average OSM inspector was about 32 years old at the time of his employment.[2] Eighty-seven percent came from rural or small town backgrounds ($n = 109$), and 80% grew up in households whose heads did not work in the coal industry ($n = 100$). Still, 63% had some experience in the regulation of coal mining before joining the OSM ($n = 79$).

Seventy-five percent of the inspectors held bachelors degrees ($n = 94$), primarily in environmental management ($n = 47$) and plant and animal sciences ($n = 31$). Generally, these areas emphasize a conservationist or environmental protection perspective. As a group, the inspectors espoused a strong environmental protection approach. Given their undergraduate education, this is hardly surprising.

Before assignment to one of the agency's five regions, inspectors attended a formal OSM training school. This training lasted two weeks and focused primarily on familiarizing inspectors with the agency's mechanics (e.g., filling out inspection forms). In addition, our questionnaire data show that inspectors averaged 4 months of on-the-job training before they were certified to conduct inspections. Throughout this period, new inspectors accompanied and observed their co-workers during mine inspections. Once certified, inspectors normally were assigned to specific areas within their region. In general, 8 to 15 inspectors were assigned to each OSM office. The small number of inspectors facilitated direct supervision.

### INSPECTOR SUPERVISION

Consistent with the act's mandates for uniform inspection and automatic citation of all violations, OSM supervisors employed formal and informal control mechanisms to minimize inspector discretion. To avoid undue familiarity with specific coal operators and mines, supervisors rotated these areas among inspectors. Also, supervisors regularly examined inspectors' files, photographs, and reports for discrepancies. Periodically, supervisors followed up by conducting their own inspections of the mine sites.

Many offices posted statistics on enforcement activities for their inspectors as well as those of the other regions. Though no formal policies were associated with these statistics, often they operated as an informal means of self-evaluation. A number of interviewed inspectors expressed a need to meet or exceed the quotas. They viewed the quotas as the "agency's" rates. Clearly, the inspectors were aware

[2]Because the OSM inspectors are almost entirely white men, we omitted questions on sex and race.

of the agency's stringent enforcement preferences. As one regional manager told us: "They [the inspectors] were told, 'goddamn, you're a cop. Get your ass out there and enforce the law.'"

## INSPECTING A MINING OPERATION

Ignoring interoffice variation, our interview data and analysis of agency statistics permit a general overview of inspectors' daily routines. Inspectors averaged between three and five inspections per week, depending upon the distance between inspection sites and the size of the mining operation. Each inspection normally required one to two hours of preparation. The preparation time was spent reviewing an operation's mining plans. Analysis of the agency's weekly inspection statistics from July 1, 1978, to June 30, 1982, show that its inspectors averaged 1.54 NOVs per 10 inspections (Office of Surface Mining, 1978–1982).

Inspectors generally followed a routine during an inspection. Arriving unannounced at the mine site, they first reviewed the operation's log books and mining records. Following this, inspectors "walked" the mine site, usually with someone from the company. Inspectors took notes and photographs for use later in documenting the inspection.

After walking the site and noting violations, the inspector met with the company's representative to review any enforcement actions. Violations and abatement requirements were discussed, and a copy of each NOV was given to the company. The inspector then set a deadline for correcting the violation. At the end of this period, the inspector conducted a follow-up visit to determine if the company had corrected the violation. The inspector terminated the NOV if the violation was abated properly within the set time period. However, the assessed fine was not affected by this action. If the company failed to meet the time deadline, the inspector (1) extended the deadline; (2) issued an additional NOV; or (3) issued a CO if corrective measures were not forthcoming.

Inspectors devoted one to two days of each week to filing reports for completed inspections. The reports documented the technical aspects of the violation. Additionally, they provided information on the violation's actual or potential damage to the surrounding area and the degree of corporate responsibility for its occurrence. These documents were sent to the Washington Assessment Office and provided the basis for determining the amount of civil penalty assessed for each NOV.

## DOCUMENTING INSPECTOR DISCRETION

### THE NATURE OF INSPECTOR DISCRETION

Research on regulatory inspectors indicates that discretion, regardless of the agency's enforcement provisions, is not only a common but a critical job element for "street level bureaucrats" (Lipsky, 1980). Faced with the task of applying general rules to situational cases, field-level enforcement agents routinize their work by employing "gaming strategies" to induce compliance from their clientele (Hawkins, 1983; Mileski, 1971; Schuck, 1972). In surface mining enforcement, these discretionary practices are visible at three stages of the inspection process.

The first occurs when an inspector decides whether to issue a NOV for an observed violation. All inspectors insisted that serious violations never were ignored. However, five respondents acknowledged that on occasion they ignored minor violations (e.g., missing entries in log books, fallen perimeter markers). Moreover, a majority of inspectors stated that if the violation could be corrected before the inspection was completed, a NOV usually was not issued.

This tactic was a common gaming strategy among OSM inspectors. For example, inspectors said that they often pointed out a minor violation to the company's representative indicating that it would result in a fine if processed. Then, the inspector tacitly offered to overlook the violation if the company corrected it immediately. Several inspectors told us that this tactic also enabled them to extract company promises to abate quickly more serious violations. The five respondents who admitted to ignoring minor violations indicated that this latter "trade-off" rationale was their motive for overlooking minor violations (Hawkins, 1983).

Second, the outcome of inspectors' discretion was apparent when they set the time period for abating violations. All of the interviewed inspectors told us that this could be used to punish or reward companies. When operators were perceived as cooperative toward rule compliance, inspectors normally gave them a longer abatement deadline for correcting the violation. Often, inspectors "punished" uncooperative companies with short deadlines.

This strategy was effective, especially when companies failed to meet the abatement deadline. In this instance, the inspector generally extended the deadline for more cooperative companies. Companies considered to be recalcitrant offenders were sometimes issued an additional NOV (or even a CO). In fact, inspectors found this strategy particularly useful in extracting a more cooperative stance from mine operators who were hostile to the OSM's regulations.

The final outcropping of inspectors' discretion is visible in their documentation of violations. Inspectors confidently asserted that they could influence the size of the fine by the wording of their reports. This finding is supported by our questionnaire data. Seventy-two percent of the respondents felt that the wording of inspector reports influenced the amount of penalty assessed for a violation.

When asked how their reports influenced fines, inspectors suggested that the OSM assessors were responsive to certain words or phrases. By invoking such linguistic devices, without adjusting the "facts" or technical aspects of the violation, inspectors employed their discretionary powers within the regulatory structure. Thus, not only were inspectors aware of their reports' impact on the determination of fines; but also they were cognizant of *how* to effect this impact!

> *Environmental harm* is one word that will really send the fine sky-rocketing. If you've got environmental harm, you put that in the report, that'll really send it up there. Another thing is *lack of reasonable care*—which is negligence—and that's another thing that'll send the points up there.

Although the "new style" regulatory agencies emphasize a proactive, nondiscretionary stance, our analysis of the OSM points out the problems apparent in such policies (Thomas, 1980). The OSM's literal application of the act's stringent mandates represents an attempt to restrict field-level discretion. Nonetheless, inspectors regularly employ discretion at several stages in the inspection process. But what is the impact of inspector discretion for the regulated?

## THE IMPACT OF INSPECTOR DISCRETION

In examining our sample of civil penalties imposed by the OSM, we found that smaller mining companies paid higher fines than larger corporations (Shover *et al.,* 1982).[3] Even when other influencing variables were controlled, company size was related inversely to the size of the fine ($r = -.16$). Stated differently, our analysis reflects a differential advantage for the more powerful sectors of the industry.[4]

This modest inverse relationship between company size and the magnitude of the fine suggests the presence of informal mechanisms of corporate influence on agency decisionmaking. Because the OSM's penalty assessment process is based on inspector reports, the fines elicited by the reports reflect systematic inspector perspectives toward offending corporations. We hypothesize that the social organization of agency-client encounters is structured by increased corporate complexity—a function of the power differentials rooted in corporate size (Long, 1979). Our data show that larger mining companies benefit from the fact that inspector-client confrontations are a match between salaried technicians in which large, but not small, industry has the upper hand. How does this process work?

## INFLUENCES ON INSPECTOR DISCRETION

Research on the police (Muir, 1977; Sacks, 1972; Sykes and Clark, 1975) and regulatory inspectors (Hawkins, 1983; Kagan and Scholz, 1984) indicates that enforcement personnel develop and employ typifications of their clientele to organize their work (Lipsky, 1980; Manning, 1977; Piliavin and Briar, 1964; Scheff, 1966). In fact, the invocation of discretionary strategies is largely a function of the stereotypic conceptions that enforcement agents develop about their clientele (Gregorio, 1978; Lipsky, 1980; Nivola, 1978).

Our analysis supports this finding. When we asked 24 inspectors to distinguish

[3]From all mining corporations that received at least one NOV from October 1978 through March 1980, we drew a purposive sample of 83 mining companies. The sample was drawn to ensure approximately equal numbers of NOVs for small, mid-, and large-size coal mining companies. The 83 firms received a total of 735 NOVs during the 18 months. Using records maintained by the OSM's Assessment Office, we coded variables related to the nature of the violation, the magnitude of the assessed fine, and the company's response to the assessed penalty. We focused on the relationship between the size of the offending corporation and the amount of the assessed fine (Shover *et al.,* 1982).

[4]Research by Clinard *et al.* (1979: 142) supports this position.

"types of operators," 22 did so on the basis of company size. For example, one inspector told us:

> There's basically your *large companies* that are often cold to you, but you know they're going to do what you tell them. And you also know they're going to contest every violation you write them. . . . Whether they have a dog's chance or not, they'll still try. And then you've got your *small operators* that are real nice to you and bend over backwards. And as far as their image goes, they'll promise you the moon and never do anything. These are the worst of all.

As this suggests, OSM inspectors employed two perceptual distinctions between mining companies of different sizes. First, they claimed that large companies were more likely to contest violations, especially in formal, extra-agency hearings. And second, they believed that large companies were more responsive than smaller companies (hence, cooperative) with regulatory demands.

## CORPORATE RESPONSIVENESS

Like the police, inspectors expect responsiveness from their clients. Generally, OSM inspectors believed that responsiveness in abating violations and company size were related. There are structural bases for this belief. Unlike small companies, larger ones usually possess the personnel, capital, and knowledge to abate violations in a timely fashion. Also, inspectors viewed large companies as more concerned with their corporate reputation than small companies.[5] And, finally, inspectors believed that large companies were more likely than small ones to view regulatory intervention and monetary penalties simply as "part of the cost of doing business" (Clinard and Yeager, 1980: 124). As one inspector commented:

> The larger companies are aware that this is their business. They're real business oriented type people to be in this, it's a complex industry and they would like to—from what I've observed they would like to—comply. Well, I wouldn't say they would like to comply, but they don't want any violations or notices issued. And then in order to do that they need to comply to reclamations. And the small operators—a lot of them try; but they don't have the technical background or resources to know exactly what to do. . . . Larger companies will have engineering staff that they hire to look specifically at, you know, violations that's been issued and how to go about correcting them as fast as possible. The smaller operations have consulting engineers that they contract, you know, to do their engineering work. And they're not there all the time and have trouble getting them. It seems to be a problem.

Responsiveness is important to inspectors since the primary goals of any regulatory agency are rule compliance and deterrence. Companies that respond quickly to correct regulatory infractions make the inspectors' job less time consuming, and therefore easier to manage (Nivola, 1978). In sum, larger companies are perceived as being responsive to the agency's operative definitions of regulations in

---

[5]Research on this issue suggests that corporate concern over a "reasonable" versus a "tarnished" reputation, in fact, may be a primary factor in deterring corporate crime (Braithwaite and Geis, 1982; Fisse, 1971).

the field. And this responsiveness is considered indicative of a willingness to operate in a responsible, cooperative, and rational manner. As one respondent told us,

> Generally you get better work out of some of the bigger companies. I'm able to talk to them. They've got people that, they're information people, they've got their own engineers. You run into a problem, you write them up, and maybe they want me to meet their engineer or whoever and, you know, work the problem out in a rational manner. And not like some situations with maybe a small operator and you know you're the straw that broke the camel's back so to speak, and he's frothing at the mouth.

Due to their size, larger companies more often than smaller ones employ resident environmental specialists to monitor developments in the regulatory matrix, to stay abreast of advances and alternatives in reclamation practices, and to plan for reclamation in a legal, cost-effective manner.[6] Like the OSM's inspectors, these specialized personnel are fellow salaried technicians. Generally, they are well educated and tend to accept the principle, if not the specifics, of regulation. Also, their detailed and long-range understanding of mining and reclamation plans on particular mine sites gives them an advantage during negotiations with inspectors.

Research has highlighted the informal, negotiated nature of the criminal justice process (McCleary, 1975; Sudnow, 1965). Though structured by formal rules, such negotiations rely heavily on typifications that define the offender as a particular type of person to whom a specific identity and set of motives can be attached.[7] Thus, "the decision to invoke legal sanction is a process of determining the extent to which the individuals involved conform to the criminal stereotype" (Swigert and Farrell, 1977: 17). In this way, court officials selectively filter the legal and extralegal aspects of a case to negotiate a consensual, stereotyped perception of defendants and their actions. More recently, Maynard (1982) examined the process by which legal (offense-related) and extralegal (offender-related) factors are contextualized selectively in the plea-bargaining interactions of attorneys.

A similar process occurs during encounters between OSM inspectors and mine representatives. The OSM inspectors operate with the assumption that they are the reclamation experts whose task it is to insure compliance with the regulatory statutes. This assumption is challenged by reclamation specialists of large mining companies whose knowledge often rivals the inspector's. Consequently, inspectors are more likely to treat them as equals when negotiating a common definition of violations.

Thus, within an encounter over infractions of the regulations, the reclamation specialists of large companies are able to "neutralize" the violation by "legitimating" the company's violative behavior within a larger context. They can demonstrate how deviations at one point in the mining operation nonetheless are consistent with the spirit of the act—protection of the environment. Because their

---

[6]Mayhew and Reiss (1969) found that property and income are institutionalized necessities which influence an individual's contact with and use of attorneys. Similarly, company size is an institutionalized necessity which influences the company's contact with and use of specialized personnel.

[7]Research by McCleary (1975) shows how structural contexts constrain negotiations between parole officers and their clients.

knowledge of the operation's relationship to current mining technology and the regulatory statutes often rivals the inspector's knowledge, reclamation specialists, on occasion, can erode the inspector's position as "the" reclamation expert. In turn, this aspect of the inspector-specialist encounter influences the inspector's perception of the violation.

## CORPORATE INTIMIDATION

Large mining companies often challenge violations formally in agency conferences and in extra-agency forums such as the Office of Hearings and Appeals. The possibility of such challenges operates as an additional constraint. As one inspector commented:

> Usually, the larger operators aren't violent toward you or hostile; you don't fear from them. But, they'll take you to court and fight everything you do.

Apprehensive lest their actions be subjected to a formal, extra-agency hearing, inspectors are more careful, and perhaps more lenient, throughout the inspection process. For example, words or phrases used in documenting inspection reports are selected not so much for the assessors' use in determining fines but for the possibility of legal challenge before an administrative law judge. Thus, the threat of legal challenges outside the agency affects the tone of the inspector's reports.

In sum, large mining companies and their specialized personnel, while less challenging to inspectors than some smaller firms, are threatening nonetheless. Often they appear to be more knowledgeable about the regulations than the inspectors themselves. This imbalance of knowledge, together with the threat of legal challenge and the greater responsiveness (hence, civility) of larger companies, makes for a degree of trust and deference which finds expression in the inspectors' use of discretion. Completing the process of differential corporate influence, assessors, relying on inspectors' reports, judge the violations of larger companies to be less damaging to the environment, and the companies themselves as less negligent than smaller companies.

## CONCLUSIONS

The lessons here, while commonplace, are important nonetheless. First, when regulatory personnel perceive clients to be responsive to regulatory demands, their enforcement responses are more likely to demonstrate forebearance. The net result is leniency. Conversely, clients deemed unresponsive beget less forebearance on the assumption that only by such action can future problems of a similar nature be deterred (Reiss, 1971). The result is increased stringency. Second, regulatory encounters in which enforcement agents feel less knowledgeable than, and occasionally threatened by, the other party contain the potential for deferential treatment. Again, the result is leniency.

At least for the time period reported in this study, OSM promulgated and enforced regulations meticulously grounded in its enabling legislation. Nevertheless, the organization of the agency's penalty process and our data suggest that influences on inspector discretion, especially in the documentation of NOVs, was a major source of differential fines. Due to increased organizational complexity, large mining corporations possessed the resources of capital, personnel, and knowledge necessary to take responsive abatement measures. The scale of their operations necessitated the inclusion of engineers, reclamation specialists, and attorneys as full-time staff personnel, rather than contracted help on a case-by-case basis. Also, they had greater recourse to procedures for formal, legal challenge. Together these factors structured the context of inspector-client encounters. Because increased size and complexity lead to the need for and use of specialized personnel, these determinative factors may be thought of as "institutionalized necessities" (Mayhew and Reiss, 1969). So, just as the institutionalized necessities of large mining corporations promote competitive advantages over smaller firms, they provide benefits in the regulatory arena as well.

This study has documented the impact of organizational variables and processes on the exercise and impact of inspector discretion. Inasmuch as regulatory statutes are targeted for specific groups, analysis of regulatory agencies is a suitable area to assess the impact of organizational variables on sentencing and deterrence (Lempert, 1982). Such analyses would be especially interesting in light of the accepted view that corporate misconduct is deterrable (Braithwaite and Geis, 1982).

Future research is needed in two distinct but interrelated directions. First, the relationship between existing power differentials and the institutionalized necessities of regulated firms needs to be analyzed. The organization and impact of institutionalized necessities may be important determinative variables in the assessment of penalties for sanctionable activities. Second, ethnographic researchers should isolate contextual features of agency-client encounters that influence the informal mechanisms of regulatory discretion.

## REFERENCES

Bardach, Eugene, and Robert Kagan. 1982. *Going by the Book*. Philadelphia: Temple University Press.

Bernstein, Marver H. 1955. *Regulating Business by Independent Commission*. Princeton: Princeton University Press.

Braithwaite, John, and Gilbert Geis. 1982. "On theory and action for corporate crime control." *Crime and Delinquency* 28: 292–314.

Caudill, Harry M. 1963. *Night Comes to the Cumberlands*. Boston: Little, Brown.

Clinard, Marshall B., and Peter Yeager. 1980. *Corporate Crime*. New York: Free Press.

Clinard, Marshall, Peter Yeager, J. Brissette, D. Petrashek, and E. Harries. 1979. *Illegal Corporate Behavior*. Washington: National Institute of Justice.

Erikson, Kai T. 1976. *Everything in Its Path*. New York: Simon and Schuster.

Fisse, W. Brent. 1971. "The use of publicity as a criminal sanction against business corporations." *Melbourne University Law Review* 8: 107–150.

Gregorio, David J. 1978. "Enforcement is the name of the game: an essay on the immigration inspector at work." *Sociological Focus* 11: 235–246.

Hawkins, Keith. 1983. "Bargain and bluff: compliance strategy and deterrence in the enforcement of regulation." *Law and Policy Quarterly* 5: 35–73.

Kagan, Robert A., and John T. Scholz. 1984. "The 'criminology of the corporation' and regulatory enforcement strategies." In *Enforcing Regulation: Policy and Practice,* edited by Keith Hawkins and John M. Thomas. Boston: Kluwer-Nijhoff.

Lempert, Richard. 1982. "Organizing for deterrence: lessons from a study of child support." *Law and Society Review* 16: 513–568.

Lilly, W., and J. C. Miller. 1977. "The new 'social regulation'." *The Public Interest* 47: 49–61.

Lipsky, Michael. 1980. *Street-Level Bureaucracy.* New York: Russell Sage.

Long, Susan B. 1979. "The Internal Revenue Service: examining the exercise of discretion in tax enforcement." Paper presented to the Law and Society Association, San Francisco.

McCleary, Richard. 1975. "How structural variables constrain the parole officer's use of discretion." *Social Problems* 23: 209–220.

Manning, Peter K. 1977. *Police Work.* Cambridge: MIT Press.

Mayhew, Leon, and Albert J. Reiss, Jr. 1969. "The social organization of legal contacts." *American Sociological Review* 34: 309–317.

Maynard, Douglas W. 1982. "Defendant attributes in plea bargaining: notes on the modeling of sentencing decisions." *Social Problems* 29: 347–360.

Mileski, Maureen. 1971. Policing Slum Landlords: An Observation Study of Administrative Control. Unpublished Doctoral Dissertation, Yale University.

Muir, William K., Jr. 1977. *Police: Streetcorner Politicians.* Chicago: University of Chicago Press.

National Coal Association. 1976. *Coal Facts.* Washington: National Coal Association.

Nivola, Pietro S. 1978. "Distributing a municipal service: a case study of housing inspection." *Journal of Politics* 40: 59–81.

Office of Surface Mining. 1978–1982. Inspection Activity Reports. Washington: Division of Inspection and Enforcement.

Piliavin, Irving, and Scott Briar. 1964. "Police encounters with juveniles." *American Journal of Sociology* 70: 206–214.

President's Commission on Coal. 1980. *Coal Data Book.* Washington: U.S. Government Printing Office.

Reiss, Albert J., Jr. 1971. *The Police and the Public.* New Haven: Yale University Press.

Sacks, Harvey. 1972. "Notes on police assessment of moral character." In *Studies in Social Interaction,* edited by David Sudnow. New York: Free Press.

Save Our Cumberland Mountains. 1978. *A Study of Tennessee Strip Mining Enforcement, 1972–1977.* Knoxville: East Tennessee Research Corporation.

Scheff, Thomas J. 1966. "Typification in the diagnostic practices of rehabilitation agencies." In *Sociology and Rehabilitation,* edited by Marvin B. Sussman. Washington: American Sociological Association.

Schneider, David A. 1971. "Strip mining in Kentucky." *Kentucky Law Journal* 59: 652–672.

Schuck, Peter. 1972. "The curious case of the indicted meat inspectors." *Harpers Magazine* 245: 81–92.

Shover, Neal, Donald A. Clelland, and John Lynxwiler. 1982. Constructing a Regulatory Bureaucracy. Research report submitted to the National Institute of Justice.

Sudnow, David. 1965. "Normal crimes: sociological features of the penal code in a public defender's office." *Social Problems* 12: 255–270.

Swigert, Victoria L., and Ronald A. Farrell. 1977. "Normal homicides and the law." *American Sociological Review* 42: 16–32.

Sykes, Richard E., and John P. Clark. 1975. "A theory of deference exchange in police-civilian encounters." *American Journal of Sociology* 81: 584–600.

Thomas, John M. 1980. "The regulatory role in the containment of corporate illegality." In *Develop-*

*ment of a Research Agenda on White-Collar Crime,* edited by Herbert Edelhertz. Seattle: Battelle Human Affairs Research Centers.

U.S. Department of Energy. 1982. 1981 Annual Report to Congress. Volume 2: Energy Statistics. Washington: Energy Information Administration.

U.S. Department of the Interior. 1967. *Surface Mining and Our Environment.* Washington: U.S. Government Printing Office.

# LAW AND OTHER SOCIAL CONTROL

# 19

# PRIOR OFFENSE RECORD AS A SELF-FULFILLING PROPHECY

RONALD A. FARRELL
VICTORIA LYNN SWIGERT

The use of official records of arrest and conviction as indices of criminality has long been a controversial issue in sociology. Many studies utilizing such documents have shown that lower-class persons are overrepresented in criminal populations (Shaw, 1929; Shaw and McKay, 1931; Caldwell, 1931; Glueck and Glueck, 1934). Based on these findings, a theoretical tradition has developed that explains crime and delinquency in terms of the characteristics of lower class life (Merton, 1938; Shaw and McKay, 1942; Kobrin, 1951; Cohen, 1955; Miller, 1958; Cloward and Ohlin, 1960). Differentials in legitimate and illegitimate opportunities, institutional disorganization, the conflict of cultural values, and the predominance of norms conducive to criminal behavior have all been offered as explanations of official rates of criminality among the poor.

At the same time, however, it has been argued that law enforcement agencies exercise selective bias against lower class and minority populations (Robison, 1936; Warner and Lunt, 1941; Useem *et al.,* 1942; Sutherland, 1949; Stinchcombe, 1963; Goldman, 1963; Cameron, 1964; Chambliss and Liell, 1966; *UCLA Law Review* Editors, 1966: 686; Skolnick, 1966; Chevigny, 1969; Black, 1970). Saturated patrol of slums and lower class neighborhoods, detention of suspicious persons, and harassment of deviant and delinquent groups are illustrative. The self-fulfilling effects of these practices appear in the form of inflated arrest rates and criminal records among the black and the poor (Robison, 1936: 228; Swett, 1969: 93). In this view, official statistics become indicators of official processing decisions rather than of actual criminality.

Evidence generated by self-report and victimization surveys lends support to this argument (Nye et al., 1958; Akers, 1964; Empey and Erickson, 1966; Gold, 1966; Ennis, 1967; Blankenburg, 1976). These studies suggest that crime levels are several times greater than the officially recorded rates, and that there may in fact be no significant relationship between criminal behavior and socioeconomic status. Statistical differences in criminal involvement, therefore, may only reflect variations in the reporting of offenses and differential law enforcement practices.

In spite of the questionable validity of official data, explorations of differential justice continue to treat arrest and conviction records as indicators of prior criminality. Such studies conclude that apparent relationships between class, race, and legal treatment are explained by the more extensive criminal histories accumulated by lower class and minority groups, and not by overt discrimination (Green, 1961; 1964; D'Esposito, 1969; Willick et al., 1975; Burke and Turk, 1975).

Such a conclusion overlooks the fact that the explanatory variable—criminal history—may itself be a product of differential justice. For "although a disproportionately large number of . . . lower [status] offenders have a . . . record, there is at least the possibility that the legal treatment initially given these offenders was influenced by their social status" (Farrell, 1971: 57).

An understanding of prior record and its role in the legal process requires an exploration of the factors that lead to a determination of guilt. Unfortunately, research on differential legal treatment has focused almost exclusively on sentencing (for a review and discussion of the literature, see Swigert and Farrell, 1976: 15–17; Greenberg, 1977). An exception, however, is the work of Chiricos, Jackson, and Waldo (1972), who have studied adjudication itself, thereby making the construction of what will become a "prior record" a dependent variable. Their analysis indicates that where judges have the option of not entering a felony conviction on a defendant's record, persons who have a prior record, as well as those who are older, black, poorly educated, and defended by appointed counsel, are more likely to be denied this privilege. Thus, in addition to the social characteristics of defendants, prior contact with the law itself affected subsequent elaboration of a criminal record.

These findings have important implications. Since present adjudications influenced by status criteria become part of criminal histories, it may be inferred that prior record is itself a product of the differential dispensation of justice. It would appear, furthermore, that the official designation of individuals as career offenders may influence subsequent decisions of law enforcement agents. Once criminality becomes the dominant prophecy, a sequence of events may be set into motion that serves to preclude outcomes inconsistent with the original presumption of guilt. Guided by the theoretical tradition of W. I. Thomas (1923) and Robert K. Merton (1957: 421–436), we would suggest that prior offense records, as public definitions (prophecies or predictions), become an integral part of the situation and affect subsequent developments, regardless of the factual basis upon which these definitions are built.

The focus of the present work is an examination of the antecedents of criminal adjudication. Using the convictions of defendants as the dependent variable, an effort will be made to specify the process by which prior records are constructed.

## THE SAMPLE

The data utilized for this research were part of a larger study of the differential legal treatment of homicide defendants. Cases were drawn from the files of a diagnostic and evaluation clinic attached to the court, and from the indictment records maintained by the Office of the Clerk of Courts in a large urban jurisdiction in the northeastern United States. Four hundred and forty-four defendants were selected for analysis, a 50% random sample of all persons arrested on general charges of murder from 1955 through 1973.

As an offense type, criminal homicide provides a valuable opportunity for the study of legal treatment. Homicide defendants are more representative of persons who commit homicide than are defendants accused of any other crime of persons who commit that crime. The visibility of the offense and the high clearance rate of deaths due to homicide suggest that individuals charged with murder exemplify persons who actually commit murder; other offenses display a much greater disparity between crimes known to the police and arrests recorded.[1]

The seriousness of the offense is also controlled by the use of a single offense type. This is particularly true in the jurisdiction in which this study was conducted, where defendants are arrested on general charges of murder and indicted for both murder and voluntary manslaughter. The degree of the offense, along with guilt or innocence, is determined at the trial.

The court clinic from which the records were obtained is charged with the evaluation of all persons arrested for homicide. Within 72 hours of the alleged offense extensive psychiatric and social histories are compiled for each defendant. If the accused is subsequently adjudged insane, proceedings are initiated for his commitment to a mental hospital. Otherwise, the clinic report is summarized and forwarded to the presiding judge for use in presentence investigation. If the defendant is found not guilty, or if the case is dismissed, the sealed evaluation is returned to the clinic unopened.

The clinic files included information from a number of diverse sources. FBI and police reports; military, occupational, and educational records; medical histories; social service investigations; and psychiatric evaluations were available for all defendants.

---

[1]Of all homicides known to the police, 82% are eventually cleared by arrest. Clearance rates for other crimes are much lower: forcible rape—57%, aggravated assault—66%, robbery—30%, burglary—19%, larceny—20%, auto theft—17% (see Quinne, 1975:19).

Information regarding the legal aspects of the case was obtained from the Office of the Clerk of Courts, and included the type of legal representation, results of bail hearings, plea, and conviction.[2]

## METHODS

Previous research concerning the effects of prior record on legal treatment has traditionally noted the presence or absence of a criminal record (Farrell, 1971; Burke and Turk, 1975) or the number of crimes of which the defendant was found guilty (Bullock, 1961; Green, 1964; Chiricos *et al.*, 1972). Given the reported significance of the variable, a more sensitive index seemed desirable. In the present study it has been operationalized as the sum of the maximum penalties prescribed for each prior conviction. The selection of this measure was guided by a number of considerations. The legislatively determined maximum sentence constitutes the most objective determination of the severity of an offense. Robbery is more serious than bookmaking because the state authorizes a maximum penalty of 20 years for the former and 5 years for the latter. Records of previous arrests or time actually served introduce subjective considerations. Arrest records are affected by administrative practices such as stacking (the filing of multiple charges in preparation for bargained settlements). Sentence actually served, on the other hand, is a product of the bargaining skills of defense, the capacity of the system to absorb new prisoners, and the presentence evaluation of the defendant's characteristics and circumstances. To be sure, conviction is also a product of the nature of the original arrest and agreements between prosecution and defense. Yet in all succeeding adjudications, the official determination of guilt of a particular offense stands as a decontextualized indicator of prior criminality. The seriousness of a record measured in this fashion describes the crime itself, as legislatively quantified, and not the special circumstances affecting time served. The second degree murderer who serves 5 years and the one who serves 10 years are equally guilty of an offense carrying the maximum penalty of 20 years. We maintain that the records of both are equally serious from the point of view of legal officials.[3]

The severity of a prior record was measured by summing the maximum penalties for each conviction. A defendant with an earlier conviction for robbery (maximum penalty 20 years) and one for bookmaking (maximum penalty 5 years) would receive a score of 25. Penalties ranged from 0 to 20 years; no defendant had a prior conviction for first degree murder. Sentences of less than a year were given fractional scores.[4]

[2]The characteristics of the sample and the circumstances of the offense did not differ significantly from those reported by earlier studies, cf. Wolfgang (1958); Bensing and Schroeder (1960); Porkorny (1965); Voss and Hepburn (1968).

[3]Evidence that this is actually the court's logic can be found in the fact that the record of relevant *convictions* is utilized by this jurisdiction during bail hearings to determine eligibility and amount.

[4]Defendant scores ranged from 0 to 219.25, with a mean of 17.12 and a standard deviation of 31.675.

In the first stage of the analysis we assessed the impact of the prior offense record and social characteristics of defendants, including age, sex, race, and occupational prestige,[5] upon conviction severity. Since defendants were sometimes found guilty of charges other than the two degrees of murder and two degrees of manslaughter, the disposition was scaled as first degree murder, first degree felony (including second degree murder), second degree felony (including voluntary manslaughter), first degree misdemeanor (including involuntary manslaughter), acquittal, and dismissal (including *nolle prosequi* and demurrer sustained.)[6]

The second stage of the analysis sought to specify the influence of criminal record within the legal process. Here, we tried to determine the role of private at-

---

[5]The distribution of the social characteristics of defendants is presented below. Occupational prestige was measured in terms of Treiman's (1977) classification system.

Race and Sex of Defendants

|  | Sex | | | | | |
|  | Male | | Female | | Total | |
| Race | *n* | % | *n* | % | *n* | % |
|---|---|---|---|---|---|---|
| White | 134 | 30.5 | 26 | 5.9 | 160 | 36.4 |
| Black | 215 | 49.0 | 64 | 14.6 | 279 | 63.6 |
| Total | 349 | 79.5 | 90 | 20.5 | 439 | 100.0 |

Age and Occupational Prestige of Defendants

|  | Range | Mean | Standard deviation |
|---|---|---|---|
| Age | 13–81 | 35.73 | 14.796 |
| Occupational Prestige | 5–71 | 25.34 | 11.606 |

[6]Although disposition is ordinally scaled, multiple techniques appear to be robust enough to handle the violation of the method's interval assumption, see Bohrnstedt and Carter (1971:118–146). The distribution of cases across the dependent variable is depicted below:

Disposition

|  | *n* | % |
|---|---|---|
| Dismissed | 38 | 8.96 |
| Acquitted | 67 | 15.80 |
| First degree misdemeanor | 40 | 9.44 |
| Second degree felony | 126 | 29.72 |
| First degree felony | 110 | 25.94 |
| First degree murder | 43 | 10.14 |
| Total | 424 | 100.00 |

torney, bail, and trial by jury in mediating the effects of prior convictions upon disposition.

The highly structured nature of the judicial system lends itself to a systematic analysis of legal processing. The discrete ordering of events—the social characteristics of the defendants prior to their entry into the system, their accumulated criminal histories, the type of legal representation, pretrial release, the mode of adjudication, and final disposition—constitutes a series of stages that allows the researcher to assert the causal sequence of relationships. The path analytic technique is particularly suited to such an exploration. Having established causal priority among a system of variables, paths of direct as well as indirect influence may be assessed. Based on multiple regression techniques, path coefficients represent the relative contributions of the several independent variables to predicting the dependent variable (Lin, 1976: 315). Where a coefficient failed to reach 0.100 the variable was dropped from the equation and all coefficients were recalculated.

In addition to standardized path coefficients, the multiple correlation coefficient ($R^2$) is also presented. This statistic indicates the total portion of the dependent variable explained by the combined effects of all independent variables.

## FINDINGS

The path model presented in Figure 1 depicts the relationships among the social characteristics of defendants, the severity of their prior convictions, and the final dispositions.

Age and sex are antecedents of a defendant's prior record (see also Table 1). Males and older defendants are more likely to have severe conviction histories. These relationships are presumably the result of the greater opportunity that older persons have had to accumulate conviction histories and of the more frequent application of criminal labels to men. Whether the latter reflects more criminal activity (cf. Adler, 1975) or the unwillingness of legal authorities to recognize female criminality (cf. Harris, 1977) requires further investigation. We have argued elsewhere (Swigert and Farrell, 1977a) that the overrepresentation of males in offender populations may be a function of the applicability of a criminal imagery to this group (see also Harris, 1977). The relationship between sex and disposition lends support to this argument: even when males and females are charged with the same offense, males are more likely to be convicted of more serious charges. In this way the imagery of the violent male is reinforced by statistics concerning violent criminality, statistics that reflect the failure of officials to perceive and label females involved in violent crimes.

Occupational prestige also influences the development of a prior offense record. There are two competing explanations of this relationship: lower-status persons may actually have committed more crimes, or their more extensive records may indicate differential treatment in the past. In order to choose between these explanations, it is sufficient to observe that in the present adjudication defendants of

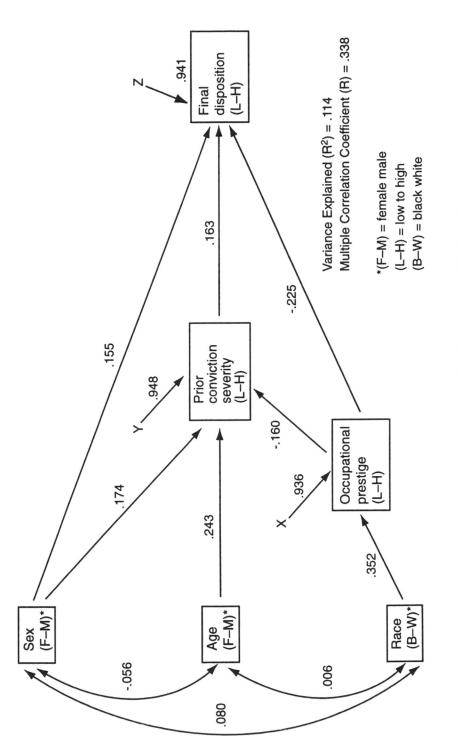

FIGURE 1 Final Disposition By Defendant Characteristics and Prior Conviction Severity

**TABLE 1**  Correlation Coefficients among All Variables Included in the Analysis

| Variables | 2 | 3 | 4 | 5 | 6 | 7 | 8 | 9 | 10 | 11 |
|---|---|---|---|---|---|---|---|---|---|---|
| 1. Age (L-H)* | -.056 | .006 | .077 | .221 | -.050 | -.064 | -.046 | .209 | -.057 | -.052 |
| 2. Sex (F-M)* | — | .080 | .057 | .151 | .034 | -.065 | .093 | .155 | .024 | .167 |
| 3. Race (B-W)* | | — | .352 | -.081 | .057 | .042 | .034 | .160 | -.063 | -.032 |
| 4. Occupational prestige (L-H) | | | — | -.131 | .316 | .153 | .104 | -.302 | .306 | -.237 |
| 5. Prior conviction severity (L-H) | | | | — | -.162 | -.161 | -.010 | .738 | -.155 | .215 |
| 6. Private attorney (No-Yes) | | | | | — | .230 | .016 | -.199 | .607 | -.165 |
| 7. Bail (No-Yes) | | | | | | — | .108 | -.212 | .681 | -.293 |
| 8. Jury trial (No-Yes) | | | | | | | — | -.030 | .549 | -.171 |
| 9. Occupational prestige and prior conviction severity (P-N)* | | | | | | | | — | -.201 | .267 |
| 10. Legal resources (L-H) | | | | | | | | | — | -.306 |
| 11. Final disposition (L-H) | | | | | | | | | | — |

*(L-H) = low to high.
(F-M) = female-male.
(B-W) = black-white.
(P-N) = positive to negative.

lower status still receive more severe sanctions when we control for prior record. Given this finding, it is reasonable to assume that occupational prestige may also have affected previous dispositions. Since today's conviction decision is tomorrow's record, a relationship between social status and prior offense record must be expected.

Race was found to have no independent effect on either prior record or disposition. Rather, race operates in the legal process through its association with occupational prestige. Blacks tend to have lower status and thus to have acquired more extensive records and to receive severe dispositions.

Of particular interest is the effect of prior convictions on further elaboration of a criminal record. If a defendant comes to court with a history of criminality, the probability of exacerbating that history increases. On the other hand, if the defendant's record is minimal he is likely to be spared the more severe dispositions. Given this pattern, it is possible to envision that the present adjudication is likely to have a similar effect on future contacts with the law.

It is important to point out that an accused person must be judged by evidence of the crime with which he is charged; prior offenses are supposed to be irrelevant, and admissible only for the purpose of impeaching the credibility of a defendant who testifies in his own behalf. The path from prior record to disposition, though it may reflect that limited admissibility, therefore deserves further investigation.

In order to specify the effects of criminal record on disposition, it was necessary to examine several intervening events: the type of counsel retained, whether the defendant was released on bail, and the mode of adjudication.[7] The influence of each of these variables on disposition has received abundant empirical support. The differential resources available to private and public attorneys for investigation of the case have been shown to affect the outcome of legal proceedings (Ehrmann, 1962, Chiricos et al., 1972). Similarly, studies have shown that, among

---

[7]Type of attorney is a two-category variable: privately retained and state subsidized. The latter category includes court appointed private attorneys who are compensated by the state at a fixed rate per case, and salaried public defenders.

Persons without pretrial release may remain incarcerated either because bail was denied or because it was set at a prohibitive level.

Mode of adjudication was dichotomized into jury and no jury trial. In most cases, the absence of a jury trial was the product of the defendant's plea to the original or reduced charges. In a few, it represented a decision to be tried by a judge. The distribution of cases across each of these variables is as follows:

Intervening Events

|  | Private attorney | | Bail | | Trial by jury | |
|  | n | % | n | % | n | % |
|---|---|---|---|---|---|---|
| Yes | 192 | 48.7 | 125 | 33.0 | 147 | 39.8 |
| No | 202 | 51.3 | 254 | 67.0 | 222 | 60.2 |
| Total | 394 | 100 | 379 | 100 | 369 | 100 |

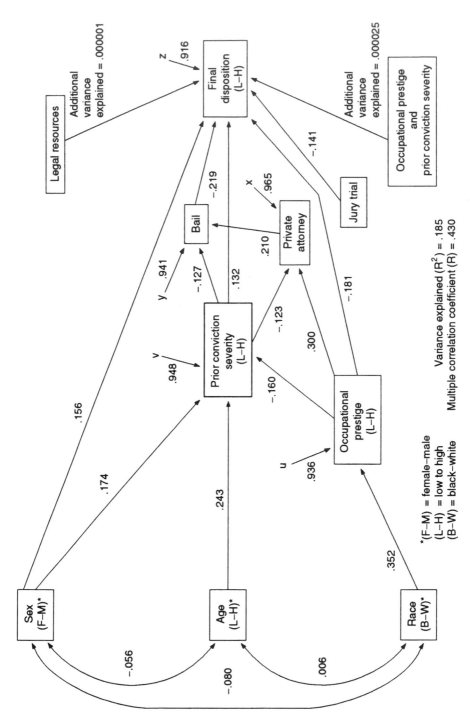

FIGURE 2  Final Disposition by Defendant Social Characteristics, Prior Record, and Intervening Events

defendants charged with similar offenses, those jailed before trial are more often convicted than those released on bail or on their own recognizance (Foote, 1959: 47; *Louisiana Law Review* Editors, 1961; Ares *et al.,* 1963: 83; cf. Clarke and Koch, 1976: 83). Finally, the defendant has a right to trial by jury, but may also choose to be tried by a judge or to plead guilty. In fact, more than 90% of all convictions involve the negotiation of a guilty plea between defense and prosecution (Newman, 1956; Blumberg, 1967; Alschuler, 1968). This may defeat the ends of justice, for not only are the guilty neither prosecuted nor sanctioned for the offense originally charged, but the innocent are often encouraged to enter a plea of guilt and accept a certain but slight penalty rather than run the risk of a more serious conviction (Rosett, 1967).

In an effort to determine the interrelationships among prior record, the several legal variables, and disposition, a second path model was generated. As shown in Figure 2, prior record is an important determinant of the ability to retain private counsel and to secure pretrial release, but not of the mode of adjudication.

The influence of prior record on access to a private attorney is independent of the defendant's occupational status and may be a product of the presumption of guilt implied by a criminal history. Private attorneys, sensitive to the importance of prior record in arriving at negotiated settlements and fearful of loss of payment when incarceration appears to be the inevitable outcome, may refuse to accept defendants whose earlier experiences with the law are seen as predictive of career criminality. But occupational prestige also exerts a strong independent influence on access to private counsel. It becomes apparent, then, that the failure of lower class persons to retain private counsel is a product of their financial inability to purchase such services as well as of the more extensive criminal histories found in this group.

A defendant with a record of serious convictions is also more likely to be detained before trial. Such a pattern may likewise be a consequence of the presumption of guilt created by a criminal record. The belief that individuals previously convicted of violating the law are more likely to be guilty of the present offense is institutionalized in the standards recommended for granting bail.[8] Access to bail is also influenced by the type of legal representation: private attorneys are more successful in securing pretrial release.

---

[8]In the jurisdiction studied, because the degree of the offense is determined at the time of the trial, homicide defendants are eligible for pretrial release. The purpose of bail is to ensure the presence of the defendant at subsequent proceedings. The official standards include:
   i. the nature of the offense charged and any mitigating or aggravating factor that may bear upon the likelihood of conviction and possible penalty;
   ii. the defendant's employment status and history and his financial condition;
   iii. the nature of his family relationships;
   iv. his age, character, reputation, mental condition, *record of relevant convictions,* and whether addicted to alcohol or drugs; and
   v. any other facts relevant to whether the defendant has strong ties with the community or is likely to flee the jurisdiction.
[Criminal Code Manual issued by the state in which this study was conducted, italics added]

An assessment of the effects of bail on disposition reveals that pretrial release directly results in greater leniency. The effects of type of attorney on disposition, on the other hand, are not direct but mediated by the ability of private counsel to secure pretrial release for their clients. Persons with private attorneys are more often awarded bail, a resource which in turn produces the more favorable dispositions.

There are no significant relationships between the social characteristics of defendants, prior conviction severity, access to a private attorney, and bail, on the one hand, and the mode of adjudication selected by the defendant, on the other.[9] Persons who waive their right to a jury *are* found guilty of more serious charges. But it must be remembered that most defendants who waive a jury trial plead guilty to the original or a reduced charge. Since a plea of guilty is virtually synonymous with an adjudication of guilt, the path coefficient between this variable and conviction severity would necessarily link more serious convictions to nonjury trials.[10]

On the basis of these findings, it is possible to assert the nature of the relationships that exist among prior offense record, intervening legal variables, and adjudication severity. Defendants with histories of repeated criminality have less access to a private attorney or bail. This latter relationship is not only a product of the immediate influence of criminal record, but is also an indirect result of the inability of defendants represented by publicly paid counsel to obtain pretrial release. Finally, persons who are incarcerated pending adjudication are convicted of more serious charges.

It should be emphasized that though part of the impact of criminal history on disposition is mediated, a significant direct effect remains evident. Explanations of this relationship must remain speculative, given the limitations of the data. It may be suggested, however, that though the law requires a determination of guilt without reference to a defendant's background, such information actually influences the legal process at a number of stages. Prosecutors, defense attorneys, and judges do have access to the prior record. The vehemence with which defense counsel will press for acquittal and the prosecutor for conviction, or the weight a judge accords to evidence in a bench trial, may in fact be influenced by their familiarity with the defendant's criminal history. It is an issue certainly deserving of empirical attention.

The remainder of the analysis involves an assessment of the interactive effects of several variables on disposition. A significant interaction was anticipated between occupational prestige and prior record—that dispositions for persons from

[9]Elsewhere we have shown that the extent to which the defendant resembles criminal stereotypes affects the availability of a jury trial (Swigert and Farrell, 1976; 1977a).

[10] An analysis of the effects of mode of adjudication on sentence severity, not reported here, shows that persons who are found guilty following a jury trial are penalized more severely. This supports the contention that defendants who make greater demands on the scarce resources of the legal system are treated more harshly (Tiffany *et al.*, 1975).

the lowest occupational levels would be most affected by extensive criminal histories. For while the imagery of guilt created by prior criminal involvement might lead to a less favorable disposition, both directly and through the mediating variables, persons of higher status might be able to compensate for these disadvantages. Likewise, we thought that the combined influence of private attorney, bail, and jury trial upon disposition might exceed the sum of the effects of each. In both cases, however, the additional variance explained is insignificant. This would suggest that the effects of each variable are additive, which supports our original interpretation.

## CONCLUSION

In their study of the application of the felony label, Chircos *et al.* (1972: 569–570) have noted:

> the privileged status of first offenders before the law is neither surprising nor uncommon. In fact, many statutes explicitly provide harsher penalties for repeat offenders. A reasonable—though not necessarily correct—interpretation of these findings would be that judges recognize the self-fulfilling character of the formal convict label and purposely withhold it from first offenders in the interests of possible "rehabilitation."

But the pattern observed in this research has even more important implications. The use of a prior record as meaningful information in the disposition of a criminal case compounds the discretion of prior adjudications.

We have seen that lower status offenders are more likely to have accumulated long histories of criminal conviction. Similar observations have led researchers to conclude that the relationship of class to differential criminal justice is explained by the greater involvement of lower status persons in lives of crime. Thus it is argued that if blacks and members of the lower classes are more severely sanctioned for their offenses, it is because of the judicial decision to penalize the repeat offender.

We have also seen, however, that each criminal conviction is itself influenced by class. Lower status defendants, independent of their prior criminal involvement, receive more severe dispositions. The relationship between social status and prior record is therefore not simply the result of a tendency toward criminality on the part of the lower classes, but is also a reflection of the influence of class on those previous convictions. Furthermore, prior record, both independently and through the three mediating legal variables, was found to be associated with the severity of disposition. Since occupational prestige affects severity of disposition directly and also indirectly, through its historical influence on prior record, the introduction of that record into the criminal process may amplify its class bias.

The influence of prior record within the legal system produces a cyclic reconfirmation of criminality. Prior record, itself partly a product of discretionary treatment, becomes a salient factor in the accumulation of additional convictions. This occurs not only through its direct effect on disposition but also through its influence on access to private counsel and bail, themselves important determinants of outcome.

Such findings are obviously significant for the criminal justice system. Prior record is presently an important source of information at a number of stages in the legal process. The use of previous convictions in habitual offender laws, in eligibility for suspension of sentence and probation, in the standards for granting of bail, and as evidence of a defendant's credibility, are an official sanction of discretionary treatment. More important, such practices constitute an institutionalization of prior record as a self-fulfilling prophecy. The lower classes, by virtue of social and economic disadvantages, more often accumulate more serious convictions. These convictions, in their turn, serve to justify differential treatment in any succeeding adjudication. The process is continuous and serves to fulfill the original prediction that the lower classes are dangerous classes, prone to lives of criminality.

## REFERENCES

Adler, Freda. 1975. *Sisters in Crime: The Rise of the New Female Criminal.* New York: McGraw-Hill.

Akers, Ronald L. 1964. "Socioeconomic status and delinquent behavior: a retest." *Journal of Research in Crime and Delinquency* 1: 38–46.

Alschuler, Albert W. 1968. "The prosecutor's role in plea bargaining." *University of Chicago Law Review* 36: 50–112.

Ares, Charles E., Anne Rankin, and Herbert Sturz. 1963. "The Manhattan bail project: an interim report on the use of pre-trial parole." *New York University Law Review* 38: 67–95.

Bensing, Robert C., and Oliver Schroeder, Jr. 1960. *Homicide in an Urban Community.* Springfield, Illinois: Thomas.

Black, Donald J. 1970. "Production of crime rates." *American Sociological Review* 35: 733–748.

Blankenburg, Erhard. 1976. "The selectivity of legal sanctions: an empirical investigation of shoplifting." *Law and Society Review* 11: 109.

Blumberg, Abraham S. 1967. "The practice of law as a confidence game: organizational cooptation of a profession." *Law and Society Review* 1(2): 15–39.

Bohrnstedt, George W. and T. Michael Carter. 1971. "Robustness in regression analysis." In *Sociological Methodology,* edited by Herbert L. Costner. San Francisco: Jossey-Bass.

Bullock, Henry Allen. 1961. "Significance of the racial factor in the length of prison sentences." *Journal of Criminal Law, Criminology and Police Science* 52: 411–417.

Burke, Peter J., and Austin T. Turk. 1975. "Factors affecting post-arrest dispositions: a model for analysis." *Social Problems* 22: 313–332.

Caldwell, Morris G. 1931. "The economic status of the families of delinquent boys in Wisconsin." *American Journal of Sociology* 37: 231–239.

Cameron, Mary Owen. 1964. *The Booster and the Snitch: Department Store Shoplifting.* New York: Free Press.

Chambliss, William J., and John T. Liell. 1966. "The legal process in the community setting: a study of law enforcement." *Crime and Delinquency* 12: 310–317.

Chevigny, Paul. 1969. *Police Power: Police Abuses in New York City.* New York: Vintage Books.

Chiricos, Theodore G., Philip D. Jackson, and Gordon P. Waldo. 1972. "Inequality in the imposition of a criminal label." *Social Problems* 19: 553–572.

Clarke, Stevens H., and Gary G. Koch. 1976. "The influence of income and other factors on whether criminal defendants go to prison." *Law and Society Review* 11: 57–92.

Cloward, Richard A., and Lloyd E. Ohlin. 1960. *Delinquency and Opportunity: A Theory of Delinquent Gangs*. Glencoe, Illinois: Free Press.

Cohen, Albert K. 1955. *Delinquent Boys: The Culture of the Gang*. Glencoe, Illinois: Free Press.

D'Esposito, Julian C., Jr. 1969. "Sentencing disparity: causes and cures." *Journal of Criminal Law, Criminology and Police Science* 60: 182–195.

Ehrmann, Sara B. 1962. "For whom the chair waits." *Federal Probation* 26(1): 14–25.

Empey, Lamar T., and Maynard Erickson. 1966. "Hidden delinquency and social status." *Social Forces* 44: 546–554.

Ennis, Phillip H. 1967. "Crime, victims and the police." *Trans-Action*. 4(7): 36–44.

Farrell, Ronald A. 1971. "Class linkages of legal treatment of homosexuals." *Criminology* 9: 49–68.

Foote, Caleb. 1959. "The bail system and equal justice." *Federal Probation* 23(3): 43–48.

Glueck, Sheldon, and Eleanor T. Glueck. 1934. *One Thousand Juvenile Delinquents: Their Treatment by Court and Clinic*. Cambridge: Harvard University Press.

Gold, Martin. 1966. "Undetected delinquent behavior." *Journal of Research in Crime and Delinquency* 3: 27–46.

Goldman, Nathan. 1963. *The Differential Selection of Juvenile Offenders for Court Appearance*. New York: National Research and Information Center, National Council on Crime and Delinquency.

Green, Edward. 1961. *Judicial Attitudes in Sentencing*. New York: St. Martin's Press.

———. 1964. "Inter-and-intra-racial crime relative to sentencing." *Journal of Criminal Law, Criminology and Police Science* 55: 348–358.

Greenberg, David F. 1977. "Socioeconomic status and criminal sentences: is there an association?" *American Sociological Review* 42: 174–176.

Harris, Anthony R. 1977. "Sex and theories of deviance: toward a functional theory of deviant type-scripts." *American Sociological Review* 42: 3–16

Kobrin, Solomon. 1951. "The conflict of values in delinquency areas." *American Sociological Review* 16: 653–661.

Lin, Nan. 1976. *Foundations of Social Research*. New York: McGraw-Hill.

*Louisiana Law Review* Editors. 1961. "The institution of bail as related to indigent defendants." *Louisiana Law Review* 21: 627–638.

Merton, Robert. 1938. "Social structure and anomie." *American Sociological Review* 3: 672–682.

———. 1957. *Social Theory and Social Structure*. Glencoe: Free Press.

Miller, Walter B. 1958. "Lower class culture as a generating milieu of gang delinquency." *The Journal of Social Issues* 14(3): 5–19.

Newman, Donald J. 1956. "Pleading guilty for considerations: a study of bargain justice." *Journal of Criminal Law, Criminology and Police Science* 46: 780–790.

Nye, F. Ivan, James F. Short, Jr., and Virgil J. Olson. 1958. "Socioeconomic status and delinquent behavior." *American Journal of Sociology* 63: 381–389.

Porkorny, Alex D. 1965. "A comparison of homicides in two cities." *Journal of Criminal Law, Criminology and Police Science* 56: 479–487.

Quinney, Richard. 1975. *Criminology: Analysis and Critique of Crime in America*. Boston: Little, Brown.

Robison, Sophia. 1936. *Can Delinquency Be Measured?* New York: Columbia University Press.

Rosett, Arthur. 1967. "The negotiated guilty plea: an evaluation." *Annals of the American Academy of Political and Social Sciences* 374: 70–81.

Shaw, Clifford R. 1929. *Delinquency Areas*. Chicago: University of Chicago Press.

Shaw, Clifford R., and Henry D. McKay. 1931. "Social factors in juvenile delinquency." *Report on the Causes of Crime*. Washington, D.C.: National Commission on Law Observation and Enforcement.

———. 1942. *Juvenile Delinquency and Urban Areas*. Chicago: University of Chicago Press.

Skolnick, Jerome H. 1966. *Justice Without Trial: Law Enforcement in Democratic Society*. New York: Wiley.

Stinchcombe, Arthur L. 1963. "Institutions of privacy in the determination of police administrative practice." *American Journal of Sociology* 69: 150–160.

Sutherland, Edwin H. 1949. *White Collar Crime.* New York: Dryden Press.

Swett, Daniel H. 1969. "Cultural bias in the American legal system." *Law and Society Review* 4: 79–110.

Swigert, Victoria Lynn, and Ronald A. Farrell. 1976. *Murder, Inequality, and the Law.* Lexington, Massachusetts: Lexington Books.

————. 1977a. "Normal homicides and the law." *American Sociological Review* 42: 16–32.

————. 1977b. "The legal disposition of inter-and intra-group homicides." Presented at the Annual Meeting of the Society for the Study of Social Problems, Chicago.

Thomas, William I. 1923. *The Unadjusted Girl.* Boston: Little, Brown.

Tiffany, Lawrence, Yakov Avichai, and Geoffrey Peters. 1975. "A statistical analysis of sentencing in federal courts." *Journal of Legal Studies* 4: 369–390.

Treiman, Donald J. (editor). 1977. *Occupational Prestige in Comparative Perspective.* New York: Academic Press.

*UCLA Law Review* Editors. 1966. "The consenting adult homosexual and the law: an empirical study of enforcement and administration in Los Angeles County (Part III - enforcement techniques)." *UCLA Law Review* 13: 686–742.

Useem, John, Pierre Tangent, and Ruth Useem. 1942. "Stratification in a prairie town." *American Sociological Review* 7: 331–342.

Voss, Harwin L., and John R. Hepburn. 1968. "Patterns in criminal homicide in Chicago." *Journal of Criminal Law, Criminology and Police Science* 59: 499–508.

Warner, W. Lloyd, and Paul S. Lunt. 1941. *The Social Life of a Modern Community.* New Haven: Yale University Press.

Willick, Daniel H., Gretchen Gehlker, and Anita McFarland Watts. 1975. "Social class as a factor affecting judicial disposition: defendants charged with criminal homosexual acts." *Criminology* 13: 57–77.

Wolfgang, Marvin E. 1958. *Patterns in Criminal Homicide.* Philadelphia: University of Pennsylvania Press.

# 20

# THE IMPACT OF VICTIM ASSESSMENT ON PROSECUTORS' SCREENING DECISIONS: THE CASE OF THE NEW YORK COUNTY DISTRICT ATTORNEY'S OFFICE*

## ELIZABETH ANNE STANKO

### INTRODUCTION

Prosecutors, armed with the power to charge a suspect with a criminal offense, allocate their limited resources to those cases which, they believe, constitute the most "trouble" for society (Blumberg, 1967; Emerson and Messenger, 1977; Miller, 1970; Myers and Hagan, 1979). Not surprisingly, what is defined as trouble corresponds with the organizational goal of achieving a high conviction record.

Earlier studies have examined prosecutors' use of legal and social criteria for handling serious criminal offenses. The seriousness of crime and its evidentiary strength influence the prosecutability of particular cases (Blumberg, 1967; Eisenstein and Jacob, 1977; Mather, 1979; Miller, 1970; Neubauer, 1974). Defendant characteristics, such as the existence of a prior criminal record, are also important

*This is a revised version of a paper delivered at the Northeastern Political Science Association Annual Meeting, 1980. I would like to thank Lindsey Churchill, George Cole, Cynthia Enloe, Joel Grossman, Jim Thomas, Gaye Tuchman, and the anonymous reviewers for their helpful comments on this chapter.

components of prosecutorial strategy (Mather, 1979; Neubauer, 1974; Swigert and Farrell, 1976). Some attention has also been given to the victim and the impact of victim characteristics on prosecutorial decision making (Hall, 1975; Myers and Hagen, 1979; Stanko, 1977; Williams, 1976).

Myers and Hagan, in finding that "the troubles of older, white, male and employed victims" are considered more worthy of public processing, suggest that certain *types* of victims affect the allocation of prosecutorial resources (1979: 448). Stereotypes about victims assist them in the sorting (Swigert and Farrell, 1976) of serious cases (those deserving full prosecution) from less serious ones.

This paper explores prosecutors' use of victim stereotypes during the screening and charging stage of serious felony prosecutions. It concludes that the character and credibility of the victim is a key factor in determining prosecutorial strategies, one at least as important as "objective" evidence about the crime or characteristics of the defendant.

Prosecutorial focus on victim character is particularly evident in the early stages of the criminal justice process. As a gatekeeping function to limit prosecutors' workloads, the sorting of serious felony cases is a necessary and routine function of a prosecutor's office. With an eye to assuring a high conviction rate, screening prosecutors are likely to devote limited resources to those felony cases with "good" victim/witnesses; "stand-up" witnesses' overall credibility lends strength and legitimacy to the sure case. Throughout my 13 months of observation, it was frequently the victim—not the facts of the case, the seriousness of the crime, or the dangerousness of the defendant—upon whom the prosecutor focused for the *prediction* of an assured conviction.

## THE RESEARCH SETTING AND ITS ORGANIZATIONAL CONTEXT

The setting of this study is a bureau within the New York County (Manhattan) prosecutor's office that is devoted solely to the screening of felony arrests. This particular office screens a high volume of cases 365 days a year. Focusing only upon serious offenses, assistant prosecutors assigned to this bureau review all the arrest circumstances, assess the evidence against the arrested individual, interview the complainant, and draw an affidavit summarizing the case against the defendant.

For approximately 13 months (March 1975 through March 1976), I observed this felony arrest screening process, recording descriptive accounts of the interactions among the assistant prosecutor, arresting police officer, and complaining witness(es). During the last 6 months of observation, I was able to transcribe the dialogue among these actors.[1] Of the roughly 1000 felony screenings I witnessed, I

---

[1] I was able to examine the screening work of all the prosecutors in the Early Case Assessment Bureau. The data collected include verbatim dialogue in the roughly 100 conversational accounts of case

transcribed over 100 conversational exchanges regarding felony case assessment for assault, rape, and robbery offenses.[2]

Prior to 1975, assistant prosecutors assigned to the complaint room reviewed the arrest charges and prepared an affidavit that served as the charging instrument in arraignment proceedings. Determinations about the merits and eventual outcome of a case were rarely made at this time.[3] In 1975, a newly elected District Attorney (following Frank Hogan, who controlled the D.A.'s office for over three decades) began restructuring the process of prosecution. One of his priorities was to establish an early case assessment bureau (ECAB), whose primary purpose was to review all incoming felony arrests, to weed out those cases that would not lead to convictions, and to forward only solid, convictable cases to the supreme court bureau.[4]

The new D.A. believed that establishment of early case screening would enable his office to predict the probability of successful prosecution. Screening prosecutors now prepare incoming felony arrests for prosecution along selected routes. They scrutinize each arrest for its evidentiary strength, seriousness, and witness credibility. At this point in the process, prosecutors determine whether a particular case warrants supreme court prosecution; all the remaining cases are disposed of in the lower court.

During the period of my observations, ECAB was staffed by nine assistant prosecutors: a bureau chief, four senior prosecutors, and four junior prosecutors. The senior prosecutors came to ECAB from the trial bureau. Their experience, the bureau chief felt, enabled them to assess how a felony case would be received in supreme court. As described by one ECAB prosecutor, this alleged predictive capacity was the result of "acquired experience in how the case is processed throughout the whole system. Then we can use this [information] to determine what is a

---

screening. Descriptions of the setting and other screening incidents were also collected. In all I spent approximately 300 hours observing the research site.

Generally I would sit next to one D.A. each day I observed, making note of each robbery, rape, and assault case he handled. In the beginning, I was collecting descriptions of the offense, the questions the D.A. would ask, and the predicted outcome. As I became more familiar with the operations and quicker in my note taking, I was able to transcribe the dialogue in shorthand.

[2]After six months, I began limiting my data collection to the crimes of assault, rape, and robbery, for a number of reasons. First, I was primarily interested in what is assumed to be the most serious threat to public safety—crimes against persons. Second, after months of initial observation, I noticed the particular focus by prosecutors on the victims. Whether a similar analysis to that put forth in this paper applies to crimes against property is merely speculation at this point. To the extent that socially relevant factors are incorporated into prosecutorial decision making, determinations concerning property offenses would be affected by a similar process.

[3]Prior to 1975, the prosecutors rotated through the Complaint Room from other bureaus. The drawing of affidavits involved little prospective screening on the part of the prosecutors. I observed this process of screening during the first six months, prior to the founding of the felony screening bureau.

[4]This restructuring was in part due to a reorganization of the office to achieve a more efficient, accountable bureaucracy. Another factor that contributed to the creation of the Early Case Screening Bureau was the availability of L.E.A.A. [Law Enforcement Assistance Administration] funds. It would be interesting at some point to examine the impact of L.E.A.A. funding on bureaucratic decision making.

legally prosecutable case." Not only did the senior prosecutors possess the organizationally acquired skill suitable for identifying solid cases, but they had an awareness of what Dill (1980) refers to as a "laundry list" of other institutional considerations: knowledge about resource limitations, competence of other bureaus within the prosecutor's office, judge and jury reactions to different types of cases and witnesses, likely sentences, and so forth.

Through a process of organizational socialization, junior prosecutors learned this predictive skill from the senior prosecutors. "After all," commented one senior prosecutor, "he's been to law school and he's got common sense." With these basic skills, junior prosecutors then become members of the prosecutor's subculture (Rosett and Cressey, 1976). Developed within a bureaucratic setting geared only to selecting convictable cases, knowledge shared among this subculture includes a tacit understanding of how victims and their credibility are a key to predicting solid cases.

## THE VICTIM AS AN ORGANIZATIONAL CONSIDERATION FOR SOLID CASES

How do prosecutors actually make screening decisions? As noted earlier, New York County prosecutors utilize a convictability standard against which each felony case is assessed (Alschuler, 1968). Similar to what Mather (1979) describes as a "dead bang" serious case, screening prosecutors refer to their sure cases as solid cases.[5]

After lengthy discussions, ECAB prosecutors could not agree on formal criteria to define a solid case. They turned instead to a series of questions they asked of each case. As told by one senior ECAB prosecutor, they were:

(1)  Is the matter of law sufficient?
(2)  If sufficient, does it establish a felony offense in the eyes of society?
(3)  Am I (the prosecutor) personally assured of the defendant's guilt?
(4)  Can the case be persuasive to a jury?

(Note how these criteria blend both legal and organizational requirements: legal sufficiency and socially recognized "trouble" are important aspects of solid cases.)

Prosecutors were particularly concerned with evidentiary matters, with the defendant's guilt, and with predicting the organizational success of the case—its persuasiveness to a jury. This latter concern is pivotal. If a case has strong evidence and an apparently guilty defendant, but is nonetheless not persuasive to a jury, then the outcome is not likely to be successful. In crimes against persons, especially, the victim is both witness to and object of the offense. In these types of crimes, then, the case's persuasiveness to a jury is integrally linked to the victim's credi-

---

[5]All other cases were termed "garbage" cases by prosecutors. These were not considered truly "serious" matters.

bility. In short, the credibility of the victim becomes an *organizational* problem for screening prosecutors: whether the victim's story is sufficiently believable to assure a "solid" case.

Victim credibility is less important in cases slated for disposition in the lower courts, since most of these cases will be resolved through plea bargaining. But if those cases forwarded to the supreme court go to trial, then the victim or complaining witness is likely to be subjected to severe cross examination ("impeaching the witness") by defense attorneys (Holmstrom and Burgess, 1978). Prosecutors must predict how a judge and jury will react to the victim under these circumstances. And they often base these predictions on common-sense evaluation of how judge and jury will assess a victim's life style and moral character, and derivatively their honesty and trustworthiness as witnesses. Moreover, prosecutors are prone to attribute credibility to certain *types* of individuals, those who fit society's stereotypes of who is credible: older, white, male employed victims (see Myers and Hagan, 1979). In Goffman's (1963) sense, this is what constitutes *stereotypical credibility*. Indeed, prosecutors are no exception to the generalization that organizations are particularly prone to the use of stereotypical thinking (Swigert and Farrell, 1976). Bureaucracies routinely structure the interaction of participants and, as Goffman notes, this structuring is often without "special attention or thought" (1963: 2).

The process of selecting "solid" cases, therefore, focuses on identifying problems that reduce the chance of a successful prosecution. Such problems are likely to be perceived in a victim's appearance or character, or in the defects or weaknesses of a *category* of individuals of which the victim is a part. Gender, race, and occupation have important social meanings; power and status are often accorded on these grounds. A pleasant appearance, residence in a good neighborhood, a respectable job or occupation, lack of nervous mannerisms, and an ability to articulate clearly, are decided advantages. Inferences that a victim might be a prostitute or pimp, a homosexual, or an alcoholic, on the other hand, may seriously damage a victim's credibility. All of these factors must be carefully weighed.

The seven case studies which follow illustrate how prosecutors explore the "problems" of victims in otherwise solid cases. In each case, the screening prosecutor (D.A.) discusses the case with the arresting officer (A.O.), another D.A., or the victim (C.W.). These cases are not a random sample of prosecutorial screening activity, but they do illustrate the process of victim assessment in the selection of solid cases.

## EXAMPLE 1: ROBBERY IN THE FIRST DEGREE

Three individuals were arrested and charged with robbery in the first degree. The two complainants in the case had not yet arrived at the D.A.'s office. The D.A. began questioning the arresting officer about the case before the complainants arrived. Here, a prior relationship did not seem to be a problem.

D.A. Does the complainant know the defendant?

A.O. No, never seen him before.

However, the address of the complainant was not in a neighborhood the D.A. considered
an "upstanding" one. Finally, the question was asked:
    D.A. What do we know about the complaining witness?
    A.O. He's a Columbia University student.
    The D.A. told the arresting officer to bring in the complainants as soon as they arrived.
Later, the complainants walked in: two white, articulate graduate students. The D.A. remarked to me after he briefly interviewed them: "Stand-up complainants—I knew they
were stand-up—I marked it [to be forwarded to the grand jury] before I saw them."

The use of the term "stand-up victim" appears frequently in prosecutor's talk.
It describes the ideal victim for the solid case: one who can *stand up* before any
jury or judge and present him/herself as a credible witness. As noted by Myers and
Hagan (1979) and others (Hall, 1975; Miller, 1970; Stanko, 1977), when evidentiary strength is held constant, higher-status victims are likely to increase the prosecutability of a case.

Note the stereotypical imagery. The prosecutor assesses this victim on the basis of what is "known" about the typical Columbia University student. It is assumed that these students are, as a category, "law-abiding" citizens with no noticeable character flaws that undermine their credibility. Indeed, if the victim
seems categorically credible, the prosecutor may view the criminal incident more
seriously than the arresting officer did. For instance, in the following example,
prosecutorial attention focuses primarily on the victim, altering the arresting officer's definition of the criminal offense.

### EXAMPLE 2: ROBBERY IN THE THIRD DEGREE

The complainant is an elderly woman. The incident involved a purse snatching by a
16-year-old male. The complainant chased the defendant through a park after the purse was
taken. The prosecutor admired the complainant as an individual least deserving of harassment. After the complainant reported the incident, she was excused from ECAB; the prosecutor became excited about the potential case: "I'm going to write it up as a robbery one
[first degree] with a tree branch [as the dangerous weapon]. I only wrote up one rob[bery]
before with a tree branch [as a weapon] and that was because the victim was John F.
Kennedy, Jr. These are the cases that try themselves. Any case that has a stand-up complainant should be indicted. You put her on the stand—the judge loves her, the jury loves
her—dynamite complainant!"

Although the arrest charge was robbery in the third degree, the prosecutor
changed the affidavit charge to read robbery in the first degree by defining a tree
branch as a "dangerous weapon." In such instances (rare but not unheard of), sympathy for the victim and the prosecutor's positive assessment of the victim's credibility will result in upgrading to a more severe charge. Presumably, if that same
tree branch had been wielded against another teenage male, it would have been
viewed as less threatening and thus less likely to sustain a first-degree robbery
charge.

In the next example, the vulnerability of a victim's life style is explored for its
possible detrimental effects on the seriousness (and thus prosecutability) of an offense.

## EXAMPLE 3: ROBBERY IN THE FIRST DEGREE

The complainant is a professional man who works for the Better Business Bureau. He entered the Early Case Assessment Bureau with his Sunday *New York Times* tucked under his arm. His recall of the incident was clear, and he presented his story articulately. After the complainant had received instructions to appear before the grand jury the next morning and had then left the room, the D.A. remarked to the arresting officer:

D.A. Do you think the defendants know the complainant is a homosexual?
A.O. No.
D.A. Would have been a great alibi [for the defendants]. They could claim that they had met and the complainant invited them up for a drink.

Essentially, the prosecutor indicates that, on second thought, he might have accorded this case nonfelony status (and thus deny it a supreme court hearing), because the victim's homosexuality raised questions about his credibility. Being labeled a homosexual, prosecutors recognize, casts doubt upon the victim's credibility; stereotypes about homosexuals, and the kinds of encounters they are alleged to have, can jeopardize the chances of winning the case. Yet in this particular instance, other factors such as the clarity of the victim's recall and his professional status compensated for this vulnerability. The charge was not altered.

As Goffman (1963) notes in his study of social stigma, characterizations such as those associated with homosexuality inherently carry with them suspicion of deviousness or dishonesty, which in turn invites disbelief of accounts reported by such people. Applying some character labels to victims implies a participation in other activities that are not "law-abiding." Similarly, during the screening of another robbery complaint, the prosecutor specifically addressed the problem with victims who were prostitutes. Reducing the charges, the prosecutor stated: "I have to deal with two complainants who will get up on the stand and say they work the streets." One prosecutor described this practice as turning "complainants into defendants."

Anticipating problems with a victim's character is an organizational strategy where prosecutors predict that a witness will be successfully impeached; they must commit their resources accordingly.

## EXAMPLE 4: ROBBERY IN THE SECOND DEGREE

A young black complainant was accosted by two males. The defendants stopped the complainant and told him they wanted money. One put his hand on the complainant's chest and told him if he didn't produce "they could 'cap' him." The prosecutor asked the complainant what 'cap' meant. The complainant replied that he didn't know; all he knew was that he didn't want to be hurt and he assumed that whatever capping was, he didn't want to find out. He gave the defendants his money—included was one ten dollar bill torn in half, which was found in the possession of the defendant. The complainant was not harmed. The prosecutor reduced the charges from robbery in the second degree to grand larceny in the third degree, stating that if the grand jury asked what 'cap' meant he couldn't answer and therefore wouldn't be able to prove the threat of force in the robbery charge.

Rather than concern himself initially with the circumstances of the actions of the defendants, here the prosecutor questions the victim's actions and explanations. The prosecutor reduced the seriousness of the original arrest charge by anticipating the reactions of the grand jury. But how is it possible for the prosecutor not to accept the victim's definition of the encounter as threatening, involving sufficient force to compel him to cooperate with his assailants' demands? Perhaps, as Swigert and Farrell note, "institutionalized conceptions of crime and criminality" influenced the prosecutor's view of the victim's actions (1976: 18). He may suspect, for example, that the victim was in the area for other illegal activities such as the purchase of illegal drugs. Whatever the rationale, the prosecutor, relying upon stereotypes about the probable actions of victims in this situation, concludes that this particular victim cannot be one who is *clearly* classified among those who have been threatened during a robbery (certainly the victim would not have given up his money without a threat of force!).

In another similar incident, the prosecutor's first question to the victim was: "What caused you to be in the area when you were robbed?" As in Example 4, the victim is being asked to justify his presence in a location, including his possible motives for being there, and his actions throughout the criminal incident. The prosecutor's mandate to forward only solid cases requires selection of cases with victims whose reactions to a criminal offense somehow fit the assumed reactions of victims in "real" criminal encounters. The prosecutor must anticipate similar reactions from the judge or jury and therefore prepares the case for what "will happen," not according to what happened (Hostica, 1979).

In the next example, the prosecutor questions the case's seriousness because of the assumed relationship between the complainant and the defendant.

### EXAMPLE 5: ROBBERY IN THE FIRST DEGREE

D.A. How long have you known the defendant?

C.W. I was a counselor in a drug program—Neighborhood Thing—in 1971–72, and I met her there. I've seen her around since then. She was a Muslim and had a boyfriend and I didn't see her much then. But since she split I've seen her around.

. . . D.A. then asks the complainant to go out to the waiting room while he draws up the affidavit in the presence of the A.O.

A.O. He's the best complainant I've had in two years.

D.A. The people in Supreme Court don't like prior relationship cases. I think he was going out with her. The jury wouldn't like this. It's just a feel for the case. I don't like it.

This unknown but assumed prior relationship between the victim and the defendant somehow "normalized" this encounter, relegating it to the range of typical everyday interactions that might occur between the victim and the defendant. The victim, in order to be seen as a "real" victim, must at least convince the prosecutor of the irregular character of the event. (Other studies, too, indicate that the relationship between the victim and the defendant is an important element in the presumed prosecutability of a felony case [Cannavale and Falcon, 1976, Miller, 1970; Newman, 1966; Stanko, 1977]).

Even the slightest hint of implausibility in the victim's story imperils conviction by a jury which must be convinced of the defendant's guilt "beyond a reasonable doubt." What could be only a criminal act between strangers looms as possibly less so between persons who have experienced a prior relationship. The law does not distinguish between the two, of course, but juries often do.

## EXAMPLE 6: ATTEMPTED MURDER; RECKLESS ENDANGERMENT

During the day, people had talked about a Chinese gang case that one ECAB D.A. had marked for further investigation while another ECAB D.A. had changed its status to a non-felony case. A D.A. from the arraignment court entered ECAB and could not believe that the case was not to be sent to the grand jury.

The case is as follows: a major Chinese gang had split into two factions. One faction had attacked members of the other faction as they were walking down one of the busiest streets in Chinatown. Several shots were fired. No one was injured, and the defendant was arrested for attempted murder.

During the police investigation, two different bullet fragments were found in an ice cream shop. An account of one witness, who had identified the defendant as being at the scene of the incident, revealed that someone said "Get ready, here they come," but that witness did not observe the firing of shots. Another witness, one from the ambushed faction, identified the defendant as the individual who fired the shots and was willing to cooperate with the prosecution.

The ECAB D.A. who assessed the case as a nonfelony cited the witness's credibility as the major problem in this case. The witness from the rival faction, the one who could identify the defendant as the person who fired the gun, had a prior record of several assaults. Yet, the D.A. handling the case in arraignment could not believe that the incident itself did not warrant more serious treatment by the prosecutor's office. "After all, they [the police] found fragments [of bullets]." But the ECAB D.A.s began to raise issues that would weaken the strength of the case. "How do you know they [the bullets] came from the gun? You can't prove it. It's not a grand jury case. You'll be lucky to get an A mis [demeanor] on the thing [in the lower court]."

The arraignment D.A. would not give up, and he continued to question the ECAB D.A.s. "But the witness [who could identify the defendant]," repeated the arraignment D.A. "What witness," replied the ECAB D.A., "You've got one guy who hears someone say 'here they come' and a complainant who's got a rap sheet all over the place. Go ahead, put him on the stand. They'll tear him to pieces. If you want to send it to the grand jury, go ahead. That is, if you want [the indictment bureau head] to send a pack of wolves after you." But the arraignment D.A. continued to argue with the ECAB D.A.s, particularly about the fact that someone could have been injured. "What do we do about this? They'll wind up killing each other," stated the arraignment D.A. "Good," retorted the ECAB D.A. "So what," replied the other ECAB D.A. "But what about innocent people; they could have shot someone innocent," continued the arraignment D.A. "Not them, they're too good a shot," retorted the ECAB D.A. [Forgetting, of course, that even when firing at close range, the defendant shot into a store and missed the complainant.] "They'll kill each other," stated the ECAB D.A., hoping to end the discussion.

This case had many problems. How strong was the evidence (were the bullet fragments from the gun used in the shooting?)? Would the victim's prior record affect his credibility? Would the court regard this as a criminal encounter, or "merely" a violent encounter between warring gang factions? A recurring encounter between gangs is often assumed to be unworthy of full prosecutorial effort, particularly where no serious injuries were reported, and no "innocent" people were involved.

Does the prosecutor's assessment of a particular witness actually become pivotal in determinations of seriousness? In the last example, we see the prosecutor's screening activity as a fluid one—one that may alter definitions of seriousness in light of additional information about the victim.

### EXAMPLE 7: ROBBERY IN THE FIRST DEGREE

The complainants were a young, white couple. The male was the primary story teller. He stated that he was delivering furniture in the area. His girlfriend accompanied him occasionally on his deliveries and was with him the night of the robbery. As they parked on the street, three individuals approached them, displayed knives, took them inside a building, and robbed them of $80. He had never seen these individuals before. The police arrived on the scene as the defendants were fleeing the building. The young woman was not able to report many of the details of the robbery. She could not estimate the amount of time they were held in the building or the amount of money that was taken from her. However, she was visibly shaken, attractive, and concerned about the case. The D.A. attended to the woman, focusing his attention upon her. He determined that they were an innocent young couple; the case was slated for the grand jury. About two minutes after the case was sent to the typist, the male complainant returned to the D.A. and stated that he was in the area to buy heroin. He did not want his girlfriend to know about the buy. The D.A. recalled the papers and reduced the charge to a misdemeanor.

The above example illustrates the flexibility of the prosecutor's definition of a serious crime. The robbery offense was determined to be legally sufficient and the witness credible. However, after the male complainant described his motives for being in the area, a felony prosecution was no longer tenable. An individual seeking to purchase drugs places himself "at risk," and—at least as a practical matter—the culpability of the defendants is reduced. It is no longer a "solid" case.

## CONCLUSION

One essential concern of a critical approach to criminal justice processing is the assumption that the legal system does not apply the law impartially (Chambliss and Seidman, 1971; Quinney, 1970; Janovic, 1978). Social class, sex, race, and life style are factors often taken into account in the application of the law (Chambliss and Seidman, 1971). But the implicit (never explicit, of course) use of such attributes in the charging process is not—or at least not only—a measure of outright prosecutorial bias. More often, it emerges as the pragmatism of a prosecutor intent on maximizing convictions and using organizational resources efficiently. Convictions are maximized when only solid cases are brought to trial. A "solid" case must be not only legally sufficient, but also based upon a credible complainant or victim. A victim must be credible not only in the eyes of the prosecutor, but also to the judge and jury. Thus an essential element of the charging decision is the determination of perceived victim credibility.

Credibility is not, however, only a matter of the personal characteristics of the victim. It also pertains to the situation, and to the congruence between situation and individual. Moreover, what emerges most clearly from the cases which I have described, and from my study, is the stereotypical quality of all such attributions. Prosecutors assume that judges and juries—particularly the latter—will find certain *kinds* of victim claims credible and acceptable, others not. It matters less that a victim with a prior record *may* have been robbed and beaten than that a jury may be dubious about such a claim, or merely unsympathetic to the victim. Prosecutors may rely on such stereotypes because of their own ideologies, but may also be influenced in accepting them by bureaucratic self-interest. A high batting average for convictions is a dominant organization goal in many prosecutors' offices. Doubts are resolved against the victim except in cases involving glamorous legal issues or particularly notorious crimes. The result may be that victims' quest for justice is often determined more by stereotypes than by the actual harm rendered against them by their assailants.

## REFERENCES

Alschuler, Albert W. 1968. "The prosecutor's role in plea bargaining." *University of Chicago Law Review* 36: 50–112.

Bittner, Egon. 1967. "The police on skid row: a study of peace keeping." *American Sociological Review* 32: 699–715.

Blumberg, Abraham. 1967. *Criminal Justice*. Chicago: Quadrangle.

Cannavale, Frank J., and William D. Falcon. 1976. *Witness Cooperation*. Lexington: D.C.: Heath.

Chambliss, William, and Robert Seidman. 1971. *Law, Order and Power*. Reading: Addison-Wesley.

Chiricos, Theodore, and Gordon P. Waldo. 1975. "Socioeconomic status and criminal sentencing: an empirical assessment of a conflict proposition." *American Sociological Review* 40: 753–772.

Dill, Forrest. 1980. "Reasons for felony dismissals." Paper presented at the Annual Meeting of the Law and Society Association, Madison, Wisconsin.

Eisenstein, James, and Herbert Jacob. 1977. *Felony Justice*. Boston: Little, Brown.

Emerson, Robert M., and Sheldon L. Messenger. 1977. "The micro-politics of trouble." *Social Problems* 25: 121–134.

Goffman, Erving. 1963. *Stigma: Notes on the Management of Spoiled Identity*. Englewood Cliffs: Prentice-Hall.

Hall, Donald. 1975. "Role of the victim in the prosecution and disposition of a criminal case." *Vanderbilt Law Review* 28: 931–985.

Holmstrom, Lynda Lytle, and Ann W. Burgess. 1978. *The Victim of Rape: Institutional Reactions*. New York: Wiley.

Hostica, Carl J. 1979. "We don't care about what happened, we only care about what is going to happen: lawyer client negotiations of reality." *Social Problems* 26: 599–610.

Janovic, Ivan. 1978. "Social class and criminal sentencing." *Crime and Social Justice* 10: 9–16.

Mather, Lynn. 1979. *Plea Bargaining or Trial?* Lexington: D.C. Heath.

Miller, Frank. 1970. *Prosecution: The Decision to Charge a Suspect with a Crime*. Boston: Little, Brown.

Myers, Martha A., and John Hagan. 1979. "Private and public trouble: prosecutors and the allocation of court resources." *Social Problems* 26: 439–451.

Neubauer, David. 1974. *Criminal Justice in Middle America*. Morristown: General Learning Press.

Newman, Donald J. 1966. *Conviction: The Determination of Guilt or Innocence without Trial*. Boston: Little, Brown.

Quinney, Richard. 1970. *The Social Reality of Crime*. Boston: Little, Brown.

Rosett, Arthur, and Donald R. Cressey. 1976. *Justice by Consent*. New York: J.B. Lippincott.

Stanko, Elizabeth A. 1977. These Are the Cases that Try Themselves. Unpublished doctoral disserta-
   tion, City University of New York.
———.1981. "The arrest versus the case." *Urban Life* 9: 395–414.
Swigert, Victoria Lynn, and Ronald A. Farrell. 1976. *Murder, Inequality, and the Law*. Lexington: D.C.
   Heath.
Utz, Pamela. 1978. *Settling the Facts*. Lexington: D.C. Heath.
Williams, Kirsten M. 1976. "The effects of victim characteristics on the disposition of violent crimes."
   In *Criminal Justice and the Victim,* edited by William F. MacDonald. Beverly Hills: Sage.

# 21

## SHEATHING THE SWORD OF JUSTICE IN JAPAN: AN ESSAY ON LAW WITHOUT SANCTIONS*

### JOHN O. HALEY

Law in Japan, writes Kawashima Takeyoshi, is like an heirloom samurai sword; it is to be treasured but not used (Kawashima, 1967: 47). The simile is apt. No industrial nation has weaker formal law enforcement. Sanctions taken for granted in the West, in Europe, as well as in the United States, either do not exist or remain unused in Japan. Although the contrast between Japan and the United States is the most stark, because differences between the two often reflect features unique to the United States rather than Japan, the contrast with Germany is even more instructive. What is important, however, is not simply the comparison itself but the consequences that the differences suggest.

At the outset several general propositions should be stated. It should be emphasized, first, that no set of formal legal sanctions, short perhaps of a regime of absolute terror, can be perfectly effective in any society. All legal orders rely predominantly on voluntary compliance with the law. The absence of effective sanctions and the consequent need to rely totally on voluntary conformity with legal norms reduce, however, the legal order to a purely customary one in which community consensus controls. Legal rules and standards remain vital or change and die out depending upon the aggregate effect of individual whim or the efficacy of nonlegal customary or "social" sanctions as a substitute. Moreover, the range of formal sanctions available in any legal order is quite limited. The catalogue of rewards and punishments at the disposal of the formal institutions of a legal system is short. There is little besides "life, liberty, and property" against which they can

*This article is based on a paper delivered at the Third National Conference of the Asian Studies Association of Australia, Brisbane, Queensland, August 24, 1980.

be invoked. Only the infliction of physical pain (or denial of its relief) can be added as a theoretical possibility, then excluded in most Western-based legal systems as a matter of public policy. In no legal system are the available legal sanctions completely effective. All are subject to significant limitations.

Finally, again at least in Western-based legal systems, the formal categories of law relate only in part and imperfectly to particular sanctions available and their severity. We speak of civil versus criminal versus administrative sanctions to denote both the persons—private individuals or the government agencies as private litigants, police and prosecutors, and administrative officials—who possess the discretion to activate and control the course of the sanctioning process as well as the variety of sanctions (including remedies) that can be imposed—attachment of property, imposition of a fine, or imprisonment. The effect is to give those who exercise such discretion the ability to disregard and not enforce legal norms they do not accept. On their attitudes and views depends the efficacy of legal rules, the living law.

## THE LACK OF FORMAL SANCTIONS

Few meaningful sanctions or effective legal remedies exist at all in Japanese law. Although other jurisdictions share some of the limitations of Japanese law, none share so comprehensive a failure to provide effective sanctions or remedies for violation of legal norms. In civil cases in Japan, as elsewhere, the ultimate formal sanction is to attach property. The propertyless or those who are able to hide what they have—for instance, by false registration of land—are thus beyond the law's reach. Even those with accessible assets, however, are not easily subjected to legal compulsion. For example, in Japan as in other civil law jurisdictions, such as Germany and France, the general remedy for a breach of contract is a court order to the breaching party requiring performance. In the case of a sale of personal property, say a painting, should the seller violate his duty to deliver the painting, in theory the buyer can obtain a court decree ordering the seller to hand it over. Only if the buyer, as plaintiff, knows where the painting is actually located and can direct the bailiff there without interference can the court order be effectively enforced. Otherwise, the buyer is able only to recover damages to compensate for the monetary loss, which must be proved and can be enforced only if the seller has property that can be attached. A sale of land is easier to enforce. All land is registered and a court judgment effecting the prerequisites for a registry transfer of title is possible. To force an obstinate seller off the land even after title has been transferred can be a costly and time-consuming effort. What on the surface appears to be an effective remedy may in reality be of little or no avail.

Nor do the government and other public authorities in Japan have more effective means to enforce the law. Several years ago at a dinner in Tokyo with several former students and other University of Washington graduates, I happened to sit next to a Japanese lawyer whose father is a prominent psychiatrist. Our conversation turned to the topic of his father's practice; he mentioned that it was tax audit time and thus his father was exceptionally busy. "I suppose," I said, "that quite a few taxpayers seek psychiatric relief." "Oh no," he quickly responded, "Psychiatrists are busy with tax collectors not taxpayers." My surprise showed, so he went on to explain. In the case of small firms, more often those that belong to trade associations affiliated with one of the opposition parties, especially the Communist Party, tax auditors are frequently barred from even entering the premises by members of the association and others who surround the building and block the entrances. Incredulous I asked, "What do the auditors do?" "See their psychiatrists," he replied.

The civil process offers little help. Civil fines may be provided as a sanction for violation of an administrative order or regulation, but collection will depend upon attachment or registry transfers—in other words, the private party's capacity to pay or willingness to abide by the court order despite refusal to obey the agency order.

In contrast, in the United States and most other common law jurisdictions, the courts' contempt powers make available in the civil process both the threat of prompt imposition of a fine of unlimited amount or imprisonment for an indefinite term, or both. By failing to obey a court order to deliver a painting, vacate land, or to obey an administrative order, the defendant faces the possibility that he will be fined whatever amount the judge believes will provide sufficient compulsion, or that he will be jailed until he complies. Although in many cases judges may be reluctant to resort to contempt, its threat is ever present, and its importance should not be underestimated. Judicially enforced subpoenas to compel disclosure of documents or other information provide only one of many examples of the critical role contempt plays in American public law enforcement. Moreover, since agencies do not have contempt powers under American law, the courts perform an important supplementary role in administrative law enforcement. An agency anticipating that a party may disobey an agency order will seek an enforcing court order. Both orders will be identical in legal effect, both requiring the same conduct and both equally binding as a matter of law. The only difference is that the court order is backed by contempt. The importance of contempt is thus illustrated each time an American agency seeks a judicial enforcement order. Lacking contempt powers, Japanese courts have no role in civil enforcement of administrative regulations except in terms of appeals from agency actions. One consequence is that the Japanese judiciary tends to be less sympathetic to the government.

Judicial contempt is also unknown in other continental legal systems. It is viewed as too dangerous a power to place in the hands of the least accountable branch of government and as inconsistent with fundamental notions regarding the need for certain and legislatively-fixed penalties.[1] Nonetheless, German law at least has an analog to contempt. Under the German Code of Civil Procedure,[2] court injunctions can be enforced either through a fine up to 500,000 DM (approximately

[1]See, e.g., Duren, 1974. Also, *Grundgesetz für die Bundesrepublik Deutschland* (Basic law for the Federal Republic of Germany), 23 May 1949 (BGBI. S. 1), article 103.

[2]*Zivilprozess Ordnung* (Code of Civil Procedure), 30 January 1877 (RGBI. S. 83) as amended, article 890.

$250,000) or confinement up to two years. Moreover, administrative officials have the authority in most instances to enforce administrative orders by levying fines or attaching property without resort to the civil process or criminal proceedings (see Forsthoff, 1973: 290–296). There are no similar provisions in Japanese law.

Until the Allied Occupation and the postwar reform of Japan's legal system, administrative officials in Japan could resort to an extensive variety of sanctions under special legislation,[3] repealed in 1947 without effective substitute.[4] Moreover, the police had broad jurisdiction to adjudicate cases involving infractions defined as "police offenses" (see Ames, 1981: 9–11). Today, however, the Japanese must rely almost completely on criminal prosecution for enforcement of court orders and of almost all public law. Most Japanese regulatory legislation, for example, includes provisions at the end for criminal penalties, both fines and imprisonment. These may appear to be adequate, yet in reality, they are rarely invoked. In over thirty years of antitrust enforcement, for example, there have been only six criminal prosecutions. Three were begun in 1949. The successful prosecution on September 26, 1980 of Japanese oil companies and their executives for illegal price-fixing in the Tokyo High Court[5] was thus an extraordinary event. One culls the statistics and records in vain to find more than a handful of prosecutions under other statutes. This dearth is only in part explained by limitations in applying criminal sanctions to economic misconduct found in most other jurisdictions or institutitonal barriers to effective enforcement, described below; it is also a product of the inherent incapacity of the Japanese legal system to rely effectively on criminal sanctions.

Confession, repentance, and absolution provide the underlying theme of the Japanese criminal process. At every stage, from initial police investigation through formal proceedings, an individual suspected of criminal conduct gains by confessing, apologizing, and throwing himself upon the mercy of the authorities.

The experience of a long-time American resident of Tokyo is illustrative. His *bessō* or vacation home was destroyed by arson late one Sunday evening an hour or two after he and his family had left to return to the city. Learning that a few weeks earlier he had increased the insurance on the house, the local police asked him to meet with them the next day. Upon his arrival the police ushered him into a room reminiscent of an early James Cagney film—small table, uncomfortable wooden chair for him on one side, two or three policemen sitting or standing at ease on the other, glaring light overhead. What made the scene uniquely Japanese were the three portraits, at either side and facing him but tilted slightly to ensure

[3]*Gyōsei shikkō hō* (Administrative execution by proxy law), Law No. 84, 1900.
[4]The *Gyōsei daishikko hō* (Administrative execution by proxy law), Law No. 43, 1948, permits execution against property but does not authorize taking persons into custody. For a brief discussion in English on the background to this reform, see Government Section, SCAP, *Political Reorientation of Japan* (Washington, D.C., 1952), pp. 226–227. See also Hosokawa, 1980.
[5]Japan v. Sekiyu renmei *et al.,* Case No. 2 (Wo) 1974 (Tokyo High Court, September 26, 1980). All jail sentences were suspended. The defendants were acquitted in the companion case on the output restriction charge for lack of criminal intent.

direct vision from where he sat. They were of Buddha, the Emperor, and Christ. Then in a somber but pleading voice the principal investigator said: "Now, Mr.—, why don't you just confess."

Such incidents illustrate the significance attached by the Japanese authorities to confession and apology.[6] I should note quickly that the confession does not provide a shortcut to conviction as in the United States. It does not save the police and prosecutor the time and effort of obtaining other evidence to prove guilt. There is no guilty plea in criminal cases in Japan; there is no plea bargaining. In every case brought, the prosecution must prove that a violation was committed by the defendant. A summary procedure that avoids oral hearings and defense is available and much used at the discretion of the prosecutor if there is confession, but for each case that goes to court the prosecutor must marshal evidence other than the confession to prove the accused guilty.

Held out to each suspect, however, is the promise of absolution if he does confess and apologize, and Japanese authorities respond in predictable fashion. Under article 248 of the postwar Code of Criminal Procedure (article 279 of the prewar code) the procurator may suspend prosecution after taking into consideration three factors: (1) the age, character, and environment of the offender; (2) the circumstances and gravity of the offense; and (3) the circumstances following the offense. The first two do not necessarily surprise us. To treat leniently a case involving a minor first offense would not be unusual in any legal system. In Japan, however, the third is equally, if not more, important. For the Japanese prosecutor the accused's attitude—in other words his willingness to confess and apologize— is critical to the decision whether to prosecute or not. In 1972, 94% of all persons formally charged with a crime admitted guilt (Bayley, 1976: 147), and in approximately 33% of all cases involving nontraffic offenses prosecution was suspended (Ministry of Justice of Japan, 1978: 26).[7]

Judges repeat the pattern. The rate of conviction in the cases that do go to trial is currently 99.99% (Ministry of Justice of Japan, 1978: 23). In less than 3% of convictions, however, do the courts impose a jail sentence; and 87% of these are terms of less than 3 years (ibid: 24). Moreover, the courts regularly suspend more than two-thirds of all jail sentences. In 88% of all cases, all with confessions, the prosecution availed itself of the summary procedures described above (Anonymous, 1975: 48). The penalty in such instances is restricted by law to 200,000 yen.[8] In 65% of these cases, however, the fines were less than 50,000 yen (ibid: 48). Consequently, the overwhelming majority of offenders in Japan confess and are either not prosecuted or are penalized by a fine of less than 250 U.S. dollars.

[6]The best account of the role of confession and apology in the Japanese criminal process in English is Bayley, 1976: 134–159.

[7]The prewar pattern is basically the same. Out of 228,693 cases from 1912–1916, 73,864 were suspended; from 1917–1921, 84,618 out of 307,035; from 1922–1926, 105,575 out of 330,539; from 1927–1931, 150,562 out of 402,339 (Brever, 1940: 125).

[8]Law for Temporary Measures Concerning Fine (*Bakkin to rinji sotchi hō*), Law No. 251, 1948, article 7.

The determinative factor for the judge, as for the prosecutor, in deciding the sentence to impose or whether to suspend sentence is the attitude of the offender. Confession is demanded and repentance rewarded. Japanese judges tell of a veteran of the bench who refused to permit convicted defendants to leave the courtroom even after sentencing until they had confessed and apologized. A primary purpose of trials in Japan, Japanese judges emphasize, is to correct behavior, not to punish. Nor, one might infer from the conviction rates, to determine guilt.

While the overall leniency of the Japanese criminal process for all categories of crime—assuming confession and apology—must be kept in mind, it would be a mistake to conclude that all offenders are treated alike. Although the differences are not as great in terms of sentencing, rates of prosecution differ widely depending upon the offense involved. For example, in 1968, prosecutors suspended 87.1% of all cases involving abuse of authority by public officials, 81.2% for negligent injury and manslaughter, 63% for robbery, 52.4% for larceny, 26% for arson, 22.5% for bodily injury, 8.4% for homicide, and 6.9% for traffic law violations (Dando, 1970: 525). These percentages are representative for other years as well (see Ministry of Justice of Japan, 1980: 140–143). While the average rate of prosecution for statutory crimes (conduct made criminal under various statutes excluding the criminal code) is roughly 33%, in 1977, 71% of all pollution offenses, 66% of bribery cases, and 97.3% of road traffic violations were prosecuted (ibid: 11, 12, and 19). As noted above, the ultimate sentencing does not show this variance. In 93.2% of all bribery cases, for instance, the court suspended sentences imposed by law (ibid: 12).

The criminal process also operates to provide compensation for victims. In this sense, there is an addititonal informal sanction. One indication of true repentance is the defendant's attempt to make matters right with the victim. Typically a monetary payment is made in return for a letter absolving the offender of further blame. Nothing in Japanese law requires such action, but it is a factor to show that an apology is real.[9] The sign of repentance remains the critical factor.

A Japanese attorney recently related to my law class at the University of Washington his experience in defending two American servicemen accused of raping a Japanese woman. She had charged the two with the crime in an affidavit to the prosecutor, but then left Japan with a third U.S. soldier. The affidavit was the sole basis of prosecution. The attorney advised the two defendants first to obtain a letter from the woman stating that she had been fully compensated and had absolved them completely. As advised the accused paid her $1000 and obtained the letter. The lawyer then argued that to convict the accused solely on the basis of the affidavit constituted an unconstitutional denial of a fair trial since they had had no opportunity to cross-examine the witness. After listening attentively to the argument, the judge leaned forward and asked the soldiers if they had anything to say. "We

[9]The idea of compensation is not unique to Japanese law; see, e.g., sections 437 and 438 of the New South Wales Crimes Act of 1900. But we tend to codify such systems and make compensation legally mandatory, a telling distinction as shown above.

are not guilty, your honor," was the immediate reply. The lawyer cringed. Although few Japanese attorneys are as knowledgeable as he about American law, it had not even occurred to him that the defendants might not offer apologies. The time and money spent on the letter were wasted. The judge sentenced the two soldiers to the maximum term of imprisonment, not suspended. More telling, Japanese students need only hear what the servicemen said to the judge to react. They know what happened next. Only Americans have to be told.

The success of the Japanese system of criminal justice in terms of correction is unquestioned. Crime rates in all categories except for traffic violations are far lower than in any other industrial nation and are decreasing. (In all others they are rising.) In only one respect do the Japanese and U.S. statistics coincide. The rate of recidivism is steady in Japan and, as a ratio of persons who commit further crimes after release from prison, is almost the same as in the United States (Bayley, 1976: 140). The difference between the two countries is that less than 2% of all those convicted of crime ever serve a jail sentence in Japan as compared with more than 45% in the United States. As a Japanese prosecutor told a prominent Philadelphian investigating Tokyo's low crime rate, "We do not believe in imprisonment; jails are the schools for crime."

In summary, the few formal sanctions that do exist in Japan are rarely used. The lack of sanctions in the civil and administrative process is thus compounded by the disregard of those that are available in the criminal process.

## INSTITUTIONAL BARRIERS TO EFFECTIVE LAW ENFORCEMENT

Added to the lack of formal sanctions, however, are a variety of institutional barriers that diminish the efficacy of those that do exist. In all but a few cases the imposition of sanctions is a judicial task. An obstructive debtor can, in most instances, force formal adjudication of even the strongest claim. Yet even to enforce instruments, such as notarial deeds, that do not require a preliminary judgment or to collect a court award or an administrative fine may require further judicial assistance. No court can fulfill such tasks adequately unless it is accessible and can act promptly and efficiently.

On these counts the state of the judiciary in Japan is woeful indeed. Governmentally imposed restrictions limit total entry into the legal profession—private attorneys, government lawyers, and judges—to less than 500 persons a year. As a result Japan has fewer lawyers and judges per capita today than it did in the mid-1920s. The number of judges has remained almost constant since 1890. Today there is approximately one judge for every 60,000 persons in Japan as compared to one judge for every 22,000 persons in 1890 (Haley, 1978: 382). This is not, I must emphasize, the result of any lack of demand. Japanese judges handle caseloads that would stagger an American judge—nearly double the number of cases decided by judges in "litigious" California and five times that of the Federal bench (ibid: 381).

Often overlooked is a similar lack of government lawyers—or procurators. All cases—civil, criminal, or administrative—in which the government of Japan or any public agency is a party require involvement if not direct representation by the procuracy. (In the case of most minor local government cases, private attorneys are retained.) Yet there are only about 2000 procurators. For purposes of comparison, Los Angeles County alone has more than 400 lawyers in its district attorney's office.

The comparison with Germany is even more revealing. With less than two-thirds of Japan's population, Germany has nearly six times as many judges as Japan (approximately 15,500 to 2700) and the ratio of judges to the population has steadily decreased: from one judge to 6080 persons in 1911, to one judge to 4840 persons in 1951, and to one judge to 3963 persons in 1979. There are also nearly three times as many private attorneys (approximately 28,800 to 10,000) in Germany today as in Japan, and a third more procurators (approximately 3330 to 2100.[10] It should be noted, however, that the German procurator (*Staatsanwalt*) handles only criminal cases. In administrative and civil cases the government is represented by private attorneys.

Aside from the shortage of judges, lawyers, and procurators, there are other obstacles to prompt and efficient justice in Japan. The continental system of disconnected hearings, trials *de novo* upon first appeal, the appeals of right to the Supreme Court rather than by court discretion, filing fees, bond posting requirements, stringent requirements of evidentiary proof, the unwillingness of judges to discipline lawyers for unnecessary delays—all combine to foreclose the courts as a viable means of obtaining relief. "The litigation of a small claim," say two of Japan's leading civil procedure scholars, "tends to be an economic disaster" (Kojima and Taniguchi, 1978: 692). What is remarkable about the Japanese legal system is not that people are reluctant to sue but that they sue at all. Despite these hurdles, the demand for legal relief, for sanctions, strains the legal resources of Japan to their limits.

## SUBSTITUTE SANCTIONS

The dearth of formal sanctions is balanced by an enduring set of informal, extralegal means of compulsion. The most persuasive is "loss of face" or damaged reputation. In explaining why the apology works as a means of inducing conforming behavior, the Japanese almost invariably say that to apologize in public carries with it the stigma of loss of reputation.

Examples of threats to reputation as an effective sanction abound. Antitrust enforcement provides one example. Firms will agree to Japanese Fair Trade Commission recommendations tacitly admitting their violation and subjecting them-

---

[10]*Statisches Jahrbuch für die Bundesrepublik Deutschland,* 1959–1980; *Statisches Jahrbuch für die Deutsche Reich,* 1971, p. 336.

selves to possible damage actions, rather than prolonging the case because of fears of a damaged company reputation. This, however, may reflect more the weakness of the formal sanction—no damage action has been successful—than the strength of adverse publicity. A better example is found in the pollution and drug cases, where the primary hurdle delaying settlement was the plaintiffs' uncompromising demand for public apologies by the presidents of the firms involved. It was far easier apparently to reach agreement on the amount of damages than for the defendants to comply with such a demand. In the SMON litigation,[11] the one case involving a foreign party, I am told by the attorneys that the officers of the company were incredulous at this attitude by the Japanese plaintiffs and defendants. It was as if the amount of damages—over 100 million U.S. dollars—was of no consequence compared with the apology.

Adverse publicity is a tool of law enforcement in most countries. The threat of public condemnation is often the most effective means to force compliance that is available to an administrative agency. "Jaw-boning" by the president of the United States to keep a firm from raising prices, or labor from demanding wages in excess of a benchmark figure, is often little more than an exercise in the persuasive effect of adverse publicity. Officials enforcing antitrust laws in both the United States and Germany agree that adverse publicity is their most effective sanction.[12] Yet upon close scrutiny, where effective, a tangible financial loss rather than mere reputation is usually at stake. It is easy to understand why the threat by the Food and Drug Administration or the Department of Agriculture to release a report that a certain drug or food product may be hazardous is apt to cause consternation and a rapid, positive response by the manufacturers. Reputation is important because its loss involves other types of deprivation. Although the same argument may be said to apply to Japan, the role of reputation in Japan appears to be a more subtle and complex matter.

## THE SOCIAL IMPACT OF SANCTIONLESS LAW

Few of the many enigmas of Japan are as acute as the paradox it presents of a society so free from crime, rule-abiding and cohesive with such overt thuggery,

---

[11]The SMON (Subacute-Myelo-Optics Neuropathy) cases involved a nationwide series of suits against one foreign and two Japanese pharmaceutical companies and the Ministry of Health and Welfare for injuries attributed to the drug dioquinol. The principal reported cases include the following: Yagi v. Japan, Hanrei Jihō (No. 879) 26 (Kanazawa Dt. Ct., Mar. 1, 1978); Ōyama v. Japan, Hanrei Jihō (No. 899) 48 (Tokyo Dt. Ct., Aug. 3, 1978); Ochi v. Japan, Hanrei Jihō (No. 910) 33 (Fukuoka Dt. Ct., Nov. 14, 1978); Aoyama v. Japan, Hanrei Jihō (No. 920) 19 (Hiroshima Dt. Ct., Feb. 22, 1979); Ishikawa v. Japan, Hanrei Jihō (No. 950) 53 (Sapporo Dt. Ct., April 10, 1979); Iwada v. Japan, Hanrei Jihō (No. 950) 87 (Kyoto Dt. Ct., June 2, 1979); Ōki v. Japan, Hanrei Jihō (No. 950) 199 (Shizuoka Dt. Ct., June 19, 1979); Sasaki v. Japan, Hanrei Jihō (No. 950) 241 (Osaka Dt. Ct., June 30, 1979); Arai v. Japan, Hanrei Jihō (No. 950) 305 (Maebashi Dt. Ct., Aug. 21, 1979).

[12]Observation to author by Professor Thomas C. Armitage, former director, Seattle Regional Office, Federal Trade Commission. On the German experience, see comments by Helmut Gutzler, former vice-president, Federal Cartel Office, in Gutzler, 1974.

widespread flouting of law, and virulent conflict. Although not the complete or even certain answer, such riddles begin to unravel by viewing Japan as a society of law without sanctions.

A legal order without effective formal sanctions need not grind to a halt. Legislators, bureaucrats, and judges may continue to articulate and apply, and thus legitimate, new rules and standards of conduct. The norms thus created and legitimized may have significant impact. To the extent no legal sanctions apply, however, their validity will depend upon consensus and thus, as "living" law, become nearly indistinguishable from nonlegal or customary norms. As to those norms the community accepts as necessary or proper, the absence of legal sanctions is likely to produce extralegal substitutes and to reinforce the viability of preexisting means of coercing behavior. Thus the legal order relies increasingly upon community consensus and the viability of the sanctions the community already possesses. The evolution of Japanese law exemplifies this process.

The coincidence of Neo-Confucian values and the demands of polity ensured that Tokugawa justice remained as inaccessible as possible. The fragile equilibrium of the early Tokugawa settlement made indirect rule and local autonomy a necessity. Each unit of the society, the lesser communities and the whole—whether han, village, guild, or family—were left alone so long as taxes were paid and outward order maintained. This was in stark contrast with Angevin England where the monarchy achieved dominion by extending the king's justice, through greater access to the king's courts and by fashioning new and more effective remedies. In England the consequence was a common law for the nation and a vigorous judiciary as well as a central monarchy. In Japan, community autonomy and weak government remained hidden behind a veil of ritualized deference to authority.

It is unlikely that the draconian penalties that adorned the *ritsuryō* codes and that appalled nineteenth-century Europeans were ever as important as the simple group sanction of ostracism and expulsion, especially when joined to the notion of vicarious liability. Social control develops new dimensions when landlords are made responsible for the conduct of their tenants, community leaders for the activities of its members, or parents for the conduct of their children, and when expulsion from the community and its resources is an ever present threat.

The absence of formal sanctions in modern Japanese law has had direct impact on both the retention of these earlier forms of social control as well as the creation of new ones. Boycotts, refusals to deal, and other forms of modern *murahachibu* are among the most prevalent means by which social order is maintained. The Japanese financial clearinghouse, for example, has a rule that no bank is allowed to transact business of any type with any individual or firm that defaults twice on promissory notes or checks. Since no firm could long stay in business without at least a bank account, promissory notes in Japan are almost as secure as cash (and indeed are used as collateral).

The combination of refusals to deal and other forms of ostracism with vicarious liability produces an even more effective deterrent to nonconformity. One of the first graduates of a new university to be allowed even to apply for employment with a large Japanese manufacturer turned down an offer by a foreign firm, that in monetary terms amounted to more than he could ever expect to make, at least in part because he feared that such a display of "disloyalty" to the Japanese firm would result in its refusal to hire another graduate of that university.

Community or group cohesion is inexorably intertwined with such informal sanctions. Ostracism is not effective in a mobile society in which the benefits of membership in one group can be easily had by independence or by joining another. However, where one of the primary benefits of the community is its capacity to maintain stability and order, its ability to sanction reinforces its cohesion. Independence becomes a risky alternative and access to other groups becomes more difficult. Clientage too is the product of a demand for security by those who are unable to fend for themselves and whom the general community is unable to protect. In any society where the state fails to secure its citizens against lawlessness by those who exercise physical, economic, and social powers, there may be no choice but to attach oneself to those who can. The inability of the formal legal system in Japan to provide effective relief, to impose meaningful sanctions, thus tends to buttress the cohesion of groups and the lesser communities of Japanese society and to contribute to the endurance of vertical, patron-client relationships. The use of private mediators, the procuracy, and police in dispute settlement; the role of the *yakuza* and organized crime; the reliance on banks and other large enterprises; all fit this pattern of conduct.

Witness, for example, Japanese approaches to contracts. The literature is replete with descriptions of the Japanese penchant for informal, ambiguously worded agreements in which the parties rely more on "goodwill" and personal relations than carefully drafted documents. This is precisely the behavior one would expect where the parties anticipate that legal enforcement of the contract may be of no avail. Without legal sanctions, the words in a contract are just words, no matter how carefully drawn. Although the party whose bargaining power remains strong perhaps need not be concerned, the weaker party has little choice but to rely on the "fairness" or "benevolence" of the other. Thus both sides—strong and weak—come to the contract with the same conclusion: if the agreement is reduced to writing at all, a vaguely worded document will suffice. On the other hand, when dealing with a foreign enterprise that can be anticipated to enforce the contract in court, Japanese firms negotiate and draft with extreme care. They will make certain that every "t" is crossed and every "i" is dotted. Similarly, a Japanese firm will assiduously abide by adverse commitments to its contract partners in cases where sanctions—either informal, arising out of either their relative bargaining positions or the promise of an on-going relationship, or formal, such as the likelihood of legal action—are strong. Yet where sanctions of either sort are weak, the same firm is just as apt to disregard indisputable contractual promises.

Nor is the Japanese government immune from the effects of weak sanctions. The inability of government agencies to enforce the law by formal means forces reliance on an imperfect combination of consensus, voluntary compliance and, in some but not all instances, a variety of indirect carrots and sticks. In some contexts administrative law enforcement can be very effective, giving the impression of a monolithic and powerful bureaucracy that needs merely suggest to achieve obedience. Upon closer examination, however, few examples of such power exist apart from customs and immigration controls, areas in which government officials have little difficulty in obtaining actual possession of persons and property. (Consequently, government regulation is relatively effective in the areas of foreign trade, foreign enterprise, and immigration, hiding from most foreigners the inherent weakness of Japanese government over domestic conduct.) Administrative guidance is thus exemplary as a process of negotiation and compromise to achieve voluntary compliance dictated by government weakness rather than strength.

Trying to explain the difficulties of collecting debts in Japan to an exasperated foreign client, who wanted to recover the sales price of goods sold to a small Japanese firm, a Japanese attorney finally said, "You should just write it off. The fellow was untrustworthy and that's that." A Japanese banker, asked about the problems the bank had faced in foreclosing security interests, retorted, "We don't lend to people who default."

Such incidents illustrate the nexus between reputation and weak law enforcement. When sellers and lenders cannot expect to obtain relief in the event of default, either they do not sell on credit or make loans, or they take great care to ensure that they are not selling or lending to "people who default." In other words, one's reputation for trustworthiness can become a necessity of life. Furthermore, where the lesser communities and patrons provide the most important substitutes for formal sanctions, one's reputation will depend in part on affiliations and sponsorship. Thus in Japan, as most foreign businessmen and scholars know from personal experience, introductions are essential. Even law firms regularly, if politely, turn away potential clients who do not have proper introductions. Businessmen, government officials, libraries, and schools are often inaccessible without introductions.

Implied in such practice is a type of informal suretyship, that is, the reputation (but not formal legal liability) of the group and patron depends in part on the conduct of the member and the client. In fact, few practices are more ubiquitous in Japan than the use of such suretyship. Letters of guarantee are unusually common as the prerequisite for an extraordinary variety of activities: immigration, loans, employment, and leases. One can hardly enter a legal relation in any context without having someone as guarantor. Such contracts have little legal significance despite (and to some extent because) of their breadth. Few would even think of enforcing most of these guarantees in court. They are demanded instead on the premise that the loss of reputation the guarantor suffers as a result of any misconduct of the person vouched for will itself restrain if not prevent such misconduct. In other words, reputation is vicarious. The conduct and reputation of the members of the group or the client affect that of the group or patron. Thus the benefits of group membership and clientage come to depend in part on the capacity of the group (including the family in extreme cases) or patron to deny access or expel those who damage reputation. Again the pattern repeats: such needs reinforce the cohesion of the group and the power of the patron and thus the effectiveness of the informal sanctions they wield.

It should be apparent that in this process the concern of the group or patron focuses on loss of reputation, not the conduct itself. To the extent that the group accepts the norm and wishes to enforce it for its own merits, there is no need to be concerned with reputation. To protect against loss of reputation, the group must enforce norms that other groups or the community at large see as legitimate and important regardless of its own attitude. As a result, it is not the misdeed that is condemnable but the loss of reputation resulting from outside knowledge of the misdeed. Consequently, one discovers in Japan that failure to abide by the law may be known to, but not condemned by, the group. Yet as soon as this becomes public, group condemnation follows. One result is a pattern of pervasive nonconformity masked by outward conformity. Legal rules may be outrageously flouted so long as all appear to be punctilious in their observance. Another result, however, is the capacity of formal legal norms to become effective without necessarily full consensus. To the extent that private litigation and especially the criminal process disclose violations of the law and reputation suffers, this threat may produce a positive reaction.

In conclusion, Japan is the paradigm of a society of law without sanctions. Features of Japanese society, both good and bad, that fascinate and intrigue, that seem so uniquely Japanese, can in the end be explained by a very basic although long-standing fact: the inability of the formal legal system to provide effective sanctions. It is, I suggest, this fact that explains the ultimate enigma of Japan—its capacity to preserve outward cohesion and tradition within the context of rapid economic and technological change. The institutionalized legal system enables Japan to create new norms, to meet new demands, but their viability requires consensus and a process for sanctioning that continually reinforce the existing social structure. A final caveat: this process is not itself inexorable and unchangeable. To strengthen legal sanctions, to make the courts more efficient and judicial remedies more effective, or by any means to broaden the enforcement of law through the legal process, would inevitably corrode the social structure that now exists. What the Tokugawa shogunate did for Japan, a Henry II could undo.

## REFERENCES

Ames, Walter L. 1981. *Police and Community in Japan*. Berkeley: University of California Press.

Anonymous. 1975. *Crime Prevention and Control National Statement: Japan*. Fifth United Nations Congress on The Prevention of Crime and Treatment of Offenders.

Bayley, David H. 1976. *Forces of Order: Police Behavior in Japan and the United States*. Berkeley: University of California Press.

Brever, Richard. 1940. *Die Stellung der Staatsanwaltschaft in Japan*. Berlin: Junker & Dünnhaupt.

Dando, Shigemitsu. 1970. "System of discretionary prosecution in Japan." *American Journal of Comparative Law* 18: 518–531.

Düren, Wolfgang. 1974. *Contempt: Das Rechtinstitute des Contempt in der politischen Realität der USA*. Munich: de Smet.

Forsthoff, Ernst. 1973. *Lehrbuch des Verwaltungsrechts* (10th ed.). Munich: G. H. Beck.

Gutzler, Helmut. 1974. "Die ermittlungstatigkeit des bundeskartellamtes." *Grundlagen der Kriminalität* 13: 529.

Haley, John O. 1978. "The myth of the reluctant litigant." *Journal of Japanese Studies* 4: 359–390.

Hosokawa, Toshihiko. 1980. *Kōhōjō no saimushikkō to kyōsei shikkō* (Enforcement of public law duties and execution). *Minshōhō Zasshi* 82: 641–660.

Kawashima, Takeyoshi. 1967. *Nihonjin no hōishiki* (Legal consciousness of the Japanese). Iwanami.

Kojima, T., and Y. Taniguchi. 1978. "Access to justice in Japan." In *Access to Justice,* edited by Mauro Cappalletti and Bryant Garth. The Hague: Sijthoff.

Ministry of Justice of Japan. 1978. *1978 Summary of White Paper on Crime.* Tokyo.

———. 1980. *Hōmusho hōmu sōgō kenkyūsho, Shōwa 55 nenpan hanzai hakusho* (1980 White Paper on Crime). Tokyo.

# INDEX